LANDSCAPED AREA
(OPEN TO SKY)
DOUBLE HIGHT PORTION
1800 X 1200 NITCH AT 1350 LVL
NITCH
UP
MAIN COMPUTER ROOM
CAPACITY- 56 NO.
BOARD
ENT. COMPUTER CENTER
LIBRARY ENT.
PHOTO-STAT
CHECKING COUNTER
SITTING
DRG. NO. A-15
DISPLAY
PERIODICAL/ MAGAZINES
LOBBY
CATALOGUE TERMINAL
(DOUBLE HIGHT PORTION)
ENT. HALL
INFORMATION DESK
ISSUE & RETURN COUNTER
CATALOG TERM.
W.M. BOARD
CONF/LIBRARY RM.
ROOM
SYS. MANAGER
STORE 2770 x 2580
GENTS TOILET
L TOILET
WATER COOLER
PANTRY
A.H.U 2770 x 2300
DISPLAY OF BOOKS
READY REFERENCE STACK
INTERNET
STORAGE
1800 WIDE PASSAGE
SYSTEM ANALYST
HIGH END COMPUTING
OPENING 3020
1800 WIDE PASSAGE
CATALOGUE TERM.
SERVER RM.
MULTIMEDIA LAB
GEN. STACKS
7' HIGH STACK

CPKA: *Five Decades of India's Built Environment*

Authored by

Arunima Kukreja

Dikshu C. Kukreja

राष्ट्रीय समर

Locations

The firm has worked with clients from:

USA
Canada
UK
Ukraine
Saudi Arabia
France
Germany
Italy
New Zealand
Nigeria
Austria
Finland
China
Switzerland
Kenya
Japan
Korea
Australia
Sweden
Bhutan
Brazil
Russia
Denmark
Singapore
Sri Lanka
Bangladesh
Nepal
Spain
Malaysia
Mexico
Poland
Oman
United Arab Emirates
Iraq
Iran
Qatar
Israel
Turkey
Syria
Jordan
Kuwait
Bahrain
Netherlands
Belgium
Vietnam

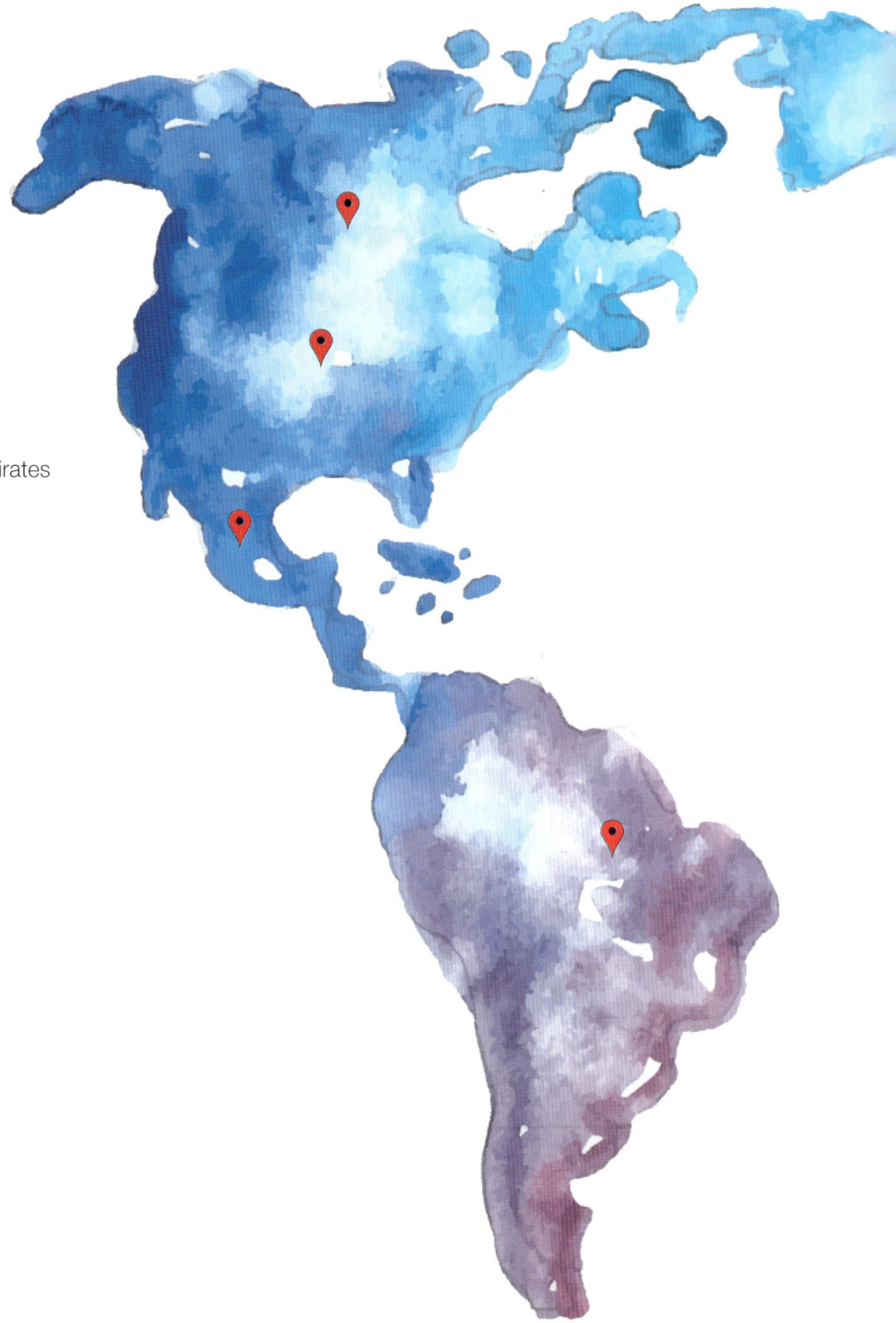

Previous spread: *Proposal for the National War Memorial, New Delhi*

Contents

Foreword

Dr. Shashi Tharoor
Member of Parliament for Thiruvananthapuram, Kerala, India; Lok Sabha
Chairman, Parliamentary Standing Committee on Information Technology
Chairman, All-India Professionals' Congress

Even as Indian design has embarked on countless evolutions and changes throughout the millennia, there remains one common thread in our creative aspirations which stands out, one that is certainly worth recognizing. And this has to do with a unique capacity to take art, philosophies and traditions from the past, and harmonize them with the practices of the present and innovations of the future. Indian designers are reimagining today's products by evoking the spirit of India's age-old traditions. This quality is quite exclusively Indian.

In all of this – the conceptualization and communication of the essence of our nation in a globalized world – design and art play vitally important roles. But what is design and why is it so important? What are we doing to enhance our understanding and appreciation of design, and how do we take it a step further so that the capacity to deliver design is embedded in each of us?

Everything we do, every single action, be it the way we walk or the way we speak, has two elements to it: there is the motive to it, its intention or purpose, and then there is the execution of it, the performance of the action. It is in the performance of the action that we see the design. Through the design, we see what materials have been used, how have these been arranged and what method has been used to arrange or combine them with one another. It is through the design of the action that we judge the appropriateness of the action to its motive and purpose. Design also plays an immeasurably important role in how a country is perceived by its global neighbours and its own citizens. Given that the world of the twenty-first century will increasingly be a world in which the use of 'hard power' (armies or economic muscle) carries with it the odium of mass global public disapproval, we need to double-down on our strengths within the ambit of 'soft power'.

It is in this context that the designs captured in *Five Decades of India's Built Environment* present an insightful compendium of not just iconic architecture in post-independent India and the visionary hands behind it, but a journey of how the very image that India has presented of itself to the world has evolved radically since Independence. And perhaps that unassuming but significant change of how the world looks at India in itself offers a fitting tribute to the late C.P. Kukreja, a doyen of the architectural world whose life's work is chronicled in this magnificent publication.

Though he may have left this world, his commanding work offers an eternal legacy to a man who was the force behind many of our iconic and visually arresting architectural marvels — from the sprawling campus of the Jawaharlal Nehru University, which seamlessly blends into its calming natural environment, to the suave and sophisticated Master Plan of Delhi's Aerocity, a towering set of structures that are impossible to miss as you make your way to or from the airport. His creations have left behind an inspiring amalgamation of design, sustainability and visual brilliance that are instructive to all who admire this field and those who take it up themselves. I am pleased to commend this volume to all who are interested in the recent history of Indian architectural design.

Facing page: *Central University Rajasthan, Rajasthan.*

Preface

Thomas Vonier, FAIA RIBA HonFRAIC
President 2017–21, Union Internationale des Architects (UIA), Paris
President 2016-17, American Institute of Architects (AIA), USA

If Winston Churchill's aphorism is true that 'we shape our buildings and thereafter they shape us', then, surely, C.P. Kukreja and his descendants have had a very strong hand in shaping today's India.

The breadth and influence of the design practice of CP Kukreja Architects (CPKA) is extraordinary. Any review of modern influences in the country's architecture must include his wide-ranging works such as university buildings, embassies, temples, hospitals, hotels, and housing complexes, as well as urban plans and large commercial and mixed-use development schemes. His work also extends beyond India's borders to Bangladesh and Nigeria, among many other countries.

Five Decades of India's Built Environment is an account of a lifetime spent in architecture. It also documents the legacy of a visionary man and a master architect. The thriving firm C.P. Kukreja established, which is now run by his son, Dikshu Kukreja, embodies principles and ideas that have inspired generations of design students and fellow architects, and will likely continue doing so.

In an era of deepening environmental crises, we know that it is urgent for us to build more responsibly. We know that we must conserve resources, employ more efficient construction methods and promote sustainable practices. Many good architectural solutions are available now, ready to contribute to more resilient communities and improved ways of life.

The sustainable development goals established by the United Nations define the challenges humankind must overcome if we hope to create a better world for the future. The design and construction professionals who produce the built environment – planners, architects, landscape designers, engineers, surveyors – all have an influence on how well our buildings perform.

As an architect, C.P. Kukreja seemed to have anticipated many of these challenges and imperatives. Surely, that is why his firm today encompasses and integrates so many of design disciplines. Master planning, urban design, infrastructure planning, architectural design, and interior design are all here, of course, but we also find the engineering disciplines, including structural, mechanical, electrical and fire protection, along with the key project management and administration functions.

This exemplary approach to the practice offers lessons for 3.2 million architects around the world. As the International Union of Architects (UIA) pursues its main purposes: to *unify* architects worldwide, *influence* public policies on building, and *advance* architecture in service to society, we constantly seek to bring excellent architecture from one part of the world to the attention of all parts of the world. And indeed, that is what this book by CPKA does.

A rich source of inspiration and progress, this is a wonderfully comprehensive view of architecture produced by a firm during the last half a century in one of the most important countries on earth. It shows many inspiring examples of how buildings have helped to make living better for people in India. In sum, it demonstrates how the great promises of architecture can be delivered.

Facing page: *India International Convention Centre, New Delhi.*

A Serendipitous Journey

Olivier Vidal

Architect, Paris–New York

Many years ago, I was fortunate enough to win a competition in India. It was a large hotel in Goa. I had no clue how easy or difficult it would be to work in that country. India was a mystery for me. The idea that I could discover a culture and a whole lot more intrigued me. In addition to the project was hidden a trove of discoveries and people that changed my life for the better. My client offered me to team up with his architect. He had worked on the hotel I was staying at and I really liked it. I was a little afraid it would be a clash of egos as he, too, seemed to be a well-established and competent guy. The wicked smile of C.P. and his bonhomie made my stays in Delhi more than a business trip. Not only could he teach me a lot about making buildings in his country, but he also made it a pleasant journey. There used to be lunch rituals at his office during which he would tell me stories about his youth and schooling in Canada. I grew to anticipate with relish the entertaining and educational lunchtime. He made me laugh about the guy on the street who was teaching us about God. He knew so much about tropical architecture; he made my understanding of many things grow. During that time, he asked me if he could send a young intern to my Paris office. This young intern was Dikshu, his son. Without hesitation I accepted, hopeful that this young man could glean some European training to complete his American journey. I was interested in seeing what his son was like. I got more than I bargained for. This person humbly got seated in a small office downstairs in my building, and soon he got saddled with shopping centre work. He had to make a model for a specialty shopping centre for Louis Vuitton et al., in Guam, USA, and also worked on a Parisian one, 'Passage du Havre'. I really liked those projects and needed good material for presentation. I do not know how much of a mentor I was or how much I tormented him... but his work was exceptional as I might expect, and I also learned that he had the charm of his father. Soon he became one of us. I was amazed by his thirst for learning, and I decided to include him in some trips I had planned to try and make his experience broader in terms of acquiring a feel of European culture. My wife had a thirteenth-century castle in Savoye, where we were trying to rehabilitate some parts that were falling apart. I thought he could benefit from a trip there; he could enjoy the changing landscape between Paris and Savoye and the experience of staying in this thirteenth-century folly might teach him something about scale and landscape management. As expected, he embraced the whole experience and seemed to be learning more every step of the way. He was eager to listen and to understand, which in itself is a rare talent. We enjoyed many fascinating discussions. The setting, far away from the formality of the office, allowed a new kind of openness. That part of the world is charged with European culture – it is where the great thinkers of the Middle Ages lived and theorized about the world. For some strange reason, the landscape allows you to meditate and clear your head and make it fresh for new ideas. Eventually Dikshu went back to India to finish his studies and take over the company from his beloved father. He succeeded in taking this large firm to increased capabilities and performance. I appreciate the fact that we could have open discussions about the state of architecture and noticed he would take my criticisms positively. I have been teaching in many universities around the globe; it is easy to recognize a winner. He knew I was not partisan when criticizing and that I was trying to pass on my knowledge. He was gracious enough to ask for my advice along the way.

I must say it is a rare pleasure to see somebody listen and take steps when and if necessary, leaving his ego aside and with the understanding that the quality of a job is the only important thing and that it takes a lot of humility and fortitude to nurse a large project to fruition. The worldwide experience he gathered will always accompany him and lead him to bigger and better things. To this day, I feel blessed I met Dikshu and C.P. – they helped me try and understand India to the benefit of my own personal growth.

Facing page: *Internal courtyard of the Secretariat building – Central Vista Redevelopment (proposal), New Delhi.*

Building Beyond Time

Suneet Paul

Editor-in-chief, *Architecture + Design*

The post-Nehruvian era in India, when architect C.P. Kukreja set up his practice, was one when architecture in the country was at its infancy. It was in such restrictive environs that, driven with passion for making a mark, he with a one-track mind, successfully pursued his dream to contribute and bring recognition to the field of architecture with conviction, hard work and a cheer. Backed with international architectural degrees and an understanding of the Indian cultural context, he made his presence felt very strongly through his architecture of Indian Modernism. His design methodology portrayed a pulse throbbing with sensitivity to climatic sustainability, tradition and art.

C.P. Kukreja, in the seventies and eighties, took upon himself the significant task of establishing credibility and respect for the profession of architecture in the country. Very assiduously, brick by brick, he built one of the largest practices in India, and thus, simultaneously added depth and a vibrant vocabulary to Indian architecture. The inherent robust character in his architecture won him numerous prestigious awards, national and international, and accolades. Indeed, to be listed in the top 100 architecture firms in the world is no small feat.

An architect with a vision, C.P. Kukreja's firm was one of the few firms then which intelligently structured a large, self-sufficient office with all allied services under one roof. His constructive forays not only extended to the practice of architecture, but also to architectural education and journalism. In the eighties, he was the key initiator and then a founding member of the Sushant School of Architecture and the journal *Architecture + Design,* respectively.

And then, after equipping himself with the diverse design exposure and liberal approach to architecture at Taliesin and Harvard, Ar. Dikshu C. Kukreja, his son, joined the firm and incorporated newer perspective towards an architecture driven by technology with a slant towards global vocabulary and rejuvenated interpretations to the narrative of tradition. Charged with a strong pulse for design and to address architecture with a contemporary idiom, he lost no time in entrenching himself to evolve a methodology that attempts to root out modern day environmental concerns. Dikshu imaginatively carries forward the future Indian vision of working towards smart design that is responsive and appropriate for a large and fast developing country. Anchored to the basics in architecture and culture, he now heads the legacy created by C.P. Kukreja, taking further strides to be involved with meaningful architecture and gracefully posturing Indian architecture.

A firm which has, over the years, intelligently handled mega-scaled projects in all typologies – institutional, residential, retail, hospitality, religious, educational and recreational – can but be a massive resource of knowledge for budding young practicians and students. Whether it be their earlier projects, like the all-encompassing Jawaharlal Nehru University or the recent Gautam Buddha University, interpreting Buddhist architecture in the twenty-first century, CPKA's strength is demonstrative in the mature handling of material, form and function. Dexterously treating the exteriors, as in the Ambadeep Towers or the Hamidia 'Smart' Medicity Hospital, they have incorporated traditional Indian architectural elements with prudence. Spontaneous evolution with time has been their hallmark, as well demonstrated in the design and architecture of the Surat Multi–Modal Transportation complex and the Transit–Oriented Development Hub. Their JCB Manufacturing Blocks' end-product image is one that adds an architectural elegance to industrial architecture. A positive, radiant approach to design is what classifies their style and design belief.

This monograph, I'm sure, is a stimulating insight into the design philosophy of the firm, bringing forth the truth that passion and innovation can, no doubt, yield results beyond comprehension. Their architecture has purposefully responded and dramatically evolved over the period with society's changing requirements, while simultaneously stimulating improved results for energy conscious design. If one of the aims of architecture is, albeit a challenging one, to provide an aesthetic, functional and sustainable habitat, then the firm CPKA sails through with a gigantic applause.

India International Convention Centre, New Delhi.

Introduction

Dikshu C. Kukreja

Above: *Ar. C.P. Kukreja, founder of CPKA, showcasing the winning entry of Jawaharlal Nehru University (JNU), New Delhi, to Mrs. Indira Gandhi, former Prime Minister of India.*

While some cities seemed adept at offering international standards of living, the dawn of post-independent India presented a bittersweet opportunity. The country embarked on a mission to de-colonize itself and re-introduce its architectural identity. At this time, with not many schools to offer the required training for the subject, there were a few who educated themselves, and by gaining international work and educational experiences, would return to the country. Among these few stalwarts was Ar. C.P. Kukreja, who founded CP Kukreja Architects (CPKA), New Delhi.

In the late sixties, there was a proposal to set up a world class, greenfield university, named after our first Prime Minister, Jawaharlal Nehru. The highly prestigious national competition for the design of JNU was won by Ar. C.P. Kukreja, and it put him in the spotlight. This project, the Jawaharlal Nehru University – or JNU as it is fondly known – spread across a 1,000-acre campus, served as a blank canvas for the architect and his team to set a precedence of an architectural language in the country. JNU's design was representative of the University's ideology – independent and empowering. The project also placed immense value on the scale of this colossal contoured site, and used context to create a new paradigm of humane architecture.

The 1970s witnessed the firm treading

Left: *Ar. C.P. Kukreja during his educational years in Canada.*

Below: *Ar. Dikshu C. Kukreja being felicitated with the Bharat Shiromani Award 2018–19 for Excellence in Architecture by Lord Swraj Paul in the presence of Ambassadors of Iceland and Slovenia.*

further and acquire more government projects. At the time, there was an upsurge in large scale housing projects. From Assam to Gujarat, and from far ends of south to north, the firm was involved in the design and execution of stupendous residential townships. The humility and proximity to nature that brick construction was able to instil in spaces enamoured the Architects and became a preferred material of construction. It also inspired elements such as brick arches, semicircular openings and *jaalis*, which soon became a signature style of the firm. C.P. Kukreja's strong resolve to work with sustainable practices, also elaborately explained in his book *Tropical Architecture* (published in 1978 by Tata McGraw-Hill), reflected in his reinterpretation of *aangans* and verandahs; *chhajjas* and *chhattris*; and use of forms and materiality in his designs.

By the end of the seventies, the firm had asserted its stronghold in the Indian landscape. This fuelled the Architects' dream to test international grounds, leading to fruition of projects such as the Parliament Building in Baghdad, Iraq; a five-star hotel in Ekaterinburg, Russia; hospitals in Nepal and Bangladesh; projects across Middle East Asia and Iran; embassies in Africa, etc. Back in the country, with state-owned as well as private companies investing in designs of office complexes and housing, the array of projects expanded for the firm. Household economies were also

Right: Tropical Architecture, *authored by Ar. C.P. Kukreja, is a much celebrated book on 'Environmental Architecture' and is a popular reference book in the libraries of prestigious institutions like Harvard University and MIT.*

Below: *Ar. C.P. Kukreja being felicitated by the Former President of India, Shri. K.R. Narayanan, for his lifetime contribution in architecture and environmental awareness.*

improving, enabling common people to spend on personal luxuries and qualifying CPKA to lead hospitality and retail projects as well.

Indian Institute of Management (IIM), Lucknow, and Rumtek Monastery, two of the most significant projects in the early eighties, saw the firm unfold a gallant character. The projects were diverse and exhibited the firm's desire to explore new paradigms in architecture. While IIM Lucknow's design fused modern design sensibilities and traditional Awadhi architecture, Rumtek Monastery in New Delhi, built for his Holiness the Dalai Lama, incorporated intricate craftsmanship and a detailed artistic sensibility into its design. Growing from a two-man setup into a multidisciplinary architectural and engineering firm opened up new avenues as large industrial projects made way into the company's portfolio. This added a significant achievement for the Architects and heralded a revolution for the architectural fraternity into a field which was previously being helmed by engineers. One could gauge a stark difference this shift made as monotonous industrial sheds were replaced with compassionate designs illustrated with *jaalis*, curtain glazing, skylights and cantilevers and projections on façades. The Architects even successfully transformed utility and service buildings such as water tanks, warehouses, paint shops, etc., infusing design expressions and aesthetics.

C.P. Kukreja's commitment towards architecture was deep and unparalleled. Though by the eighties the Architects had established themselves as a reputed design firm, C.P. felt the profession was sorely missing a platform for documentation, exchange of knowledge and critical thinking. He felt that a vast and diverse country such as ours, with a plethora of contemporary architecture being created, had no medium for sharing these developments. He put in a pioneering effort of establishing the first Indian architecture magazine – *Architecture + Design (A+D)* in 1984. Thirty-six years later, *A+D* continues to

be at the forefront of architectural journalism. Mr. Kukreja's attention then moved to address another serious concern in the profession – quality of architectural education. He believed that to enrich the future of the architectural profession, it was important to inculcate the right knowledge in our future generations who enter this profession. His strong belief in contextually relevant, climate responsive, vernacular architecture that imbibes the arts led to the establishment of Sushant School of Art and Architecture (SSAA) in 1989. Over three decades later, SSAA continues to be recognized amongst the leading architectural schools in the country.

Similarly, early on in its journey, in the 1970s, when the profession of architecture in India primarily looked inwards for projects to engage in, the Architects chose to venture overseas. In a world which is today often referred to as a 'global village', we might not be able to appreciate the enormity of this feat. As a nation, we were only seen to produce migrant labour, which could travel ashore to follow instructions of foreign architects and engineers to build. Here was an Indian architect who ventured overseas, competed against global design firms, and against all odds, established not one or two but almost a dozen offices across Middle East Asia, Iran and Iraq. Another

Above: *CPKA, being a multi-disciplinary set-up, encourages discourses between different departments.*

Left: *Ar. Dikshu C. Kukreja being felicitated by Dr. Manmohan Singh, Former Prime Minister of India, with the GPS Achievers Award 2014 – Excellence in the field of Architecture (Young Architect).*

Left: *With a robust in-house structural team, the firm is one of the pioneers of engineering innovation in the country.*

unusual feat was when C.P. Kukreja, in a deep urge to propagate the virtues of environmentally sensitive principles of design, penned down many of his philosophies in his book *Tropical Architecture*, which is a much celebrated book on environmental architecture and is a popular reference book in the libraries of prestigious institutions such as Harvard University and MIT. Altogether, a completely new revolution was started by him in the field of post-independence Indian architecture that prioritized concepts like sustainability, energy efficient design, renewal of natural resources, responding to natural context and blending tradition with modernity, which made his projects contextually relevant.

With the nineties, India ushered in an era of economic liberalization, permitting multinational companies (MNCs) into the Indian market. A boom in infrastructure ensued with these MNCs requiring improved office designs and facilities. The design sensibilities shifted from a subdued modern language to fully embracing vertical expansion and bold ideas of structural engineering. Ambadeep Towers was a first-of-its-kind landmark project where the Architects imbibed the western concept of high-rise architecture and remodelled it to an Indian context. Path-breaking and striking, the Towers redefined office design and broke away from dull and boxed cuboids. It exhibited the largest mural on its façade accomplished over any of the buildings at the time. The firm also used this opportunity as a social endeavour, using glass elevators to provide visitors with a lifetime experience of witnessing magnificent views of their city from an elevated level. Sir Banister Fletcher's well-known encyclopaedia, *History of World Architecture*, selected Ambadeep Towers as one of the most notable buildings of the twenty-first century. Ending the nineties on a high note, design of the flamboyant curtain-glazed Signature Towers in Gurugram was significant for two reasons – CPKA was an internationally acclaimed Indian design firm, and it was synonymous with bringing technological innovation to the country. The economic liberalization and India opening its doors to the world in the early nineties were defining moments in the country. The Architects saw this as an opportunity to redefine the contours of architectural profession. With a strong belief that the meaning of great architecture is an outcome of collaborative thinking, CPKA stepped forward to forge new alliances with the best international design practices from across the world.

A new century brought with it a new confidence for the Architects to acknowledge their sombre, sustainable concepts and to boldly manifest them in colossal projects. This would also be a time for a new generation to become involved in the practice, which brought with it a drive to allow technology to empower vernacular understanding of architecture. My international education and work experience – first-hand exposure to design values from across the world, infused a new energy into the firm. The underlying philosophy still remained strong, of introducing a built intervention which can successfully co-exist with its natural environment – a contextually responsive architecture. This is best exemplified by projects such as Pathways World School at Aravalli Hills in Gurugram, which celebrates the topography of the site by creating an ensemble of buildings around a natural depression that gets transformed into a magnificent lake. At the bottom of this lake is a mosaic artwork inspired by the 'rangoli' patterns designed by the nearby village folk. With a plethora of other design innovations, this project blended effortlessly into the Indian design landscape and became the first LEED Platinum certified institution in the country and was also selected amongst the best institutional designs in the world in New York. Army College of Medical Sciences followed the array of achievements by being enlisted amongst the five best designed buildings in Delhi. While integration of technology would be the new high in the field, the firm completely changed the rules of design with Gautam Buddha University, and introduced and cultivated a new understanding in institutional design and a holistic approach for projects, along with bringing an essence of spiritual learning. That also became a threshold to signify the firm's endeavour to constantly evolve and innovate, and through it showcase the finesse of Indian design and engineering expertise on international ground. After my early years of architectural education in India, followed by traversing the West through academic and work experiences, an underlying thought and concern has remained – while I have chosen a profession that allows us to 'create' a built environment – are we creating something which contributes to what already exists or is it at the cost of nature's ecological balance?

My father's architectural legacy and ideology have undoubtedly inspired me. While I am deeply impressed by many architectural legends, my idol remains my father, Mr. C.P. Kukreja. His passionate and determined commitment towards his work, his compassion towards society, his humility towards success and sacrifice for others are qualities that I not only admire but strive to emulate. As a child, I was fascinated by the longevity and permanence of the tombs and forts I visited.

Below: *Teamwork is an essential process during design ideation, allowing the best designs to flourish.*

Bottom: *Various conference and meeting rooms become areas for brainstorming and exchange of ideas.*

Above: *Team CPKA.*

Facing page: *The architectural studio.*

To me, architecture is the largest unwritten historical document, and even at a tender young age, as I wondered at the solitude and beauty of the ruins that I was surrounded by, they would evoke a curiosity in me as to what life would have been like all those years ago. Pioneer Ludwig Mies Van der Rohe has astutely remarked: 'Architecture is the will of an epoch translated into space.'

The twentieth century has been predominantly led by the western world. But on the other side, China has been able to make a huge imprint in the design world. Globally recognized icons in the design field have sprung across cities like Singapore, Tokyo, Shanghai, Beijing, Dubai and London, and across the United States. In this dominating spirit, for an Indian design firm to achieve global recognition is a matter to be proud of. The firm's ease to adapt and constantly strive to excel at each project plays a tremendous role in the firm being at the forefront of every opportunity and task at hand. Through its rigorous work ethic and attention to detail, it has been constantly ranked amongst the best design firms in the world. The firm has been able to not only create its own identity of sustainable, contextual architecture, but has also been in the vanguard in acquiring an international design firm, a feat unheard of. The deal undertakes to redraw the architectural landscape in India as the Architects expand their operations and focus further on sustainable infrastructure. It reinforces the firm's ever-existent vision of creating environment-friendly buildings, which is needed now more than ever.

I cannot help but feel concerned about the design practices today and their impact on our planet. I strongly believe that both society at large and the architecture profession have to rethink their actions towards our environment – both built and natural. Why are words such as 'iconic' and 'striking' common in architectural parlance rather than 'responsible' and 'sensitive'? My early experiments with 'underground architecture' were an outcome of a desire to be more frugal of land and its resources, to search for a design language which is more 'humble' and rooted rather than soaring into the skies and screaming for attention. More recently, these concerns towards our environment have resulted in CPKA, again in its continued spirit of innovation and redefining the boundaries of architectural practice, to acquire and integrate global talent in sustainable design into its design office. This endeavour of having in-house expertise in sustainability is aimed at creating a design thinking which at its core, revolves around an environment-friendly, climate conscious, sustainable design – one where any intervention of our built environment only enhances our natural environment and no other way.

While CPKA's five decade journey so far has had a profound impact on the built environment, a fact which visibly manifests in their buildings, a lesser known notion, is of their

indomitable spirit of innovation and redefinition of boundaries of architectural practice. The practice of architecture in India has always been understood as one where a client selects an architect, who then cobbles a team together of various independent professionals who deliver the project. This reliance on many separate design practitioners, such as civil, structural, electrical, mechanical engineers, landscape architects, interior designers, cost consultants and others, more than often leads to challenges of unison and coordinated team work. The firm created a unique setup where all such diverse design professionals are brought together under one roof and the outcome is of a truly comprehensive design consultancy where a single office team deals with the project. This unique design approach continues to draw awe and admiration from clients and redefines the contours of an architectural practice.

I am proud to say that currently CPKA is spearheading some of the most coveted and prestigious projects in the country, the likes of which include mixed-use developments, international embassies, Master Planning (townships, railway station redevelopments, transit-oriented developments, bus terminals, etc.), and office complexes. In our constant endeavour to find balance between the built and natural ecosystem, we are pushing boundaries with projects such as Gautam Buddha University, felicitated with multiple national and international awards for best green institutional design; a 100-storey tower (tallest building in India) at India's first transit-oriented development; India International Convention and Exhibition Centre, Delhi with the world's third largest Convention Centre of 10,000 capacity for hosting the G-20 summit; the Extension Complex to the Madhya Pradesh Secretariat, etc., to name a few, which have won national and international accolades as best architecture in office design. These achievements also empower one with a deep understanding of the power of architecture to influence one's life. We have also started a unique programme for students of design to encourage ideas from youth for improving our cities: the 'CP Kukreja Awards for Design Excellence', awarded through the CPKA Foundation, which gives the highest cash prizes to design students and opportunities for them to intern abroad.

At CPKA, we believe that design is a process and not the end product. It is a journey of discovery, innovation, evolution, and eventually, creation. With each project, we aim to 'read' and 'respond' to the built and unbuilt contexts of the urbanscape. The most important exercise in the design process is to read the salient gestures of forms and spaces, to converse with the natural environment and then translate those gestures into architectural ensembles. We refer to this as 'Responsive Architecture' – a philosophy which advocates architecture as a response to the various existing forces and systems like nature, climate, society, technology, economy and culture. Our primary objective is to create architecture that is a collective of all these blended seamlessly as a physical manifestation with the existing geographical setting, and at the same time, containing within itself a strong potential to live up to future developments and urban standards.

Timeline

1969
Firm established by Ar. C.P. Kukreja

1970

National competition winning entry – Jawaharlal Nehru University, New Delhi

Opened offices across Middle East Asia, Iran, Iraq

1978
Book authoured by Ar. C.P. Kukreja

1984
Atrium Palace Hotel, Ekaterinburg, Russia

1988

Ambadeep Towers, New Delhi

Rumtek Monastery, New Delhi

1997
Delhi Metro Rail Corporation

1999
United Hospital, Bangladesh

2000
Signature Towers, Gurugram, Haryana

2001

Indian High Commission, Nigeria

2004

The Lalit Golf & Spa Resort, Goa

2005
Former President of India, Shri K.R. Narayanan, felicitates Ar. C.P. Kukreja with Lifetime Contribution in Architecture & Environmental Awareness

2006
US Embassy Diplomatic Residences, New Delhi

2007

Gautam Buddha University, Greater Noida, Uttar Pradesh

2007
CNBC
Best Architects for Residential Building

Ar. C.P. Kukreja felicitated by Building Industry Leadership Award

2011
Lifetime Achievement Award for contribution in architecture felicitated to Ar. C.P. Kukreja (received by Ar. Dikshu C. Kukreja on his behalf)

2012

Shiv Nadar University, Greater Noida, Uttar Pradesh
LEED Gold Rating (IGBC)

2012
5GIREM LEADERSHIP AWARDS
Best Architecture Firm of the Year

Baburao Mhatre Gold Medal Award presented to Ar. C.P. Kukreja

2013

120-storeyed building in Sri Lanka – Tallest in South Asia

2014
Aerocity, New Delhi

2014

GPS Achievers Award for Excellence in the Field of Architecture presented to Ar. Dikshu C. Kukreja

Bharat Seva Ratan Gold Medal to Ar. Dikshu C. Kukreja for Outstanding Individual Achievement in Architecture

2015

Awarded Architect of Sustainable Design for Eldeco Ananda

Ar. Dikshu C. Kukreja selected amongst the 101 Notable Personalities

2017

India International Convention Centre (IICC), New Delhi, for G-20 Summit

2018

CPKA awarded the APAC Excellence Award

First Indian Architects to acquire a US design firm

2018

CPKA featured amongst top 100 global architects

2019

Redevelopment of Pragati Maidan, New Delhi

2019

Mumbai Metro Rail Corporation Limited

Gomtinagar Railway Station Redevelopment, Lucknow

2019

CPKA listed amongst top 5 architects in Asia

Opened office in New York

2019

CPKA wins design for the prestigious HRRL Township in Barmer, Rajasthan

2020

Opened office in Tokyo

World Architecture Community Award for Central Vista Redevelopment proposal

2014

Infra & Realty Sutra Award for Best Designed Residential Skyscraper

2015

Perto Industrial Facility, Jaipur

Society Interiors Honors Award for Outstanding Contribution to Architecture

2016

Innovation in Institutional Architecture in India

Best Eco-friendly Indian Institutional Project, Gautam Buddha University, Uttar Pradesh

2017

Best Architecture & Urban Design Firm–India

BUILD Excellence Award for Healthcare Projects 2017

2018

CPKA awarded Most Innovative Indian Architectural Design Firm

Vallabh Bhawan Secretariat – Architectural Design of the year 2018

2018

Hamidia Hospital Medicity Bhopal – 3,000-bed hospital

2019

India Pavilion, World Expo 2020, Dubai

2019

Bharat Shiromani Award for Excellence in Architecture presented to Ar. Dikshu C. Kukreja by Lord Swraj Paul

Gautam Buddha University – Winner in the Institutional Category (BUILT)

2019

Most Outstanding Urban Design Firm in India

2020

HUDCO Design Award for HRRL Township under 'New and Innovative Town Design Solutions / Eco Cities'

East Delhi Hub – Tallest building in Delhi

An exquisite landscape fronts the Secretariat building, creating avenues for recreation.

INSTITUTIONS

Institutions and their inhabitants constitute a distinct kind of community. With their special mix of permanent and transient populations and a shared sense of purpose, these communities are defined and sustained by traditions, goals and common experiences that profoundly influence their architecture. Great institutions are contingent upon the act of a thoroughly integrated, multiparty process of development. Institutional design is not just about creating an architectural style but using a palette of materials, forms and colour, creating an inspiring architectural character.

Gautam Buddha University

Location **Greater Noida, Uttar Pradesh** Site **511 acres** Built-up area **80,00,000 sq. ft.** Year of completion **2012**

Winner of the Award for ***'Innovation in Institutional Architecture – India'*** *and* ***'Best Eco-friendly Indian Institutional Project'*** *at the* ***BUILD 2016*** *Architecture Awards; winner in the* ***'Institutional Category (Built)'*** *at the* ***International Rethinking the Future 2018*** *Competition*

With a number of universities coming up across the country, what is needed is a pledge to create institutions that will contribute towards a society characterized by the wise and learned. It was with such a vision that the design for Gautam Buddha University was conceived. The aim here was to create a globally acclaimed academic and research institution that could nurture a vibrant community of intellectuals, endowed with character, creativity, competence and commitment, and also inspire meaningful transformations to ensure holistic growth and social development.

To imagine an environment of learning, wisdom and creativity that would infuse a sense of cultural ethics and ecological harmony with a respect for history, it was necessary to base the design of the campus on philosophies stemming from different cultures, all of which teach humans 'simple living and high thinking'. The essence of this design philosophy lay in respecting both continuity and change, and aligning it with teaching and learning practices within the University.

With Schools of study such as Management, International Law, Information and Communication Technology, Environmental Sciences, Applied Sciences, Biotechnology, Humanities, Buddhist Studies and Development Studies, the campus is dedicated to learning in an environment that truly engenders intellectual growth.

The iconic meditative pose of Gautam Buddha is Dhyana Mudra. This has been used as the primary design inspiration for the campus, with various buildings constructed in a way that superimposes them on this image. At the 'head' of Lord Buddha sits the library, the ocean of all knowledge; the eight faculties are located in the 'body', where they form the backbone of the University and represent Buddha's eight-fold path; the administrative office, which serves the University in terms of

Facing page: *The meditation centre is a magnificent domed structure, echoing the architectural symbolism of a stupa.*

Below: *Iconic image of Lord Buddha in Dhyana Mudra is translated onto the site. Buddhist chakras overlap linearly to form the basic components of the Master Plan.*

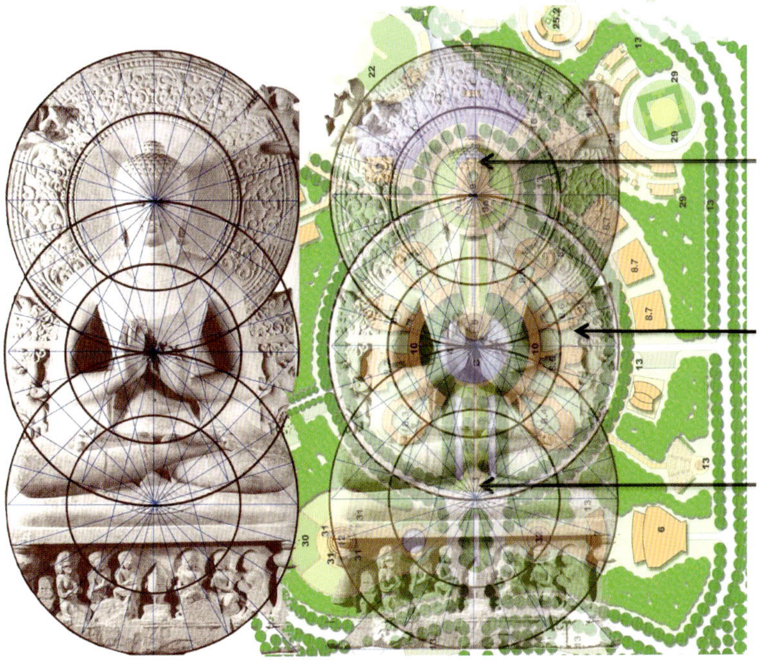

At the head is the **Library**

The body comprises the **Faculties**

At the feet is the **Administration** which serves the University

Above: *An aerial view of the campus highlighting the entrance promenade axis.*

Facing page above: *An initial sketch of the Buddhist stupa element used as a design inspiration.*

Facing page centre: *A magnificent statue of Lord Buddha, situated at one end of the entrance promenade axis, becomes the centre of gravity.*

Facing page bottom: *An elaborate natural stream at the foot of Lord Buddha's statue, which helps maintain ecological balance at the site.*

logistics and scholarly practicalities, is located at the 'feet'.

The very understanding and realization of 'Enlightenment' has been propagated globally by Gautam Buddha, the Enlightened One. The most ideal aspects of life, as it is to be lived, are derived in Buddhism through the middle path, which teaches marriage between binaries like *dhatu* (matter/solid) and *shunya* (antimatter/void), existence and non-existence, *bhog* (consumption) and *tyag* (detachment), and it is the balance between these respective binaries that keeps the wheel of life turning, causing birth and rebirth.

The abstraction of overlapping chakras, which form the different spatial entities in the Master Plan, brings a rhythm into the dialogue between the spaces. This also stands as a metaphor for the rhythm of life and death, success and failure, light and dark, and all the binaries which, as the middle path of Buddhism advocates, contribute to the creation of the universe. Indeed, much like the hierarchy of activities one observes in daily life, the activity pattern of life in the campus, comprising education, sports, meditation, recreation and leisure, has been distributed according to this very rhythm. The result: an academic complex, sports facilities, an indoor stadium, a convention centre and hostels for 5,000 students and 500 faculty members over a built-up area of 80 lakh sq. ft.

Consistent attempts were made to align the principles of the middle path with the design concept of Gautam Buddha University. By interweaving green landscape with different and carefully planned campus blocks, the Architects consciously mediated the central Buddhist tenets of life into the very fabric of the University. An understanding of spatial dynamics and its influence on the human psyche – the ability to seamlessly translate this knowledge into the overall felt and lived experience of the campus – is one of its many strengths. It is a design that respects the balance between binaries of open spaces and built forms, nature and man-made architecture, and is a harmonious conjunction of symmetrical patterns and subtle asymmetries. A dynamic hierarchy of spatial and visual sequences consequently recurs throughout the campus and is able to present a futuristic and competent example of a centre for holistic development.

Entering the campus through the majestic main gateway, one is greeted by a forest that acts as a noise and visual buffer from the Yamuna Expressway, along which it is located. The forest also creates a tranquil environment, metaphorically depicting the threshold between the chaotic worldly life of hectic frenzy and an orderly environment of peace and discipline. It further helps in regulating the microclimate of the area.

Above: *An evening panoramic view of the spectacular statue of Lord Buddha with the monumental edifice of the library in its background.*

Facing page below left: *Interiors of the meditation centre use a subtle palette of materials, which soothes the eyes and illuminates the space with natural light.*

Facing page below right: *A day view of the meditation centre.*

Inset: *The translucency in the ceiling of the meditation centre allows natural light to flush its interiors.*

A magnificent statue of Gautam Buddha is positioned along the entrance promenade axis; visible from any point within the campus, it serves as the centre of gravity of the academic environment. At the foot of the statue is a striking lake that not only functions as an ecological water system but also as a vibrant meeting place for students and members of the faculty. The faculty blocks are strung around this lake like gems on a necklace and are connected by an impressive colonnade. The academic blocks have faculty rooms, classrooms and lecture rooms assembled around a green space. This helps the teachers and students in sharing knowledge and utilizing the facilities the campus is endowed with, while enjoying the vast open area. The main administration building and meditation centre are located on either side of the main promenade.

The meditation centre and library imbibe the teachings of balance within its very design. The meditation centre is a sublime domed structure that echoes the architectural symbolism of a stupa, integral to Buddhist architecture. In particular, the spire or the pillar erected on the structure takes inspiration from the older versions of stupa design in which it acted as a source of unifying the cosmos with all of humanity. Elevated on sloped greens, it sits atop the subterraneous library and reading rooms, which receive natural daylight through a continuous light-well that covers the circumambulatory path on the mound. The meditation hall is a large, column-free structure clad in local stone and is a visually powerful building, designed in a manner that almost seems to tie the earth with the sky when viewed at the horizon. The landscape that surrounds it is designed to mimic the concentric circles of the *dharmachakra* (wheel of spinning energy), symbolizing the teachings and path that were expounded by the Buddha. The entire edifice is outlined by a water body, which adds to the calm and spiritual experience that is palpably disseminated through the university campus.

Certain design features incorporated in the planning of the campus have set it apart as a model for an ecologically sensitive, green development. At a time when our planet is facing substantial loss of green cover due to felling of trees, the Architects emphasized on saving and respecting nature through

abundant plantation across the university campus. Complete water recycling, through the creation of natural lakes and water bodies, makes the water balance at the site self-sustaining. Along with this, the buildings have been designed to receive maximum natural lighting and ventilation, making the University energy efficient. Architectural elements such as *jaalis* (ornate lattices) and *chhajjas* (overhangs), which reduce mechanical heat and lighting requirement of the building, are an essential part of the design. In addition to this, use of materials like locally sourced natural stone saved on building costs, with local craftsmen and masons encouraged to recreate *jaalis* and other vernacular architectural elements familiar to this region. With the execution for the design as per the GRIHA (Green Rating for Integrated Habitat Assessment Council) guidelines, the University sets a leading example of successful green campus design.

Gautam Buddha University is a fine example of a modern, twenty-first century interpretation of Buddhist architecture in an institutional design. It is also a testimony to the conscious balance of natural and man-made habitats, a pressing need in the present world. The strong emphasis on environment, with its introduction of greens, lakes and local craftsmanship, has transformed a flat and featureless site into a fine melody of buildings and landscape. The magnificent vistas and dramatic skyline have arguably created one of the finest masterpieces of campus architecture, both in India and beyond.

Facing page: *An evening view of the academic blocks; the building screened by an intrinsic* jaali *pattern.*

Above: *An evening view of the meditation centre as seen from the entrance of the site.*

Below: *Elevation of the Buddhist Research and Museum Centre.*

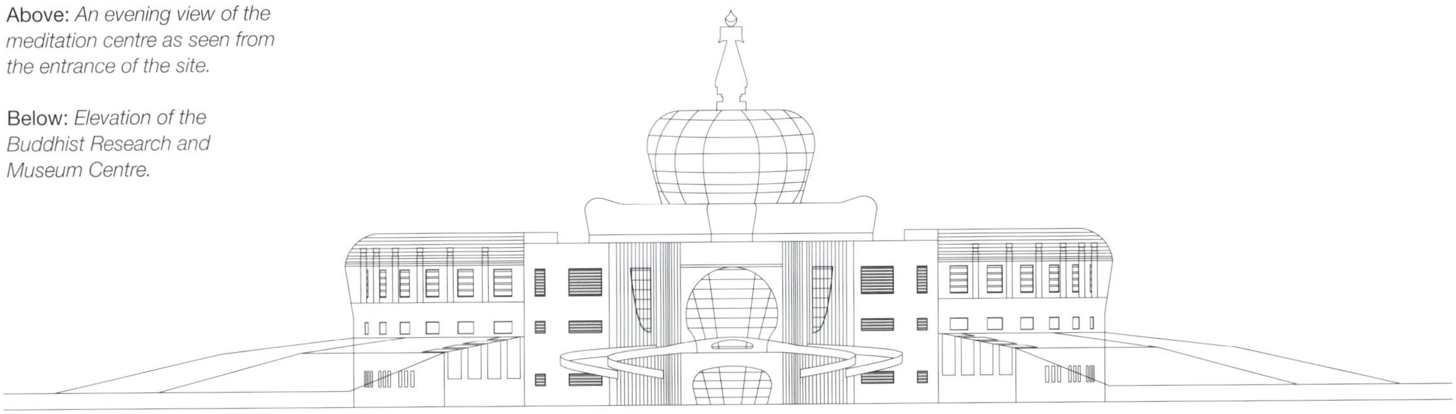

Central University of Kashmir

Location **Ganderbal, Jammu and Kashmir** Site **600 acres**

Built-up area **40,00,000 sq. ft.** Year of completion **Ongoing**

Won as a national competition design entry *and thriving on vernacular design sensibilities*

The Central University of Kashmir is a one-of-a-kind greenfield project and attempts to make a strong statement regarding sustainable use of landscape in developing eco-sensitive educational campuses. The design, a winning entry in a national competition, was highly appreciated for its concept, namely, 'landscape as a tool for enhancing sustainability and cultural awareness'. With the pressure of the real estate market rising everyday in India, the natural landscape of the country, especially in critically eco-sensitive regions, is threatened by overpowering, rampant urbanization. Jammu and Kashmir, with its treasure trove of lakes, rolling uplands, valleys and pastures is a region which is vulnerable to this force.

With 7,000 students, 350 faculty and 400 non-teaching staff, the design of the University aims to fulfil a high quality of life and learning for a large population, with state-of-the-art infrastructure that does not compromise on environmental considerations. The campus consists of academic and administrative blocks, a convention centre, hostels, a central library, faculty departments, development centres, faculty and non-teaching accommodations, guest houses, club buildings, health centre, and other amenities.

The design process advocated a study of the existing geographical character of the site. Its natural form, landscape, flora and fauna were documented and analysed to derive a

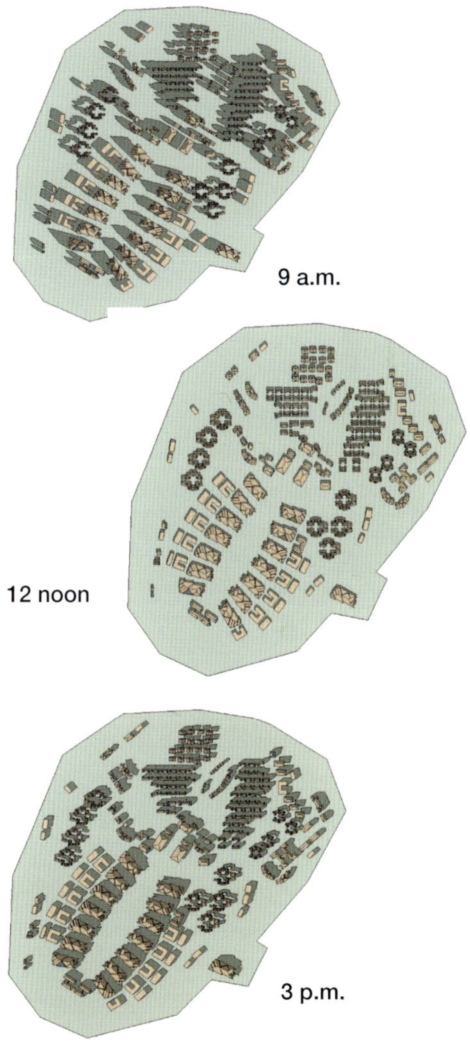

Facing page: *An aerial view of the academic complex.*

Above: *Simulation drawings to study shading at the site.*

Below: *Master Plan of the University.*

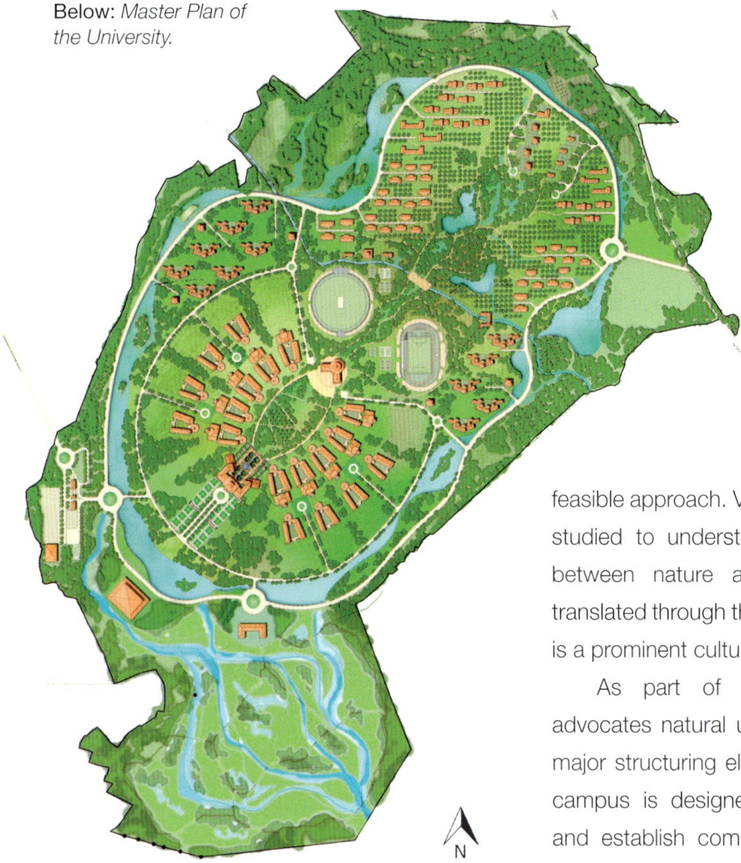

the low-lying terrain. Inspired by regional architecture, low-rise structures have been given preference to provide resilience against earthquakes. Furthermore, low-height buildings respect the horizontality of the landscape, creating a serene skyline.

A 'pedestrian spine' has been conceived as a pleasant tree-lined avenue that shades the walking path through the day, its thick canopy animated with the colours and life of the biodiversity housed within. Designed to open on to play fields, the informal gardens and shaded courts become student activity zones, discussion areas and leisure spaces. The landscape has been extensively tapped into as both – a cultural symbol and connection between major built complexes. The built masses occupy central space in a compact manner to minimize distance and enhance walkability. Forest-like buffers line the site boundaries, and trees with dense canopies wrap around the buildings and clusters, creating a comfortable microclimate. This helps in natural humidification, preventing the extreme cooling that takes place in Kashmir.

feasible approach. Vernacular architecture was studied to understand how the relationship between nature and built environment is translated through the local architecture, which is a prominent cultural image of the region.

As part of a design strategy that advocates natural urbanism, nature is also a major structuring element within the site. The campus is designed to promote walkability and establish common areas of interaction. The buildings are placed in a compact manner on higher ground to avoid interference with

In addition, water presents itself in many forms in Kashmir's landscape – lakes, rivers, canals and natural reservoirs. Existing depressions and watery marshes on the site were studied and strengthened through design developments like a freely flowing waterway, punctuated by pools, fountains and reservoirs. This water system also provides the opportunity of on-site storing, recycling and re-charging water. *Shikaras* (houseboats) have been planned as an energy-efficient and environment-friendly mode of transport.

The design approach has also helped create an opportunity for surrounding villages to come together and be a part of the campus design. The traditional design language of Kashmir was studied to understand how the architecture of the region responds to the local context of climate and geography through material gestures of form and space. Since the buildings have been designed to follow these parameters, they are characterized by green, sloping roofs, stepped forms and towering canopies. The long, pitched roof steeply slopes down, resulting in the buildings almost merging with the landscape. The extensive use of gardens as a tool to blend outdoor with indoor spaces is inspired by the Mughal gardens of Kashmir.

Engravings and sculptural massing have been incorporated into the building elevations, which are reminiscent of the local art. Lattice screens and window shutters, intricately carved wooden brackets, eaves boards (locally called '*morakh patt*'), pendants (locally called '*dour*') are architectural details borrowed from the traditional art and architecture of Kashmir. This built cultural language of the land has been integral, both aesthetically and practically, to the University's overall form.

Top: *A panoramic view of the academic complex.*

Above: *Typical hostel elevation drawings.*

Shri Vaishnav Vidyapeeth Vishwavidyalaya

Location **Indore, Madhya Pradesh** Site **51 acres** Built-up area **2,86,000 sq. ft.** Year of completion **Ongoing**

Envisaged to be a ***Green Campus,*** *the design incorporates compact axial planning to create an evident and efficient circulation network*

Located in the commercial capital of Madhya Pradesh, Shri Vaishnav Vidyapeeth Vishwavidyalaya embodies the rich heritage of Indore city in a modern and practical style. This is the result of the architectural vocabulary of the campus design, which involves a contemporaneous interpretation of the traditional architecture of Madhya Pradesh. Jewels of Indore architecture, such as *chhatris* (umbrella shaped roofs), *jaalis* and *chhajjas,* have influenced the campus' modern edifices. Ultimately, exposed brick façades reflect a grounded and vibrant academic institution that is quintessentially Indian.

The University as a 'green campus' strongly promotes walkability and universal accessibility in a variety of ways across the site. Compact axial planning has been adopted to create an efficient circulation network, punctuated by greens and play fields. The academic complex has been planned around a central square; the built form invites the open area to permeate through its apertures, encouraging a seamless interaction between the exterior and the interiors.

Below: *A visualization of a thriving central courtyard leading to the library and flanked by academic blocks.*

Maitreyi College, University of Delhi

Location **New Delhi** Site **10 acres** Built-up area **4,00,000 sq. ft.** Year of completion **1987**

Maitreyi is a first-of-its-kind ***women's college*** *in Delhi and is* ***designed for an intake of 1,500 students***

Maitreyi College, established in 1987, is located in the prestigious Chanakyapuri area of Delhi. It is one of the constituent colleges of University of Delhi's South Campus, and therefore, draws from an urban design layout that is commonly identifiable. It is part of a larger urban statement that forms the design vision of Chanakyapuri.

The college campus is flanked by plots of international embassies, all of which follow the urban layout of 'villas in the garden'. The landscape plan also followed the 'urban garden' typology – its basic structure is defined by a central court, which all buildings of the campus can look into. The physical solidity of the buildings is balanced with the void created by the open spaces, bringing harmony into the design. The building also uses solid blocks with deep arches, creating an interesting interplay of light and shade, which changes as the sun moves.

The architecture of the campus captures the very essence of Indian Modernism. The sculptural composition of the architecture is due to the solid massing's exposed brickwork. Brick was chosen not only as a tool to create aesthetic appeal but also to protect the interior and exterior environment of the campus from the extremes of Delhi climate. An earthy material, it reflects incoming heat and also acts as an insulator, keeping indoors cool in summer and warm and cozy in winter.

Below: *The front façade of Maitreyi College with its iconic arched windows.*

'When I started in 1972, I was drawn towards the warmth and human scale that exposed bricks projected. In addition, it is a material that is economical, besides being ideally suited to our domestic architecture. From there, to the design of JNU situated on the rocky terrain, the use of brick as a natural material was an instinctive move.'

Ar. C.P. KUKREJA

Architecture + Design, 1992

Jawaharlal Nehru University

Location **New Delhi** Site **1,000 acres** Year of commencement **1972**

Winning cntry in a national competititon *of the* ***largest university campus in the country,*** *it is helmed as a* ***pioneer in sustainability***

In 1969, the Government of India founded Jawaharlal Nehru University (JNU) to realize India's first prime minister, Pandit Jawaharlal Nehru's vision of an ideal university. This was to be an institution that, in his words, *'[stood] for humanism, for tolerance, for reason, for the adventure of ideas and for the search of truth.'* The campus of JNU, therefore, was aimed to be characterized by values that were both deeply social and spatial, realized through a form that could recall the earthly spirit of modern India. This called for a superior design vision of a modern structure impregnated with values of learning and enlightenment, well-suited to a trailblazing and independent nation. CPKA's design was ultimately the winner of the first national architectural competition to be held in post-independent India – selected from sixty-eight entries submitted by the nation's top architects at the time.

Located in South Delhi and spread over an area of 1,000 acres, the campus occupies some of the northern-most reaches of the Aravalli Hills. The Ridge is home to more than 200 species of birds and animals and has very rich and interesting patterns of biodiversity. This demanded a singular planning of the university campus that was both nature-inclusive and capable of moulding the unique rocky terrain into a sustainable and welcoming space for human habitation and scholarship.

Other than these social and environmental values, the concept of the campus also intended to incorporate economically efficient designs within a recognizably Indian context. This was fulfilled through the productive use of space, cost-efficient materials and local methods of construction. Open, developable land in Delhi – considered to be a highly scarce commodity since the Partition – needed to be used without wastage and as judiciously as possible, maintaining a reasonable balance between man-made and natural ecologies.

The campus contains an academic core with six academic blocks known as schools, a computer centre (one of the first-of-its-kind), a nine-storeyed library, a conference, a lecture

Facing page: *The computer centre, which forms the apex of the academic complex, has screen walls around it which help in passive cooling.*

Below: *The form of the hostel block is an accentuation of the steeply contoured site.*

Above: *View of the landscaped courtyard of the Department of Bio-Technology (DBT) building.*

Facing page above: *A play in light and shadow of the pergola pattern of the library centre.*

Facing page below, left and right: *A distinct departure from the brick architecture of the academic complex, the administrative block has been designed with façades in stone: one wing in Red Agra (left) and the second in Dholpur (right).*

and a theatre complex, an administrative centre and a students' activity complex. The academic complex is a quadrangle surrounded by walkways, covered with creepers, and leads to each of these buildings. The whole setting is laid out in a traditionally Indian manner along the slope of the high terrain, well-suited to the surrounding landscape.

JNU also consists of sixteen residential sectors, comprising 1,500 faculty residences and hostel facilities for 10,000 students. Each of these residential complexes is named after major geographical divisions of India, and student hostels are named after the major rivers of each of these sectors, including Ganga, Godavari, Kaveri, Narmada, Jhelum, Brahmaputra, Tapti and Sutlej. The campus is self-sufficient with its own primary and secondary schools, a shopping centre, recreational spaces, and other important infrastructural facilities.

The six academic schools at JNU are the School of Life Sciences, Schools of Social Sciences I and II, School of International Studies, School of Languages and School of Environmental Sciences. Each school has a constructed area of 60,000 to 70,000 sq. ft. Furthermore, each building is planned around a court and is generally four-storeyed. The internal planning of these built forms, including these vertically recessing courtyards, caters to the variegated requirements of different functional rooms on different floors.

The design approach relied on an architecture that seeks to foster a harmonious and intellectually refined society of students, professors and adjunct staff. The assembly of forms and spaces, holistically put together, created a true environment of learning. Traditional methods of education, such as learning in close contact with nature, were also considered alongside provision of advanced educational infrastructure such as laboratories, a computer centre, conference, lecture and theatre complexes, and the library. Since its construction, the JNU library has become one of Delhi's many educational landmarks, and has been designed to stack over 10 lakh volumes in a vertical block. There are two base floors in which most of the major reading and reference areas are located. Each floor in the tower is subject-oriented, and caters to a vast spectrum of undergraduate and postgraduate needs across the subjects of science and humanities.

Careful thought was also given to the choice of materials to be used at every step of the campus' construction. During the discussion over the mode of JNU's construction, brick was neither seen nor understood as simply a material made from clay. It was, recognizably, a Modernist symbol within the discourse of Indian architecture. While considering the value of brick as one of the chief building materials for the project, its nature as a down-to-earth, environment-friendly, low cost and locally available material quickly came to the fore. It is crucial to note that never before had a project of this scale in India attempted to use exposed brick as a unifying material. However, its use throughout the campus created a strong urban character that was highly distinctive and distinguished at the time of construction, and arguably has since remained so.

Another bold step taken while creating the campus was a conscious interplay between natural and built forms. The natural landscape was allowed to flow effortlessly throughout the campus, and it continues to do so with as much success as the built form that creeps

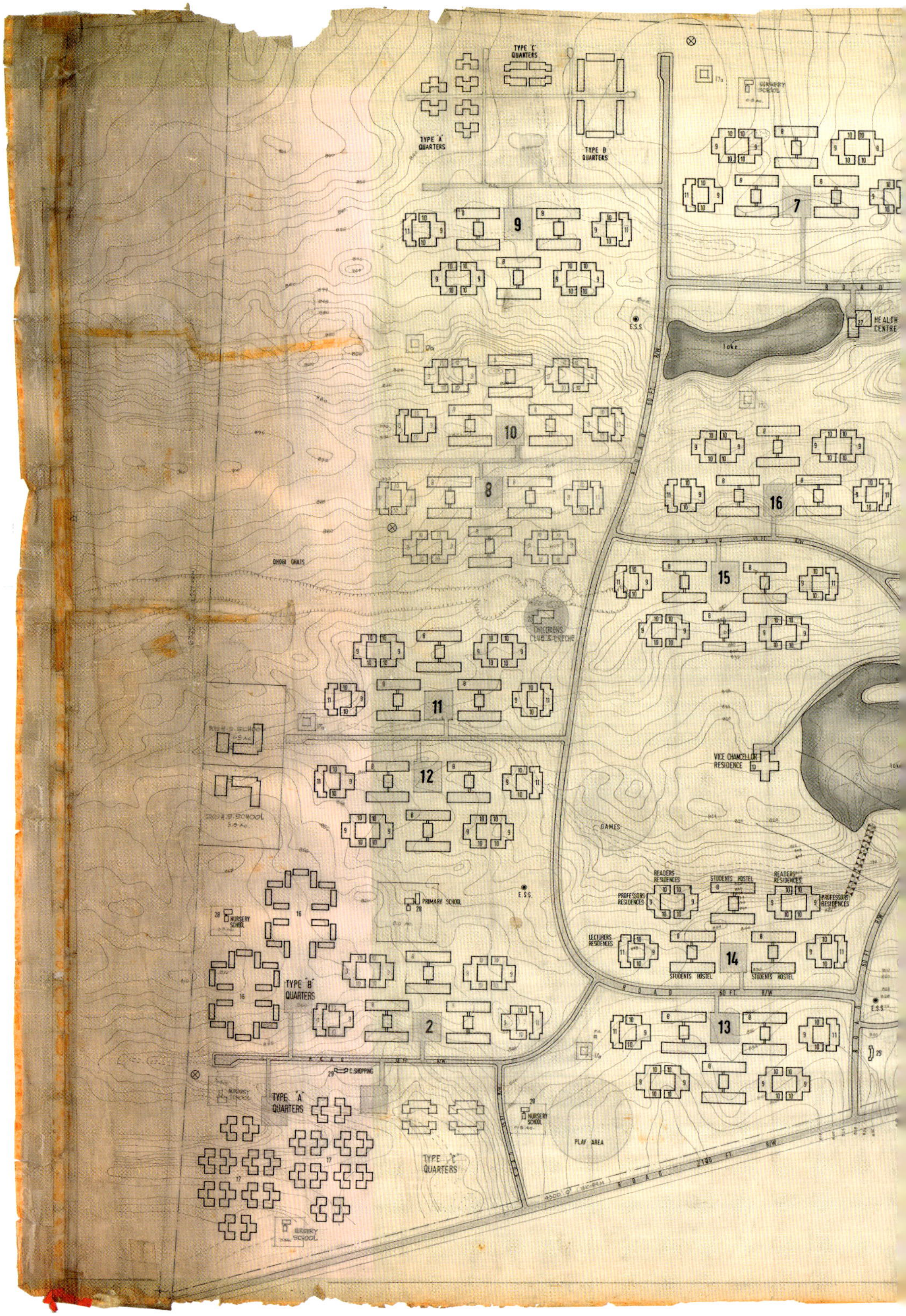

Hand-drawn archival plan of the 1,000-acre site. The design uses the lake as focal point to plan the academic complexes, the administration building, the library block and the student and faculty residences around it.

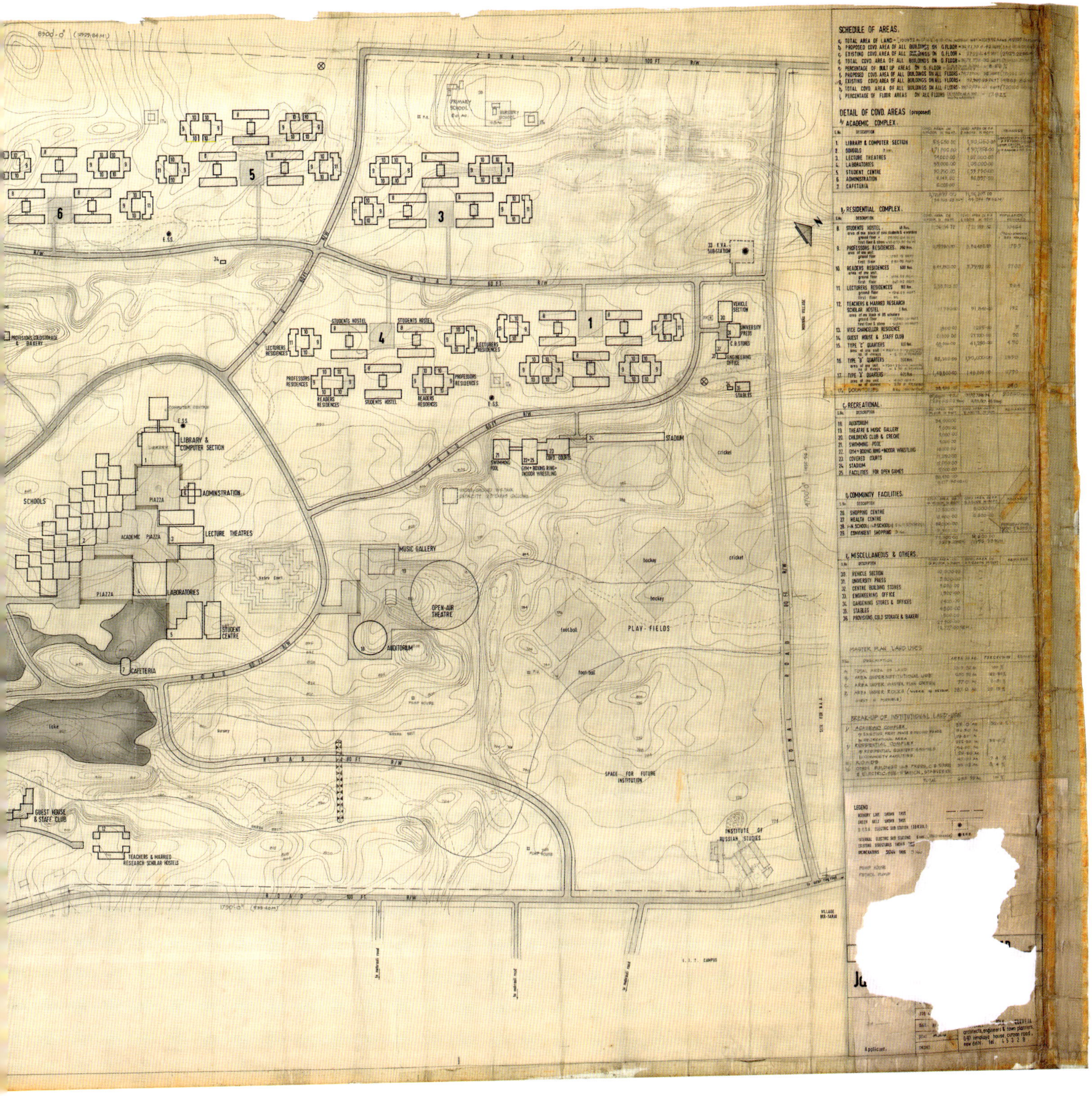
SCHEDULE OF AREAS.
DETAIL OF COVD. AREAS (proposed)
ACADEMIC COMPLEX.
LIBRARY & COMPUTER SECTION
SCHOOLS
LECTURE THEATRES
LABORATORIES
STUDENT CENTRE
ADMINISTRATION
CAFETERIA
RESIDENTIAL COMPLEX.
STUDENTS HOSTEL
PROFESSORS RESIDENCES
READERS RESIDENCES
LECTURERS RESIDENCES
TEACHERS & MARRIED RESEARCH SCHOLAR HOSTEL
VICE CHANCELLOR RESIDENCE
GUEST HOUSE & STAFF CLUB
RECREATIONAL.
AUDITORIUM
THEATRE & MUSIC GALLERY
CHILDRENS CLUB & CRECHE
SWIMMING POOL
COVERED COURTS
STADIUM
FACILITIES FOR OPEN GAMES
COMMUNITY FACILITIES.
SHOPPING CENTRE
HEALTH CENTRE
CONVINIENT SHOPPING
MISCELLANEOUS & OTHERS.
VEHICLE SECTION
UNIVERSITY PRESS
CENTRE BUILDING STORES
ENGINEERING OFFICE
GARDENING STORES & OFFICES
STABLES
PROVISIONS, COLD STORAGE & BAKERY
MASTER PLAN LAND USES
BREAK-UP OF INSTITUTIONAL LAND-USE
LEGEND
ZONAL ROAD 100 FT R/W
ROAD 60 FT R/W
ROAD 80 FT R/W
PRIMARY SCHOOL
NURSERY SCHOOL
33 K.V.A. SUBSTATION
STUDENTS HOSTEL
LECTURERS RESIDENCES
PROFESSORS RESIDENCES
READERS RESIDENCES
VEHICLE SECTION
UNIVERSITY PRESS
C.B. STORES
ENGINEERING OFFICE
STABLES
PROVISIONS, COLD STORAGE & BAKERY
LIBRARY & COMPUTER SECTION
ADMINISTRATION
SCHOOLS
PIAZZA
ACADEMIC PIAZZA
LECTURE THEATRES
LABORATORIES
STUDENT CENTRE
CAFETERIA
lake
MUSIC GALLERY
OPEN-AIR THEATRE
AUDITORIUM
SWIMMING POOL
GYM + BOXING RING + INDOOR WRESTLING
COVD. COURTS
STADIUM
cricket
hockey
foot.ball
PLAY - FIELDS
SPACE FOR FUTURE INSTITUTION
INSTITUTE OF RUSSIAN STUDIES
GUEST HOUSE & STAFF CLUB
TEACHERS & MARRIED RESEARCH SCHOLAR HOSTELS
VILLAGE BER-SARAI
I.I.T. CAMPUS
Applicant
architects, engineers & town planners

spontaneously into the background of hills and forests. Within JNU's topography, vegetation and rocky outcrops, it is as if the buildings have gradually evolved from the earth, with red brick edifices emerging from the red soil at the site. The noteworthy manner in which the built fabric intertwines with its natural landscape sends a powerful message that is even more significant today, fifty years later: the idea that we must co-exist with our natural environment, and not at the expense of it.

Though the overall concept was conceived much before the advent of green buildings, a nature-centric design elevated the JNU project to an early venture in green architecture, or at least, an environmentally responsive architecture. Several of its design approaches were ahead of its time: natural lighting, ventilation and passive cooling methods were all greatly facilitated and enhanced by the infrastructural performance of the project, making it a futuristic assemblage of art and technology.

In an era when campuses were designed with the notion that faculty housing and student hostels had to exist in different parts of the campus, JNU introduced the novel idea of creating sixteen residential zones, improving the quality of the residential spaces visualized for a revolutionary campus design. Each was to have a mix of 600 students and 100 faculty members and foster greater interaction between the two groups, helping to establish a more proactive and collaborative environment for academic learning.

All the hostels are designed as load-bearing structures with exposed brick work, and the stepped form of the hostel block is an accentuation of the steeply contoured site. A typical hostel in JNU houses 200 students in two linear, parallel wings, and the dining and common room facilities serve as a link between the two. In each wing, the rooms are planned on either side of an atrium, flanked by corridors on two sides. These corridors strategically regulate cooling through cross ventilation. The design also enables provision of open air, sit-out spaces for residents without adding to the overall cost. Built form of the hostels illustrates a rhythm in terracing that not only helps students maintain privacy but also allows each of the students' rooms to have a balcony that brings them closer to nature.

Today, JNU is more than just a university campus. As the nation's first truly 'sustainable' campus, it has successfully stitched its natural ridge landscape and the surrounding

Facing page: *A view of the DBT Building.*

Left: *The academic schools with a vertically recessing courtyard.*

Below: *A model of the Master Plan of the academic complex.*

urban cityscape and stands out as an iconic architectural masterpiece in Delhi NCR region. Its open spaces, corridors and lawns continue to provide an inspiring sanctuary for national debates and budding leaders in politics, art and business.

This project has confirmed the Architects' position as one of the most forward thinking architectural firms in India, possessing an undeniable sense of artistry and technological intelligence in their design philosophies – visible in the very design of JNU itself. Though the firm has journeyed a long way in its architectural practices since then, the campus remains one of its best designs, continuing to inspire creative scientific thinking in the future institutional projects.

Pathways World School Aravali

Location **Gurugram, Haryana** Site **30 acres** Built-up area **5,00,000 sq. ft.** Year of completion **2003**

*Recognized as the **first platinum-rated institutional project** in the country; awarded the **'Most Innovative Institutional Design'** at the **Designshare Award in New York,** USA, in 2003*

Facing page: *View of the academic block as seen through an old architectural archway.*

Above: *The school passages are lined with dense foliage.*

Pathways World School Aravali was established in 2003 with the objective of introducing a new dimension in the field of education. At its outset, the Architects sought to create a physical environment that would not conform to conventional design stereotypes, but instead allow natural surroundings to be an essential aspect of its learning spaces. The project, however, begins with an interesting story. The Client possessed a 30-acre parcel of land in the midst of the Aravalli Hills of Haryana, south of Gurugram. The site has an engaging topography with plenty of contours and some rocky outcrop; bound by roads on two sides, it slopes inwards which forms a natural depression towards the centre of the site. The Client, unsure of how to put this land to use, invited a few of India's leading architects to propose how to best utilize this space. The varied options that were suggested included turning the site into a resort, weekend cottages, a market place, a healing centre, or a school.

In offering this final option, the Architects were certain that the unique setting of the land offered an opportunity to introduce a new kind of educational paradigm – one that would expose children during their early, formative years to holistic learning with special focus on environment, culture and global advances. The close interaction between the Architects and the Client, and the high value of their dialogue, brainstorming and mutual trust became the foundation for successful creation of the school. The results have been outstanding, with the campus being recognized as the first platinum-rated institutional project in India. In 2003, the design was selected as the 'Most Innovative and Environment-Friendly Institutional Design' in New York, and in 2018, it achieved the first rank in Infrastructure Provision parameter in Education World C Fore Survey. The design approach was unconventional, innovative and sensitive towards the current needs of the society. Its pragmatism lay in the fact that the rocky, hilly and almost inaccessible site would have to be transformed into a comfortable

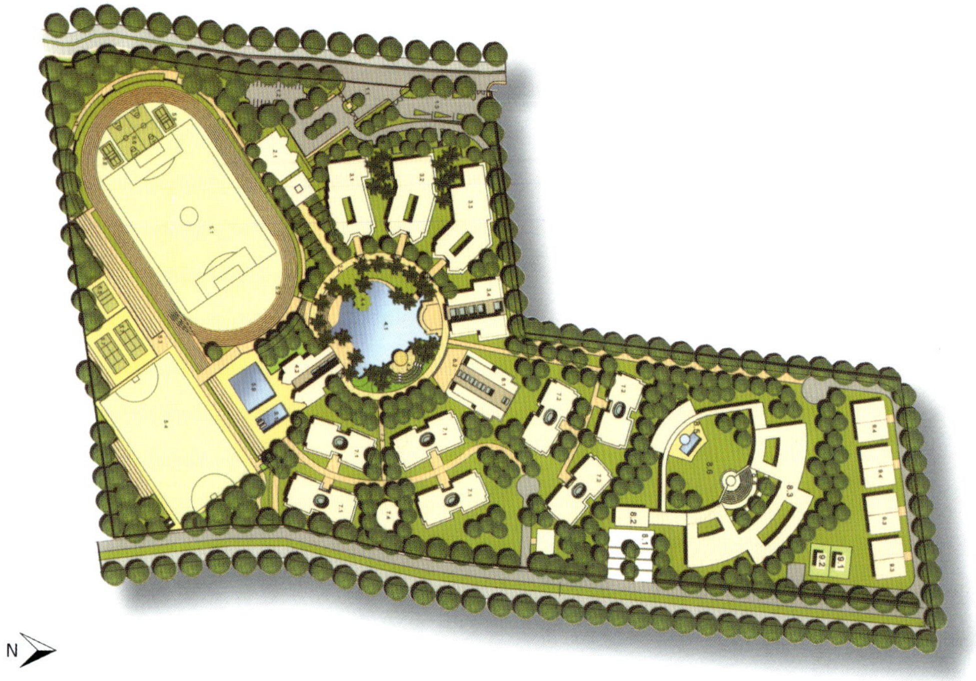

and state-of-the-art campus within twelve months, all in a highly cost-conscious manner. The architectural design was also sensitive to preservation of the site's fragile ecosystem, with the Architects treading carefully, both physically and intellectually, during the planning and construction stages of the project.

The Master Plan was generated organically with a deep consideration of the site's singular topography. The first major design decision was creation of a central lake in the natural depression that existed at the centre of the site. This magnificent lake was then kept as the central focus, and all the school's buildings were slowly configured in a circular manner around it. The lake had been conceptualized as an ecological water body that collects water run-off throughout the site. It also serves as a backup water resource in case of a fire emergency, since the site is in a remote location with no crisis resources, such as a fire station, available in its vicinity.

The school campus is strung together by a circular colonnade, which also serves as a circulation spine. Different buildings in the campus are designed along this colonnade. Each building, having a different function, was planned separately. This avoids creation of large blocks of buildings and allows shorter spans of travel for students and faculty members. It also creates an interesting interplay of built mass and open spaces, encouraging students, teachers and staff members to pause and enjoy the natural landscape as they move from one building to another.

As one enters the campus, they are greeted by an entrance forecourt flanked by flags of various countries, representing nationalities of the diverse community of students. Across the forecourt is a grand administration building, which is the focal point of contact between students, parents, visitors and faculty. On entering the atrium of this building, one is able to view the school's impressive sports facilities,

Above: *Master Plan of the project.*

Facing page above left: *Entrance to the Primary School.*

Facing page above right: *The pergola acts as a connecting spine throughout the site.*

Facing page below: *A view of the dining hall and library block as seen from the amphitheatre.*

complete with an international level athletic track that is among the very best in the country. Walking down the slope from the administration building towards the main campus, one is drawn towards the central lake and its beautiful floor mural. As one approaches the lake, they are able to appreciate the panoramic view of the campus that unfolds. This panorama begins with two academic buildings towards the left, followed by the media centre, dining hall, two hostels and a student centre. All these buildings meet world-class standards at an institutional level; the centrally air-conditioned school is equipped with state-of-the-art learning equipment, building management systems and wireless internet technology.

The Architects were keen to transform the barren, rocky campus into a lush, green environment. For instance, the edge of the lake has been treated in multiple ways: from sloping grass turfs to stepped planters, the stone wall of the media centre and the charming amphitheatre. It is gratifying to observe the lake, particularly as it is visited by many exotic birds from the Aravalli Hills. The areas around the water body have become a popular meeting spot for both students and visitors. In addition, plenty of trees and play on levels throughout the site add to a burgeoning eco-campus.

The environment-friendly design approach also includes deep overhangs on the façade, grey water recycling, solar panels, provision of adequate natural lighting through design features of the buildings, low energy illumination, and roof and wall insulations. Furthermore, the Architects selected natural and locally available materials for construction, such as clay-brick and local stone, which give the buildings a dignified, institutional appearance, and a permanent finish that also complements the landscape. Interestingly, the stone used was procured from the site itself since quarrying is banned. In this way – and so many more – the architectural identity of the campus is an inextricable part of the natural site area, and vice versa.

The project is truly a standing example of how incorporating environmentally conscious design ideologies can create iconic, long-lasting structures. Without having to compromise on any of its facilities, Pathways World School Aravali is a blend of modern and vernacular elements.

Above: *Front panoramic view of the campus showcasing the striking mural design inside the lake, around which stands the amphitheatre.*

Facing page: *Roof structure above the swimming pool.*

Indian Institute of Management, Lucknow

Location **Lucknow, Uttar Pradesh** Site **200 acres** Year of completion **1999**

*Selected as the **Best Designed IIM by the Outlook magazine;** the **computer centre,** housed in a spacious 75,000 sq. ft. area, was **a first-of-its-kind** centre to be designed in any institution across the country*

The Indian Institute of Management (IIM) at Lucknow is a proud part of India's premier league of educational institutions. In the decades since its inauguration, it has continued to uphold the strong legacy of management studies in the country.

Lucknow is one of the most distinctive cities in north India, with a rich socio-cultural and architectural heritage – from its stunning *imambaras* and royal palaces to sturdy buildings that have long served to house the common man. Widely used local materials, such as bricks and natural stones, reflect a naked urban ruggedness, simultaneously creating a tangible sense of Lucknow's renowned resilience and history of social expression. The design for the Institute was conceptualized to be respectful of the landscaping and planning philosophies of the region, which is characterized by lush green gardens, open courts and pavilions. Lucknow's extreme weather also called for a climate-sensitive approach that could effectively foster and maintain passive cooling and natural ventilation. The resolve for such requirements lay in Awadh architecture, a singular style of design followed in Lucknow, in addition to many other contemporaneous cities in north India.

The firm's design is characterized by an interplay of solids and voids within the entire built form to facilitate natural lighting and ventilation, giving the building a balance of solidity and porosity. Elements such as false walls, double walls and networks of corridors efficiently induce passive cooling and air circulation, and have been used extensively throughout the design. The overall physical image of the campus presents a collage of different enclosed and semi-enclosed spaces – courts, terraces, atriums, pavilions and colonnades that attempt to emulate the architectural character of the city itself, and reflect its Mughal heritage. The buildings have been set amidst landscaped gardens, integrating them with the topography of the site.

An orchard serves as the welcoming entrance of the campus. There are both static and flowing water bodies, while connections between the buildings are established through shaded walkaways and criss-cross paths, punctuated by common public spaces that guide one from one building to the other in a pure, rhythmic sequence. A conscious sense of play between the organization of buildings and open spaces takes monotony away from the campus. It allows closed and open spaces to

Facing page: *Atrium of the library and computer centre.*

Below: *Housing blocks in the Institute.*

Above: *Typical* jaali *screen detail.*

Above right: *An archival hand-coloured pencil drawing of the layout plan of the academic complex.*

Facing page above: *Hand-drawn archival plan of the iconic library and computer centre (dated 1998), a first-of-its-kind to host computers in an educational facility. The roof design accommodates a dome in the centre, flushing the interiors with natural light.*

Facing page below: *Hand-rendered elevation of faculty block.*

unify the design of the entire campus into one holistic ensemble. The buildings are screened with an outer layer of *jaalis* and rich indentations in the brick work to protect the campus against the harsh summers of Lucknow. It prevents the structures from being directly exposed to the sun and also offers a subdued interweaving of light and shade that is as visually delightful as it is practical.

What brings a thoroughly hard-wearing yet beautiful expression to the architecture is the use of Kota stone, a locally available material. Used with bricks, and with occasional reliefs created by marble patterns, it lends a superior quality to the aesthetics of the design, while maintaining a low cost in construction. This exposed brick work with Awadh reliefs was used in building both the exteriors and interiors throughout the campus, consisting of faculty building, classroom blocks, library, computer centre, administration building, auditorium and conference centres, hostels (for 2,000 students) and faculty residences (with a 500-person capacity).

Deriving inspiration from the traditional architectural elements of the rugged and rustic city that the campus calls home, albeit with a vision that is notably forward thinking and futuristic, IIM Lucknow stands as a truly distinguished blueprint for future educational institutions in India.

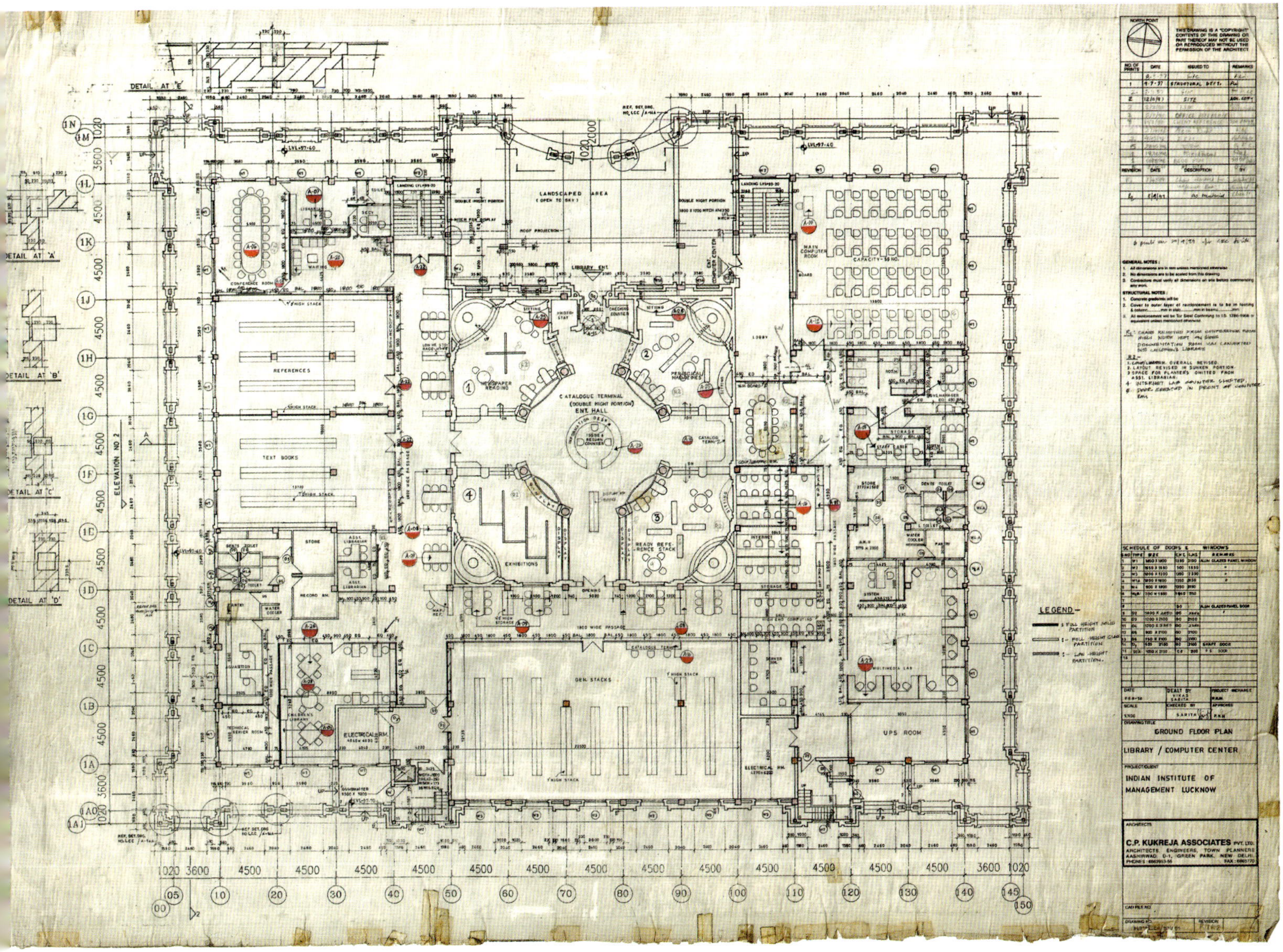
GROUND FLOOR PLAN
LIBRARY / COMPUTER CENTER
INDIAN INSTITUTE OF MANAGEMENT LUCKNOW
C.P. KUKREJA ASSOCIATES PVT. LTD.
LEGEND
CATALOGUE TERMINAL
ENT. HALL
GEN. STACKS
UPS ROOM
REFERENCES
TEXT BOOKS
EXHIBITIONS
LANDSCAPED AREA
ELEVATION NO 2

National Archives of India

Location **New Delhi** Site **3 acres** Built-up area **1,00,000 sq. ft.** Year of completion **1981**

National competition winning entry *located on the iconic Rajpath, its design harmoniously unifies with the existing Lutyens' buildings*

The Imperial Record Department was first set up in Calcutta in 1891 but was later shifted to Delhi in 1911. After Independence, this institution came to be known as the National Archives of India. The design was awarded to the Architects as the result of a winning entry in a national competition.

After independence, when a strong wave of national cultural revival was sweeping the country, many old buildings of the British Era underwent significant alteration and retrofitting due to changes in functional demands and social outlook. The National Archives witnessed a second phase of construction during this time, which sought to build new amenities, such as an auditorium, a canteen, research scholars' wing and other technical facilities that could serve archival and scholarly purposes.

The challenges for this particular project included respecting the newly emerging national movement within the capital city. The Architects also sought to interpret its gravity through an architectural design that could simultaneously respond to the radical urban design vocabulary set by Sir Edwin Lutyens through the urban fabric along Rajpath boulevard. Hence, the design approach undertaken for this project primarily sought to create an architectural style that was neither purely British nor Indian, but rather suggested the emergence of a modern Indian nationalist statement from, and not despite, its colonial roots.

The architectural typology was, therefore, conceptualized on the basis of the urban block and volume proposed by Sir Lutyens, while its substantive and intricate design details contained Indian elements, such as arches, frames and recessed windows, which sit upon a sturdy façade with stone finish. The rhythm of the colonnaded façade on the existing block was also borrowed and applied within the array of arches of the newly designed buildings in the complex.

The new facilities constructed during the second phase of construction of the National Archives successfully merged with the original architectural composition. Today, this institution stands out as a singularly holistic design that celebrates the marriage of Indian and British architectural ethos in Delhi.

Below: *A view of the library block as seen from the adjacent lake.*

Bihar Police Academy

Location **Rajgir, Bihar** Site **133 acres** Built-up area **8,50,000 sq. ft.** Year of completion **2018**

Designed for training members of the Indian Police Force, it has been ***awarded a GRIHA 4-Star rating***

The Academy was envisioned as a training institute for the members of the Indian Police Service, one of the primary defence services in India. The project site for the Academy spreads over an area of 133 acres and is strongly influenced by a splendid array of biodiversity owing to the plant wildlife sanctuary situated less than 10 km away, and for this reason, the site also presented the challenge of preserving the sensitive site surroundings. Nonetheless, the setting provided unparalleled scenic beauty for the campus, and the unevenly contoured landscape was dedicated to the manifold activities required during police training.

The design approach sought to create a low-rise campus with two- to three-storeyed buildings sheltered under a crown of trees, thereby preserving the landscape's rural character. The entire campus continues to be bordered by thick groves of trees that reduce sound and air pollution, and merge the site effortlessly with its surrounding natural landscape. The strong emphasis that the design places on nature has led to its 4-star rating as per the GRIHA Council.

The design is conceptualized along the lines of Classical style. The campus comprises training blocks, an administration building, a hospital, residences, schools, reserve offices and a guest house. This makes it self-sufficient and has allowed it to become a mini-city dedicated to the police force. Among the training facilities provided are long and short firing ranges, marching and drilling grounds, and even equestrian and canine training areas, which have increased the diversity of the landscape.

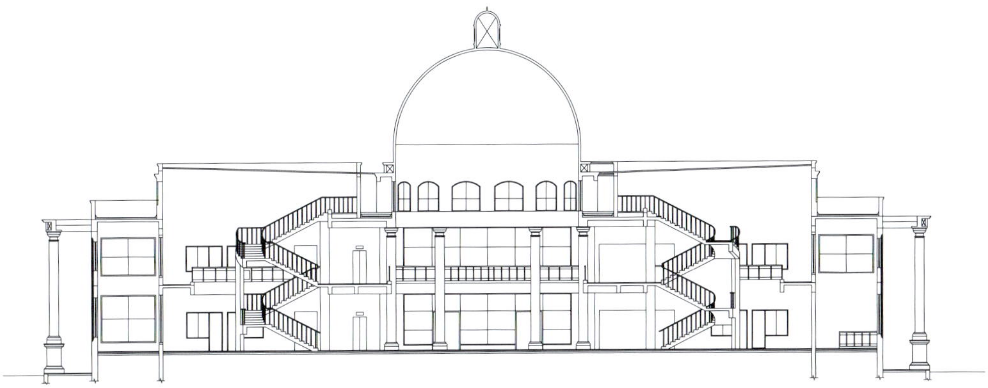

Above: *Cross-section of the academic block.*

Below: *A view from the front of the campus.*

I D P S INTERNATIONAL

Delhi Public School International

Location **Gurugram, Haryana** Site **5 acres** Built-up area **4,50,000 sq. ft.** Year of completion **2014**

The school redefines and ***reintroduces the Classical order of architecture*** *on Indian soil with a fresh perspective*

A nationally and internationally significant urban centre, adjacent to Delhi–Gurugram, has gradually emerged as an area furnished with advanced infrastructure facilities and technologies. With this very understanding of the city shaping the design process, a campus branch of Delhi Public School (DPS), a highly recognized name among educational institutions in India, was developed in Gurugram's Sector 45. Indeed, through an expansive low-height design, the Architects have been able to break away from the monotonous high-rise character of Gurugram's famous urbanscape.

DPS International, Gurugram, was visualized possessing a distinct personality in its architecture – one that was profound in depth, stability and progress in all their manifestations, and with a unique structure that could captivate the first-time as well as regular visitors. The Client's idea was to realize a vision by bringing back the old world charm of learning spaces that could nurture young minds towards a futuristic mode of thinking.

To present a design that captured an entire school in a moment of timelessness while also accommodating a functional embrace of technology was certainly a challenge. The answer appeared in pursuing the footsteps of Classical Architecture, which is both immortal in its appearance and is able to incorporate the advanced technological provisions of present day education. The centrally air-conditioned school for 2,000 students over a built-up area of 4,50,000 sq. ft., with an eye-catching architecture and proportions, is reminiscent of true Classical imagery.

Within a high-functioning infrastructure, the school follows the globally renowned International Baccalaureate (IB) curriculum and contains 'smart' classroom facilities. The school's curriculum, therefore, resonates equally with the principles of Classical Architecture – those of balance, proximity, alignment, repetition, contrast and space – and, through pedagogy, sets its own strong foundation stone for the formative years of a child's growth and learning.

Fronting the school with a vast greenscape has allowed visitors to witness the grandeur of the school in one length, with the campus rising

Facing page: *View of the school entrance.*

Below: *Wall panelling detail of the reception lobby.*

as an edifice of imperial finesse as one moves closer. Furthermore, the presence and growth of native flora during the students' initial years of education gives them an understanding of the value of nature and the balance required to have a sustainable lifestyle.

The height of the main building could not be very high, owing to the standard Classical proportions that were followed. It was then adjusted by sinking the ground floor and sloping the top floor by creating dormer windows. This balanced the height in scale with an aesthetically pleasing elevation being created at the front. To further accentuate the front elevation of the building, a clock tower – a significant element of Colonial-Classical Architecture – was introduced at the front façade. This clock tower not only added a remarkable detail to the building but, beyond architecture, is a powerful urban marker in the skyline, visible from a distance.

The site, being extremely linear, presented certain setbacks during attempts to create a harmonious balance between the open and built-up spaces. This issue was effectively addressed by the creation of several building blocks, separated by open spaces in-between. This allowed the segregation of activities among primary, secondary and kindergarten classes, with separate play areas for little kids on one hand, and young boys and girls on the other. The classrooms' location on the front face of the design allows ample natural light, proven to benefit the health and performance of children. The filtered natural light also adds to the school's nurturing ambience. Aided by pastel hues of the campus, a playful and radiant environment is created, making learning fun. The Architects understood the value of bright and optimistic surroundings, essential to mould and develop the personality of a child from an early stage.

Similarly, the central courtyard was conceived to encourage student activities. It is a common space for all kinds of school activities – be it for morning prayer sessions, lunctime hustle, prize distribution ceremonies or Christmas parties. Yet, even as they encourage movement and play, the courtyard and the campus remain a distraction-free and calm environment, with their interiors also contributing to the airy and spacious ensemble, and complement the carefully hand-picked furnitures.

DPS International, Gurugram, is an example of an institution that has effortlessly managed to blend the timelessness of classical design with the innovative spirit of contemporary architecture. The unmatched architectural mastery and magnificence of the school is reflected in the much-lauded distinction that the design has been able to achieve for itself.

Above: *The use of Classical Architectural elements is evident from this striking panoramic shot of the front façade of the school.*

Below: *Front elevation drawing.*

Shiv Nadar University

Location **Greater Noida, Uttar Pradesh** Site **286 acres** Built-up area **18,00,000 sq. ft.** Year of completion **2012**

Thriving on ***water conservation and regeneration strategies,*** *the project has achieved* ***LEED (Leadership in Energy and Environmental Design) Gold Rating from IGBC (Indian Green Building Council)***

The Shiv Nadar Foundation nurtured a vision to foster an intellectual environment that would encourage freedom of enquiry, criticism and creativity. Ultimately, intelligent site planning, thinking and urban landscape design strategies gave birth to the holistic design of Shiv Nadar University, which fulfilled the vision of the Shiv Nadar Foundation.

The site is located on a vast, green field – adjacent to the Grand Trunk Road in Gautam Buddh Nagar, Greater Noida – and so the eco-sensitive geography of the area had to be taken into consideration at each design stage. The Master Plan was imagined in a manner that allowed the campus to merge seamlessly with the surrounding greens. The campus was envisioned to be an epitome of environmental design and was, therefore, planned according to the principles of compact urbanism, which encourage concepts such as a walkable and cyclable campus. The inner part of the site is kept as a pedestrian space, making walking and cycling within it feasible, and which in turn supports the compact nature of the campus. The buildings are organized within close proximity of each other, leaving most of the site free for landscaping. The vehicular road runs all along the periphery of the site and gives access to the campus buildings successively.

This close circuit of buildings is further 'stitched' together by a vibrant public space network. This comprises a main public spine, punctuated intermittently with open spaces, to create a variety of experiences and control the hierarchy of activities. This variety of open and semi-open spaces was proposed in order to control the degree of privacy enjoyed at different points within the campus. The specific urban form and typology of blocks for the hostels was also an important component of the overall design. Judicious amounts of space have been left to accommodate any future

Facing page: *The overarching trellis around the library block.*

Above: *Façade of the hostel block.*

Above: *A rendered site plan of the campus.*

Facing page above: *An evening shot along the path to the library block with the hostel blocks in the background.*

Facing page below: *Panoramic view of hostels and the dining hall.*

expansion plans and have been placed in a manner that will not hinder the current design structure of the University in any way.

The natural depressions on the site were carefully studied and many of them were designed to be reservoirs for harvesting water. One proposed design idea was a large 'eco-lake', from which thin, informal water channels would flow between the building blocks and percolate into the green landscape, merging the water body effortlessly with the architecture of the site. Punctuated with fountains between academic blocks, this created a serene environment that is highly conducive for peaceful learning. The eco-lake also acts as a natural reservoir that can harvest water during the hot and dry periods of climate.

In order to achieve a sustainable environment in economic terms, passive engineering principles were key in the development of the campus design. An early proposal was planting an array of trees with thick canopies, lining the footpaths and bicycle-tracks to keep the grounds shaded from the sun, which becomes especially necessary during the city's harsh summer months. In fact, the extensive planting of trees and groves on the site also indirectly made up for the carbon footprint generated during construction of the campus. In addition, the water from the eco-lake cools the campus during summers by means of evaporative cooling: saturated winds, channelized by the lined trees, flow over the eco-lake from the south and into the open courts, keeping the area cool and ventilated during hot months.

The compact arrangement of buildings and courts enables self-shading during summers, thereby cooling the indoor and outdoor spaces. Play fields complement the orientation of the blocks well, easing the entry of north light inside the buildings. Such passive design strategies appreciably cut down air-conditioning costs in summer and electrical heating costs in winter.

Landscape is, therefore, not only the chief element in controlling microclimate within the site, but is also the unifying element between architecture and nature in the Master Plan. It has been designed to 'flow' in the open and semi-open spaces as well as, occasionally, within the buildings themselves. The large central *maidan* serves as the primary social space amidst the hostels, becoming a major breathing lung for the site. Green arms glide out from the *maidan* and extend between the buildings to join hands with the eco-lake on the other end of the campus.

The visual corridors within the site have been designed to provide a breathtaking view of the eco-lake to maximum number of buildings. The radial layout of the academic blocks around the eco-lake also serves to make the latter the focal element within the campus. These visual linkages are designed with the aim of enhancing communication and public interaction within the campus, while simultaneously minimizing the felt distance between the buildings. The variety of open

spaces thus created accounts for a large number of public spaces, which, added to the fabric of the city, encourage vibrant social and cultural interactions amongst the vast diversity of students.

Finally, the play fields on one end of the site act as the University's distinctive sports hub, with outdoor sports facilities such as tennis courts, a cricket ground with practice nets, basketball courts, volleyball courts and a football ground. Moreover, the sports hub contains a high-class gymnasium, along with indoor sports facilities for badminton, table tennis, chess and carom. Besides these facilities, the site also offers yoga gardens for meditation, as well as extensive jogging trails and cycling tracks as part of the 'daily keep fit' network on site.

The design strategies behind Shiv Nadar University bring to life the ideal model of an urban educational institution: one that harnesses a futuristic and environmentally conscious architectural design with efficient building technologies and passive engineering. The architecture of the University owes its successful design to smart environmental and landscape planning aided by cutting-edge urban design concepts, which have helped the campus to develop into a smart and economic institution within the urban Indian landscape.

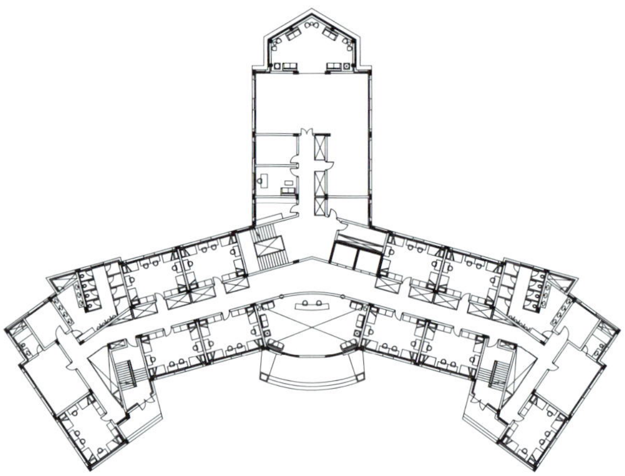

Top: *The extended shell of trellis around the edifice induces a play in light and shadows.*

Above: *A typical hostel plan.*

Facing page: *The eco-lake created on-site acts as a natural reservoir.*

Iconic School

Location **Bhopal, Madhya Pradesh** Site **20 acres** Built-up area **4,50,000 sq. ft.** Year of completion **2016**

A harmonious combination of natural materials, *inspiring and providing a learning experience for the students*

The Architects were approached to create an inspiring school campus on the fringes of Bhopal, Madhya Pradesh. The Master Plan incorporated the necessary requirements of a dedicated primary school, an administration block catering to primary and senior schools, laboratories, an art centre, a library, a dining hall and outstanding residential quarters for both students and faculty. A large derelict structure that stood nearby – originally an Information Technology (IT) building with a rather unimaginative façade – was also revamped into an academic block for the school upon request by the Client. Deep structural improvements were made to this building, such as the incorporation of an additional floor for better functional efficiency.

The institution's use of vernacular brick architecture with Indo-Saracenic influence is a particularly noteworthy design element. The school has been planned around a system of courtyards, with colonnaded corridors opening out into them. Richly landscaped, a correlation between the open and built spaces is marked by these colonnades and courtyards, which serve as semi-open spaces, creating a seamless transition between the two zones.

Below: *Looking towards the middle school block from the landscaped court.*

Gyan Bharati School

Location **New Delhi** Site **7.5 acres** Built-up area **1,50,000 sq. ft.** Year of completion **1980**

*One of the forerunners to **helm the trend of exposed brick work** in institutional design, the project is a **celebrated design of Modern India***

Gyan Bharati School is an English medium, co-educational school located in Saket, an upscale neighbourhood in South Delhi. It was established in 1980 and has a strength of more than 2,000 students. It was developed with a strong and proactive vision to impart an integrated and comprehensive education to its students, which would prepare each and every one of them to lead the world, armed with a balanced and dignified understanding of the rapidly evolving society in which they live. The school believes that the holistic development of a child leads to better results in terms of their growth and general decision-making, and this is facilitated through its efficient and appealing design.

The site, located amidst the kerfuffle of the nation's capital, is nothing less than an academic oasis. A buffer of trees and rich vegetation was designed along the site edges, revealing the buildings of the school only when one enters the premises. The buffer acts as a noise and air pollution barrier while also visually protecting the school from the continuous activity outside. This careful engagement between the built form and the surrounding greenery makes the children understand, from a young age, the value of coexistence with nature.

The buildings were designed with brick as the prime construction material. Left exposed, they embody the grounded design sensibilities of post-modern India: imparting a rugged, dignified look that conceals their identity as low-cost, low-maintenance material. Openings in the shapes of circles and semicircles dominate the façade curving at their edges and playing with the built mass. The harmony between solids and voids is maintained with recessed arches, sloping walls, sweeping pergolas and ramps. These varying geometries create an exuberant space for children to ideate creatively whilst pursuing intellectual activities.

The school's infrastructure includes state-of-the-art buildings, sixty-four spacious and well-ventilated classrooms, smart classes with computer-aided learning, Wi-Fi, round-the-clock internet, cutting-edge laboratories, play and activity rooms, well-stocked libraries, an assembly court and two covered auditoriums. However, equal emphasis has also been placed to create areas for extracurricular and sporting activities for the students to receive a holistic education. The design for the school condenses the built structure to the entrance area of the site, providing large and open grounds for recreational sports. The expansive playgrounds contain high-quality facilities for cricket, basketball, football, badminton, volleyball, table tennis, and many more.

Above: *A combination of exposed concrete and brick gives a dramatic entrance to the nursery wing.*

Management Development Institute

Location **Gurugram, Haryana** Site **40 acres** Built-up area **1,60,000 sq. ft.** Year of completion **1983**

Recognized as one of the ***Most Innovatively Designed Business School*** *in the country by* **Business Today,** ***2013***

The design for the Management Development Institute (MDI) is a landmark in modern architecture that honours the legacy of age-old institutions in the country by adopting a contemporary interpretation of the same, infused with technology and engineered finesse of tomorrow. This vision placed the Institute much ahead of its time.

The design for the campus, an area of more than 40 acres and located on the junction of MG Road and National Highway near Gurugram, was devised on principles and design of famous Indian institutions like Vikramshila, Nalanda and Takshila during ancient times. Like many of these historical institutions, the campus' layout plan follows an axial plan where all major functional elements fall on the primary axis while other facilities are dotted along the secondary axis, branching out of the former.

This planning ideology has also helped the functional areas of the campus to be aggregated and arranged within a compact footprint along the major circulation corridors. The main focal points on the primary axis are the academic complex and the students' hostel wing; the secondary axis bears facilities such as staff and faculty residences, the chairman's residence, an ancillary block and various club facilities.

Since the built footprint was confined to a compact ground area, the majority of the site was left for landscaping. This provided an opportunity of harnessing a huge volume of greenery within the campus. A dense and richly landscaped campus inspired construction of avenues alongside the internal roads and created an environment of serenity and repose, one that is conducive to the holistic development of students' personalities.

The variation between the landscape elements creates a harmonious rhythm, ensuring that the campus exists as a successful reminder of historical education methodologies.

Facing page: *The academic complexes follow a series of arched openings.*

Below: *The courtyard fronting the library building.*

The campus was further planned in a way that created different activity zones that could generate public interaction and activity during the course of the day, and also serve as a common space for meeting and recreation of students and faculty members.

The landscape design aimed to segregate the open spaces within the whole campus into different public and private zones depending on the functions and activities required, such as academic, residential, recreational, or simply for circulation purposes. It plays a crucial role in bringing balance to the entire campus.

The underlying objective was to weave a structural connection between all the elements within the site and unify them as part of one holistic campus design. In this respect, private courts within each block open out through paved pathways into a larger, central open space shared by multiple facilities. This area, in turn, empties itself into the large flowing greenery of the campus, merging gradually with the sprawling golf course in the southwest.

This design concept acts as a green buffer, reducing sound and air pollution generated from the vehicular traffic outside the site boundaries. In addition, the abundance of protective foliage canopies in the landscape plan help in keeping the open spaces within the site humidified: comfortable and cool in summers and warm in winters. As a result, the foliage acts as a natural climate controlling factor in the overall design, emphasizing successful accommodation of requirements of the Indian landscape within the planning ideology.

In addition, elements such as *aangans* (shared courtyards) and verandahs help crochet a climate-friendly campus. The courtyards allow the buildings to merge effortlessly with the landscape and facilitate passive ventilation in the surrounding buildings. This helps the areas to act as 'breathing lungs' within the built complex of the campus. They are also the defining element of a building's entryway, which are exquisitely landscaped. Through this interspersed network, these green pockets are able to balance the built and unbuilt volumes of the design.

The buildings are double-storeyed blocks, their low-rise stature respecting the horizontality of the ground. Besides this, the buildings are rendered in exposed brickwork that makes them appear as earthly extensions of the ground itself. Bold arches adorn their façades, and their elevation builds a sense of character for the institution's architecture. Sculptured forms, such as arches, *jaalis*, coffers and pergolas, reinforce details into the otherwise unostentatious exposed bricks. Arched columns span the entire length of the buildings, introducing a sylvan charm to the campus. The semi-covered corridors act as shared spaces of recreation for students, also easing the movement across different blocks. They act like a double-wall for the buildings, thereby controlling the climate of the rooms during summers and winters. The design of the columns varies in nature, exhibiting finesse in brick as an architectural and engineering building material.

Arcaded corridors, which are 6-feet-wide, run all along the periphery of the courtyards. They form an edge between the building and the open space while creating circulation networks that connect the buildings in both the academic complex and the students' hostels.

The Institute's built structures are seamlessly integrated into the green landscape,

with a system of courtyards punctuating the site at different nodes. This is particularly visible in the agglomeration of the academic complex, where a large central court leads onto smaller internal courts, encompassed by academic and administrative facilities. The Architects' endeavour to emulate the values of a truly collective learning environment has helped develop this specific language of design – one that also evokes a sense of modernity and tradition.

MDI remains one of the most revered institutional designs in modern Indian architecture. The approach of bold built forms set amidst a lush, green landscape creates a magical juxtaposition of buildings and open space. It has resulted in a tranquil academic setting within the heart of a city, and is the perfect example of how architecture can shape its own unique environment.

Facing page left: *The corridors are open, allowing natural ventilation through the buildings.*

Facing page right: *Entrance court of the library building.*

Above: *View of the academic block.*

N
0
100
250
500M

Indian Institute of Technology, Jodhpur

Location **Jodhpur, Rajasthan** Site **840 acres** Built-up area **14,40,000 sq. ft.** Year of completion **Ongoing**

The architectural form ***thrives on passive design strategies*** *to regulate thermal comfort*

The Indian Institute of Technology (IIT), Jodhpur, has been conceived as a self-sufficient campus for 8,000 students. It is viewed by the Indian government as an emerging seed of development that can bring Jodhpur a step closer to its ambition of becoming a Smart City in the future. In this spirit, it is intended to be a smart eco-campus, and a shining example of an institute that imparts knowledge, promotes technological research and facilitates a sustainable lifestyle. The Architects won the prestigious design competition for comprehensive design solutions in Phase I of the campus development, comprising architecture for the building zone, hostel zone and related utilities and services. For the hostels, the vision was to design a vibrant building for students to live, work and relax in, and to encourage interaction amongst them.

The compact arrangement of building blocks helps in combatting external climatic conditions, thereby creating a comfortable microclimate within. The close proximity of the buildings to each other also allows self-shading. Further, the blocks in the residential zone are arranged in a manner that creates a street system within the complex, inspired by the *nukkads* or labyrinthine street corridors found in the old city of Jodhpur. Being narrow, these alleyways in the city often remain shaded and open up into *aangans* or courts, which become common meeting places, playgrounds for children and centres for celebration within the community.

The architectural morphology of the buildings is, therefore, largely derived as a spontaneous response towards the local climate and culture of Jodhpur. Architectural details, such as deep overhangs, recessed windows, heavy massing on the western and southwestern façades of the blocks and double wall construction techniques, have been adopted with this perspective. Other passive climate control strategies adopted include placement of water bodies (kunds), use of thick green groves as buffers and for shading, stepped terraces and designing of staircases and vertical shafts as pneumatic channels to induce ventilation through 'stack effect'. Local vernacular architectural elements in the design, like kunds, *jharokha, chhatri,* pot, *jaali, johad* and *wadi,* suit the geographical, climatic and social context of the site.

Facing page: *An elaborate Master Plan for the project done in association with SHiFt Architects.*

Below: *A visualization of the students' accommodation.*

Biswa Bangla Biswavidyalaya

Location **Bolpur, West Bengal** Site **18.5 acres** Built-up area **7,20,000 sq. ft. (Phase I)** Year of completion **Ongoing**

National competition winning entry, modelled on the lines of the famed Shantiniketan, *the concept uses art as an influence to guide the design*

Inspired by Rabindranath Tagore's philosophy of education as an open learning system, exemplified in his founding of the iconic Shantiniketan, Biswa Bangla derives inspiration from a Gurukul concept of learning. Tagore's philosophical influences have been materialized in the design, evident in the way that areas have been divided into uncluttered zones and how the facilities have been uniquely set up.

The site is lined with a thick grove of trees that provide a natural buffer against the inevitable noise coming from the State Highway, running along the site's northwest border. However, the main challenge of this project was the provision of entry and exit points as the State Highway itself was not a feasible option. An alternate route was devised in the form of an 18-metre-wide road that perpendicularly cuts across, running on one side of the University.

Different buildings have been placed on a high ground in a compact manner to cause least intervention on the low-lying terrain. The seamlessness of the built and unbuilt environment makes the campus a modern interpretation of vernacular design. Water has always been associated with purity, and historic educational settings in India generally had a natural source of water. Therefore, a central lake has been designed for this institution as well. This eco-lake acts as a water reservoir and maintains the microclimate of the site. Further, an interplay of building materials diffuses the light penetrating the buildings, with no glare issues. The use of bamboo lends an earthiness to the façade, which is also decorated with different paintings and motifs.

A visual axis cuts the site into two, emerging between the library and the multipurpose hall. Faculties of Education, Social Science and Science have been clubbed together to form an informal village setting on one side of the central axis, while student facilities have been placed around the lake. The administration building is placed at the entrance, and towards the northern part of the site is a sports field with a football playground in the middle surrounded by running tracks.

Tagore believed that nature fulfills the criteria of an educator better than enclosed spaces do. The creation of spaces that emphasize the significance of education and its practicality has been of utmost importance to the design team. Through the design of this University, the Architects have attempted to re-create the ancient ways of imparting education, integrated with today's technologies and requirements.

Facing page above:
The academic complexes showcase different types of artwork.

Facing page below:
An eco-lake creates an environment of harmony and serenity within the campus.

Below: *An aerial visualization of the entire campus through the entrance road of the site.*

Vidya Sanskar International School for Holistic Learning

Location **Faridabad, Haryana** Site **13 acres** Built-up area **4,00,000 sq. ft.** Year of completion **2007**

The building typology of the institution has been ***influenced by passive engineering technologies***

The underlying vision for this school was to encourage and promote independent thinking and decision-making from a young age. The facilities have been provided according to the latest technological and infrastructural advancements, allowing academics, sports, art, dance and drama to thrive in newer forms.

The client brief called for a design that could accord vastness to an otherwise modest site area and easily present the various physical components of the school's infrastructure to students, staff and visitors. The design responded by placing the school facilities against the length of the site, which exhibit at a single glance all that the institution strives to offer: academic blocks, library, dining hall, hostels and other socio-cultural amenities. A pedestrian street connects these physical components like a microcosm of a city. The buildings create a city skyline and form backdrop to the large open space comprising entrance courts, play fields and a herbal garden. This also successfully fulfilled the Client's desire to amplify the scale of the land parcel.

The design of the school campus is ultimately aimed towards utilizing eco-friendly methods and designing by reduced energy usage. This is achieved by cutting down lighting and air-conditioning costs through maximum utilization of natural lighting during daytime and passive ventilation. The green engineering technologies that define the building typology also control harsh climatic variations. The courtyard typology, in particular, was deliberately chosen to induce a comfortable microclimate that could counter the extremes of summer and winter and maintain desirable humidity and temperature conditions all year round. Continuous *chhajjas* were introduced on the façade to allow apertures to catch the oblique rays of the sun.

An expansive open lawn thrives as a vibrant zone for the children, encouraging shared recreational activities and also contributing towards a reduced built footprint of the overall design. The play field also acts as a multipurpose space utilized by students for physical fitness training, yoga and marching sessions. The school is a worthy example of eco-institutional architecture that has done much to help redefine the manner in which educational institutions are designed in the State.

Above: *A panoramic view of the front façade of the project.*

Translational Health Science and Technology Institute

Location **Faridabad, Haryana** Site **79 acres** Built-up area **6,00,000 sq. ft**. Year of completion **Ongoing**

The design is conceptualized to adhere to ***Green Building Principles as per LEED and GRIHA***

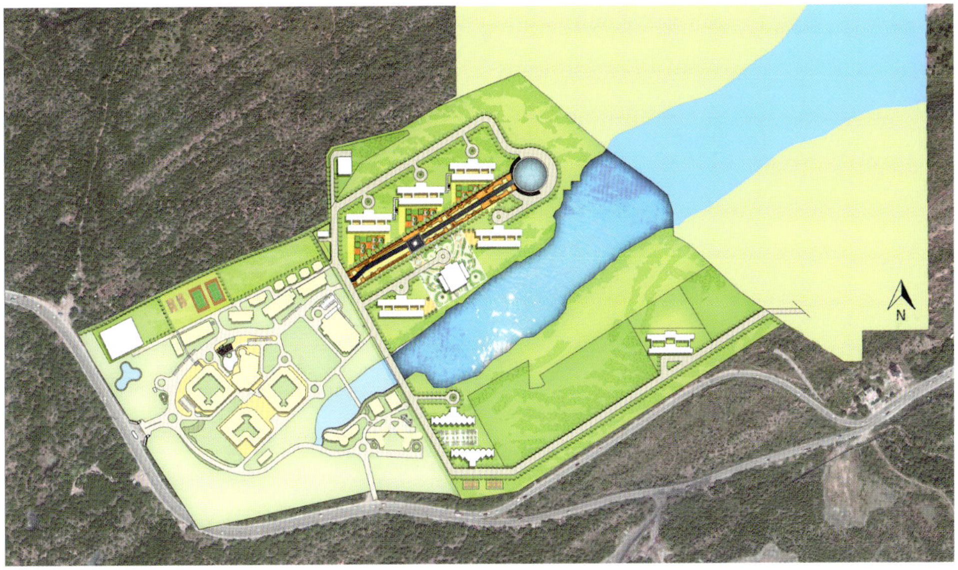

Translational Health Science and Technology Institute (THSTI) is a highly anticipated campus expansion project on the busy Gurugram–Faridabad Highway. The primary planning objective is to initiate a building cluster for institutes such as THSTI, Regional Centre for Biotechnology, National Institute of Plant Genome Research, National Brain Research Centre and National Institute of Immunology. The project is designed as per the highest level of LEED and GRIHA certifications.

The site planning is sensitive towards the organic water channels that exist on location. The building placements are configured in such a way that they do not disturb these existing water collection and movement paths. Alongside such precautions, the cluster will have a rainwater collection tank, as well as a sewage treatment plant to recycle water for slushing, irrigation and cooling needs.

The building façade has been developed using advanced energy simulation tools, with the final design comprising a combination of overhangs, skins and tapered walls. The orientation of buildings is predominantly north to south; the façade on the south side is tapered to ensure as little direct solar exposure as possible. These combinations guarantee that the façade is 100 per cent shaded in summer but receives adequate amounts of sunlight in winter, when it is most required.

In the same vein, the window-to-wall ratio, which has been selected based on simulation studies, ensures that sufficient daylight is received with minimal heat gain. In addition to this, heat-minimizing strategies of stone cladding with insulated walls and double glass units, and the star photo voltaic (PV) panels on the rooftop have been incorporated to generate and support 100 per cent of the lighting load. Simultaneously, buildings will have radiant cooling technology, reducing electricity consumption from air-conditioning by 30 per cent. Indeed, with the design following Energy Conservation Building Code (ECBC) and green certification norms, the overall energy consumption will be 20 per cent less as compared to conventional design.

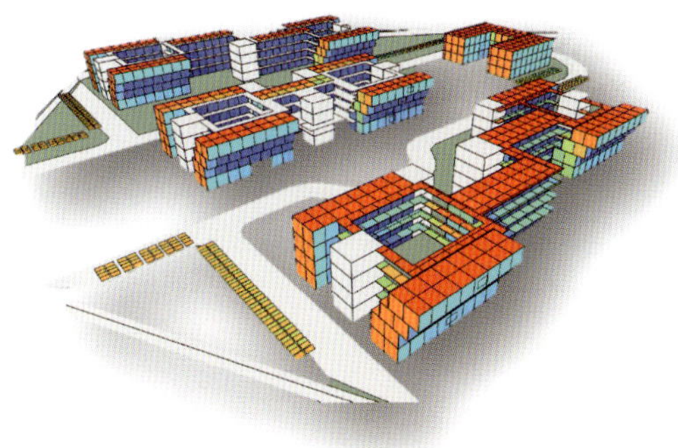

Top: *A rendered Master Plan of the site.*

Above: *Simulation drawing of solar insulation.*

'The most important exercise in a design process is to read the salient gestures of forms and spaces, to converse with the natural environment and then translate those gestures into architectural ensembles.'

Ar. DIKSHU C. KUKREJA

India International Institute of Democracy and Election Management

Location **New Delhi** Site **5 acres** Built-up area **6,00,000 sq. ft.**
Year of completion **Ongoing**

National competition winning design *reflects the philosophy of democracy and election management in contemporary India*

The India International Institute of Democracy and Election Management (IIIDEM) campus is a national design competition winning entry. It was selected for its futuristic ideas in terms of sustainability parameters, innovative architectural details and grand building design. The 5-acre site holds 6,00,000 sq. ft. of built-up area and comprises the main institutional building, an auditorium block, residential blocks, training halls, exhibition galleries and cafeteria, and is consciously planned to maintain pleasant harmony between built and open spaces.

The Master Plan of IIIDEM was inspired by the symbol of the Election Commission of India, which consists of rectangular bars and circles. The rectangular bars are represented by buildings, while the circles are formed with the circular shells of the auditorium blocks. Furthermore, the site plan is organized around a central open space, surrounded by the built blocks. The site is rectangular in shape with the longer edge overlooking the abutting road. To respond to such a site alignment, the main building has been designed as a poised structure, with a landscaped ceremonial entrance marked by a grand colonnaded majestic façade.

Left: *A visualization of the inner courtyard space.*

In keeping with the accessibility and security requirements of a landmark public building, there are two entries, for reasons of convenience and safety. The first is primarily for dignitaries, visitors and staff, who are greeted at and by the ceremonial entrance. The second entrance is to the residential campus, with common amenities dedicated to the government officers.

Since the site organization depends on an open space structure, landscape design has played a crucial role in controlling hierarchy and public spaces. Indeed, landscaping has been used to unify the entire design. The grand central court encloses a semi-covered *jan aangan*, which unfolds as one enters. This *aangan* acts as 'people's court' and represents the freedom every citizen is entitled to, in democratic India. It is a place of gathering, shaded by tree-like columns, which impart a unique character and identity whilst filtering natural light into the court. The age-old symbol of the banyan tree, representing grace and shelter, under which an elected panchayat carries out their decision-making, is recalled by these futuristic sculptural canopies. The other important open space on the site is the *jan upvan*, an informal garden created especially for residents. In addition, small-scale private courts between buildings and double height spaces create breezeways.

FORM EVOLUTION

VIEW

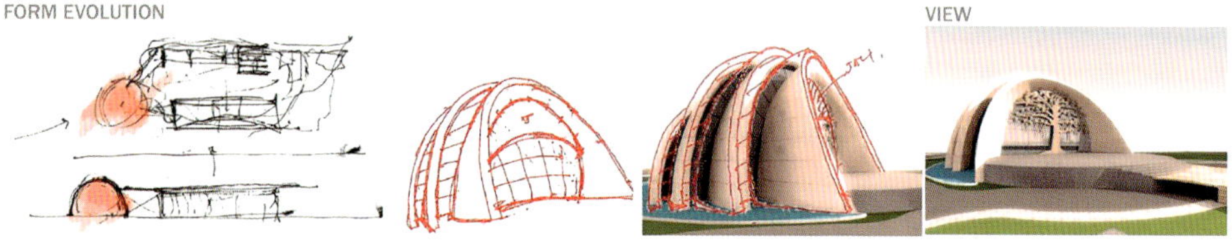

Top: *The imposing front façade of the Institute.*

Above: *A concept sketch illustrating the form evolution of the auditorium block.*

These spaces give a sense of privacy to the residents during leisure hours.

A natural lake at one end of the site regulates wind entering from one direction to cool down and flow along the aerodynamic-shaped shells, and into the institutional court to ventilate and refresh its air quality. The landscape is a perfect co-existence of natural and built environment – it reflects every human being's yearning to be close to nature. The auditorium reflects the overall design concept, with the outline of a banyan tree adorning its entrance and a water body extending as an exquisite landscape design element. It fulfils the need of a well thought out entrance design while highlighting its majestic persona. The building glows at night, spreading its light across the campus and through its outline.

The planning and design of IIIDEM is based on the principles of ecologically neutral and sustainable architecture. Being located in Delhi, which experiences extreme weather conditions, several sustainable design principles have been adopted to create a comfortable micro-environment at the site. For instance, trees with thick canopies have been planted along the edges of the site and open spaces to create passive cooling and humidification. The foliage also prevents sound and air pollution as it traps the dust coming from roads and acts as a sound barrier. The plantation creates shaded spaces that encourage movement and interaction within the campus.

Furthermore, the design typology responds to the site's climatic conditions. Residential courts are planned in a way which provides shade in summers and allows people to bask in sunlight during winters. The façades incorporate details like recessed windows and *jaalis*, which cut off the sun's blaze. The central area is surrounded by buildings, creating a common open space, where daylight filters through tree-like pods, its glare diffused by the pods' membrane. In addition, roofs of the buildings have solar panels that harness sunlight and cut cooling costs. Hence, the entire roof area contributes to storage of solar energy.

The project understandably harnesses Classical Architecture, a product of the British era, as the most commanding image of the seat of power in the country. This is blended with modern appeal through dynamic, slender edges on otherwise mundane rectangular blocks. The building typology is derived out of these compact, solid blocks that leave a smaller built footprint, with majority of the site used for landscaping. Their solid appearance also creates a bold architectural statement. A curious interplay of solid and void makes the difference in elevation appealing from a distance.

The front elevation of the main building is etched with typical British Era details – a double-height colonnade, raised podium, grand stairs, symmetrical façade and heavy stone texture – and the overall elevation of the building is punctuated with sculptures and *jaalis*. The rhythm of the colonnade over elevation creates a pattern as one moves along the abutting road. The vintage aspect of the elevation, created by the classical elements and visible from the road, is broken by the auditorium block, which resembles an aquatic animal.

Below: *A rendered Master Plan of the project.*

Bottom: *Different elevation drawings for the auditorium centre.*

SCI Maritime Training Institute

Location **Mumbai, Maharashtra** Site **44 acres** Built-up area **2,00,000 sq. ft.** Year of completion **1985**

Training students to lead shipping companies as future GMs and CEOs, the Institute ***flourishes in its natural surroundings*** *and offers tranquility and serenity*

The Maritime Training Institute provides not only knowledge-based training but also practical competence in the field of marine engineering. It is located in Powai, one of Mumbai's most eco-sensitive regions, which is characterized by an undulating landscape impregnated by streams and lakes. The design vision for the project sought to encourage eco-sensitive urban development and conserve the natural systems of Powai's geography.

Placed adjacent to Powai Lake, the site has a soft and hydrated soil profile that possesses little bearing capacity. The height of the buildings was kept low, ensuring shallow foundations that did not dig too deep into the malleable ground and did not disturb the hydrological system, which exists below the ground level. The low height also helped in merging the built form with the openness of the site by respecting the horizontality of the ground. In order to further emphasize the appearance of the buildings, emerging in layers parallel to the ground, the entire façade was rendered in bold stone finish, with a striped pattern that embodies the surrounding environment's geographical aesthetics.

The Master Plan further took into account the existing contour profile of the site such that little cutting and filling work was required, and this became a cost-effective design strategy. One of the site's major depressions was conserved as an eco-lake that now serves as a natural water reservoir within the campus. The architectural design was, to a large extent, influenced by marine vessels like ships, boats and submarines. These marine crafts have strongly inspired key details of the campus' material form and expression. For instance, the rhythmic patterns of the oars found in sea-vessels are reflected in the arrangement of circular columns on the front façade of the Institute.

Above: *The entrance drop-off area of the Institute.*

To further articulate the built form, deep recesses, punctures, overhangs and porches were incorporated. These architectural details cast an attractive interplay of patterned shadows on the buildings during the day. The riveting composition of solids and voids in the architectural massing allows for the buildings to be passively ventilated by the breeze flowing from the nearby Powai Lake, thereby also making the architectural design climatically responsive.

The design for the SCI Maritime Institute was one of the earliest projects for the firm. It was truly futuristic in its approach to preserve the site, and in its promotion of sustainability as a feasible design concept.

BML Munjal University

Location **Gurugram, Haryana** Site **40 acres** Built-up area **7,00,000 sq. ft.** Year of completion **2014**

***Harmonious use of conventional and modern materials** displays a contemporary design language*

BML Munjal University, developed under Haryana State Private Universities Act, 2006, is a premier institution that offers high-quality, specialized courses in management and other technical disciplines. It was envisioned as a self-sufficient institution and is fully furnished with residential and public facilities. The aim of the project was to create a stimulating environment conducive to learning and research, and which would help develop and nurture a community of intellectuals who can excel in every sphere of their lives.

The site is located along the Delhi–Jaipur Expressway in a peri-urban area, and has a number of historic villages, such as Kapdiwas, Joniwas, Siddrawali, Mao and Maipura in its vicinity. The design ideates a seamless integration of built academic spaces for the campus within a tight-knit built footprint, leaving larger areas available for recreational purposes. These expansive recreational grounds allow the University to offer a variety of sports activities, including tennis, football, basketball, volleyball, badminton and cricket.

The campus is also equipped with residential facilities, such as student hostels and staff housing quarters. Each facility has either a common courtyard or open space for special functions, festivals and daily activities. The landscape is designed in a manner that provides students, teachers and visitors with specially curated outdoor spaces for socialization. The campus cafeteria, a well-equipped and popular food joint, is also a common meeting point.

The campus has been designed in a way that walking and cycling, rather than vehicular movement, are strongly encouraged amongst students, faculty and non-teaching staff. A major consequence of this has been considerably low air and sound pollution throughout the campus, which has helped create an atmosphere of learning and living that is both peaceful and dynamic. This innovative ethos is reflected in the very materials used for construction of buildings, with refreshing use of steel and glass alongside traditional concrete and brick. As a modern development within a village setting, the University is a ray of hope, uplifting the quality of education, especially for students coming from surrounding areas.

Below: *The front elevation of the gateway building.*

Central University of Rajasthan

Location **Ajmer, Rajasthan** Site **500 acres** Built-up area **21,53,000 sq. ft.** Year of completion **2014**

The University was ***honoured at the GRIHA Summit 2014 for exceptional design thinking in 'Integrated Water Management'***

The Central University of Rajasthan is considered one of the finest examples of institutional design in India, where the traditional meets the modern. In the year of its completion, the project was awarded for its exceptionally good design in the field of urban sustainability at the 2014 GRIHA Summit. It was selected for its exemplary performance in water management and conservation of landscape and biodiversity. Located along the Jaipur–Ajmer road in Rajasthan, it is a collection of striking architectural ensembles including academic blocks, an administration block, a library building, hostel facilities for 10,000 students and faculty housing for 1,000 faculty members.

A university is a sanctuary that maintains an environment conducive to peaceful learning, observation, criticism, questioning and, above all, inclusive discussions. The principal vision behind the development of this University was, therefore, to create a distinguished, eco-friendly learning campus that can culturally, socially and financially enhance the living experience of its students. The University also wanted to

Facing page: *An aerial visualization from the entrance of the University, highlighting the axial planning.*

Right: *Intrinsic* jaali *pattern, followed through the entire campus, facilitates natural temperature.*

achieve a campus that would take the least and give back the most – in other words, achieve maximum sustainability through least possible disturbance of environmental balance, along with minimal wastage of energy and resources.

Rajasthan's capital, Jaipur, is arid, hot and dry. Considering this geographical context, native drought-tolerant plants were sown to reduce the amount of water consumption. Existing trees were protected and local vegetation was selected for plantation to turn the campus into an urban oasis amidst the desert. Parks and green plazas at important nodes served as transitional elements in the design.

Being mindful of the arid climate, the built mass was also kept to a minimum. The Architects used radial planning, with the administration block centred in the middle and the different academic blocks expanding outward up to a radius of 800 metres. The middle spaces were left as circulation buffers, supported by avenues developed with dense vegetation.

Urban clusters were preferred to control the built footprint as well as the hierarchy and flow between spaces. Each residential cluster consists of student hostels and faculty housing, while academic clusters consist of classrooms, laboratories, audio-visual rooms and faculty rooms. These clusters also have a variety of landscaped spaces with ornamental groves, gardens and grass courts. Small unit courtyards flow into cluster courts which, in turn, enter into the green pedestrian spine and, finally, join the major central green space.

The naturally undulating contours of the site called for organic planning that would not only ensure the least cutting and filling of soil, thereby bringing down the landscape treatment costs, but also help in creating informal spaces, which are desired assets in any campus design. Thus, open public areas and vegetation were planned to flow casually between built masses, creating comfortable open and semi-open spaces for recreation and public gatherings.

The compact planning also helped in creating a microclimate that combats the extreme weather through passive cooling, humidification and ventilation, as well as local breeze control. The minimum built footprint left an ample amount of unbuilt space, which has been judiciously utilized for landscaping. The resulting playgrounds, gardens and meditation spaces not only act as sound and pollution controlling buffers, but also compensate for

the carbon footprint of the construction by producing enough oxygen to balance it.

The buildings are oriented in such a way that their height and breadth shade the pathways traversed by pedestrians, resulting in ambient cooling and ventilation through most of the open spaces in the campus. The natural contours of the site were utilized to the maximum and natural depressions were converted into water bodies wherever possible, much like the *nahars* or natural reservoirs of Rajasthan. Most of the lower and flatter contours were used for the built footprint, leaving the higher contours for grove plantations that channelize breeze in desired directions. Traditional screens called *jaalis* were used as elevation elements, especially for the western façades to cut off intense sun rays. *Jharokhas* or hanging balconies and turrets were used for self-shading of the built mass. These *jharokhas* also create interesting architectural punctuations in the elevation.

Identity and culture, if harnessed properly, can be introduced into a physical environment through design. With this thought in mind, public art has been incorporated in the urban design to add a sense of heightened usefulness to plazas, open spaces, buildings and, most importantly, public life on campus. The accommodation of public art was also considered as a tool to revive the cultural symbols of Jaipur, which are currently endangered due to rampant development.

The geographical and cultural context of Jaipur, therefore, teaches basic principles of sustainability through conservation of resources. The urban landscape of the region is a conscious reflection of Rajasthan's harsh climatic conditions, and this is visible in local architectural details such as *nahars, jaalis, jharokhas,* and more. This approach, adopted in the design of the Central University, is both an eco-friendly path towards a large-scale building project, and a major tool for harnessing and conservation of natural resources.

Facing page: *The soaring roof over the dining hall visually expresses all the structural elements.*

Above: *Drop-off area fronting the admin block.*

South Campus, University of Delhi

Location **New Delhi** Site **75 acres** Built-up area **8,00,000 sq. ft.** Year of completion **1980**

Creating an urban ensemble that would help in the ***conservation of environmental quality and biodiversity*** *of the area as well as to create a modern image of the rising, independent nation through an architectural interpretation*

After Independence, the Nehruvian vision of a new India inspired the development of many institutions across the country to improve the educational standards of modern India. University of Delhi, keeping up with this growing demand within the educational sector of the capital, established its second campus in South Delhi.

The major concerns while planning the design of South Campus revolved around creating an urban ensemble that would conserve the biodiversity of the area and cement the image of a rising, independent nation. The urban pattern of the campus was designed to be organic, merging effortlessly with the natural reserves of the ridge adjacent to the site. This enabled the campus to grow within the urban forest and vice versa, setting an example of how a city can co-exist with its forest surroundings. The built footprint of the campus was kept to a minimum, leaving maximum ground area free for landscaping and plantation. This decision also helped in creating a lot of open spaces in the campus that encourage recreational activities, sports and public life to thrive. The extensive greenery of the foliage within the campus keeps these open spaces shaded and humified, making them comfortable despite the extreme climate of Delhi.

Spread across 75 acres, South Campus is almost like a city within a city. It contains specialized departments such as Faculty of Arts, Faculty of Interdisciplinary and Applied Sciences, Faculty of Management Studies, along with buildings that house the administrative block, examination block, central library and cafeteria. In addition, there are residential quarters and hostels for faculty members, non-teaching staff and students, with supporting amenities like a health centre, banks, a post office and more. These amenities have been rhythmically woven together to create on-site activity networks.

The buildings, constructed with local Delhi quartzite, appear to rise naturally from the earth, composed effortlessly amidst the rocky outcrop of the ridge, creating a poetic ensemble of nature and built form. The campus design is a fresh departure from the era of the British Raj and explores a new design paradigm – one where modern Indian architecture must be sensitive to context and climate.

The design for South Campus was one of the first post-Independence projects completed at such a large, urban scale. It paved the way for future communities of architects and urban developers to invest in a coherent design, and also helped in highlighting how peri-urban natural reserves around the city could be preserved and conserved without engulfing them into a web of concrete.

Above: *A view of the academic blocks.*

Indian Institute of Technology, Roorkee

Location **Roorkee, Uttarakhand** Site **365 acres** Built-up area **1,00,000 sq. ft.** Year of completion **2007**

A sophisticated design conceptualized as the ***epitome of knowledge centres in the country***

After Roorkee College became IIT, Roorkee, in 2001, the need for a new library facility was felt. With its extant plethora of materials – 9,000 archived and out-of-print documents, over 7,000 online journals, 3,20,000 documents, and much more – a new, state-of-the-art central library and computer centre, with a combined area of 1,00,000 sq. ft., was designed and completed in 2007. The building functions on fiber-optic network technology and has sophisticated IT facilities. As one ascends the steps to the library, they are engulfed with a feeling of veneration.

Muted tones of the sandstone material used for the building's exterior blend well with the extensively landscaped campus, making the built form a natural extension of its surroundings. The edifice is nestled in a dense greenscape, ensuring a peaceful environment for its students. The water and green in the landscape help soften the imposing demeanour, moulding it into an iconic architectural ensemble.

The front façade of the building has curtain glazing, providing the students, faculty and visitors with a panoramic view of the entire campus from inside the building. The monumental scale is justified by the row of columns lined on the front façade. Once inside the building, the magnificent double height atrium space, with a dome on the top, allows natural light to flush the centrally air-conditioned interiors.

These interiors are spacious and well-laid out to allow unobstructed movement around the seating area. It also enabled the arrangement of books and journals in an accessible manner. An open plan facilitates a sense of freedom to both move and acquire knowledge, and efficiently utilize any and all space to accommodate as many study areas as possible. The Architects were conscious to plan the space in a manner that allowed different study areas to exist within the same building. Finally, the building rests on a high ground, paying homage, by its way of design and planning, to the library as the highest centre of knowledge.

Above: *A view from the flight of steps fronting the library block.*

Sri Aurobindo College of Commerce and Management

Location **Ludhiana, Punjab** Site **12 acres** Built-up area **82,000 sq. ft.** Year of completion **2004**

A playful volumetric concept juxtaposed on a low-rise design, *imbibing the humble teachings of Rishi Aurobindo*

This Institute was established in 2004 in Ludhiana with a vision to become the finest college for education in Commerce and Management. It aimed to follow the teachings of Rishi Aurobindo, who encouraged 'Integral Education' as a necessity for building social community with the potential to contribute sensitively towards the environment it exists in.

The building blocks on the site are organized in such a way that they merge with the existing geographical setting. Indeed, special attention was given to environmental planning in the project, so it minimally affected the eco-sensitive balance of Jhande village, where the Institute is located. The campus is dominated chiefly by the presence of lush green lawns and paved and unpaved open spaces, as well as play fields. The extensive greens designed around the building blocks are utilized for both teaching and multipurpose public activities.

The architecture of the buildings respects Indian Modernism through its extensive use of Kota stone, along with Udaipur green and white marble finishes, helping the project attain an elevated grandness. Teakwood has been used extensively for fine detailing in louvres and screens, which also allows the buildings to maintain a comfortable indoor climate through the facilitation of passive ventilation and natural lighting. Classrooms are designed in an amphitheatre style, easily accommodating seventy students and maximizing utilization of interior spaces.

Below: *A panoramic view of the main academic building.*

Institute for Indian Council of Social Science Research Complex

Location **New Delhi** Site **5 acres** Built-up area **1,50,000 sq. ft.** Year of completion **1985**

Creating interesting spaces** by introducing a harmonious **balance of the built and the unbuilt

The natural ridges of Delhi have long been home to a number of significant educational and cultural institutions. This includes the esteemed JNU, whose greenery and open landscapes have, for long, preserved the biodiversity of the South-Central Ridge. The complex for the Institute for Indian Council of Social Science Research (ICSSR), located along Aruna Asaf Ali Marg, is one of the South-Central Ridge's other prestigious institutions.

With keen consideration to conserve ecology that governs the geography at the site, the architectural design of the ICSSR campus was derived from a sustainable perspective, keeping in mind the need to protect existing flora in particular. The underlying concept for the design was, therefore, bolstering a natural flow of greenery and open spaces as structuring elements within the campus. The overall volume of the Institute was broken and a staggered form achieved, which not only reduced built footprint but also induced a playful character to the design. The built space extensively embraced open areas in the form of courtyards, plazas and green courts, which also became interactive public spaces on the campus, boosting learning both inside and outside the classrooms.

The architectural form of the campus was imagined to be low-rise, in a vertical continuation of the rocky ridge, and yet eye-catching. The solid textures of the stone surface complement this vision, with the beige blend of the stones on the buildings' exteriors making the built form appear largely monochromatic, while simultaneously standing out in perfect contrast to the greenery of the site. Traditional Indian architectural elements, such as *jaalis* and *chhajjas*, along with deeply recessed balconies, pergolas and double height enclosures form an aesthetic sculptural statement, while also helping the buildings combat the extreme weather conditions experienced in the city by invoking passive cooling technologies. The Institute – with its research and seminar facilities, an auditorium, a computer centre, a guest house, students' and faculty residences – presents both a vision and reality of a campus design in Delhi, and indeed India, that is much ahead of its time.

Above: *The Institute imposes its colossal demeanour with extruded columns and externally colonnaded corridors.*

Indian Institute of Management, Bodhgaya

Location **Bodhgaya, Bihar** Site **73 acres** Built-up area **12,40,000 sq. ft.** Year of completion **Ongoing**

***National competition winning entry** to be designed in the historic and sanctorium city of Bodhgaya in Bihar*

The design for the prestigious project was awarded to the Architects through a national competition. The site is located in the historic and sanctorium city of Bodhgaya, Bihar. The concept behind this institution emanates from a search for progression in the field of Management Studies. Different areas in the campus are unified through a single thread of ribbon, which acts as the connecting spine.

The different cloisters in the campus are conceptualized with themes, creating unique atmospheres. The faculty cloister is themed around wisdom, meditation and tranquility; the academic cloister supplies an exchange of knowledge and life experiences; and the student cloisters offer vibrancy, dynamism and colour. Each cloister is uniquely defined not only by its surrounding landscape, but also by the people who are able to exhibit freedom in expression.

An abstract frame of edifice imitating the Bodhi Tree – under the shade of which the Buddha attained enlightenment – will be erected at the entrance. It will be a sustainable feature that would filter the water run-off, generate energy and harness heat, cool the area with chilled water pipes, cast within the Super Tree, and also dehumidify the air before cooling.

The library is another iconic feature in the campus. The form of the library block takes inspiration from a stack of books. The intention of the Architects was to project the library as a space containing a vast array of knowledge, making it available through intriguing spaces and activities, and at the same time, providing individual detachment from the daily rituals, much like how one is able to transport oneself to a different state of being through the act of reading a book.

The Architects have ideated the campus in a manner that consciously embraces the site's context. The design seeks to enrich the overall educational experience, aspiring for holistic human development.

Facing page: *The inner courtyard looking out to the overarching Super Tree.*

Below: *Concept sketch showing the inspiration and development of the library block.*

Human Resources Development Centre and Delhi Public School

Location **Greater Noida, Uttar Pradesh** Year of completion **2019**

Site (HRD) **5 acres** Built-up area **2,15,000 sq. ft.**

Site (DPS) **7 acres** Built-up area **3,22,000 sq. ft.**

Human Resources Development (HRD) Centre has been felicitated as ***'Outstanding Concrete Structure, 2019'*** *by the* ***Indian Concrete Institute of Uttar Pradesh***

Human Resources Development Centre

The HRD Centre, located in Knowledge Park V of Greater Noida, a sub-urban area of National Capital Region (NCR), is the educational nerve centre of DPS Society for the 'In-service Teachers' Capacity Building' programme. The striking design of the project breaks away as an extension of the neighbouring DPS whilst being able to exude a colourful design language of its own.

With Greater Noida expanding as a thriving upcoming urban development at an accelerating rate, the Architects felt it was imperative to weigh factors such as effective land-use and inclusion of sustainable design features, like energy efficiency, water recycling and rainwater harvesting.

A self-contained, barrier-free complex and the bright and cheerful demeanour of the edifices allow the centre to be spotted from afar. The centre acts as a beacon of knowledge that seeks to prepare and coach the future teaching staff of the DPS Society. The project included the design of an administrative cum academic block, a multipurpose hall, a gym building, a hostel building and accommodation for the lecturers as well as the support staff.

Keeping in mind the functionality of the centre, the Architects wanted the design language to be reflective of the balance between an educational habitat and high-spirited learning endeavour. The use of exposed brick as a primary building material expresses an earthy outlook, however, to break the monotony of the same, bands of amber radiate throughout the campus, highlighting areas such as the grand entrance porch of the admin block, a string of differently sized window openings, interspersed over the façade, and an overarching roof structure. This magnanimous roof overhang acts as a shade, engulfing the premises and regulating passive cooling. The entrance porch of the administrative cum academic block is an extruding element, imposing in style with massive columnar elements to support louvres on the roof. The design of the multipurpose hall, however, with a striking arched entrance, displays a fine

Facing page: *The seamless RCC archway inspires an innovative and futuristic way of learning in the campus.*

juxtaposition of architectural and engineering prowess. An intricate *jaali* pattern used over the arch element softens the robustness of the entrance and invokes art to fuse in to the campus' environment. The Reinforced Concrete Cement (RCC) archway seamlessly extends from one end of the building to the other, spanning an impressive 80 feet. With large window openings through the design, the Architects have been able to channelize natural daylight into the interiors, thereby regulating thermal cooling and reducing the load on mechanical means of cooling (air-conditioners) by a considerable margin. The Architects have also paid careful attention to landscape design within the campus. Wide circulation pathways in-between and around the different blocks create an interactive as well as engaging space for visitors. Native trees have been planted all over the campus, establishing a deep connection with nature.

The design of the HRD Centre achieves a unique mark in the perception of educational institutions in the country and presents a high-spirited way to break the mould. The project was felicitated as an Outstanding Concrete Structure 2019 by the Indian Concrete Institute, Uttar Pradesh.

Facing page above: *The presence of a water body within the campus regulates temperature.*

Facing page below: *Spanning 80 feet seamlessly, the RCC archway exudes a harmonious balance of art and architecture.*

Top: Rhythmic pylons at the entrance project a magnificent and imposing demeanour.

Above: *Windows have been generously interspersed across the façades, allowing natural light inside the edifices.*

Top: *DPS School and HRD Centre coexisting harmoniously as seen from the front of the site (placed right to left).*

Following page left: *An entrance to the central courtyard of the school.*

Following page right top: *Central courtyard of the school provides an expansive recreational area for students.*

Following page right bottom: *Front façade of the auditorium exhibits a structural robustness of the design.*

Delhi Public School, Greater Noida

The latest addition to the thriving DPS Society, DPS Greater Noida has been garnering attention for its striking architectural design. Located in Knowledge Park V, the sprawling 7 acres of campus has been perceived with a vision of creating a distinct institutional architecture, one that embraces profoundness and stability in all its manifestations. With a unique conceptualization, it captivates the first-time visitors. The Client's idea was to realize such a vision by bringing back the old world charm and nurturing young minds towards futuristic thinking.

The Architects sought to present a design which captured the essence of the entire school in a moment of timelessness while also accommodating, and being identified with, technology in its function. The design treads on Classical Architecture, and yet, is able to imbibe vernacular harmony by infusing elements of lattice screens and extended slabs in the design. The generous use of amber across the landscape of the campus instills a dynamic character.

Through an irregular façade design, the institution breaks away from the stereotypical box-typology, and instead allows the imagination and creativity of the students to dwell in an aesthetically pleasing and uplifting space. The front side of the academic building breaks inwardly, directing the eyes of a visitor towards the imposing clock tower, which becomes the identity and focal point of the institution. The colonial character of the exposed clad edifices are juxtaposed with intricately detailed lattice screens, held by hefty frames of Dholpur stone on the lower floor, which act as a parasol and create a shaded corridor behind. The buildings have been meticulously planned, keeping in mind the location of circulation areas, which increases functionality of the spaces and makes them easily accessible for the students.

With its immaculate design and colour filled spaces, the project outshines as a successful example of education's playful spirit reflected through the design of the campus.

Left: *Angular form of the school building assists in regulating natural daylight inside.*

Complete Listing of Institutional Projects

Jawaharlal Nehru University (JNU), New Delhi
A 1,000-acre campus on a rocky terrain, it was won through a nationwide architectural design competition. Major buildings are academic schools, a computer centre, a nine-storeyed library building, conference, lecture and theatre complexes, an administration centre and a students' activity complex. Sixteen residential sectors, each comprising hostel facilities for 600 students and 150 faculty residences, were also designed. The campus is self-sufficient with its own primary and higher secondary schools, a shopping centre, recreational and other infrastructural facilities.

Indian Institute of Management (IIM), Bodhgaya, Bihar
Spread on a site of 73 acres, IIM Bodhgaya's design concept aspires to provide a sense of holistic learning and personality development of students through its educational facilities. The library design stands as an iconic feature, translating the concept of an open book for its roof design.

National Rail and Transport Institute (NRTI), Vadodra, Gujarat
NRTI has been proposed as a solution for research and model conceptualization for resolving railway transportation woes being faced in the country. The concept for the University is one-of-its-kind – it is the third such university in the world. It would be a centre to help, equip and train students, and to better prepare them with the upcoming technical services and advancements for smooth functioning of the Indian railway network.

Shiv Nadar University, Greater Noida, Uttar Pradesh
The University is spread over an area of 286 acres. The campus accommodates schools of Technology, Business Studies, Management, residential sectors for students and faculty members, and a spacious cafeteria.

National Archives of India, New Delhi
The construction was in two stages. The first stage comprised an eight-storey library-cum-stack block. The second phase included, among others, technical facilities for archives, an auditorium, research scholars' wing and a canteen. The entire complex is centrally air-conditioned. The project was awarded to the Architects as a winning entry in an architectural design competition.

South Campus, University of Delhi, New Delhi
South Campus is affiliated to University of Delhi and is spread over an area of 75 acres near Dhaula Kuan in South Delhi. It comprises academic institutions, such as the Arts and Science faculties, a library, an auditorium, an administration block, a students' hostel, faculty housing, a shopping centre, a recreational complex, etc.

Exim Bank Library and Data Centre, JNU, New Delhi
An independent facility attached to the Centre for Economic Research, JNU, the Exim Bank Library, funded by Export Import Bank of India, has stacking provision for 2,500 volumes, a plethora of data bank and well organized reading areas.

N.B.K.R. Institute of Science and Technology, Vidyanagar, Andhra Pradesh
The project involved design of the Master Plan as well as of academic buildings for this technical college at Vidyanagar. It consists of the science and technical college block, laboratory and workshops, a hostel, staff housing, etc.

North-Eastern Regional Institute of Science and Technology (NFRIST), Itanagar, Arunachal Pradesh
This 400-acre campus is the regional centre for technical education for the seven northeastern states of India. The project comprises academic blocks for sciences and engineering, along with faculty housing and students' residences.

Indian Institute of Technology (IIT), Guwahati, Assam
The IIT in Assam near Guwahati is the sixth premier institution of its kind in the country. The Master Plan for this 200-acre campus has been developed with an academic complex, faculty and student housing, and a uniquely innovative technology park.

Manipur University, Kanchipur, Manipur
The project involved design of the Master Plan, including design of various academic buildings, administration, canteen and health centre. A distinctive feature of the campus architecture, particularly the centre of Manipuri studies, is the thoughtful amalgamation of traditional and modern architecture.

Higher Secondary School, Krishak Bharati Cooperative Limited (KRIBHCO), Surat, Gujarat
Central School has been designed for a student

population of 2,000. The design accommodates classes and facilities for a 10+2 central school system.

Indian Institute of Technology (IIT) Roorkee, Uttarakhand
Designed at IIT, Roorkee, are a new state-of-the-art central library and computer centre, which comprise an area of 1,00,000 sq. ft. The facility is completely fibre-networked and has sophisticated IT services.

Management Development Institute, Gurugram, Haryana
Spread over an area of 40 acres, the project consists design of academic buildings, hostels and faculty residential units. The arcaded brick structures have been designed and meticulously detailed to provide effective climate control and protection.

Gautam Buddha University, Greater Noida, Uttar Pradesh
This prestigious University is developed on an area of over 511 acres. The University will also have foreign institutions included in the undergraduate and postgraduate programmes in Information Technology, Bio-Technology, etc. Other facilities include an academic complex, sports facilities, and hostels for 5,000 students and 500 faculty members. It has been lauded as a sustainable campus, winning various national and international awards.

Data Centre for Historical Studies, JNU, New Delhi
A small library and data centre with storage facilities for 2,000 volumes.

Maitreyi College, University of Delhi, New Delhi
Named after the vedic sage, Maitreyi, it is a first-of-its-kind all-women's college in Delhi with an intake of 1,500 students, offering undergraduate and postgraduate studies in Arts, Humanities and Science under Delhi University.

Research and Development Complex (for Union Carbide India Limited), Bhopal, Madhya Pradesh
A landmark in Bhopal, the project consists of R&D buildings, a material handling warehouse, a high pressure laboratory, a green house complex for a plant breeding, plant extension, an office block, a health centre, a guest house and club facilities.

Iconic School, Bhopal, Madhya Pradesh
The project is spread over an area of 20 acres with an approximate built-up area of 4,50,000 sq. ft. The school has been planned around a system of courtyards, with colonnaded corridors opening out into them. This institution's use of vernacular brick architecture with Indo-Saracenic element is truly unique.

Motilal Nehru Training Institute, Allahabad, Uttar Pradesh
It serves as the residential training institute for educating farmers in modern systems of agriculture and farming. It is located within the Indian Farmers Fertilizer Cooperative Limited (IFFCO) Complex at Phulpur.

Computer Centre at Aligarh Muslim University (AMU), Aligarh, Uttar Pradesh
This is an ultra-modern computer centre for AMU with a dust-free, air-conditioned environment. It is finished in exposed brick work with a façade in arches, compatible with the existing campus architecture.

Assam Agricultural University, Jorhat, Assam
A World Bank sponsored project, this was the first full-fledged university in Assam. The designing involved complete Master Plan and utility service networks.

Assam Agricultural University, Guwahati, Assam
Another project sponsored by the World Bank. Besides Master Plan and utilities, the assignment also included design of all the academic buildings. A novel modular planning concept was evolved in the design of the campus building.

Jain Happy School, New Delhi
A senior secondary school for about 1,200 students with classrooms, laboratories and ancillary facilities in the heart of Delhi.

Mata Sundri Engineering College, New Delhi
A new campus for the engineering college comprising an administration block, academic blocks, an auditorium, workshops, hostels and recreational facilities.

Indian Institute of Mass Communication, New Delhi
This premier Institute is designed on a 15-acre site adjoining the JNU Campus in Delhi. The expansion programme of the Institute comprises an auditorium to seat 1,500 people, lecture halls and a seminar complex, an air-conditioned guest house for eighty persons and faculty housing.

Sri Aurobindo College of Commerce and Management, Ludhiana, Punjab
An institution of higher learning being developed on 12 acres of land on the outskirts of Ludhiana city, the campus comprises a learning centre, an auditorium for 1,000 students, a hostel for 500 students, faculty residences, a meditation centre, house and club facilities.

International School, Faridabad, Haryana
The school, located in Eros Gardens, has been designed with forty classrooms, six labs, four activity centres, a swimming pool, sports and recreation facilities.

SCI Maritime Training Institute, Mumbai, Maharashtra
The project comprises an academic block, staff housing, hostel blocks, a gymnasium, a guest house and specialized survival training facilities. It has been designed for the Shipping Corporation of India Limited.

Engineering College, Jaipur, Rajasthan
The campus for 1,000 students in different engineering disciplines comprises an administration block, academic facilities, a media centre, hostels, faculty residences and sports facilities.

Management Development Centre and Officers Training Institute (for Oil India Limited), Assam
These important complexes for the training facilities for Indian Oil executives are located in Assam, and are designed using the traditional Assamese architectural design elements.

Institute of Engineering and Technology (for Apeejay Group), Greater Noida, Uttar Pradesh
The campus is planned on an area of 30 acres. It has schools of Education, Architecture, Business, hostels and an auditorium with the capacity for 2,000 students.

Indian Institute of Management (IIM), Lucknow, Uttar Pradesh
Among the premier management training institutes in India, this IIM is a 200-acre campus near Lucknow city. The academic complex comprises a faculty building, classroom blocks, a library, a computer centre, an administration block, an auditorium and conference facilities. Hostels for 2,000 students and 500 faculty residences are also part of the complex. The campus was selected amongst the best designed IIMs in the country.

Nitrogen Fixation Lab (for Department of Science and Technology, JNU), New Delhi
This is a centrally air-conditioned, ultra-modern and unique laboratory, which is one-of-its-kind in India. The lab is located within the JNU premises.

Institute for Indian Council of Social Science Research (ICSSR) Complex, New Delhi
ICSSR Complex consists of air-conditioned research and seminar facilities, an auditorium, a computer centre, a guest house, students and faculty residences.

Research and Development Complex (for Hindustan Insecticides Limited), Gurugram, Haryana
This is a United Nations Development Programme (UNDP) sponsored project with research laboratories, workshops, an auditorium, a guest house and ancillary facilities.

International Centre for Alternative Dispute Resolution, New Delhi
A modern and elegant complex with juxtaposition of different buildings which accommodate the varied requirements of the centre including administration, teaching, business centre, residential and recreational facilities, amidst a lush and extensively landscaped campus setting.

Water Technology Centre (for Indian Agricultural Research Institute), New Delhi
The project, sponsored by the Ford Foundation, was built in a record time of eight months. The entire building is designed by using load bearing precast RCC wall, floor and roof panels.

Army College of Medical Sciences, New Delhi
A new medical college attached to Army Base Hospital with 500 beds in Dhaula Kuan, and with an annual intake of 100 students. The college was designed in such a manner that it could support modern facilities, such as a 1,200-seater auditorium and hostels for 600 students.

Research and Development Complex (for Union Carbide India Limited), Kolkata, West Bengal
A three-storeyed office and laboratory complex, the building is distinctive in its innovative application of solar louvres through the complex.

Residential School, Jaipur, Rajasthan
A residential school for 1,500 students with advanced facilities for teaching, and fully equipped with on-campus housing for both students and faculty.

Shri Vaishnav Vidyapeeth Vishwavidyalaya, Indore, Madhya Pradesh
Located in the commercial capital of Madhya Pradesh, this University, spread over 51 acres, is envisaged to be a 'Green Campus' that promotes walkability, sustainable design and universal accessibility. The design and planning of the campus embodies the rich heritage of the city in a contemporary style.

Higher Secondary School, Gas Authority of India Limited (GAIL) Township, Vijaipur, Madhya Pradesh
Designed on a 10+2 pattern, the school has classrooms for 1,000 students, an auditorium, an open air theatre, laboratories, activity rooms and related facilities as per central school norms.

Integrated Polytechnic Complex (for Delhi Sikh Gurudwara Management Committee), New Delhi
The polytechnic campus offers courses in Fashion Design, Computer Science, Business Management, Hotel Management and Education.

Higher Secondary School (for Delhi Sikh Gurudwara Management Committee), New Delhi
A school for classes starting from nursery to class XII with laboratories, an assembly court, a multipurpose hall and sports facilities.

Gyan Bharati School, New Delhi
The school, with its student strength of more than 2,000, consists of sixty-four classrooms, laboratories and an assembly court. The building is clad in exposed brick and has an attractive façade with arched openings.

International Institute of Information Technology (IIIT), Hyderabad, Telangana
A premier institute in the country for imparting higher education in Information Technology. The campus is designed for a student strength of 2,500 with an administration block, the main academic block, IT research labs, a library, a computer centre, student hostels and faculty residences. In addition, the campus also has incubation centres and a mini campus for IT based companies such as IBM, Satyam and Wipro. The campus is planned as environment-friendly and is fully equipped with all IT technologies including wireless networking, video conferencing, distance learning and optical fiber network.

Central School Complex, New Delhi
The project, sponsored by National Council of Educational Research and Training (NCERT), serves as an apex higher secondary school teaching facility and includes workshops, a library, laboratories, an auditorium, and science labs. It has the capacity for total 2,500 students.

Oral Polio Vaccine Complex, Bulandshaher, Uttar Pradesh
A premier research and development complex for the development of indigenous expertise, and the first factory to manufacture polio vaccine in India, the project has a built-up area of 2,00,000 sq. ft. and primarily consists of super clean rooms of classes for a total 10,000 students.

Pathways World School Aravali, Gurugram, Haryana
A residential school conceptualized on a sprawling 30-acre campus, situated in the picturesque Aravalli Hills. The centrally air-conditioned school includes academic facilities for 1,500 students along with international level sport facilities, a media centre, hostels and housing for the staff. The school is affiliated to the IB curriculum. The design was adjudged amongst the most innovative designs by Design Share, USA, from over 100 entries received from all over the world. It is the first LEED Platinum rated institution in the country.

German School, New Delhi
A model school for the children of expatriates in Delhi, the school has an interesting layout of classrooms in a European pattern. In addition, it also has labs and student activity rooms for 1,000 students.

National Institute of Information Technology (NIIT) University, Neemrana, Rajasthan
An eco-friendly university campus located at Neemrana, Rajasthan, its design is a benchmark for sustainable and environment friendly campus design. The University is spread over 75 acres of land and is planned for 10,000 students and faculty housing. The campus has successfully demonstrated the latest technologies in sustainability.

Vidya International Girls School, Greater Noida, Uttar Pradesh
This all-girls international school provides a world-class campus. It has large classrooms, a library, a auditorium, an administrative building, faculty and staff housing, and a commercial complex, among others. It is spread on an area of about 30 acres. Total built-up area is 12 lakh sq. ft.

Delhi Public School International School, Gurugram, Haryana
A centrally air-conditioned school designed on a prominent site in Gurugram for a student intake of 2,000, the school has a distinctive architectural style and follows the IB curriculum. The total built-up area is 4,50,000 sq. ft.

Central University of Kashmir, Ganderbal, Jammu and Kashmir
The project is being developed as a greenfield project, aimed to be a world-class institution. The campus is spread over an area of 600 acres and is planned with all essential features befitting international standards. The campus comprises academic blocks, an administrative block, a convocation hall/convention centre, hostels, a central library, a faculty development centre, accommodation for the faculty and non-teaching staff, guest houses, club buildings, a health centre, a university school, etc. The campus is designed for a strength of 10,000 students and the design was a winning entry in a national level competition.

BML Munjal University, Gurugram, Haryana
The university campus is designed for 10,000 students and 800 faculty members. The University is centred on innovation and has various disciplines that are industry driven. The design of the buildings ensures flexible use of space and is unique in terms of its multifunctional character spread across the campus.

Central University of Rajasthan, Ajmer, Rajasthan
Designed to accommodate 10,000 students and over 1,000 faculty members, this University's unique green features, like thermal comfort and water management, enabled the campus to receive national recognition from GRIHA. Situated along the Jaipur–Ajmer Highway, it was envisaged as a 'Boutique Campus', which encompasses and enhances the experience of the institution through 'Product', 'Services' and 'Education'.

Bihar Police Academy, Rajgir, Bihar
The campus comprises training blocks, an administration building, a hospital, residences, schools, reserve offices, a guest house, sports facilities, a firing range, an equestrian and canine training centre, etc. The project incorporates local building materials and technologies, with the aim of making it a GRIHA 4-star rated project. The Academy has been duly vetted by the Energy and Resources Institute (TERI), and it also won the first prize through a design competition organized by the Bihar Police Building Construction Corporation.

India International Institute of Democracy and Election Management (IIIDEM), New Delhi
The campus is a national design competition winning entry, conceived as a state-of-the-art, modern building, where the blend of modern and traditional Indian architecture can be witnessed. The site, spread on an area of 5 acres with a built-up area of approximately 6,00,000 sq. ft., has been conceived as a campus with extensive landscaping.

Indian Institute of Technology (IIT), Jodhpur, Rajasthan
Boasting of a zero carbon footprint through a 'Net Zero' design concept, with zero waste generated, net zero energy and net zero water utilized at the campus, IIT Jodhpur is designed to be a self-sustainable, 'Smart Eco-Campus'. The development of the permanent campus includes buildings for residential zone, hostel zone and related utilities and services.

Biswa Bangla Biswavidyalaya, Bolpur, West Bengal
A winning entry in a national competition held in 2017, the design emphasizes on the typical setting of Shantiniketan with a modern design philosophy.

Vidya Sanskar International School for Holistic Learning, Faridabad, Haryana
A centrally air-conditioned residential school on a 13-acre site, designed for a strength of 2,000 students, the school, based on CBSE and IB curriculum, has classes from nursery to class XII. The facilities include a media centre with an audio-visual recording studio, a library, international level sports facilities, student hostels and housing for faculty.

Human Resources Development Centre (for DPS Society), Greater Noida, Uttar Pradesh
Spread over a site area of 5 acres, the centre offers training for aspiring teachers. The project consists of teaching halls, a multipurpose hall, residential facilities for the teaching and sports staff and hostel blocks for students.

Chhindwara University, Madhya Pradesh
The site allocated for Chhindwara University extends on a highly contoured patch of land of 139 acres, strewn with sparse flora. The total built-up area of the project is 8,13,000 sq. ft.

Delhi Public School (DPS), Greater Noida, Uttar Pradesh
The new campus of DPS in Greater Noida, with a site area of 7 acres, retains the iconic clock tower whilst using design elements such as pergolas and *jaalis*, juxtaposing an Indian outlook on the international design ideology followed by the campus.

Engineering College (for Apeejay Group), Sohna, Haryana
The campus is located on the outskirts of Aravalli Hills and is a premier institute for higher education in engineering and other disciplines. The campus is designed for 2,000 students.

HEALTHCARE

The new policies of liberalization have allowed the import of sophisticated medical equipment and technology. The opportunity of providing medical facilities is no longer considered the prerogative of the government. With easy access to modern hospitals, patients are demanding better quality of care. The design of these facilities, consequently, has to be modern, efficient and economical. Our firm believes that the design of a hospital has to evolve from a highly pragmatic approach. We believe a successful hospital design is one that is functional, meets the budget and creates an overall healing environment. Hospitals require careful integration of services like mechanical and electrical equipment, firefighting, air-conditioning, sound and air control, lighting, etc. Our multidisciplinary practice allows all such experts to be closely involved in designs from inception till completion.

Army College of Medical Sciences

Location **New Delhi** Site **6 acres** Built-up area **6,00,000 sq. ft.** Year of completion **2010** Beds **500**

Obtaining the status of a ***Green Building,*** *the college was rated among the* ***Top 25 Medical Colleges of India by*** **India Today** *in 2018*

Healthcare architecture or architecture related to medical services is one of the rising sectors of development in India today. With a number of development initiatives being dedicated to the health of Indian cities and their inhabitants, healthcare services are looked upon as an important way to improve the quality of life. The project is a demonstration of the discipline and care exhibited by the Indian Army for their personnel. Located at Dhaula Kuan in New Delhi and completed in 2010, the Army College of Medical Sciences, attached to a 500-bed hospital, provides education as well as state-of-the-art medical facilities to the Indian Army personnel.

The Army College of Medical Sciences, Delhi Cantonment, is a premier medical college in India, affiliated to Guru Gobind Singh Indraprastha University in Delhi. The college is recognized by the National Medical Commission and has a capacity of 100 undergraduate student admissions per year. It is supported by the Army Welfare Education Society of the Indian Army.

The 6-acre site is situated along the western slope of the Central Ridge, and hence, sits within an eco-sensitive zone. As a result of such a geographical location, the primary design approach adopted for the project was one that would harmoniously fuse the design of the buildings with the surrounding natural landscape. Besides, the huge requirement of 6,00,000 sq. ft. of built-up area had to be distributed judiciously over a plot spread in an awkward shape within the site boundaries.

The design form of the building flows organically and evolves around the complex geometry of the site and the pre-existing trees, thereby creating a dual sense of an enclosure defined by hard walls and soft foliage. Since the site had a dual frontage, with one side facing the Ring Road and the other an approach to the city from the airport, the building took the shape of sinuous curves – thereby creating a 'dual front façade'.

The main material chosen for construction was exposed bricks, a preferred choice for architectural design of institutional projects in Delhi. The Architects wanted to comply with the Client's demand for curtain walling without hampering the comfort of the patients. To achieve the same, the curtain wall on the northern side was designed to create insulation, thus reducing the heat ingress within the building and allowing natural daylight to enter freely while preventing glare. The curtain wall also created a direct visual connection from the interior spaces to the exteriors; this was complemented by a brick façade to lend an institutional feel to the building. The brick screens outlining the building were oriented towards the south, acting as a parasol of sorts for the hospital.

Facing page: *A view of the admin and hospital blocks.*

Below: *A pergola connecting the curtain glazing to the main façade.*

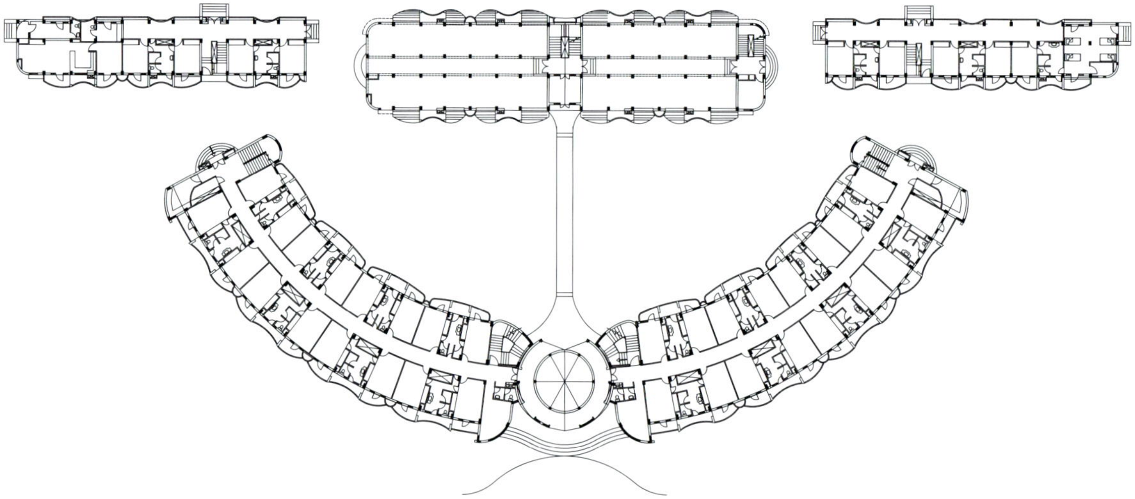

Among the facilities, alongside the college campus, a 1,200-seater auditorium and a hostel meant for 600 students contributed significantly to defining the architectural form and function of the complex.

The brick-and-glass structure can be seen on the Ring Road, as part of the army base which was the British Cantonment headquarters in the 1800s. Since it incorporates environment-friendly building technologies and materials, it was declared a Green Building in 2009.

The design for the Army College of Medical Sciences has certainly helped to establish the building as a landmark in the city, making it an essential part of its urban surroundings. The brick-screen wall makes a strong visual statement in the urban context. Functionally, the three components – the administration building, the auditorium-cum-lecture hall, and the academic block – are all separate entities, yet they are visually brought together by a sweeping roof element, transforming this complex of different buildings into a singular, imposing edifice which engages with the viewer through its sinuous form and sweeping skyline. This dramatic, unique architectural composition has received the distinctive honour of being chosen amongst the five best buildings of Delhi.

Above: *A front view of the admin block.*

Facing page above: *A front view of the boys' hostel block.*

Facing page below: *A drawing of the ground-floor plan of a hostel block.*

'Spaces should be airy, well-lit with adequate volume and should seamlessly flow into one another, thereby conversing with each other. As you experience these spaces, there should be an emotion of celebration.'

Ar. DIKSHU C. KUKREJA

Sir Ganga Ram City Hospital

Location **New Delhi** Site **12 acres** Built-up area **8,00,000 sq. ft.** Year of completion **2009** Beds **800**

Taking a cue from Brutalism, the hospital carefully ***incorporated massing techniques into its design***

Easy access is one of the most important criteria when selecting the site for a hospital, and Sir Ganga Ram City Hospital clearly ticks off that box by the virtue of its location in the very heart of Delhi. However, due to the increasing population in the capital city, it became imperative to ensure that the hospital could meet the rapidly accelerating medical needs of its patients. So, a proposal was made for an extension of the hospital, to make it better equipped for the future.

The design challenge was to revitalize, modernize and expand one of India's most respected medical facilities. Sir Ganga Ram City Hospital is truly an iconic institution, but one which had become outdated with crumbling buildings and infrastructure over the years. A comprehensive design strategy was developed not just to create new buildings but also to build a number of additional facilities and amenities for doctors, staff, patients and visitors. Buildings which could not be torn down were carefully renovated while ensuring there were no operational hindrances on floors below, above or adjacent to the area being renovated.

Massive challenges were faced by the design team, particularly for those in the engineering services. As the Architects evocatively recall, this whole revival journey at times felt like a surgical operation to them! Despite diagnosing the problem and carefully planning the surgery, as the Architects cut open the building, they encountered fresh surprises and challenges with services and building components that had not been anticipated (since there was scant or no information about the buildings, which were fifty to sixty years old and had been modified many times before).

Since the completion of its renewal in 2009, the hospital has been upgraded to an 800-bed multi-speciality facility. This includes a brand-new nine-storeyed 150-bed super-speciality facility with sixteen operation theatres, intensive care units (ICUs) and the addition of a laboratory set-up. Apart from extensions to the general and special wards and a new casualty block, the updated medical facility, with a built-up area of 80,000 sq. ft., now boasts a new oncology block with two linear accelerators,

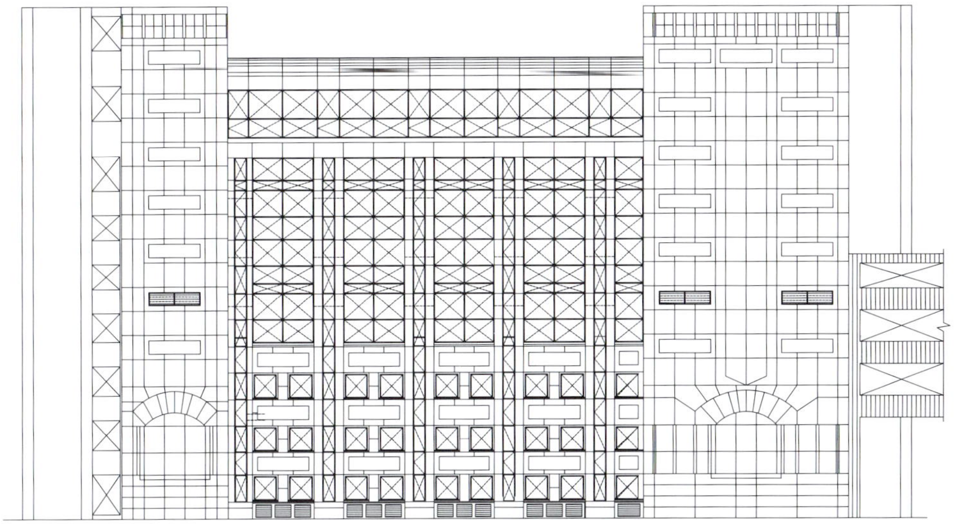

Facing page: *The entrance to the New Hospital block.*

Top: *A drawing of the front façade of the New Hospital block.*

Above: *A model scaled to represent the entire hospital site.*

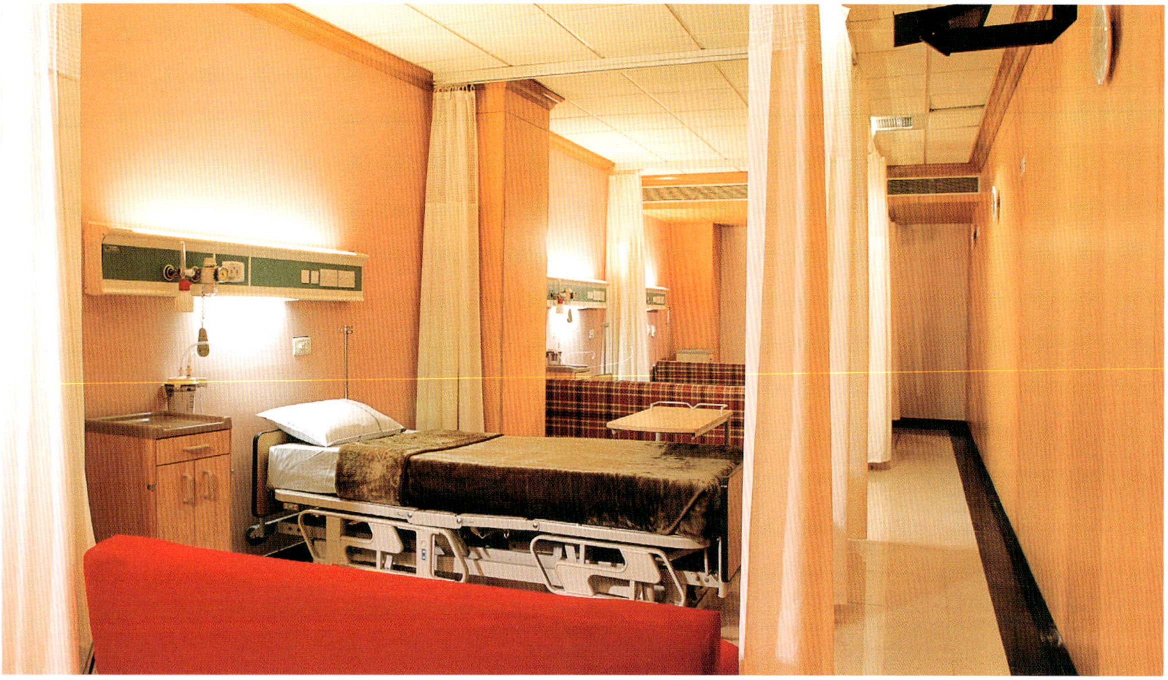

Above: *The interior of patient wards.*

Centre: *A view of the reception area.*

Facing page: *The New Hospital block conjoined to the Old Hospital block via a connecting corridor.*

simulator, brachytherapy and related facilities, including a cancer ICU.

The entrance greets the visitors with a protruding drop-off area, well-supported by massive columns. The frame of beams sandwiches a coffered ceiling, balancing the heaviness of the vertical elements. This assemblage is clad in bronze metallic finish of Aluminium Composite Panels (ACPs), which exude a contemporary element to the overall façade as well as add colour to the surroundings.

With increase in the number of patients, and consequently, their relatives, friends and caregivers, parking of vehicles would have been an issue had it not been for the foresight of the overall Master Plan of the extension site, which incorporates a multilevel parking facility for 1,000 cars. This solved the problem of vehicular congestion, easing pedestrian movement. The design team also ensured that the whole complex was made specially-abled and patient-friendly.

Rectangular in plan, the buildings are compactly designed for ease of access and movement of patients from operation theatres and ICUs to diagnostic services and rooms. The new blocks are connected to the existing buildings via elevated walkways that not only offer transparency and quick movement between various blocks, but also help establish various segments on the site as a single harmonious whole.

The interiors of the hospital were kept clean and free of obstruction creating a spacious and patient-friendly space. The wards provide state-of-the-art facilities while also leaving space for future additions. By using a subtle palette of materials, the Architects were able to create a serene environment, aware that a sensitive approach to design would go a long way in ensuring holistic treatment of the patients.

Clean lines dominate the façade, projecting the magnificence of the scale of the buildings. An otherwise utilitarian element like window glazing rises above its function. Neatly stacked in the elevation of the building, the fenestration not only defines a pattern but breaks the heaviness imposed by the structure itself.

Since the buildings are located at the edge of an expansive forest reserve on one side, the Architects designed and planned the facility in a way that enables patients to look out on to this refreshing green lung that is otherwise so difficult to find in the concrete jungle of the city. This is in keeping with the concept of inspiring healthcare.

Proximity to the dense green cover helps to manage the microclimate at the site, in addition to restraining the entry of noise and preventing distraction from the bustle outside the medical complex. The lower building footprint also allows for the accommodation of more green area on the site itself. Apart from this, the design of the extension creates integration with the dense cover, inspiring a holistic way of healing.

The parking has been provided through a multilevel facility that consolidates vehicles in one area and restricts their movement. The use of double-height drop-offs and connecting bridges, which interlink the second floor and the floors above, help to retain the openness of the ground below, thus, effectively balancing the horizontal and vertical mass.

The design of the extension adopts volumetric massing from the Brutalist style, while the Neo-Classical inspired clean lines run through the design of the façades. Local materials, which suit the city terrain and climate, have been used – a combination of ACP, glass and brick can be seen in the elevation, in conjunction with white marble grit.

With the constant new-age advancements in technology, the medical infrastructure of the new buildings was designed and developed to support the latest technological requirements of such a healthcare facility. To take care of the additional load in the new and improved facility, a completely new power distribution system with a standby Diesel Generator (DG) System (3 x 3,000 KVA) as well as a new state-of-the-art medical gas distribution system had to be installed. There are also new central sterile services department (CSSD)/laundry, kitchen and utility services for the entire hospital.

The fact that the Architects succeeded in this unusual surgical operation, is a tribute to the talent, skill and training that has been handed down from the founder, C.P. Kukreja, to the next generation.

Hamidia Hospital

Location **Bhopal, Madhya Pradesh** Site **50 acres** Built-up area **18,00,000 sq. ft.** Year of completion **2021** Beds **3000**

Conceptualized as a ***Smart Medi-city module,*** *this 'healing tissue' has been* ***designed as per the LEED (Leadership in Energy and Environmental Design) Guidelines***

One of the oldest hospitals in the country, Hamidia Hospital is a major healthcare institution in Bhopal, Madhya Pradesh. The concept of a 'Smart Medi-city', envisioned for the redevelopment of the 50-acre Hamidia Hospital complex on a built-up area of 18 lakh sq. ft., rests upon the ambition of becoming a complete urban fabric that would act like a 'healing tissue', not only through healthcare services provided by it, but also by encouraging a 'healthy way of living' through the design of its built environment. The project's success can be measured by the fact that CPKA's design for a 3,000-bed hospital with a medical college and nursing institute, hostels and faculty residences was adjudged a winning entry in a national design competition.

The hospital complex dates back to the days of the British Raj, when it accommodated 25 beds and provided healthcare facilities to British army personnel and soldiers. After Independence, the hospital became one of the most significant healthcare centres in Madhya Pradesh and contributed considerably during the Bhopal Gas Disaster in 1984.

Over time, the hospital complex grew haphazardly without any definite control or order till it became an incongruous mix of buildings belonging to different periods of time. Many of the existing structures within the complex are in a deplorable state with respect to basic services, safety and living conditions, and hence, are suffering from obsolescence. In such a situation, there was a need felt for a design that would bind the entire complex with a singular design ideology. The most important challenge, in this respect, was to conceive a development plan that would not alter the cultural fabric of the premises, dating back to the eighteenth century.

The design vision holds an ambition of converting the entire complex into an urbanscape that would attempt to heal the entire city by its dense and expansive natural cover, as well as propagate healthy practices as an integral part of one's life as well as the culture of the city.

This meant designing the complex as an extension of the city and not as an exclusive independent development. In the past, the complex had served as a fortified enclosure, detaching itself from its surrounding urban landscape. The design approach suggests

Facing page: *An aerial visualization of the entire project site.*

Below: *A perspective visualization of the project showcasing the* jaalis.

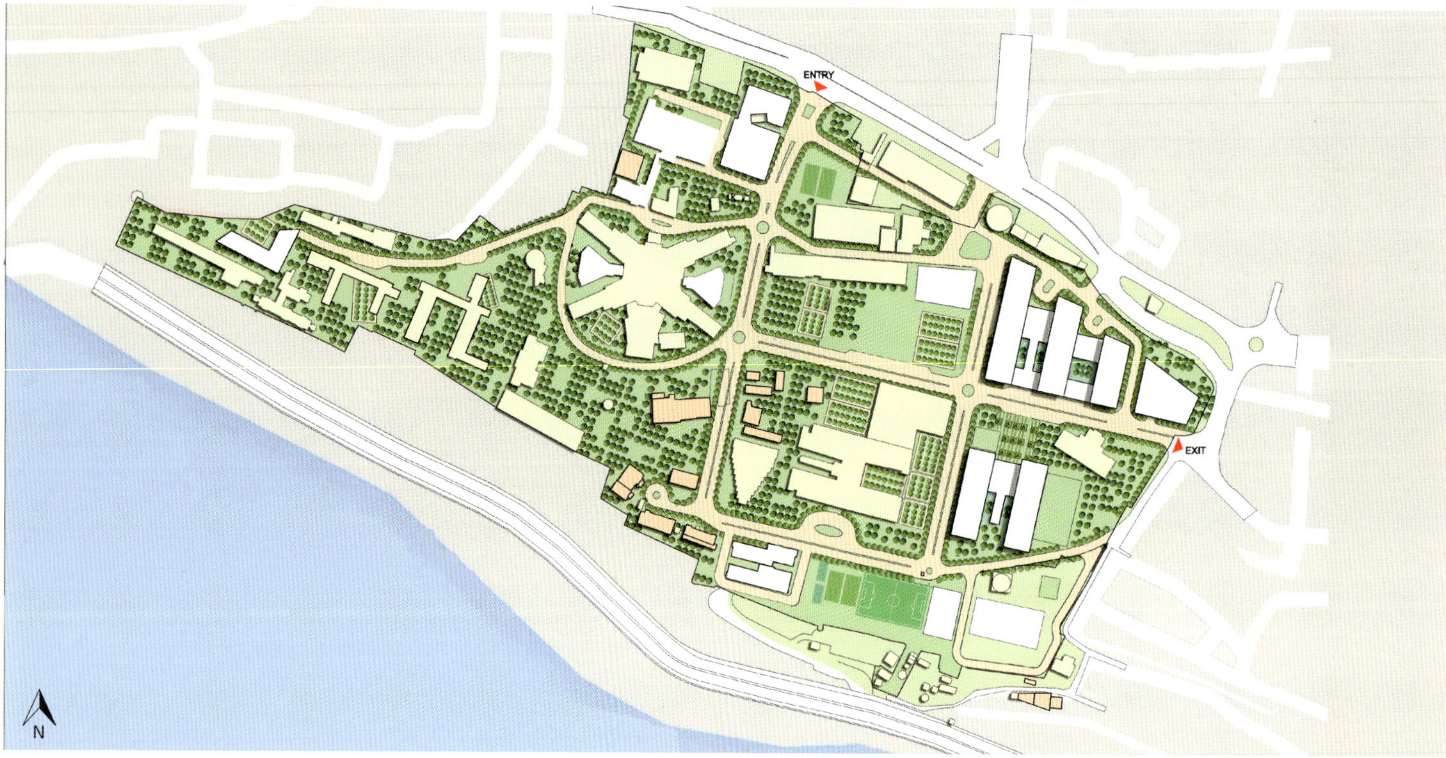

Above: *A digitally rendered Master Plan of the site.*

that public spines coming in directly from the city should be opened along the lake as a large continuous space, thereby creating a public space network as a major structuring element in the new Master Plan of the fort complex.

The medi-city so imagined is actually a 'city within a city' which contains its own functional districts, public spaces and hierarchy of streets that encourage a healthy and environment-friendly style of living. This 'healthy living' within the medi-city would be realized in the design of the Master Plan. The Architects introduced shaded avenues and bicycle lanes to encourage walking and cycling as modes of commute. Dense vegetation has been interspersed across the landscape, which helps in creating natural basins to absorb carbon dioxide, thereby processing the pollutants in the atmosphere.

Healthcare facilities have long been perceived as centres for the ailing and unwell populace. However, in current times, there is a need to think beyond these ideas and redefine medical infrastructure as quintessential design elements for a healthy economy. This concept became a motivation for the Architects' vision for Hamidia.

Condensing the built area of the development helps maintain a higher proportion of softscape, contributing to a flourishing urban space. Through these endeavours, the general public is also prompted to adopt healthy lifestyle practices. The architectural concept uses passive design strategies to naturally ventilate the interiors whilst also regulating thermal comfort. Building construction materials have been carefully chosen as per their non-polluting and non-hazardous

properties, leaving minimum carbon footprint on the environment.

Designing the healthcare complex as an organic development intends to reimagine the Master Plan of the medi-city as an organic entity which functions like a human body, that is, with a dedicated circulatory system, structural system, ventilation system, sensory system and purifying system. The circulatory system refers to the movement circuit within the complex, while the structural system refers to the structured urban networks of open space, streets and public activities. The ventilation system is composed of open green spaces that act as 'breathing lungs' for the complex, while the sensory system constitutes the urban elements and design details that appeal to the five human senses, thereby adding experiential value to the complex. Lastly, the purifying system – which is analogous to the excretory system of human body – in the Master Plan refers to the infrastructure network dedicated to recycling, treatment and reuse of water and energy that controls the sustainability in the design of the complex.

The geographical setting of the complex plays a crucial role in defining the sustainability parameters in the design. The existing social and environmental systems have been used as major structuring elements on the site. When reinforced with engineered technologies, this helps the architecture of the complex to exhibit maximized performance.

The medi-city is being developed in a region with historical significance and a cultural ethos that has evolved over time. The design approach, in this case, devises a method to respect all the cultural layers across time and finds points of coherence and convergence to achieve a result that is timeless. Hamidia's design forays into the future whilst respecting the historic nuance of the region, and initiates an idea which displays the power of eco-consciousness through an architectural manifestation.

Above: *A visualization of the front façade of the hospital blocks.*

Dr. B.S. Ambedkar Hospital

Location **New Delhi** Site **30 acres** Built-up area **3,45,000 sq. ft.** Year of completion **2022 (Estimated)** Beds **650**

The extension for the hospital ***imbibes the existing design values*** *whilst suiting the contemporary architectural character*

Dr. Baba Saheb Ambedkar Hospital, or Dr. B.S. Ambedkar Hospital, is a government hospital in Rohini in North-West Delhi that provides comprehensive medical healthcare in surgery, ophthalmology, medicine, orthopedics, pediatrics, obstetrics and gynaecology. A new 650-bed medical facility, this project is an upgradation of the existing healthcare facilities in the hospital.

A well-recognized facility in the area, the prestigious project involved the scope of addition of the following blocks: Mother & Child, Screening OPD block, Gas Manifold and Multilevel Parking. The existing blocks are conceptualized around developing a utilitarian facility inspired by modern design ideas.

The Architects were sensitive to the existing design language of the exterior and interior plan of the hospital. The new blocks, however, bring in an element of contemporary understanding. The comfort of the patients has been kept at the heart of design. Upon entering, the easy location of the Mother & Child facility segregates traffic circulation and regulates movement within the site.

Design of the Mother & Child block borrows two design elements from the existing hospital – arches and play in volumes. A vertical circulation spine has been extruded out in this block, allowing the patient rooms and consultation areas to remain private and noise-free. This vertical spine, lined with large window openings and humble skylights, disperses natural and diffused lighting into the facility's interiors. By extruding this vertical circulation spine, the Architects successfully broke the volume of the edifice whilst equally distributing the mass.

Repetition of arched windows over the façade of new blocks unifies edifices, new and old, as a harmonious ensemble. By staggering the plans, an interplay of different floors emerges over the façade, breathing a new lease of life into the overall grim and serious atmosphere of the hospital.

Planning of the hospital was one of the most important aspects for the Architects. The upgradation encourages execution of green design principles and showcases an improved understanding of designing an extension facility.

Left: *A perspective visualization of the front façade of the hospital.*

All India Institute of Medical Sciences (AIIMS)

Location **Gorakhpur, Uttar Pradesh** Site **112 acres** Built-up area **18,00,000 sq. ft.** Year of completion **2020** Beds **750**

Thriving on a ***sustainable approach,*** *the design* ***inspires natural healing and rejeuvenation of patients***

Nestled on the banks of the Rapti in east Uttar Pradesh lies Gorakhpur. It is here that the Indian government has proposed the setting up of All India Institute of Medical Sciences (AIIMS) under the Pradhan Mantri Swasthya Suraksha Yojna (PMSSY). The project is envisaged as a centre of education for undergraduate and postgraduate students, and intends to focus on providing the highest quality of patient-care services and medical education, apart from encouraging advancements in medical research.

The 112-acre site is conceptualized as a self-sustained integrated campus with dedicated zones for healthcare, institutional and residential components. The project includes a 750-bed multi– and super-speciality hospital, a medical and nursing college, auditorium, hostels, residential facilities for staff and faculty, and other ancillary requirements along with planned space for future developments.

The 18 lakh sq. ft. built-up area that houses these facilities is conceived with open spaces, and helps create synergy between patient care, research and teaching. Hospital blocks with spacious and well-lit corridors as well as ramps have been accommodated in the design to ensure mobility for patients and the physically disabled. Use of materials, like glass, instills transparency and lends a modern appearance. The Architects have been cautious about waste segregation and maintenance throughout the design, producing a holistic healthcare facility.

The complex also includes an Ayush block to inspire awareness regarding alternate therapies based on traditional methods of healthcare delivery. This facility is enriched with a healing garden that acts as a buffer space between the main outpatient department (OPD) and the building. A mix of natural medicinal herbs and trees, to be used for treatment when required, are used in landscaping the garden.

Patient care is given priority with therapy rooms being close to patient care rooms that open out into gardens. This holistic approach adopted in the design would help in fostering a culture of sustainability and in balancing, healing and relaxing of the physical as well as mental health of patients.

The Architects took the detailed design role for Larsen and Toubro, India, who were appointed as the Engineering, Procurement and Construction (EPC) agency for this project.

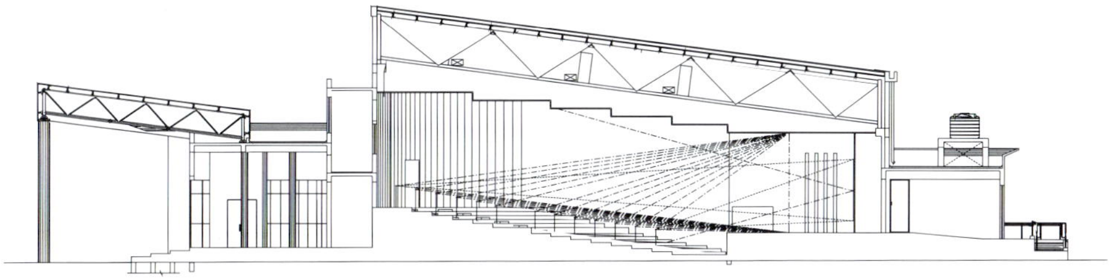

Top: *A visualization of the hospital block.*

Above: *A sectional elevation drawing of Auditorium block.*

Batra Hospital and Medical Research Centre

Location **New Delhi** Site **2 acres** Built-up area **1,50,000 sq. ft.** Year of completion **2001** Beds **200**

The hospital playfully works voids into the design to conjure a ***light-weight modern ensemble***

Immaculate, pristine white buildings stand out like silent sentinels at one end of the dense Jahanpanah City Forest within Tughlaqabad Institutional Area of New Delhi. Comprising a cardiac centre, a super-speciality block and a nurses' training centre, the buildings draw one's immediate attention to this extension of the Batra Hospital.

Completed in 2001, the new super-speciality block is equipped to deal with trauma cases and houses 200 beds devoted to intensive care. The well-equipped operation theatres are fitted with the most modern life-saving equipments that provide surgical as well as neurological operating facilities. The block boasts of ICUs and OPD clinics as well. A new cardiac wing, comprising 40 beds and additional angiographic cardiac treatment facilities, was added during the expansion.

The building is planned around a central courtyard, with the nurses' training institute set on a 2-acre plot of land, accommodating 400 in-house students, and with extensive teaching facilities. With a built-up area of 1,50,000 sq. ft., the block has enough room for an auditorium as well as facilities for advance training programmes for the resident nurses. The central courtyard is covered with a translucent material on the higher floors, increasing the volume of the space and flushing daylight into the interiors. This space has been utilized as the waiting area and appears to be spacious and airy.

The design intention was to develop a comprehensive Master Plan to transform the haphazardly developed medical complex into a vibrant, state-of-the-art modern facility. Originally, like many hospitals of yore, there were old, sporadic buildings randomly strewn across the complex with no clear circulation strategy. The medical infrastructure and engineering services were outdated and had not been optimally planned. All these

Facing page: *A view of the courtyard of the extension block.*

Above: *The atrium, which acts as the waiting area, with natural light streaming in.*

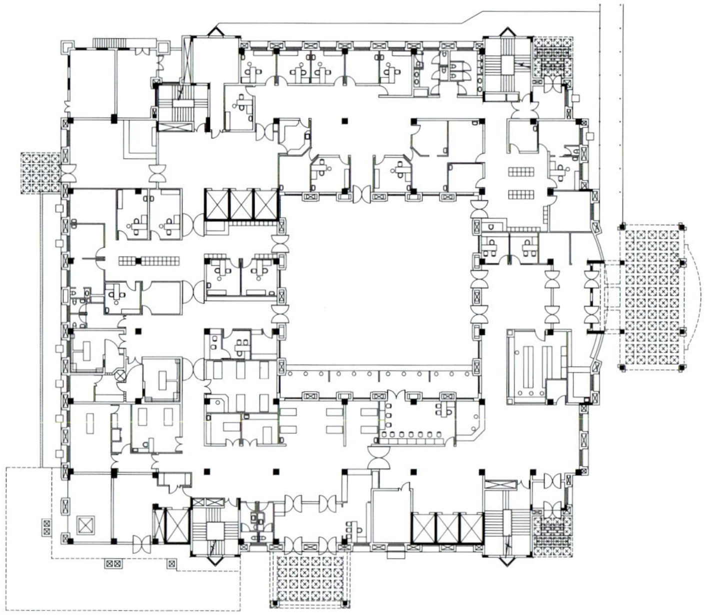

Above: *The entrance drop-off area of the hospital.*

Right: *A drawing of the ground-floor plan of the hospital.*

challenges were taken into their stride and successfully overcome by the Architects.

The biggest challenge was to keep the operations running while developing the new facilities. To begin with, a clear vision was developed to create a modern healthcare facility. The planning and design worked at multiple levels, creating new strategies for parking, circulation, landscape, visitor experience, services and utilities. Today, the hospital's architectural expression can boast of climate-sensitive buildings blessed with courtyards and, of course, the pristine white edifices that stand out like beacons in the forest.

Sustainability was also an important factor in the design intent, and it defined the overall form of the extensions. In fact, the endless expanse of forest cover that surrounds the site, almost embracing it in an environment-friendly hug, inspired the Architects to line up the rooms on the outer side of the building, providing the patients and their families with refreshing views of nature and her bounty and also ensuring their privacy during moments of distress. Thus positioned, the forest-facing rooms allowed the patients to revel in the beauty of their surroundings and simultaneously detach themselves from the inevitable bustle of the hospital's everyday routine.

Lighting being an integral aspect of good healthcare design, the corridors of the hospital are well-lit and lined with appropriate fenestrations to welcome daylight into the interiors, highlighting the healing power of daylight and reducing depression.

Even though the extension is designed to be in sync with the existing design sensibility, each of the new buildings reflect an identity and a character of its own. For instance, the entrance of the super-speciality block is through a curved face which is an imposing design element, further recessed on its two sides through stepped levels. The façade's design balances the heaviness by creating niches around the window openings, also adding elements of design and breaking monotony; a colonnaded façade supports magnificent columns.

Buffers in the form of courtyards and lawns provide an outdoor space for the visitors to relax in. A large volume of the surrounding greenery also benefits and controls the temperature of the hospital by regulating cooled air through the building's premises.

The buildings have been designed with a utilitarian design framework. Function is placed above all else – there exists an aesthetic underpinning to this project, as the Architects have used a play of forms, juxtaposing different volumes of space to achieve the overall look that is at once impressive and uplifting.

Kabliji Hospital

Location **Gurugram, Haryana** Site **5 acres** Built-up area **40,000 sq. ft.** Year of completion **1980**

The Architects used a ***vernacular design sense*** *to create a facility which effortlessly* ***blends into the rural setting*** *of Gurugram's outskirts*

Seventy-five kilometres away from Delhi and located in Gurugram, Haryana, the Kabliji Hospital – designed as a modern air-conditioned building complex with several well-equipped wards and state-of-the-art medical and surgical facilities – is set within a rural environment. Nestled in a site surrounded by thick vegetation, the single-storeyed structure seamlessly merges with the texture and colour of the dense trees of the Aravalli range that lies in the vicinity.

The hospital complex consists of different blocks placed close to each other. Connectivity from one block to another is an open walk under dense trees, an experience that inspired the Architects to make landscape an integral part of the site. Blue quartzite stone from the Aravallis is used to create pavers on the ground. The pitched roof design maintains thermal comfort for the patients in sweltering summer heat.

Executed on a shoestring budget, the design breaks stereotypes in constructing a facility which is an extension of the values of local habitation.

The choice of local materials also established the viability of construction of a project of this nature, taking a detour from the modern, conventional materials. The complexity of spaces was simplified in order to encourage availability of expertise and resources even in remote areas. The low-height edifice blends effortlessly with the surroundings, camouflaging the facility within the dense green cover of the trees. The material behaviour is in synchronization with the climate of the area.

Compact planning within the campus helps to ease the accessibility of different utilities while establishing semi-open common areas that are used for waiting. The functions and utilities have been segregated into different blocks to ease out congestion between spaces.

This project successfully demonstrates how modern healthcare, using best technologies, can be delivered through an architecture which belongs to its context.

Below: *A frontal view of one of the treatment blocks.*

QRG
Multi-Specialty Hospital

QRG Central Hospital and Research Centre

Location **Faridabad, Haryana** Site **5 acres** Built-up area **4,00,000 sq. ft.** Year of completion **2013** Beds **500**

*The **multi-speciality** QRG Hospital and Research Centre is a successful example of **juxtaposing technologically advanced medical infrastructure with contemporary healthcare design***

Spread over a 5-acre site in a bustling locality surrounded by residences, offices and commercial establishments in Faridabad, is the multi-speciality QRG Hospital and Research Centre. Completed in 2013, the 500-bed hospital is housed within a built-up area of 4,00,000 sq. ft. The building has an expansive curtain glazing distinguishing its façade, and projects an imposing demeanour when viewed from afar. The Architects intended to challenge the norms of a traditional hospital and create an all-new, contemporary identity for healthcare architecture. Indeed, the dynamic, curvilinear form of the massive portal at the entrance makes a lasting impression.

The Architects were able to plan and provide a patch of green at the rear side of the hospital, leaving the front space for entrance and parking. The overall planning is divided into two blocks connected via walkways, balancing the massing. The curtain glazing welcomes maximum natural daylight into the building – a refreshing change from the monotonous and gloomy atmosphere generally associated with hospitals.

While the exterior reflects a modern aesthetic, the interior design breaks stereotypes, taking a detour from the flat and plain colours seen in traditionally designed hospitals. Colour-filled interiors are pleasant to the eye and create a much-needed optimistic atmosphere for patients and visitors. Natural light floods the waiting and reception areas in the atrium space covered with skylights.

Most of the areas on the ground level remain shaded, as the carefully aligned north-south orientation reduces the heat-island effect. The design takes into consideration the need to insulate the buildings from solar radiation. In winters, the heating load is reduced by adequate heat gain, while summers witness less heat gain, allowing less dependency on mechanical means of thermal regulation. More than 85 per cent of public areas/common-shared spaces are planned to receive natural daylight. The Architects have been careful about reducing the glare inside too.

The facility uses a compact design strategy to make the healthcare resources and expertise easily accessible. The services are accommodated at one end on the rear of the site, and the research facility and services blocks are separated by a green space in the middle. The Architects were determined to include as many open spaces as possible on the site to balance the heaviness of the built structures.

Facing the main road, the colossal design element at the entrance spans an impressive 25 metres and instills a dramatic statement to the structure. The mammoth element lends an imposing grandeur and sculptural sensibility to the overall hospital design, and also increases the visibility of the healthcare facility when seen from a distance.

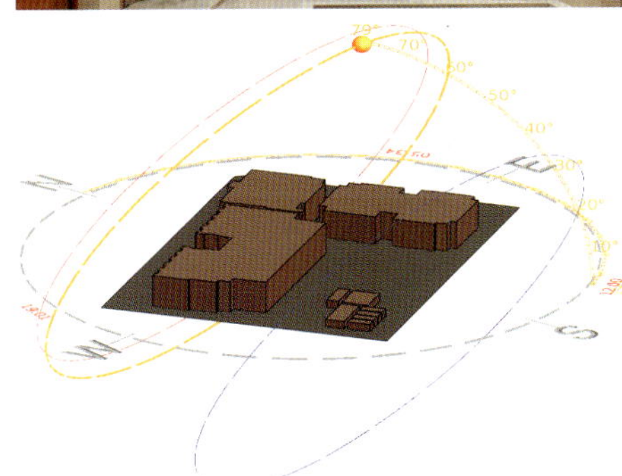

Facing page: *A visualization of the front façade of the hospital.*

Top: *The interior view of the waiting area.*

Above: *A simulation diagram exhibiting the orientation of the project design with regard to the sun-path.*

United Hospital

Location **Dhaka, Bangladesh** Site **5 acres** Built-up area **4,50,000 sq. ft.** Year of completion **2006** Beds **450**

The design successfully testifies ***brick as a light-weight building construction material***

A far cry from the box typology design usually associated with hospitals, the United Hospital in Dhaka sports a juxtaposition of different forms and levels, adding up to a landmark building. Completed in 2006, this healthcare facility makes a lasting impression on patients and their families. A magnificent pergola embodies the entrance to the hospital and the overall aesthetic is a refreshing departure from the traditional buildings in the city.

This 450-bed super-speciality hospital with state-of-the-art diagnostic and operating facilities, consists of two square blocks set around an atrium over a built-up area of 4,50,000 sq. ft. The two wings are connected by a reception that stretches from one block to the other, creating a dramatic entrance and a spacious waiting area for patients' families. The winged form equally distributes the length-width ratio of the interiors such that the different examination and treatment areas are easily accessible. A careful segregation of consultation spaces from treatment rooms on the ground floor regulates ease of movement.

The building incorporates structural finesse to execute a design with a futuristic appeal. The interiors are an extension of the meticulous detail in the form work on the exterior. A combination of yellow brick with glass and ACP columns support the roof that is structurally raised from the terrace parapet level. The different blocks of the hospital are connected via a common courtyard, partially covered with pergolas. The waiting areas in the centre of the buildings are spruced up by indoor plantation for visitors to have a pleasant experience.

The site is triangular, with the rear facing the picturesque setting of the Gulshan Lake; the Architects deliberately lined the patients' rooms on the rear side allowing them window access. Natural daylight and ventilation maintain thermal comfort within the rooms. On the external façade, one can read the grid-like design puncturing the surface with rectangular fenestrations, which regulate shading pattern and heat absorption into the interiors. Waste segregation and disposal play a vital role, ensuring that no waste (medical or non-medical) is discarded into the eco-water body.

The architecture of this hospital is regarded as one of the best in the city for its thoughtful amalgamation of vernacular ideologies with contemporary understanding of a healthcare facility at the time it was built.

Facing page: *A perspective of the front façade of the hospital as seen from the adjacent water body.*

Below: *A panoramic view of the ground-floor interiors with the waiting areas and the cafeteria.*

Expansion of Indraprastha Apollo Hospitals

Location **New Delhi** Site **5 acres** Built-up area **4,50,000 sq. ft.** Year of completion **2006** Beds **200**

*The **extension design borrows from the existing building** whilst establishing its own identity*

On the busy Mathura Road in the prime locality of South Delhi, surrounded by Jasola District Park and overlooking the lush greenery of Okhla Bird Sanctuary, is the Indraprastha Apollo Hospital campus. The Architects were approached by Apollo to visualize its expansion design programme, planned on a 5-acre plot of land within the existing complex. The project envisaged the addition of a 200-bed maternity and gynaecology block and a nursing institute with hostels meant to house 200 nurses and 50 resident doctors.

The expansion of the facility is in keeping with the stepped massing and cubic volumes of the existing structure, borrowing from its architectural vocabulary. A well-planned auditorium within the institute building was part of phase one of the construction, while the addition of the maternity, gynaecology as well as a new residential block was part of phase two. The location of the institute is ideal as the site for the new project is on the rear side of the existing hospital building, and allows students to interact with the main hospital facility and provides them with space to learn undisturbed in quiet surroundings.

The 4,50,000 sq. ft. tower-like brick-and-mortar building is reminiscent of a pylon – rising in levels and imposing in scale as one approaches it. The design guides the students and doctors through the reception porch to faculty rooms and finally to different classrooms. The rhythmic use of fenestration with window openings on the façade laid out in symmetry, and the staggering levels on the façades, arising to align the buildings in a manner that facilitates natural daylight and ventilation, are remarkable.

The presence of a significant cover of green in the vicinity ensures that the buildings remain cool through the hot and sweltering summer months. Brick and mortar were employed as primary materials, as these are best suited to extreme climate of Delhi.

A sensible yet creative use of design, form, materials, specifications, engineering technology and operational systems add up to an environment-friendly, ecologically neutral hospital campus. A combination of all these in the right proportion projects the hospital as a futuristic healthcare facility, completely furnished with modern and advanced technology to help patients recuperate in the best way possible.

Below: *A view of the entrance of the expansion block.*

Swami Vivekanand Medical College and Hospital

Location **Palampur, Himachal Pradesh** Site **50 acres** Built-up area **10,00,000 sq. ft.** Year of completion **2014** Beds **500**

Situated amidst the valley of Himachal Pradesh, the hospital is ***designed keeping in mind the spectacular view for patients***

The Swami Vivekanand Medical College and Hospital occupies a built-up area of 10,00,000 sq. ft. on a 50-acre plot in Palampur.

With a scenic mountain range as the backdrop, the environment is conducive for patients to heal by virtue of being close to the soothing effects of nature. A well-planned parking space and one-way traffic encourage pedestrian movement in the complex.

The low, multi-level blocks expand horizontally, ensuring provision of natural daylight within the interiors through *chhajjas* and cut-outs – a harmonious juxtaposition of the horizontal and the vertical. The compact planning of the buildings is a conscious decision by the Architects, as it makes movement less cumbersome for the patients.

With around 70 per cent of the land kept open and green, the facility utilized its unique location to its utmost benefit. Lush green views enable patients to dwell in nature while undergoing treatment. The contours of the site are used to the design's advantage, with spatial planning and movement properly envisioned and controlled. Distinct circulation is planned for patients, visitors and staff. Hard-paved landscaping has been kept to the minimum and is restricted to the periphery of the site. The front lawn is an open green space that is accessible to visiting family members for relaxation or waiting.

In keeping with its purpose as a medical training college and hospital, the infrastructure of the buildings supports the latest technology and state-of-the-art medical equipments that help in diagnosis and therapeutic procedures in patient care. The campus includes a 500-bed teaching hospital, medical college, nursing college as well as residential accommodation for doctors, nurses and staff. A naturopathy and wellness centre are also part of the complex.

Below: *A distant view highlighting the expanse of the hospital.*

Maharaja Agrasen Hospital

Location **New Delhi** Site **4 acres** Built-up area **1,50,000 sq. ft.** Year of completion **1999** Beds **150**

The facility is ***a well proportioned massing of healthcare design,*** *efficiently connecting its spaces*

A play of cuboids varying in volume and scale marks the design of the seven-storeyed structure that houses the Maharaja Agrasen Hospital in New Delhi. This healthcare facility is connected to important nodal points, keeping in mind ease of transportation, a residential neighbourhood and commercial retail areas in the vicinity. Within a built-up area of 1,50,000 sq. ft., the 150-bed super-speciality hospital is equipped with the finest diagnostic facilities like CT scan, radiotherapy and a cath lab (catheterization laboratory). The different areas of the hospital divide functionality floor-wise, making it more streamlined for the patients and their families.

Extruding levels on the façade influence the play between light and shade throughout the interiors. Coffered pergolas are provided on the higher floors, breaking the monotony of the structure and creating a semi-covered space that acts as a spillover healing area. The choice of white marble stone grit gives an elegant and refreshing appearance to this edifice which stands out, poised amidst a dense, urban clutter surrounding the site. The selection of this material is dictated both by its low maintenance, which avoids any repaint issues, and also by its frugality, since the Client, a charitable trust, had a limited budget. The interiors are sleek and modern, furnished with a combination of wood and stone that give an assuring natural feel and much-needed warmth.

Above: *Front façade of the hospital highlighting the drop-off area.*

The design has been formulated to suit the climate and to orient the building in such a manner that it allows most rooms to welcome natural light during the day. A careful planning of window-to-wall ratio provides natural ventilation when required. The surroundings of the hospital are extensively landscaped with thick vegetation in order to create natural noise barriers for the site. A sensitive use of brick and mortar as primary materials of construction suits the broad temperature range of the city, effectively maintaining the thermal comfort of patients. Care has also been taken to use eco-friendly, non-toxic materials to furnish the indoor spaces.

Carefully planned parking spaces help in the regulation of vehicular movement as well as in making the site more pedestrian friendly. This enables the hospital authorities to evolve and introduce safer ways for patients to move, and be moved, through the site.

Raman Munjal Memorial Hospital

Location **Gurugram, Haryana** Site **40 acres** Built-up area **1,00,000 sq. ft.** Year of completion **1998** Beds **150**

Designed in a ***rural setting,*** *the hospital* ***follows a low-height module,*** *focusing on providing ease of mobility*

A sprawling 40-acre site on the outskirts of Delhi, in Gurugram, Haryana, was earmarked for a low-rise complex housing the Raman Munjal Memorial Hospital. The hospital was planned to provide quality healthcare and to make advanced medical facilities accessible to remote areas around. The infrastructure was designed and developed to accommodate and support new-age and advanced medical technologies required to fulfill this task.

The hospital block is a single-storeyed structure and the expansion of buildings is horizontal, interspersed with vegetation cover. Various blocks are connected by means of open corridors, allowing transparency between the spaces. Huge windows, well protected by *chhajjas* that shade them from the sun, welcome natural daylight into the interiors. The design and planning of the facility around a central courtyard help to regulate the temperature, ventilation and natural daylight that enters the buildings. To maximize output from available resources, the rooms have also been designed to stay cool during summers, absorbing less heat from the exposed surfaces.

The Master Plan for the project also has provision for doctors and staff to be housed within the site, making it possible for expertise to always remain available. In addition, there are sports facilities, a vocational training centre and an auditorium for 1,000 persons within the complex.

Above: *A low-rise building with extruding forms used as drop-off porches at the hospital.*

This hospital is planned as part of the corporate social responsibility (CSR) activities of contribution to society by the renowned Hero Honda group. Ever since the group set up two large industrial facilities in the vicinity (also designed by CPKA) for the manufacture of motorbikes, they wanted to create a healthcare facility that could be used by the workers and their families.

The design approach was to create a well-equipped hospital which plays the dual role of being inviting and un-inhibiting to the rural community, yet giving the appearance of a modern healthcare facility which assures the patient and their families that the facility will treat them successfully.

The healthcare facility understands and works on the ideology of providing patients with the isolation required for recovery during treatment. Consequently, the different blocks for treatment interspersed throughout the site are surrounded by thick vegetation. The low height of the buildings are a reflection of the design ideology of the hospital, which seeks to help those who are in need but do not have access to medical facilities.

Complete Listing of Healthcare Projects

Mehrad Hospital, Iran
A 500-bed modern hospital equipped with all amenities and a full complement of specialist services. Phase one was completed in 1976.

Bagabandhu Memorial Hospital, Chittagong, Bangladesh
A 500-bed hospital with state-of-the-art diagnostic and operating facilities for University of Science and Technology, Bangladesh. The building is designed in twenty-four floors with separate storeys for doctor and staff residences in the towers.

Hospital and Medical College, Kathmandu, Nepal
An ultra-modern 500-bed super-speciality medical facility with a medical college, this state-of-the-art campus on a 35-acre undulating site also provides housing for doctors and staff.

United Hospital, Dhaka, Bangladesh
A super-speciality hospital with 450 beds and modern diagnostic and operating facilities, this project is conceived in two square blocks planned around an atrium. The construction is in traditional brickwork, typical of Dhaka.

Bir Hospital, Kathmandu, Nepal
The existing Bir Hospital at Kathmandu has been provided with an independent 200-bed extension unit with super-specialties such as cardiothoracic surgery, nuclear medicine and many others.

Institute of Human Behaviour and Psychiatric Treatment Facilities, New Delhi
The expansion programme for the Institute envisages modern diagnostic and treatment facilities, in-patient accommodation (1,500 patients), and accommodation for staff and students on an area of 100 acres.

Women's Hospital, Doha, Qatar
A 100-bed hospital with gynaecological specialities, operation theatres, radiotherapy, etc.

Ansari Memorial Hospital, Ranchi, Jharkhand
This small, 70-bed hospital, is conceived to provide ultra-modern medical facilities to the relatively affluent weavers' community in central Bihar.

Nirogi Hospital, New Delhi
This 150-bed super-speciality hospital, with four operation theatres and 16-bed ICU, also has provision for free beds, general OPD and state-of-the-art facilities for in-patients.

East West Medical Centre, New Delhi
An internationally acclaimed medical facility serving Indian and foreign nationals, this centre also has private flying rescue facilities.

Medical College, Buxar, Bihar
The proposed design is to set up a medical college for 100 admissions per year and an associated 500-bed teaching hospital, as per Medical Council of India (MCI) norms in Dumraon in Buxar, Bihar.

Madhubani Hospital, Jhanjharpur, Bihar
The design proposes to set up a medical college for 100 admissions per year and an associated 500-bed teaching hospital on a 20-acre site, as per MCI norms in Jhanjharpur in Madhubani, Bihar.

Nurses Training Institute, Batra Hospital and Research Centre, New Delhi
Built on a 2-acre land, this training institute for nurses accommodates 400 in-house students with intensive teaching facilities, auditorium as well as facilities for advance training programmes for resident nurses.

Batra Hospital, New Delhi
The new super-speciality hospital emphasizes on trauma cases with well-equipped operation theatres providing surgical as well as neurological operating facilities, ICUs and OPD clinics. The new block contains 200 beds, largely devoted to intensive care.

Bhagvan Shri Gomteshwari Cooperative Group Housing Society (CGHS) Limited, New Delhi
This Central Government Health Scheme facility is located in New Delhi and helps cater medical facilities to residents of the surrounding area.

Maharishi Valmiki Hospital, New Delhi
The 350-bed hospital was built to provide secondary or district level medical aid to the people of Pooth Khurd. It has a site area of 9 acres with a built-up area of 2,00,000 sq. ft.

Gas Authority of India (GAIL) CGHS, Gurugram, Haryana
Located in Sector 56, the medical facility was constructed to help serve families and employees of GAIL.

Yashoda Hospital and Heart Institute, Surat, Gujarat
This 300-bed state-of-the-art hospital, with a built-up area of 2,40,000 sq. ft., provides comprehensive tertiary-level care. The hospital offers diagnostic, curative and preventive services in cardiology, cardiothoracic surgery, emergency and critical care medicine including trauma, orthopaedic and neurosurgery.

Institute for the Mentally Disabled, New Delhi
As the first institute of its kind in Delhi, the complex includes residential, therapeutic, teaching and boarding facilities for nearly 400 mentally disabled children.

Moolchand Kharaiti Ram Hospital, New Delhi
The Architects were involved in the re-planning and rationalization of the existing hospital by adding a new operation theatre, ICU, birthing centre, and patients' suites and rooms as per international standards.

Raman Munjal Memorial Hospital, Gurugram, Haryana
A 150-bed diagnostic and treatment facility for the rural population; the Master Plan of this healthcare facility also has provision for doctors and staff housing.

Maharaja Agrasen Hospital, New Delhi
A 150-bed super-speciality hospital, it is a seven-storeyed structure with a constructed area of 1,50,000 sq. ft. The centrally air-conditioned hospital is equipped with the finest diagnostic facilities.

Sanjay Gandhi Memorial Hospital, New Delhi
A Government of NCT, Delhi, initiative, the project includes extension and remodelling of the existing medical facilities. The site area is 12 acres with the built-up area as 2,00,000 sq. ft., and the total number of beds is 386.

Primus Super-speciality Hospital, New Delhi
A 150-bed, centrally air-conditioned modern hospital, located in the prestigious diplomatic area of the capital. Besides advanced operating facilities and deluxe suites, the hospital also has advanced executive health check-up facilities.

Hospital in Heavy Water Project Township, Manuguru, Andhra Pradesh
A 50-bed hospital with all the facilities to benefit population of the township of 4,000 dwelling units.

Ram Manohar Lohia Hospital, Farrukhabad, Uttar Pradesh
As one of the major district hospitals in the state of Uttar Pradesh, this 300-bed complex has state-of-the-art diagnostic and operating facilities. It is planned around a landscaped court on a 10-acre site.

District Hospital, Mau, Uttar Pradesh
Constructed on a 20-acre site, this district level hospital had 200 beds in phase one, which is now being expanded to 400 beds. The hospital also provides housing for staff.

Ravishankar Shukla Hospital, Raipur, Chhattisgarh
A premier medical centre in the region, this 300-bed hospital with all super-specialties is located 15 km from Raipur city, on the national highway to Bhilai.

Life Support Heart Hospital, Agra, Uttar Pradesh
Located on a prominent site on the Delhi–Agra National Highway, the Life Support Heart Hospital is a state-of-the-art cardiothoracic super-speciality hospital with 100 beds and all other necessary facilities.

Kabliji Hospital, Gurugram, Haryana
This is a hospital in a rural environment with several well-equipped wards and modern medical and surgical facilities. The complex also includes residences for staff.

Indraprastha Apollo Hospitals, New Delhi
The expansion programme for the hospital was on a 5-acre pocket in the Apollo compound. The project envisages a 200-bed Maternity and Gynaecology Hospital and a nursing institute with hostels for 200 nurses and 50 resident doctors. The institute building is complete with a built-up area of approximately 4,50,000 sq. ft.

Rotary International Blood Bank, New Delhi
A state-of-the-art facility for collection, storing and distribution of blood plasma, this hi-tech facility is designed for Rotary International in New Delhi.

Hospital in Raghubir Nagar, New Delhi
A 500-bed hospital with state-of-the-art medical facilities.

Vardhman Mahavir Medical College Building, Safdarjung Hospital, New Delhi
A medical college within the precinct of Safdarjung Hospital, the college has a total built-up area of 4,50,000 sq. ft., including academic buildings, hostels for 500 students and faculty residences.

Hamidia Hospital, Bhopal, Madhya Pradesh
The new Master Plan for Hamidia aims to create a modern multi-speciality 'Smart Medi-city' with a staggering number of 3,000 beds, a medical college and residential quarters for staff, designed as a LEED Platinum rated complex.

Dr. B.S. Ambedkar Hospital, New Delhi
The extension and remodelling of the existing hospital, on a site area of 30 acres, includes new infrastructure facilities pertaining to Mother & Child block, Screening OPD block and multi-level parking. The hospital has a built-up area of 3,45,000 sq. ft. with the total number of beds equaling 650.

Redevelopment of Sir Ganga Ram City Hospital, New Delhi
One of the most venerated medical institutions in Delhi is being re-planned with rationalization of its various facilities as a 800-bed multi-speciality facility, with the Master Plan of the hospital complex being revised as well.

Coal India Hospital, Dankuni, West Bengal
A 50-bed hospital built for a township of 1,000 dwelling units of Coal India Limited, in Dankuni, West Bengal.

Associated Cement Companies (ACC) Hospital, Gagal, Himachal Pradesh
A hospital furnished with all amenities in Gagal Cement Works for Associated Cement Companies (ACC) Limited in Himachal Pradesh.

Swami Vivekanand Medical College and Hospital, Palampur, Himachal Pradesh
Built on a 50-acre site, this is the first medical college to be established in the state along with a super-speciality 500-bed hospital.

QRG Central Hospital and Research Centre, Faridabad, Haryana
A 500-bed multi-speciality hospital with National Accreditation Board for Hospitals and Healthcare Providers (NABH) and National Accreditation Board for Testing and Calibration Laboratories (NABL) compliance, this premium healthcare facility is built on a plot area of 5 acres.

Army College of Medical Science, New Delhi
This new medical college, with an annual intake of 100 students, is attached to the 500-bed Army Base Hospital in Dhaula Kuan. The college, with its state-of-the-art facilities, has a 1,200-seater auditorium and hostels for 600 students.

Aruna Asaf Ali Hospital, New Delhi
This 140-bed hospital is constructed on a 2-acre site with a built-up area of 1,14,000 sq. ft.

Kalkaji Hospital, New Delhi
Located in South Delhi, Kalkaji Hospital is replete with facilities to support the 100-bed facility.

OFFICES

Architecture of office buildings addresses both public and individual spaces. While the public parts of the building require a distinctive image, the inner shell needs maximum flexibility and interchangeability. New realities of globalism demand innovative methods for controlling the design's quality and outcome. Design of office buildings is more than façadism; it is about integrating landscape and interiors with the overall form. Environment friendly and ecologically neutral design technologies, which cut operating costs and create healthier work environments, are essential in the design of modern offices.

'It is a spectacular building, not least because it marks a complete volte face from all the modernist rhetoric about the iniquity of ornament. It is a sort of sultanate tower of our times.'

GILES TILLOTSON

Ambadeep Tower

Location **New Delhi** Site **5 acres** Built-up area **2,00,000 sq. ft.** Year of completion **1993**

Recognized as ***one of the most 'Notable Buildings of the 21st Century Architecture'*** *in* ***Sir Banister Fletcher's*** *well-known encyclopedia,* **History of World Architecture**

Conceptualized for the Ansal Group, this twenty-three-storeyed tower was designed to challenge the stereotype of high-rise commercial buildings in New Delhi. Strategically located at the intersection of KG Marg and Tolstoy Road in the heart of the capital, it towers above the surrounding buildings as the most eye-catching feature in the skyline of the city's prominent business centre. Due to its prime location, Ambadeep Tower opens up on three sides, welcoming traffic from different incoming roads and acting as an entry point to the heart of the city.

With a built-up area of 2,00,000 sq. ft., Ambadeep Tower has been carefully designed to allow maximum floor-area coverage. A lofty tower piercing the sky, it is fronted by two buildings placed at an angle and joined by connecting corridors nine storeys above the ground, creating an imposing atrium entrance below and marking a structural feat. The bold façade treatment in long continuous bands, broken at corners by square pilasters, uses geometric patterned glass tiles in shades of white, yellow and blue. The two smaller blocks as well as the glass-encased lifts overlook the landscaped atrium, designed exquisitely. The cavernous atrium of the tower provides one of the grandest urban scale entrances possible to an office building.

Constructed between 1991 and 1993 on a 5-acre site and at a cost of Rs. 200 million, this was the first structure in Delhi to introduce glass elevators which provide a stunning panoramic view of its surroundings. A major challenge while designing the building was to depart from the conventional style of high-rise buildings and to 'break the box', a feat that was achieved by reinterpreting traditional Indian elements, such as courtyards and terraces on upper floors along with distributing the overall built volume.

At a time when the city was still adopting and undergoing transitions with its infrastructural development, the Architects proposed a revolutionary idea with the office tower: they incorporated a glass elevator at the front façade of the building. The thought behind such a concept came from the understanding of being able to provide never-seen-before views of the city from such a height. This not only made the project one of its kind, but was also able to display the ability of architecture to act as a powerful social tool.

The Tower is a fine example of a successful marriage between art and architecture. The whole edifice has been imagined as a canvas where the intrinsic glass mosaic patterns create a unique record of art at the largest (and tallest) scale ever in the city. The building now stands as a landmark for its unique amalgamation of Indian, Persian, Neo-Classical and Modern elements of architecture. The play between different colours, in an attempt to bring art closer to the masses, is a magnificent departure from the customary, dull office buildings of Connaught Place. Highlighting the corners and folding edges of the tower with murals and by creating a hollow space in the facade, lined with rhythmic window openings, the Architects were able to balance the heaviness of the

Above: *The coffered ceiling is well-supported by extending mosaic-clad columns.*

Facing page: *Ambadeep Tower as seen from the front, highlighting the grand atrium at the entrance space.*

Left: *A view of the tower reflecting its different edges.*

structure, thereby making it appear lighter in form. Window openings have been provided throughout the façade and allow ample natural light and ventilation to flush the interiors. In doing so, the Architects were able to design and manifest a lively work environment. Along with this, the inner courtyard was left exposed to the sky.

'C.P. Kukreja put his stacks of Kahnian bricks and reminded us – in Ambadeep (1990) – that it is possible to cover the exterior of a building in coloured mosaic tiles and geometric patterns. It is a spectacular building, not least because it marks a complete volte face from all the modernist rhetoric about the iniquity of ornament. It is a sort of sultanate tower of our times.'[1]

Landscaping is an integral part of the design. Some of the strong landscape design elements that flow into the interiors are the atrium, with its terraced waterfall and planters, and a court at the rear of the building, which is overlooked by the staff canteen and the ground floor. Storage areas, the mechanical plant room, the electric substation and mandatory car parking requirements – are all housed in the three basements.

'Perhaps a first example of such strong colours in a modern building of this scale the aesthetic evolved as a result of the Architects' conviction that the art compensates for the deprivation of a natural uplifting environment

[1] *Giles Tillotson, "Continuity and Change in the Modern Architecture of Delhi: Post-Independence Perspectives." (Seminar Papers, Rashtrapti Bhawan, INTACH, Delhi, 2013).*

Right: *A close-up of the iconic Persian-inspired mosaic pattern, which adds colour and art to the building's façade.*

Below: *Blue and yellow mosaic tiles used as artistic elements for the first time on a building façade on such a large scale, making it a historical landmark.*

Bottom: *Initial concept design showcasing volumes and spaces.*

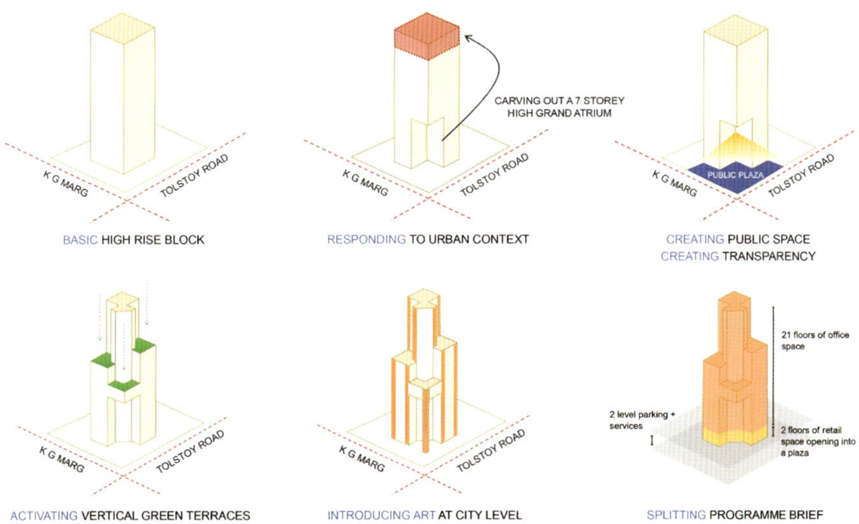

– the blocking of the sky, the sun, plants and trees – and that even a dense commercial area should be able to incorporate beauty and art and display it on a street façade.'[2]

The architectural character of the building is inspired by the exquisite Persian tile work. Aztec art patterns in full display over the façade distinguish Ambadeep Tower as one of the tallest buildings in the world to have an art mural, and thus, successfully introduce art on an urban scale for the first time in Delhi. A combination of Persian Blue with a muted yellow shade, when viewed from a distance, enhances the mural design, and over the years, it has become a visual symbol easy to spot from a distance.

The design of this landmark structure is a successful example of how statutory norms can also contribute to innovation in architecture. Delhi fire norms prescribed refuge areas to be created at certain levels in a high-rise building. Instead of viewing this as a disadvantage, the Architects turned it into an advantage, and the manifesting ensemble of volumes created terraces at levels where refuge areas are required by law. Conceptualization of these landscaped terrace courts and gardens at different alternating levels also created recreation spaces that could be shared by different offices. An added bonus was the magnificent view one would be exposed to when accessing these spaces.

It is, thus, hardly surprising that Ambadeep Tower has been recognized as one of the most notable buildings of twenty-first century architecture in Sir Banister Fletcher's well-known encyclopedia, *History of World Architecture.*

[2] *Anupam Bansal and Malini Kochupillai,* Delhi Architectural Guide *(Germany: DOM Publishers, 2013).*

'Architecture today, just like any other field, is strongly influenced by global trends. The world around us is shrinking and therefore architectural trends being followed anywhere in the world tend to have their influence across the globe. In India, the palette of available building materials has increased tremendously, and therefore, the architectural designs today reflect the choices available in terms of selection of materials.'

Ar. DIKSHU C. KUKREJA

Vallabh Bhawan Secretariat

Location **Bhopal, Madhya Pradesh** Site **25 acres** Built-up area **10,00,000 sq. ft.** Year of completion **2018**

Awarded the ***'Best Indian Institutional Project'*** *by* ***BUILD, London 2018 Architecture Awards***
Bestowed with the ***Architectural Design of the Year 2018*** *by the* ***Construction Week India Awards***

Vallabh Bhawan is the State Secretariat of Madhya Pradesh, located atop the Arera Hill in Bhopal. Flanked by a large lake on one side of the hill and a refreshing green expanse on the other, the site is blessed with the remarkable natural, scenic beauty that its vicinity is known for. These views are framed by an apparent visual axis created by Vindhyanchal Bhawan and Satpura Bhawan on both sides of the Secretariat with an exquisitely landscaped foreground.

The existing context reflects an amalgamation of modern architecture, reflected in the buildings of the Secretariat (housed within a built-up area of 10,00,000 sq. ft.) and of the traditional *charbagh* style landscaped gardens, commonly seen during the time of the nawabs of Madhya Pradesh. Completed within three years by 2018 and situated on a site of 25 acres at such a strategic location, which can be seen from the far reaches of the city, Vallabh Bhawan was imagined to be the 'crowning jewel' of Arera Hill, offering magnificent views to and from Bhopal.

Furthering the strong axial relationship of Vallabh Bhawan with Vindhyanchal Bhawan and Satpura Bhawan, also located within the site, a central promenade extends to the other end, aligning the building with the New Vidhan Sabha (Legislative Assembly), thereby creating a strong visual relationship between the legislature and the executive, an axis previously unexplored, and linking them to an integrated Master Plan. Inspired by the modern interpretation of turrets, horizontal bands and stepped forms in the architecture around it, Vallabh Bhawan imbibes these contextual influences into its own architectural vocabulary to reflect a seat of power that celebrates the cultural richness of its state hand-in-hand with contemporary styles.

The planning of Vallabh Bhawan is on the basis of a purely rational inter-relationship between various functions of the building, segregated into three distinct programme elements within a single, compact and efficient complex, namely – visitor access zones, staff access zones and VIP access zones. Some

Facing page: *An evening view of the Secretariat as viewed from across the road.*

Below: *The intricate design details on the façade of the edifice.*

Bottom: *A view of the Secretariat looking out to the expansive cityscape.*

Facing page: *An overall view of the front face of the Secretariat extensions, with the old building visible at the converging point.*

Above: *The design uses a continuous band of* jaalis *to screen the interiors from direct and harsh sunlight.*

Top: *A typical* jaali *design.*

of the facilities provided here include meeting halls, conference halls, ministers' rooms, a library, a dispensary, etc. The U-shaped form of the building not only creates an inviting entrance, but also forms a seamless loop between the three primary buildings, creating a strong correlation between them. The design frames views of the site through an interplay of scales and proportions.

Traditional architectural elements like *chhatris, jaalis* and colonnades have been given a contemporary flavour by using restraint and keeping the forms simple so that the basic shape may reveal itself. The sweeping form of the turrets – popularly referred to as the 'Beacons of Democracy' – are prominently visible from around the city, reaffirming the citizens' confidence in a strong and vibrant democratic State. In addition to this, modern elements such as fins, pergolas and solar panels keep the structure protected from harsh sunlight. Landscape strategies involve the use of trees to obstruct solar heat gain, indigenous plants that require little water and a zero-discharge rainwater system for maximum water conservation on the site.

The double glazing is recessed deep in the cavity walls, giving a depth to the building façade and a feeling of strength and dignity to the Secretariat. The stone fins in the façade create shadows that break the flatness of the stone cladding. The stone *jaalis* provide a much needed perforated barrier to the glass openings and add to the play of light

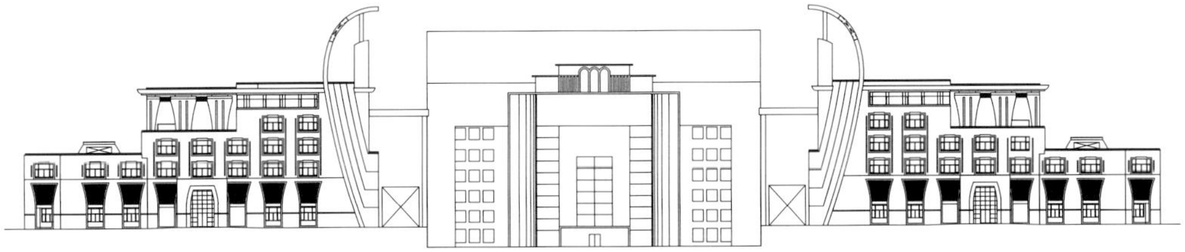

Facing page above: *Natural light pours into the reception through the expansive use of glass.*

Facing page below *The design provides sit-outs in its landscape, creating shared spaces for recreation.*

Left above: *Drawing of the Secretariat's front elevation.*

Left below: *Sweeping form of the turrets, popularly referred to as the 'Beacons of Democracy', is prominently visible from around the city.*

and shadow seen on the surface. In terms of materials used, the façade consists of a mix of the traditional (sandstone, *jaalis,* cladding, fins) and the modern (glistening metal).

The design of Vallabh Bhawan aims to translate the rich cultural fabric of the state and bring it to the global standard using contemporary styles in architecture. This amalgamation of architectural vocabularies binds the glory of the past with the aspirations of a forward-looking community to create a unique identity that embodies the spirit of Madhya Pradesh. The building is extremely popular in Bhopal and, besides winning global recognition, has also received acclaim from the local press, hailing it as a trendsetter.

Office of the Comptroller and Auditor General of India

Location **New Delhi** Site **3 acres** Built-up area **1,50,000 sq. ft.** Year of completion **1993**

*The design is a **national competition winning entry** for the prestigious headquarter building*

Located on the Deen Dayal Upadhyaya Marg in Delhi, design of the prestigious Comptroller and Auditor General's (CAG) office building was won through a national competition. Surrounded by greenery, the site is placed in an area interspersed with distinguished office buildings of the Government of India with most of them dating back to the British Era. The building's design is a blend of contemporary Indian architecture and Lutyens' style of architecture, quite prominent in the government edifices of New Delhi. Rising up to a height of five floors, the building projects a grid-like façade, which complements the design sensibility of other built structures in the vicinity.

Clad in natural sandstone, the horizontal lines along the façade of the building highlight its volume. Some lines are subdued, while others along the corners have been enhanced by using darker, earthier tones. The permanence of the stone finish lends a stately character to the building. In addition to offices for different departments, some facilities housed within the built-up area of 1,50,000 sq. ft. include a library, a club, a canteen and cafeteria, and an auditorium.

Visitors to the building are greeted by a grand entrance. The drop-off area rises from the ground level and rests under a large cantilever at the entrance. The cantilever slab projects out significantly and has a coffered ceiling that reflects its elevational design pattern. In order to break the monotony and repetitiveness in appearance of the building, two different and distinct shades of stone cladding have been used.

Poised, dignified, grand, yet modest, the office design reflects the magnificence of an institution which serves as a watchdog, discreetly managing the financial health of the government.

Above: *A view of the headquarter.*

Millennium IT Towers

Location **Visakhapatnam, Andhra Pradesh** Site **4 acres** Built-up area **4,00,000 sq. ft.** Year of completion **2018**

Constructed using green technologies, the ***towers resist wind velocity of over 200 kmph,*** *integrating a progressive design understanding and technology*

Nestled between the verdant Rushikonda Hills of the Eastern Ghats and the blue waters of the Bay of Bengal, at the heart of the Information Technology (IT) district of Visakhapatnam, Andhra Pradesh, are the Millennium IT Towers. The design brief was to integrate the progressive and technology-supported outlook adopted by the state government with an edifice that was futuristic in its functional performance and capacity; possessed a significant architectural language, complete with state-of-the-art security; and was path-breaking in the legacy of office-building designs in India.

With a built-up area of 4,00,000 sq. ft. and sitting atop a hill in Madhurawada, Visakhapatnam, the site houses offices for start-up companies or pilot incubators for small and medium enterprises (SMEs), conference halls, a cafeteria and other utilities – all of which maintain their individual significance. The sparse urban fabric of the hill is complemented by the superblocks of IT complexes, which appear as coarse grains, resulting in an uneven texture on the site. On the contrary, the settlements present in the valley appear as clusters of fine grains.

Inspired by the geometry of the surrounding hills, the buildings stand tall with their form projecting a colossal frame – an imposing character in the vicinity. The twin-tower typology of the edifices maintains harmony between open spaces and built forms with a major private open space in the middle, creating a common recreation area. Implementing this design idea also makes natural ventilation possible for most areas within the space. Seamless continuation of the façade from one end to the other produces an iconic model and supports expansive views for the employees and visitors. This complements the use of glass and makes the buildings appear lightweight.

In addition to assigning two complete floors to parking, the towers rise to ten storeys, making it one of the largest IT towers in Visakhapatnam IT Zone. Vehicular circulation has been restricted to the outer periphery of the buildings, allowing the central open plaza to connect the two towers via a bridge and green open space. The towers are IoT enabled (Internet of Things; a computing concept where physical objects are connected to the internet, and consequently, to other devices).

Constructed using green technologies, the towers are able to resist wind velocity of over 200 kmph, after the city's bitter experience following the aftermath of Cyclone Hudhud in 2014.

Left: *A view of the Towers' façade.*

QRG TOWERS
QRG
HAVELLS
ENTRY

Corporate Headquarter Office for Havells

Location **Noida, Uttar Pradesh** Site **4 acres** Built-up area **1,50,000 sq. ft.** Year of completion **2008**

The ***design of the headquarter building thrives on sustainable elements*** *which complement the spectacular form*

A 'winged' structure that seems to embrace a courtyard within its semi-circle stands out on a 4-acre plot of land in Noida. This project, with a total built-up area of 1,50,000 sq. ft., was completed in 2008 and houses the headquarters of Havells India. The brief for the corporate campus was to create an iconic building with a metal and glass skin that would symbolize the modern technologies used by Havells, and yet be a representation of green architectural design. The curvilinear office – so refreshingly different from the typical box typology form visible all around this building – is a welcome departure from the norm.

The sweeping pergola at the roof level is not only a prominent feature of the structure, it also justifies the curved planning that provides stunning views of the surroundings when seen from different parts of the interiors. Another unique feature of the design is a tensile fabric roof that has been fixed over the courtyard to form an atrium. This dynamic roof lets in natural light and blocks out the harsh weather. It is also a central visual convergence point, which allows employees placed on different floors a view of the entire office complex. The 'transparent' glass interiors symbolize the open and inclusive management style practised by the Havells Group.

As one goes past a small and thoughtfully placed water body, right behind the reception there is a stainless-steel sculpture that assumes an artistic form of the tree of life, making an impression on both visitors and staff. This sculpture is an embodiment of the values that the company has built its foundation upon – an energy-efficient ideology that promotes a sustainable vision for the future. The area thus formed, is a unique common space to relax and interact. The Architects were conscious of the need to conceptualize a design that justified the ethos of the company. Using a unique combination of elements of nature, light, water and tree, they have succeeded in achieving an integrated architectural experience. The Architects wanted the sculptural edifice to resonate the elements of innovation in a manner being helmed in the world. With a design that is exposed to natural light, the environment becomes comfortable, which goes a long way in maintaining health and productivity of the staff.

By integrating Aluminium Compressed Panels (ACP) with curtain glazing, the transparency between spaces becomes apparent, and the overall structure appears

Facing page: *Two curvilinear forms encase the atrium.*

Below: *The frontal view of the building.*

to be light and airy. Through this conjunction of materials used, the building succeeds in manifesting a splendid marvel for futuristic office designs. For the visitors, the towers seem to appear as if they are converging, projecting convex and concave shapes on the façade. The building rises to five storeys in height, without lending heaviness to the structure. Use of transparent and reflective surface materials in the interiors allow natural light to be transmitted to all corners of the space, thereby illuminating it without any mechanical means. The top floor protrudes from the façade line, creating a semi-covered recreation space. It supports a leaf-like pergola, which emerges from the outline of the office building and becomes a striking design element.

The façade's design character follows suit in the interiors as well, opening to a large atrium space. The curved module of the building design brings into play a sense of optical illusion, as one is able to view the structure with new perspectives as they move through the site. The careful combination of the colour palette of the materials exudes a majestic aura of the headquarters, whilst allowing the surrounding landscape cover to complement its design.

Eco-friendly features have been incorporated throughout the project for a green design. These features are given expression through the building's orientation as well as through material selection. Glass has been used with restraint inside the structure, and only the atrium has a glazed façade. Engineering aspects, such as the electrical system and air-conditioning, have been designed and accommodated to be environment-friendly as well. The landscaping befits the Client's principles: overlaying advanced sustainable design ideology with innovative technological finesse.

Facing page: *A striking optical illusion is created by the interiors, highlighting the 'Tree of Life'.*

Left above: *A curtain wall allows natural daylight inside the building.*

Left below: *A semi-shaded recreation space is created on the top level with the artistically flowing pergola.*

The site restricts the built from to the centre, maximizing the provision of parking space on the ground surface. With separate entry and exit points, the Architects enabled a hassle-free circulation throughout the site while also making the design pedestrian friendly.

While the metal and glass exterior of the building conveys a progressive outlook that the company believes in, the interiors project eco-friendliness and transparency they promote. As one enters, it is evident that the spaces have been designed to reflect a striking balance between technology and design. Since it houses the headquarters, Havells wanted the corporate office to be an inspiration for their employees, starting with the design – and the Architects have been successful in attaining this vision.

SIGNATURE
TOWERS

Signature Towers

Location **Gurugram, Haryana** Site **3 acres** Built-up area **6,00,000 sq. ft.** Year of completion **1999**

One of the ***first projects in India to incorporate advanced curtain-glazing system*** *and* ***Building Management System (BMS) facilities,*** *such as energy management*

A landmark project with many firsts attached to it, Signature Towers is one of the first distinct design responses at a significant scale to a new paradigm in Indian architecture. It reflected a turning point in post-Independence India, when the country ushered in globalization and liberalization in its economic policies, opening its doors to the world. The aptly-titled Tower is located on the Delhi–Jaipur National Highway in Gurugram. Built between the years 1997 and 1999 at a cost of Rs. 700 million, the eighteen-storeyed landmark office complex was a joint venture between Unitech Developers and Singapore Consortium. This commercial project, with a built-up area of 6,00,000 sq. ft., is one of the first in India to incorporate advanced curtain-glazing system and BMS facilities, such as energy management in security, billing system, car parking, etc.

Through sculpting its volume and play of mass and void, the Architects created a 100 x 60ft urban window – a metaphorical gesture to view a 'New India'. A dynamic curved façade echoes the movement along the adjoining highway and mirrors the changing moods of the sky on its reflective surface. Design of the infrastructure within the building is meant to support a high capacity of technological facilities available in the towers.

The orientation of the tower is dynamic, and projects an approachable façade from every direction. The Architects aimed for duality in design, so while the outer sides facing the highway welcome visitors, the inner sides open up to a courtyard, thus granting much-needed privacy for work. The tower superimposes elegance over magnificence, adding an artistic demeanour to the overall profile.

A combination of different forms has been used to bring together a design that is technologically advanced, aesthetically pleasant and functionally efficient. The project has emerged as a successful example of sustainable design, and has been recognized as the 'Best Design Office Complex in India' on numerous portals and occasions.

Upon its completion, this project was able to start a trend of glass-clad corporate buildings in Gurugram, and it was a precursor to Cyber City – the IT hub of this satellite city today.

While it has been designed to meet the demands of a modern office building in terms of user comfort, integration of technology, flexibility and adaptability to change, it undoubtedly became a trendsetter in the urbanscape of the city.

Facing page: *Front façade of the Towers, which are conjoined by a gallery at higher levels.*

Below: *A schematic representation of the design conceptualization, understanding planning and deriving volumes.*

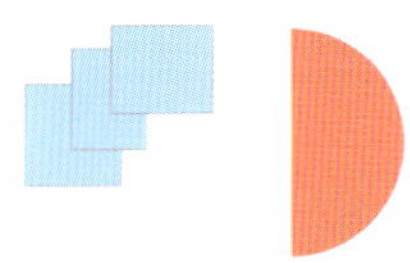

Above: Diagram showing the two distinct geometric forms as two philosophies

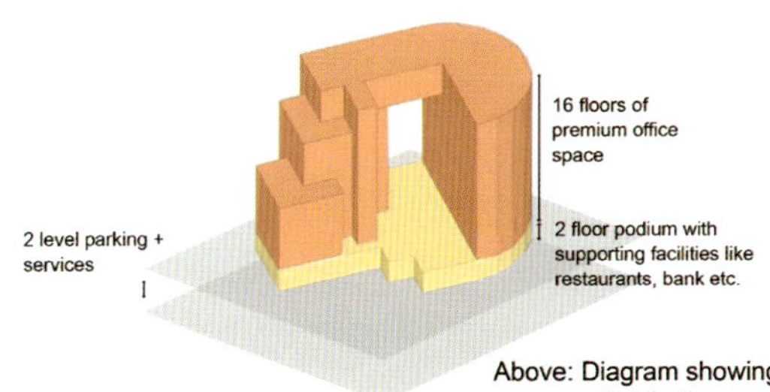

Above: Diagram showing program distribution.

Below: Diagrams showing the design process

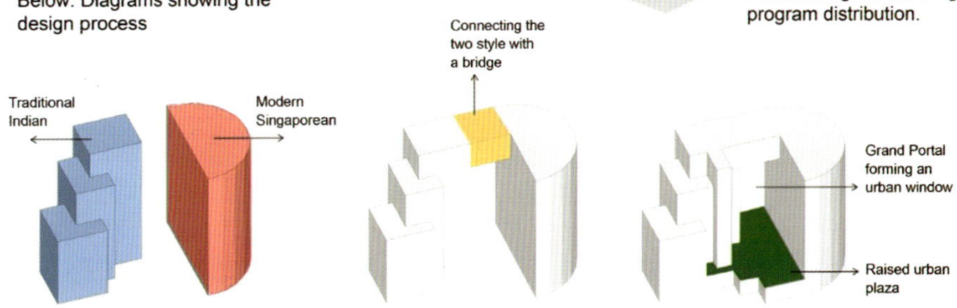

ST Microelectronics

Location **Noida, Uttar Pradesh** Site **5 acres** Built-up area **3,00,000 sq. ft.** Year of completion **2000**

*A **Design Development Centre** for a **French-Italian multinational company (MNC),** the project **imbibed Indian values** through its climatologically adept architectural conceptualizations*

This is a high-tech, energy-efficient complex that functions as a Design Development Centre for semi-conductors and microelectronics for a French-Italian MNC. The building complex has an ultra-modern communication system, networking and access control. Apart from a large number of workstations, it accommodates laboratories, a cafeteria and other facilities. The Architects were chosen for the project owing to their design ideology to create sustainable and energy efficient designs. Between 1997 and 2000, the Architects constructed a built-up area of over 3,00,000 sq. ft. across three different phases.

The overall design follows a rectangular plan, with a glass walkway joining the different blocks. The first phase of the complex has an area of 65,000 sq. ft. and was completed in 1997. The second phase of 90,000 sq. ft. was completed in 1998, and the third phase of 1,50,000 sq. ft. in 2000. The office complex is provided with an ultra-modern communications system, networking and access control, and it accommodates 300 workstations and other facilities.

The curtain glazing juxtaposed with stone provides a unique character to the buildings. While the Client wanted a curtain-glazed building, the Architects wanted the building to embrace its context and be sustainable. Thus, a unique design approach was selected where the curtain glazing acts as a second skin and is set a metre away from conventional window-wall façade.

With a water body at the bottom and an opening at the top, it becomes easy for hot air to rise and escape rather than enter inside. Local materials, such as sandstone, succeed in creating an interesting play of contrast with the glass. Pergolas, colonnades and modern *chhatris* on the roof lend an Indian touch to the architectural grammar of this landmark building.

Facing page: *A view of the office building designed in Phase 3.*

Right: *A schematic sectional representation of using water as a resource to regulate passive cooling in the offices.*

Below: *A view of the curtain glazing, a futuristic concept at the time.*

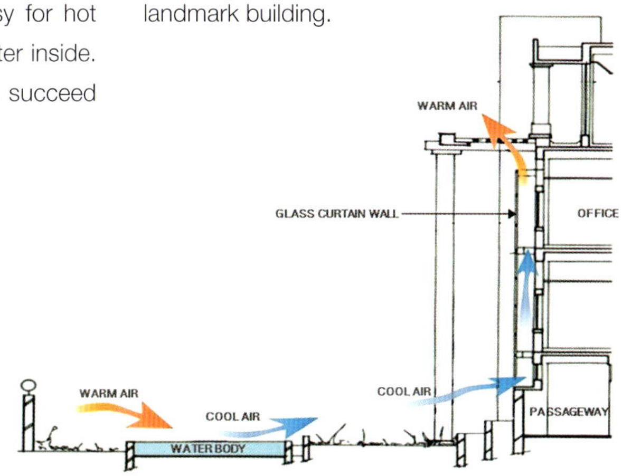

SABIC Office and Research Facilities

Location **Vadodara, Gujarat** Site **11 acres** Built-up area **90,000 sq. ft.** Year of completion **2001**

The state-of-the-art petroleum research facility functions as the ***largest research and development (R&D) centre for petroleum-based products being produced by Saudi oil industries*** *outside Saudi Arabia*

The 11-acre site lies nestled in a dense green cover of Vadodara in Gujarat. It is the meeting point between industries on one side and farmland on the other. Planned on the site is a state-of-the-art petroleum research facility with a built-up area of 90,000 sq. ft. Completed in 2001, this complex consists of centrally air-conditioned, state-of-the-art research facilities for the Saudi Arabian Basic Industries Corporation (SABIC), a worldwide R&D subsidiary of Saudi Arabian State Oil Industries. The office functions as the largest R&D centre for petroleum-based products being produced by Saudi oil industries outside Saudi Arabia.

The unique design of this complex comprises low-rise, sprawling built masses interwoven with a series of open courtyards. The brick-clad buildings harmoniously blend with the surroundings. The central courtyard, which acts as a common recreation space, has been provided with sit-outs and a centrally located water fountain.

The double-wall insulated masonry is an effective sustainable design tool and it has been used to reduce energy consumption in the harsh climate of this region. The windows open into the interiors towards the courtyards, and the connecting corridors between different blocks. The labs (Catalyst and Analytical) have been provided with a considerable length of glazing, thus welcoming natural daylight into the interiors.

Below: *A rendered landscaped site plan of the offices and research facilities.*

Bottom: *An elaborately planned drop-off area in front of the research facility.*

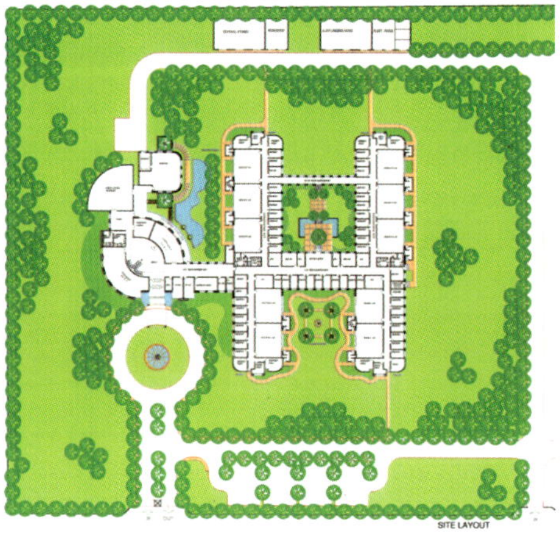

GlobeSpan Technologies

Location **Noida, Uttar Pradesh** Site **2 acres** Built-up area **40,000 sq. ft.** Year of completion **1997**

*One of the **key R&D centres of Conexant,** this office was **constructed in a record 150 days***

The extensively landscaped site of GlobeSpan Technologies, with fountains in front and a recreation space at the rear, is located in an area surrounded by office buildings. However, what makes it different are the folding facets/edges of the building, which not only help prevent overlap between the different rooms, but the staggered design also enables the rooms to welcome natural light.

The interiors are designed as a self-sufficient environment equipped with a multitude of facilities, other than 200 work-stations and electronic texting labs, like a cafeteria, a gymnasium, a crèche, an ATM and other office infrastructural facilities. The centrally air-conditioned enclosure has been provided with an efficient building service system that maintains healthy and comfortable indoor conditions with ambient temperature, light and oxygen levels.

One of the key R&D centres of Conexant, this office was constructed in a record 150 days time, including all the civil work, building services, interiors and even the landscaping! Without compromising on any of its aspects, the Architects succeeded in giving GlobeSpan a unique form.

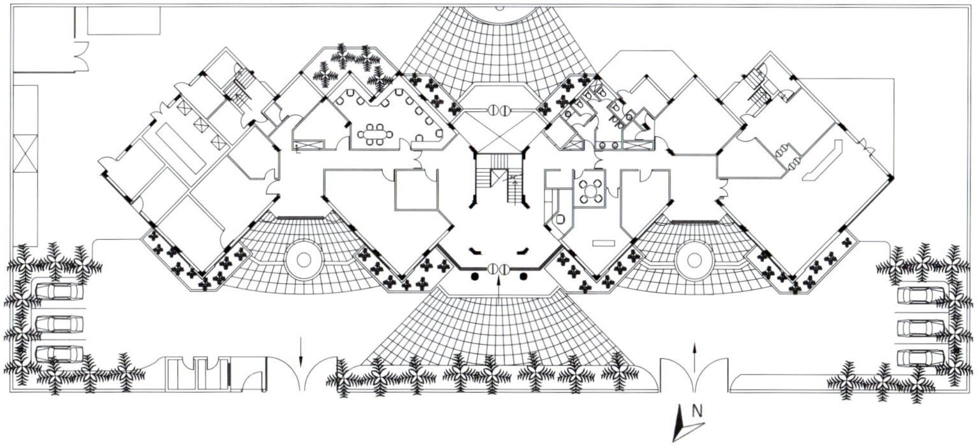

Top: *Front façade of the building combines folded edges, increasing span of the panoramic view.*

Above: *A drawing of the site plan for the project.*

39

SUN Group

Location **Gurugram, Haryana** Site **1 acre** Built-up area **70,000 sq. ft.** Year of completion **2007**

The project adopts technology to create a facility that ***deflects any audio or visual distractions***

The project is a corporate office facility for the international SUN Group. Since the 70,000 sq. ft. office is located on a 1-acre site and is flanked by other office buildings, few site constraints persisted. The Architects, however, were vigilant about providing employees with the best views, cushioning the building from exterior noise and distractions whilst accommodating greenery within the complex. To facilitate this, the office has been offset from the main building line using protruding columns and beams to provide as much shade as possible to the main glass structure behind them.

The functional volume of the building is encased within the expressive structural language of columns and beams. The design has premium finish and specifications, both for the interiors as well as for the exterior. The exterior façade is a pristine combination of glass and ACP, while the interiors are a continuation of the clean lines seen on the façade, supporting the open-plan concept of the office. Use of low-height partitions and glass cubicles for work stations provides transparency across the workplace.

This is a successful example of responding to the Client's vision of demonstrating a self-effacing, functional expression by adopting a minimalist architectural design with clean lines and abstractionism.

Facing page: *A front view of the office edifice with imposing extruded columnar elements.*

Above: *Glass acts as a screen, regulating natural light into the reception area.*

Left: *A well-designed cafeteria.*

Power Grid Corporation of India Limited

Location **Gurugram, Haryana** Site **4.5 acres** Built-up area **3,50,000 sq. ft.** Year of completion **2002**

Designed as a ***headquarter facility,*** *the project exudes a grandeur and magnificence to establish itself as a* ***landmark in its vicinity***

Headquarters of the Power Grid Corporation of India Limited is located in the Central Business District of Gurugram. The multi-storeyed office complex with two basements has a built-up area of 3,50,000 sq. ft. The centrally air-conditioned facility has been designed as a state-of-the-art, intelligent building. It has been fitted with all the accoutrements of technology, including BMS, solar-power heating, etc. It also includes office space for a minimum capacity of 900 employees, and these office spaces have been organized according to an open plan.

An octagonal design of the building enables all sides to be exposed to natural daylight, removing the possibilities of dark and dingy corners in the office. It also encloses the space efficiently, minimizing the external surface area and, consequently, the heat loss and gain, building costs, etc. In addition, it has a circular corridor in the centre, resting under the roof's dome. The atrium so created fosters vertical transparency between different floors.

Below: *Standing in the landscaped plaza, view of the stone and glass edifice.*

Hindustan Lever Limited

Location **Gurugram, Haryana** Site **1 acre** Built-up area **45,000 sq. ft.** Year of completion **2001**

The design for the ***regional headquarters*** *of India's largest fast moving consumer goods (FMCG) company is* ***a striking combination of dramatic forms and high-end materials***

Prominently located along the National Highway in Gurugram is the regional headquarters of India's largest fast-moving consumer goods (FMCG) company, with a heritage of more than eighty years in the country – Hindustan Unilever Limited (HUL). The 1-acre site, which is located at the junction of two major roads, is part of a large commercial complex. The immaculate edifice is a modern representation of an office building. A harmonious symphony of forms and design elements on the façade define a character that is synonymous with the project.

The design challenge was to create a distinct identity for the building, which is dwarfed by large office towers surrounding it. A sculptural massing, creation of a distinctive landscaped terrace on the first floor, a faceted glass façade resulting in multiple reflections and visual play – all became tools to create an identity for HUL's headquarters.

The site has been extensively landscaped with heavy and dense foliage in order to use natural elements as noise and dust barriers. A rectangular building has been scooped out from one edge, creating a remarkable visual feature for the overall design. This curved element – a result of the scooping out – also helps trace an outdoor courtyard when vertically extruded to the ground floor. An extensive cafeteria on the ground floor looks out to this landscaped courtyard, providing an intimate recreation and relaxation spot for the employees. The planning is such that the employees are seated at the rear end of the site (facing the dense green). The front façade facing the highway houses essential spaces such as the service rooms, vertical circulation areas (lift lobby, stairwell), reception and waiting areas. Use of curtain glazing, alternating with ACP throughout the building façade, bifurcates the space on the basis of functionality. This six-storeyed office has a basement and a stilted ground floor.

The project was envisioned with state-of-the-art enclosures, consisting of formal work stations and equipped with smart and user-friendly infrastructure. A highly sophisticated building service system has succeeded in making the design an example of intelligent architecture, maintaining a comfortable indoor environment through the use of auto-responsive technology.

Below: *View of the building from the highway.*

Unitech Business Zone

Location **Gurugram, Haryana** Site **6 acres** Built-up area **4,50,000 sq. ft.** Year of completion **2014**

***Staggering blocks of masses** stacked on a linear site are an opulent marvel for the office-goers*

Above: *An evening visualization of the office towers.*

Nirvana Business Zone is an IT complex for Unitech Limited, completed by the Architects in 2014. The design brief challenged the Architects to create independent leasable office modules ranging from areas as small as 1,000 sq. ft., to a single user requiring 4,50,000 sq. ft. The highly awkward shape of the 6-acre site added to the challenge. The design resolve was an ensemble of three connected towers of staggering volumes, which could be distinct yet one functional space.

The site expands in a linear manner and is located perpendicular to the main road. The narrow site opening from the main road prompted the Architects to offset the towers inwardly into the site, allowing dense trees to create a barrier around it. The variation in heights of the three glass-boxed towers imparts a visual break in the skyline exhibiting a character of its own.

Transparent walkways take on the role of connecting bridges for the different office towers and create a shared space, simultaneously providing expansive views of the city from either side. The ground floor, with its commercial spaces, food outlets and basic retail options, is designed to be functional twenty-four hours a day, also contributing to safer spaces, both, during day and at night. The infrastructure of this complex adopts cutting-edge technology and engineering to achieve a 'smart' work environment.

The landscape design has been conceptualized to act as a tool to break rigidity of the site and introduce fluidity between the built zones such as the service blocks, parking, basement entry/exits, office towers, green boulevards, etc. It was designed to provide a common ground to each of the towers and also act as a grand entrance to the complex. These common areas have been meticulously fitted out with open sit-outs, pergolas and green pavers, all centred around a refreshing water body that helps soothe the senses.

Parsvnath Planet

Location **Lucknow, Uttar Pradesh** Site **10 acres** Built-up area **15,00,000 sq. ft.** Year of completion **2019**

*A **mixed-use development,** this project consists of nine buildings*

If Mumbai is known for being India's financial capital, then Lucknow has earned the honour and privilege of being the country's cultural capital. Renowned for its culture, heritage and hospitality, the city retains its old-world charm with its havelis and heritage bungalows, but its more urbane face can be seen in the burgeoning real-estate development.

Over the last few years, Lucknow has steadily gained the reputation of being a new hotspot for investment in North India. The city earmarked a precinct, Gomti Nagar, as an area for development, led primarily by private real estate developers. The Architects had the privilege of working on three distinct projects abutting each other, Parsvnath Planet being one such project with 15 lakh sq. ft. built-up area for mixed-use development. The design consists of nine buildings, representing the nine planets, planned in crescent formation and circling a commercial hub.

The project has 3 and 4-bedroom centrally air-conditioned apartments, a commercial building, a 100-room hotel, a rooftop revolving restaurant, a shopping mall and a luxurious clubhouse with both indoor and outdoor sports.

Glass has been innovatively used in different forms, exhibiting a dynamic façade design that provides different views of the building from different angles. The design appeals to the visitors for its simplicity and high functional efficiency. A subtle palette of colours was chosen for the façade. Landscape becomes an integral part of the overall layout of the complex. The minimalistic design approach is able to create a recreation space that exudes poise and, at the same time, benefits its users.

Below: *A visualization of the commerical mixed-use tower.*

Unitech SEZ

Location **Greater Noida, Uttar Pradesh** Site **75 acres** Built-up area **75,00,000 sq. ft.**

Inclusive of IT/Information Technology Enabled Services (ITES) and commercial facilities, hotels and residential development areas, *the project's location on the Yamuna Expressway makes it easily accessible*

The Unitech SEZ (Special Economic Zone) is a state-of-the-art IT project, planned along the Yamuna Expressway in Greater Noida. The rectangular 75-acre site has been divided into two with a planned green spine, which acts as a common ground for recreation and interaction. The project, with a built-up area of 75 lakh sq. ft., includes IT/ITES facilities, commercial facilities, hotels, residential development areas and a host of other amenities. The facilities' buildings sport petal-like roof structures, which are not only major features of attraction, but also lend an element of dynamism to the overall site.

This project was an attempt to transcend the generic glass-box and concrete jungle typology of business hubs and create a Master Plan that incorporates landscape as an integral part of the IT experience. Thus, the SEZ is planned around a wide, central greenway, which is a dense tree belt that marks the central axis of the complex, and public amenities, such as conference facilities, retail outlets, etc., are located along this belt. The use of courtyard systems and landscaped terraces bring the greens into the building envelop and create interesting, vibrant social spaces across the site.

The design philosophy of developing different types of buildings (commercial as well as residential), yet being able to tie them together whilst providing a harmonious balance within the project, was essential to the Architects. The overall site is able to reflect unity in the functionality of diverse buildings through their carefully chalked out design plan and material selection.

The Master Planning strategy restricts vehicular access to the periphery of the site, allowing the pedestrians unobstructed access to the green landscape in the centre of the site. The urban planning is structured to make movement around the site and accessibility easier for visitors.

The Architects have been cautious to segregate the spaces for residents and office-goers, and develop the site holistically. The landscape spreads across the site seamlessly, intertwining the different units and reflecting the project as a single unified development.

Facing page: *A visualization of the aerial view spanning the entire site.*

Below: *The amenities buildings with petal-like roof structures add an element of dynamism.*

Logix City Centre

Location **Noida, Uttar Pradesh** Site **6 acres** Built-up area **15,00,000 sq. ft.** Year of completion **2018**

*An energy-efficient design, the project has been built to support **India's biggest superplex with fifteen screens, India's first largest Playhouse** and **North India's first 4DX nine screen premiere auditorium***

Logix City Centre is one of the first mixed-use commercial projects located in Sector 32 – the new business hub of Noida in the National Capital Region (NCR). Boasting a five-star and a four-star hotel, a retail section, one of India's biggest multiplexes, an Olympic-size ice-skating rink, high-end office spaces and extensive recreation and food court facilities, the 6-acre site is a hub of multiple activities.

The architectural expression of the mall is that of a microcosm of a city with each component distinctly expressed in the low-rise, ribbon-like form of the retail section, wrapping the lower floor from which different towers rise: the idiosyncratic tower of the five-star hotel, the 'reverse twin' four-star hotel and service apartments, and a curved office tower, punctuated by a distinct square aperture, offering glimpses into the heart of the complex.

The distinction in building volumes gives an identity to each building, which are inwardly planned around a courtyard shared between the different massings. The towers provide unobstructed views of the city, rising at significant heights and leaving their own mark on the city's skyline.

Above: *A visualization of the commercial centre, which is a harmonious juxtaposition of different forms.*

Logix City Centre houses the largest PVR Entertainment City and India's biggest superplex, with fifteen screens attached to a lavish food court. It boasts a number of 'largest' and 'first' – North India's largest Gold-three screens, India's first Playhouse, North India's first IMAX, PVR's first 4DX nine screen premiere auditorium with recliners, making it the biggest in the region. It also has one of the largest HyperCity (general store) in North India.

BHEL, SAIL, NBCC and HUDCO Offices

Location **New Delhi** Site **5 acres** Built-up area **2,00,000 sq. ft.** Year of completion **1980**

The complex serves as the ***headquarters for the four state enterprises – BHEL, SAIL, NBCC and HUDCO***

Sitting elegantly on a 5-acre site, overlooking the manicured greens of Delhi Golf Club, is a commercial complex. With a built-up area of 2,00,000 sq. ft., it serves as the headquarters for four state enterprises – Bharat Heavy Electricals Limited (BHEL), Steel Authority of India Limited (SAIL), National Buildings Construction Corporation (NBCC) and Housing and Urban Development Corporation (HUDCO). This complex has been designed with four eight-storeyed office blocks, a common podium and a basement.

The distinctive arched design of the windows is something that had hitherto not been seen in post-independent office buildings in Delhi. The buildings are offset at a considerable distance from the main road and cushioned by a thick cover of trees, creating a natural boundary wall.

Parking facilities in the complex safeguard and filter vehicular movement within the site. The unique concept of a common landscaped podium creates a green deck for office users and is also a design tool for bringing employees of the four companies together, facilitating their interaction with each other.

The 'smart office planning' creates an efficient, column-free office floor plate. Not only does this restrict columns to the periphery, which results in clean floor plates, but the glazing on the north and south façades also brings natural light into the offices.

This is a highly sustainable design initiative which, even after four decades, makes the buildings look exemplary and helps it function efficiently.

Below: *A view of the brick-clad office blocks facing the main road.*

Complete Listing of Office Projects

Council of Ministers Buildings, Baghdad, Iraq
The complex is amongst the most important projects built for the Government of Iraq. The gross built-up area is 6,00,000 sq. ft. The project comprises an auditorium, council chambers, conference and plenary facilities as well as offices for the ministers and the visiting delegations. The period of construction was 1980–83.

Signature Towers, Gurugram, Haryana
Signature Towers is a landmark office complex, promoted as a joint venture project between Unitech and Singapore Consortium. The complex has a built-up area of 6,00,000 sq. ft. spanning across eighteen floors. The complex has centrally air-conditioned, high-speed lifts and has been designed using a broad BMS.

ST Microelectronics (Phase-I), Noida, Uttar Pradesh
The project is a high-tech and energy-efficient complex for a French-Italian MNC. The building is provided with modern communication systems, networking and access control. It accommodates 300 workstations, laboratories, a cafeteria and other facilities. It was completed in 1997.

ST Microelectronics (Phase-II), Noida, Uttar Pradesh
This is a separate seven-storey office complex with a basement, and a total built-up area of 90,000 sq. ft. The office complex is, again, a high-tech, energy-efficient, centrally air-conditioned facility with more than 400 workstations. It has a large state-of-the-art auditorium, seminar rooms, and exclusive senior management areas. The project, with a site area of 5 acres, was completed in 1999.

ST Microelectronics (Phase-III), Noida, Uttar Pradesh
The third phase of the office complex consisted of a seven-storeyed building with two basements. The total built-up area of the building is 1,50,000 sq. ft., and accommodates 550 workstations, a cafeteria, a health club, and conference and meeting rooms.

Ambadeep Towers, New Delhi
Amongst the tallest buildings in Delhi, the project consists of a cluster of three towers, with the tallest of twenty-three floors grouped around an eight-storeyed atrium. Its built-up area is 2,00,000 sq. ft. The project is located at the famous 14, Kasturba Gandhi Marg.

SABIC Office and Research Facilities, Vadodara, Gujarat
A state-of-the-art petroleum-based research and development facility for a Saudi Arabian MNC with an approximate built-up area of 90,000 sq. ft. It is spread over a site of 11 acres.

Indian High Commission, Abuja, Nigeria
The project included designing for the chancery complex and high commission residence in the new capital city of Abuja, Nigeria. The project was awarded to the firm through an international competition and appreciated for the use of vernacular Indian design elements beneficial for passive cooling.

Indian High Commission, Lagos, Nigeria
This project consists of a chancery and diplomat housing. The chancery has been designed around two atriums, which, through the interesting patterns used over the façade of the buildings, forms interesting assembly areas within the building.

Power Grid Corporation of India Limited, Gurugram, Haryana
The multi-storeyed office complex with two basements has a built-up area of 3,50,000 sq. ft. The centrally air-conditioned complex is designed as an intelligent building. The facility includes offices for 900 employees.

Hindustan Unilever Limited, Gurugram, Haryana
The office complex includes a basement and a stilted floor, and comprises a built-up area of 45,000 sq. ft. A highly sophisticated building service system showcases the concept of intelligent architecture where one is able to maintain a comfortable indoor environment via an auto-responsive technology.

Ansal Bhawan, New Delhi
An office building with fourteen floors, it has two basements with shops on the ground and first floors. The total covered area of the project is 2,00,000 sq. ft. and it was completed in 1974. It is located at the famous 16, Kasturba Gandhi Marg.

BHEL, SAIL, NBCC and HUDCO Offices, New Delhi
The project comprises four independent blocks, nine to ten storeys each, with a common podium and basement. The complex serves as the headquarters for four public sector enterprises – Bharat Heavy Electricals Limited (BHEL), Steel Authority of India Limited (SAIL),

National Buildings Construction Corporation (NBCC) and Housing and Urban Development Corporation (HUDCO). Its total built-up area is 2,00,000 sq. ft., and is located on Lodhi Road.

Sikkim Legislative Assembly, Sikkim
Design for the Government of Sikkim comprises an assembly hall, committee rooms for different political parties, offices for the chief minister and members of the Cabinet, and a large conference complex. The architectural design of the buildings consists of the typical Tibetan-style windows and a swinging roof with a huge overhang, representing the traditional architecture of the region.

Headquarters for Indian Farmers Fertilizer Cooperative Limited (IFFCO), New Delhi
This five-storey building includes a basement and serves as the headquarters for IFFCO. The Architects provided complete turnkey consultancy, including design of interiors, furnishing and central air-conditioning systems. The built-up area is 80,000 sq. ft. and the construction was completed in 1977.

Vallabh Bhawan Secretariat, Bhopal, Madhya Pradesh
Vallabh Bhawan is the State Secretariat of Madhya Pradesh, located atop the Arera Hill in Bhopal. The design has been felicitated with 'Best Indian Institutional Project' 2018 by BUILD, London 2018 Architecture Awards, and also as 'Architectural Design of the Year 2018' by Construction Week India Awards.

Infocity, Gurugram, Haryana
The project, having site area of 70 acres, was sponsored by Unitech, Haryana Government and Singapore Consortium. This project included development for pollution-free, IT-oriented industrial plotted development, and construction of flatted factories and commercial buildings.

Parsvnath SEZ, Indore, Madhya Pradesh
The total site area for the project is 76 acres. It is a complete SEZ for IT/ITES facilities. The first phase of construction comprises 2 million sq. ft. The total built-up area is approximately 7 million sq. ft.

Unitech SEZ, Greater Noida, Uttar Pradesh
The total site area of the project is 75 acres. The project is planned along the Taj Expressway and consists of IT/ITES facilities, commercial and residential development, and a host of other miscellaneous amenities.

National Agricultural Cooperative Marketing Federation (NAFED) Headquarters, New Delhi
A twelve-storeyed office for NAFED, it is located near Maharani Bagh, New Delhi. The built-up area of the building is 1,20,000 sq. ft. and it was completed in 1987. The uniqueness of this building lies in ensuring full sunlight and ventilation on all the floors through a careful sustainable design technique. The arcaded façade is three feet away from the window wall to reduce direct sun, heat and glare, whilst also considerably cooling the wind passing through.

Aashirwad Commercial Complex, New Delhi
An office-cum-shopping complex for Kailash Nath and Associates has a total built-up area of 70,000 sq. ft. The complex is located in the prime area of Green Park in South Delhi. It was completed in 1985.

Software Development Complex, Gurugram, Haryana
The project was done for Global Information Systems Technology Private Limited. It is a unique data storage and processing facility for books and journals published worldwide. It has a built-up area of 16,000 sq. ft. and is centrally air-conditioned.

Commercial Office at 9 Tolstoy Marg, New Delhi
The building is designed as a twelve-storeyed tower with a five-floor high entrance lobby and total built-up area of approximately 80,000 sq. ft. The complex is owned by the Ansal Group.

R & R Tech-II, Noida, Uttar Pradesh
The project is a software technology-oriented complex located on an area of 5 acres in NCR region. It has a total built-up area of 7,00,000 sq. ft., including two basements.

Information Centre and Administrative Building for Rajasthan Atomic Power Station, Rajasthan
The project included the design of three-storeyed buildings containing offices, control rooms and an auditorium.

GlobeSpan India, Noida, Uttar Pradesh
This is an office facility for the Indian Division of US-based IT company, GlobeSpan. The facility is provided with complete BMS, workstations, computer research laboratories, a cafeteria, a gymnasium and other services.

New Delhi House, New Delhi
The project is a fourteen-storeyed office building with two basements. It was completed in 1992 and is located on Barakhamba Road.

Admin Block, Paradip Port Trust, Bhubaneshwar, Odisha
The building covers the total built-up area of 50,000 sq. ft. and is located at the banks of the Bay of Bengal. The construction was completed in 1983.

Logix City Centre, Noida, Uttar Pradesh
A prestigious mixed-use project in the prime location of Sector 32, Noida, a five-star and a four-star hotel,

retail, one of India's biggest multiplexes, an Olympic-size ice skating rink, high-end office spaces and extensive recreational and food court facilities, spread over 6 acres with a built-up area of 15 lakh sq. ft.

Corporate Headquarter Office for Havells, Noida, Uttar Pradesh
The building has a built-up area of 1,50,000 sq. ft. and is planned as twin towers around an atrium. A 'winged' structure that seems to embrace a courtyard within its semi-circle, the edifice stands out on a 4-acre plot of land in Noida.

Office of Comptroller and Auditor General of India, New Delhi
The project is a competition winning entry for CAG's office headquarters in New Delhi. The built-up area is approximately 1,50,000 sq. ft. The office has a basement, five floors, offices, a library, a recreation club, a canteen, conference rooms, etc.

Millennium IT Towers, Visakhapatnam, Andhra Pradesh
The business tower has a built-up area of about 4,00,000 sq. ft. and has general shopping, food courts, a bank, a mini conference hall, a convention hall, an incubation centre, APIIC office, IALA office and other offices, a budget hotel, space for commercial activities and other utilities.

Corporate Headquarters (NIIT Limited), New Delhi
The corporate headquarters for IT major – NIIT were completely renovated. The new centrally air-conditioned facility, with 200 workstations, was the first-of-its-kind in North India at the time.

Unitech Business Zone Nirvana, Gurugram, Haryana
The project is a modern, multi-storeyed complex for Unitech Limited, with a built-up area of 4,50,000 sq. ft. It was completed in 2014 and the design is an ensemble of three connected towers of staggering volumes, distinct in their own regard yet operating as one functional space.

SUN Group, Gurugram, Haryana
Corporate office facilities for the international SUN Group, with a built-up area of 70,000 sq. ft. It is located on a 1-acre site. The imposing ACP-clad columns envelop the main building from the heat and noise outside, reducing the intake by the interiors.

Parsvnath Commercial Complex, Lucknow, Uttar Pradesh
The complex is spread over 10 acres of land with a total built-up area of 15 lakh sq. ft. The project comprises apartments, hotel, restaurants, mall and a clubhouse.

Aerocity, New Delhi
Aerocity is spread over an area of 65 acres. It is designed as a one-of-its-kind integrated hospitality district. The total project has 5,000 rooms besides retail, a convention centre, and office spaces with conference facilities. A unique feature is a pedestrian promenade running through the district, which brings together the retail and food and beverage (F&B) elements of each individual property as a shared resource.

Corporate Office Building for Gas Authority of India Limited (GAIL), New Delhi
The office building has eight floors and two basements with a total covered area of 1,50,000 sq. ft. It was completed in 1990. The construction work included complete air-conditioning for the project as well as the interiors. The building is a part of the Bhikaji Cama Place District Centre.

Office Building for Oil Industry Development Board (OIDB), New Delhi
The project is being designed in accordance with standard green building concept guidelines for achieving 'Five-Star' of GRIHA (Green Rating for Integrated Habitat Assessment) rating system, using a 'Net Zero' concept with respect to electrical energy. It also consists of an auditorium with seating for 450 persons. The approximate built-up area is 2,80,000 sq. ft.

Paryatan Bhawan, New Delhi
Located opposite Birla Mandir, this office building is to be built for the New Delhi Municipal Council (NDMC). The sweeping pergola is the stand-out feature and creates a powerful impression, alluding to the idea of progress and development in the twenty-first century.

India International Institute of Democracy and Election Management (IIIDEM) Campus, New Delhi
The proposed IIIDEM Campus is a national design competition winning entry conceived as a state-of-the-art, modern building, reflecting a majestic image for the prestigious government office. The project has been designed for the Election Commission of India.

East Delhi Hub, New Delhi
The design is based on Smart City principles, with the project conceptualized to be the first Transit-Oriented Development (TOD) in Delhi. It comprises a 100-storeyed signature tower, the tallest in the country, luxury service apartments, affordable residential units and offices, and commercial spaces with an approximate built-up area of 15 million sq. ft. The total site area for the development is 60 acres.

Gomti Nagar Railway Station Redevelopment, Lucknow, Uttar Pradesh
The Gomti Nagar Railway Station Redevelopment Project is a railways upgradation project where a 40-acre commercial land parcel has been combined with the railway station infrastructure to create a world-class integrated development. The project shall utilize the potential of the land parcel to upgrade and modernize the railway station facilities from the revenue generated by the retail services at the station.

India International Convention Centre, New Delhi
In order for India to reap the potential benefits of the meetings, incentives, conferences, and exhibitions (MICE) market, and its share in the Asian and global market, the Delhi Mumbai Industrial Corridor Development Corporation (DMICDC) proposed the need for a large scale Exhibition cum Convention Centre in Dwarka, New Delhi. It is conceived as a smart zero-energy and world-class centre in India whose facilities are designed for a G-20 summit and other international conferences, exhibitions and trade shows.

Office Building for IFFCO, Aonla, Uttar Pradesh
Administration office building of the IFFCO Plant in Aonla is planned around an atrium. Each floor has excellent cross ventilation and full protection against the harsh

heat of western Uttar Pradesh. Reinforced Cement Concrete (RCC) structural members reflect the industrial architectural character of the building. The built-up area is 80,000 sq. ft. for the three-storeyed building. It was completed in 1988.

Commercial Complex for Unitech Limited, Lucknow, Uttar Pradesh
The complex has 250 shops and office spaces. The design is based on a *bazaar* concept, typical of North Indian towns.

Krishak Bharati Bhawan, Noida, Uttar Pradesh
The project design is the headquarters for Krishak Bharati Cooperation Limited (KRIBHCO) in Noida, Uttar Pradesh. The complex has a covered area of 1,50,000 sq. ft. including basement. It is centrally air-conditioned. The two square blocks of the complex are linked through a domed atrium over the entrance plaza of the buildings. The asymmetrical layout of blocks and the careful detailing of the façades are distinctive features of the complex.

Projects and Development India Limited (PDIL) Bhawan, Noida, Uttar Pradesh
The brief comprised designing corporate offices for PDIL. A landscaped atrium allows indirect light into the interior of the offices on all floors, rendering the building as a sustainable development model. The gross built-up area of the project is 1,00,000 sq. ft.

Cultural Centre, Chinese Embassy, New Delhi
The Cultural Centre complex within the Chinese Embassy compound is designed in ceramic tile façades and has exhibition spaces, an auditorium, an art gallery and offices of the cultural wing of the Embassy. The entire area is exquisitely landscaped and is a distinctive structure within the Diplomatic Enclave of New Delhi.

Finland Embassy, New Delhi
The design for the Embassy takes inspiration from the snow-clad mountains of both Finland and India, resulting in an iconic abstract roof of the buildings. The project consists of a chancery, ambassador's residence, and housing for the Finnish and the Indian staff. It is designed in association with architects Raili and Riema Pietila of Finland.

Redevelopment of Pragati Maidan, New Delhi
The project entails redesign and development of the Exhibition Centre Area, Convention Centre, space for public circulation and support facilities. Exhibition Halls are planned with first floor exhibition space having food outlet at mezzanine, small meeting rooms and other supporting facilities. The Architects were entrusted with the responsibility of Detailed Design of Architecture, Landscape and Engineering for the project, based on the concept by Aedas.

Stock Exchange, Ludhiana, Punjab
A seven-storeyed building, it also includes a basement. A large trading hall is the primary feature of the building. There are 250 cabins for share brokers, a bank, a library and a conference hall. The gross built-up area for the project is 1,60,000 sq. ft.

GAIL Liquid Petroleum Gas (LPG) Administrative Complex, Vijaipur, Madhya Pradesh
The new administrative complex for the LPG Plant in Vijaipur will also serve as the regional headquarters for GAIL. The three-storeyed stone and grit-clad building is planned around two atriums.

Shalimar Bagh District Centre Complex, New Delhi
The District Centre Complex at Shalimar Bagh for the Delhi Development Authority includes offices, a vast multi-level shopping centre, a hotel, offices of the city authorities, a bus terminus and other facilities on a site of 25 acres, with 2 million sq. ft. building area.

Oswal Towers, Ludhiana, Punjab
This is a six-storeyed shopping and commercial complex located on the busy Mall Road. The terraced building has a high-class shopping centre spread over four floors around an atrium. The building will have the corporate headquarters of Punjab Woolcombers Limited, a leading Ludhiana Industrial Group.

Nehru Place Office Blocks, New Delhi
The project involved construction of five blocks, each comprising eight to ten floors, with shopping arcades and offices, on Plots 47, 48, 90, 91 and 97 in Nehru Place, New Delhi. The total built-up area of all buildings is approximately 4,00,000 sq. ft. It was constructed between 1973–76.

Corporate Office Complex for Dr. Subbirami Reddy and his Companies, Hyderabad, Telangana
A multiple office and commercial centre at a prominent location in Hyderabad.

Office Building for Uttar Pradesh State Industrial Development Corporation (UPSIDC), Lucknow, Uttar Pradesh
The UPSIDC office in Lucknow uses an interesting interplay of solid and void to create a gradual passage of movement between the built and the unbuilt areas. Large semi-open enclosures redefine the traditional office experience. The use of curtain glazing and ACPs render a contemporary look to the multi-storeyed office.

East Delhi Mall, Ghaziabad, Uttar Pradesh
The multilevel, mixed-use complex includes retail shops, department stores, hypermarket, a food court, a 1,200-seater cineplex, banquet halls and a sixty-room hotel. The project also has conference facilities and speciality restaurants. The total built-up area is 4,50,000 sq. ft.

Interim Government Office, Amaravati, Andhra Pradesh
The abstract pattern on the lattice that encases the office brings a contemporary touch to the ornate Indian *jaalis*, which are an important part of the state's architecture. This second skin also performs the role of inhibiting harsh sunlight from directly hitting the glass, thus reducing heat island effect across 12 lakh sq. ft. of built-up office space.

Logix Riviera, Noida, Uttar Pradesh
With the Iconic Tower as a landmark, the design uses fluidity of form to create vibrant, interactive courts within hollow concave curves, drawing visitors from near and far.

INDUSTRIES

Industrial building design requires a different approach and expertise. Efficient planning of production sequence and speedy construction techniques determine the form and materials used for the building. Industries also require careful integration of engineering services like structure, electrical, plumbing, fire, process equipments, pollution control, and so on. Our firm, with in-house professionals from the above disciplines, undertakes industrial design comprehensively as one integral design exercise.

Perto

Perto Industrial Facility

Location **Jaipur, Rajasthan** Area **18 acres** Built-up area **6,00,000 sq. ft.** Year of completion **2017**

A multiple award-winning design ***recognized as the best designed industrial facility in India***

Perto, one of the largest ATM manufacturers in the world, is a leading Brazilian multinational corporation (MNC). For its first facility design in India, the brand wanted to make a strong architectural statement. The aim was to create a design that elevates the industrial architectural understanding to an attractive ensemble of built forms.

For a project that relied heavily on ergonomics and functionality, a band of exposed bricks on the lower edge of the building was laid, which was similar to the company's headquarters in Gravatai, Brazil. It is also the first project in India that is entirely galvanized rather than painted. Galvanizing the building complex established a uniformity in the finish of the design throughout the site whilst also protecting the steel from rusting, considering the extreme weather conditions.

The project is steel-intensive, with the material being used to the best of its testing abilities. Steel's versatility, ease of use, durability

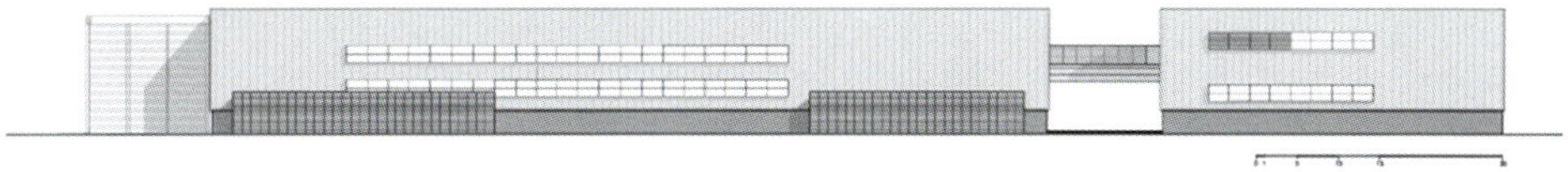

Facing page: *An aerial view of the site.*

Top: *Bands of red add life to an otherwise arid landscape.*

Centre: *Double height interiors allow natural light to flush in.*

Bottom: *An elevational drawing of the facility.*

and appealing look make it a popular building material – an ideal fit for the project. Not only is it elegant, but its tensile strength and long life also make it the go-to option for any industrial venture that requires such long spans. The project uses steel members laid out in a 20 x 10 metre grid with a hung load of 100 kg/sq.m. It is fabricated with double profile troughed pre-coated sheeting with a total coated thickness of 0.5 mm. The structures in the facility are pre-engineered buildings (PEB) that use built-up instead of rolled sections for added strength. The bold red-tinted roof of the docking yard clad in aluminium composite panel (ACP) was used to break the monotony of the otherwise disciplined architecture of the project.

The design fuses elements such as pergolas, rhythmically arranged slender columns, and carefully placed intimately sized courtyards, which create a play of light and shadow. Implemented as a design response to the hot and dry desert climate of Jaipur, these also act as buffer areas, providing breathing spaces between the steel buildings. The prismatic roof lights invite diffused natural daylight into the buildings at all times. All buildings also have forced draft ventilation (FDV) to ensure adequate air circulation.

The facility's simplicity and grace, with use of low maintenance materials, sleek finishes, bold contrasting colours and a strictly functional cubic form, define its design. With bold lines and a confident colour palette, Perto Industrial Facility is a testimony to smart and sustainable architecture for an industrial design.

Facing page above: *Vernacular design elements, such as overhanging eaves, lattice, exhibit a modern interpretation.*

Facing page below: *Well-planned and large parking spaces help regulate mobility.*

Top: *Buffer spaces between the blocks are lined with green foliage, providing a visual break.*

Centre: *Design details break the stereotype from a typical monotonous industrial facility.*

Bottom: *Different forms have been used to present a cohesive and contemporary design.*

'I feel that an architect's most meaningful role is to restore the quality of life that urbanism has taken away from him. Any single project can do this – not necessarily a major project. We must give back the spaces, the volumes, the art and aesthetics that society has been deprived of.'

Ar. C.P. KUKREJA

JCB India Limited

Location **Ballabhgarh, Haryana** Site **39 acres** Built-up area **7,75,000 sq. ft.** Year of completion **2020**

***The LEED (Leadership in Energy and Environmental Design) Gold-rated India headquarters of JCB** involved brownfield development in Phase-I and greenfield in Phase-II*

The assembly plant and India headquarters of JCB India Limited is located at Ballabhgarh, Haryana. The Architects had been involved in this brownfield facility on two occasions – first in 2006, and again in 2019 for a second, major expansion that included a massive build-up of its production facilities, including the logistics utility and administration buildings. The LEED Gold-rated building project comprises an assembly block, pre-delivery inspection (PDI), inspection and finishing sheds, a utility block, an XP shed, an IPC building and an administration building.

The new fabrication and assembly blocks, along with the new administrative headquarters of JCB were designed as composite PEB with steel and concrete construction. With JCB-manufactured engines undergoing tests to comply with international norms such as pollution, emission, etc., a separate testing facility or 'Test Cells' was designed with test labs located on its ground floor, accommodating control labs and offices on the upper floors. For the first time in JCB, the concept of movement of equipment through the ceiling with the help of conveyer belts was proposed. Different components were picked up by robotic means from the fabrication facility, and with the help of conveyer belts, these were taken first to the paint shop and then to the assembly line where the finished product was manufactured. This helped in making the aisles free for circulation. The PEB roof had to be specially designed due to the increased hung load. By anticipating the cycle of production for the next ten years, its capacity was designed to support a load of 225 kg/sq.m.

A combination of pre-coated, insulated metal sheeting with strip glazing provides for a seamless monochromatic façade incorporating the corporate colours of JCB – moor green and canary yellow. While the production facilities incorporate large steel spans of up to 40 metres, the administration building also has a column-free span of 30 metres allowing complete flexibility in office layouts.

Facing page: *Movement of materials in the facility is carried out from the ceiling, keeping the aisles free for movement.*

Below: *A night view of the metal-clad façade.*

Asian Paints

Location **Kasna, Uttar Pradesh** Area **20 acres** Built-up area **5,00,000 sq. ft.** Year of completion **1992**

An iconic design, ***one of the first to have its entire multilevel construction to be done in Reinforced Cement Concrete*** *(RCC)*

Asian Paints is an Indian multinational company engaged in the business of manufacture, sale and distribution of paints, coatings and related materials. The Kasna facility of the company was designed to emerge as an iconic design and add a modern identity to the brand.

The 20-acre complex is one of the biggest production facilities in the country and comprises a total built-up area of 5,00,000 sq. ft. The facility comprises large and complex plant buildings, such as paint house, resin house, industrial paint units, raw material and finished goods warehouses, and non-plant buildings, including a canteen and administration.

The entire multilevel construction has been done in RCC. The design sharply deviates from the box-like stereotypical typology associated with industries and instead emerges as a striking sculptural edifice. There is a play in forms and levels, resulting in a variety of structural as well as architectural layouts; this also provides an artful character to the design. Elements such as *jaalis* (lattice), an overall stepped form and a combination of materials also contribute to the striking design.

An external wall with patterns of lattices acts like a parasol, screening windows and ventilators on the parallel internal wall. While planning for the project, the Architects meticulously studied sun-shading in order to efficiently use daylight. In doing so, they were also able to regulate the placement of sensitive product-manufacturing areas. By using double-height windows, they managed to control the amount of daylight in the interiors. Abundant natural light also contributes positively towards establishing a healthy work environment for the staff.

Facing page: *A contemporary derivation of* jaalis *is used throughout the site, emerging as a striking feature.*

Below: *Double screens have been used to regulate ventilation naturally through the facility.*

Jubilant Foodworks Limited (Domino's Pizza)

Location **Greater Noida, Uttar Pradesh** Site **10 acres** Built-up area **1,50,000 sq. ft.** Year of completion **2017**

Designing a cold storage ***facility for popular food brand Domino's Pizza,*** *intricate engineering solutions were incorporated* ***as per the US Food Safety Standards***

Built in accordance with the US Food Safety Standards, the design for Domino's Factory required not only a high skillset of technical understanding of food engineering but also methodical planning of space.

The concept uses a deep understanding of factors such as insulation, preservation, maintaining optimum temperature for preparation and storage, humidity levels and ensuring safe movement of materials. The optimal temperature ranges from – 23 degrees for meat to 2 degrees centigrade for vegetables. In addition to this, the factory also boasts of a large-scale dedicated facility for mixing, kneading and production of pizza dough.

The Architects opted for PEB construction for the main facility, accelerating the overall time of construction. The warehouse and tray storage room have been placed at opposite ends of the facility, sandwiching the cooling chambers, preparation areas and assemblage in the middle. Docking spaces on the ground floor are raised to a height of 1200 mm to support hydraulic dock leveler, making stacking and parceling of materials easier. The exterior façade incorporates the universal colours of Domino's Corporation, which gives vibrancy to this industrial facility in the landscape of Greater Noida.

Below left: *The entrance is marked by a remarkable staggering form.*

Below right: *Use of electric blue is derived from Domino's Corporation's signature colour.*

Maintenance, Repair, Overhaul Facility for Aeronautics

Location **Bhiwadi, Rajasthan** Site **7 acres** Built-up area **1,50,000 sq. ft.** Year of completion **2020**

Commissioned by the Government of India under its 'Make in India' scheme, *the project is designed to accommodate maintenance, repair and overhaul facilities for Unmanned Aerial Vehicles (UAVs)*

Located in the industrial hub of Rajasthan, this highly prestigious project has been licensed by the Government of India under its 'Make in India' initiative in partnership with a Government of Israel-owned company. It is being designed to accommodate maintenance, repair and overhaul facilities for UAVs. Additionally, it provides in-house training facilities for the Indian Armed Forces personnel to operate and maintain these UAVs. The design language follows a minimalistic sense as well as judicious utilization of the open spaces needed for unhindered movement of aircraft.

Owing to the nature of the project, a technical understanding of space planning was one of the prime requirements. The hangar and annexe buildings have been placed in the centre of the site with open areas in front and rear ends, sparing space for landing and take-off of the UAVs. The Architects carefully calculated the requirements for the project and designed a robust structural system to support expansive and unobtrusive spans. The longitudinal section of the facility is segregated in three segments with two low-rise annexe blocks supporting an extensive hangar area. The overall span measures a striking 50 x 35 metres, which is sheltered by a steel truss pitched roof supported by a 1.5 tonne hangar crane. It can accommodate up to four UAVs at a time – a remarkable engineering feat. The airplane is facilitated inside the hangar through ramps and uses a 40-metre spanning sliding door to open the space. A spacious 30-metre wide demo area in front of hangar has been provided. The requirement for a robust entrance door was resolved by customizing a door spanning 40 metres with a height of 7 metres, completely sealed on all sides and specially designed for this project.

For effective handling of equipment, space for training staff has also been provided in the two wings supporting the hangar area along with facilities like crèche, dining and staff parking. While the ground floor of the two annexe buildings has a training centre, laboratories and workshops, the first floor provides areas for offices and classrooms.

The facility carefully imbues sustainability into its design and integrates aspects such as water management, sewage treatment and efficient energy management. Modular rain water harvesting pits, low-flow sanitary fixtures and electro-mechanical equipments, LED lighting across the campus, and an insulated roof for maintaining the temperature are few more of such initiatives.

Below: *An aerial visualization of the facility.*

JCB Facility

Location **Jaipur, Rajasthan** Site **115 acres** Built-up area **10,00,000 sq. ft.** Year of completion **2016**

***LEED Gold certified project** with exemplary sustainable measures in harsh desert location*

JCB (Joseph Cyril Bamford Excavators Limited) was one of the first corporate groups to establish their industrial unit in Mahindra World City, a SEZ (special economic zone) based on the concept of an 'Integrated Business City'. Today, this SEZ has become a thriving centre of economic generation in the state of Rajasthan.

The site spreads over an enormous 115 acres surrounded by major roads on all sides. The natural but uneven contouring perched the rear side of the site 4 metres higher as compared to the front side. Thus, with the site sloping to the front, rainwater drainage area gets created naturally.

The Master Plan incorporates a clear circulation system to ensure hindrance-free movement of staff, visitors and equipments. The staff and visitor vehicles traverse through the front gate while the transportation of raw materials and finished goods transpires through the rear end. Parking for large overhauls has been accommodated at the rear side and near the logistics distribution centre (LDC). Planned 1200 mm below the level of LDC, the parking's design ensures effortless loading and unloading of the backhoe loaders. The facility comprises a fabrication building, an assembly building, an administration block, a canteen, etc.

One of the key aspects that comes out strongly is how the functional requirement of a large factory, manifested through intensive mechanical engineering, has been contained in a relatively small footprint and juxtaposed harmoniously with the surrounding landscape of the factory. As a result, an interesting interplay of 'hardness' of machines against the 'softness' of the site's greenery ensues. Such a conscious blend in the design was accompanied by a subtle choice of materiality, merging the man-made structure and the natural environment into one.

The Architects preserved the natural drainage and used natural contours to create a large lake at the front. Presence of a water body, regenerated during rainfall, maintains the temperature within the site during extreme summer months. The landscape has been curated well by sculpting mounds, which create interesting volumes of spaces, and complements the low-height demeanour of the JCB backhoe loaders.

With an array of environment-friendly techniques, JCB facility in Jaipur has achieved the status of a LEED Gold certified project.

Facing page: *Presence of a natural lake within the site helps maintain the micro-climate.*

Below: *The facility expands horizontally on the site.*

Havells Integrated White Goods Manufacturing Complex

Location **Ghiloth, Rajasthan** Site **50 acres** Built-up area **6,00,000 sq. ft.** Year of completion **Phase-I: 2019; Phase-II: Ongoing**

Encompassed on a sprawling 50 acres of land in Ghiloth, the facility is a leading example of an ***industrial design thriving on sustainable aspects of energy, water and waste management***

Encompassed on 50 acres of land in the sparse and dry terrain of Ghiloth, Rajasthan, the complex consists of manufacturing plants for air-conditioners, refrigeration, television and washing machines along with a warehouse. The Master Planning ensures that the four manufacturing facilities are developed in a phased manner and operate as independent units while sharing common utilities.

Upon realizing that its branch at Neemrana had saturated its land, Havells sought to locate a new location for its expansion facility. Since Ghiloth is registered under a Panchayat system, the land cannot be sold to external authorities. For the first time in northern India, Rajasthan Industrial and Investment Corporation (RIICO) proposed leasing land from the Panchayat Samiti and developing an industrial parcel along with healthcare, institutional and commercial facilities. This would not only create job opportunities within the community but also uplift the living standards of the entire region. With this, the project became a pivotal point in initiating a social narrative through its proposal.

The now established air-conditioning plant is highly automated and its structural design assures a robust system for the conveyors. The plant is equipped with state-of-the-art injection molding machines, press shop, robots and automated guiding vehicles.

Above: *A bird's eye view of the facility.*

The facility is a leading example of an industrial design thriving on sustainable aspects of energy, water and waste management. Water is conserved and preserved by recycling and rainwater harvesting. The entire waste produced at the facility is systematically segregated into organic and inorganic before sending it off to Neemrana for recycling. Interestingly, through meticulous design strategies, almost 40 per cent of the total energy requirement at the unit is achieved through a solar photo voltaic roof, installed on the entire expanse of the roof.

The design addresses the challenges of creating multiple manufacturing facilities within a single complex, which involves clear demarcation and conflict-free movement of materials, staff and machinery. The variety of design strategies incorporated by the Architects ultimately creates a sustainable design that substantially cuts down the operational expenses of the facility.

Cummins Megasite Complex

Location **Pune, Maharashtra** Site **150 acres** Built-up area **6,00,000 sq. ft.** Year of completion **2014**

A unique manufacturing megasite with ***conglomeration of nine different plants; the design is IGBC (Indian Green Building Council) Gold rated***

TATA Cummins Private Limited is a 50:50 joint venture between TATA Motors Limited, India's largest automobile manufacturer, and Cummins Inc., USA, world leaders in design and manufacture of diesel engines. An integrated industrial complex for Cummins India Limited and its subsidiaries, the plant manufactures and refurbishes mid-range (B&L) engines. Developed as a mega-site for Cummins in India, the site had been assigned under the Maharashtra Industrial Development Corporation (MIDC).

The Architects were involved in the overall Master Planning of 150 acres of prime land and also the design of three distinct plants, along with a common utility facility for the entire complex. Careful attention was also paid to the circulation strategy, including the movement of raw materials, finished goods, staff, visitors, etc. The construction commenced in 2004 and was carried out in different phases.

The design uses a composite structure with a concrete roof supported by a steel structure. The use of a cascading roof, designed using trusses, helped with naturally illuminating the interiors. The Architects replaced conventional hydro-dynamometer technology with an eco-friendly technology. The project was awarded a Gold rating for being a 'Green Factory Building' by the IGBC.

Right: *A rendered Master plan drawing.*

Below: *A view of the facility's magnificent entrance.*

Havells India Limited

Location **Baddi, Himachal Pradesh** Site 1: Site **10.5 acres** Built-up area **2,75,000 sq. ft.** Year of completion **1996**
Site 2: Site **9.5 acres** Built-up area **3,00,000 sq. ft.** Year of completion **2009**

Developed as a sustainable facility suiting the terrain of Himachal Pradesh, *it is one of the first projects in the region that empowered locals with an industrial employment opportunity*

Being the premier brand of MCB (miniature circuit breaker) manufacturing in the country, the design of Havells India Limited at Baddi, in Solan district of Himachal Pradesh, needed to reflect a futuristic vision combined with archetypal design sensibilities. This industrial project consisted of new production facilities for manufacture of electrical low-voltage components like electrical switches, sockets, panels, MCBs, etc.

The Master Plan respects the natural undulating setting of the site. With an aim to bring about a balance in the design, the design character of the facility reflects a modern architectural language and exposes materials in their raw state without any adornment. The façade instills an element of repetition through imposing brick-clad columns, alternating with tinted and expansive spans of curtain glazing. This transparent membrane transmits optimum daylight inside the facility, whilst also complementing with lightness, the otherwise sturdy yet robust character, of the bricks.

As per the Client's requirements, it was essential to keep the aisles hindrance free. In the interiors, flat slab in RCC allows the services to be transmitted along the ceiling and down to the machines with ease. The second most important aspect was to control dust inside for safekeeping of the high-end Computer Numerical Control (CNC) machinery. Using RCC also helped achieve a seamless surface. Since the project involved production and manufacturing as its core functions, the design expanded horizontally in its planning. And this, in turn, helped in installation and function of conveyors used for material movement. One of the most difficult challenges that industrial design presents is inability of the operations to shut down for even a minute once it has begun production. Keeping this requirement of a long lasting and sturdy floor in mind, epoxy-polyurethane (EPU) was used.

Havells Baddi was one of the first projects in the region that pioneered as an industrial source of production and employment for the local population.

Below: *Design of the facility juxtaposes a variety of contemporary materials.*

Apeejay Global Logistics Park

Location **Ballabhgarh, Haryana** Site **84 acres** Built-up area **2,15,000 sq. ft.** Year of completion **2018**

The project involved ***Master Planning of a massive 85 acres of land,*** *curating a highly meticulous mechanical, electrical and plumbing (MEP) and structural design for the facilities* ***leased to international e-commerce clients***

The most important aspect of the project was its Master Planning. By definition of a logistics park, the main purpose for the Client was to build facilities for leasing purposes. Its design parameters would be synonymous with that of a transit storage hub for distribution services, fit for e-commerce businesses.

The basic requirements for the project, as per the multi-national specifications, were: leakage-proof area, high indoors (10-metre height) for ease in stacking of goods, robust and impact-resistant flooring, and use of natural daylight as much as possible.

The storage also had to be planned in a way that eased out any hindrance towards movement of goods and pacing up the time of their delivery instead. The in-and-out traffic passageways had to be separate, since these highly specific containers usually span around 12 metres in length. In such a case, the movement can get hampered, leading to considerable losses. The roads were, therefore, very carefully designed to ensure that inbound and outbound traffic had proper entry and exit points. Parking was also carefully planned and located within the site to curb the hassle for movement of trucks.

To ease out the docking and turn-around, the flooring has been invariably designed at a height between 1.2 and 1.5 metres. High-speed hydraulic and automated shutters were provided with dock sealers, ensuring ease of movement in and out of the facility and security of goods. The edifices used the PEB method to fasten the pace of construction. Almost eight different leasing companies commonly share the administration block, the utilities and security at this logistics park, which is not too far from the capital – Delhi.

Below: *A perspective view of one of the Pre-Engineered Buildings (PEB) warehouse facilities.*

'Why are words such as "iconic" and "striking" common in architectural parlance rather than "responsible" and "sensitive"? My early experiments with "underground architecture" were an outcome of a desire to be more frugal of land and its resources, to search for a design language which is more "humble" and rooted rather than soaring into the skies and screaming for attention.'

Ar. DIKSHU C. KUKREJA

TATA Cummins Limited

Location **Jameshedpur, Jharkhand** Site **25 acres** Built-up area **10,00,000 sq. ft.** Year of completion **Phase-I: 1996; Phase-II: 2020**

The facility is one of the ***first industrial buildings in the country to have its entire northern façade in curtain glazing***

TATA Cummins Limited, an engine manufacturing facility in Jamshedpur, is a collaboration between the TATA Group and Cummins Engine Co. of USA. The sprawling production facility is located in the industrial city of Jamshedpur across 22 acres and was one of the first set-ups in the region. The facility manufactures high-performance, reliable and durable mid-range (B&L) engines. Keeping with the vision of the company to create a world-class industrial hub, the Architects designed and executed a state-of-the-art facility replete with engineering and architectural prowess in line with world-class specifications in a record time of eighteen months.

The facility expands horizontally over the landscape, harmoniously blending with the natural contours of the site. The plant is divided into two major segments, bisected by a 7-metre-wide central covered aisle. The northern part consists of an assembly line, a paint shop and a test cell including storage, main offices and kitchen, besides the receiving and shipping docks. The southern part consists of block line, cylinder link, and crank and rod links with respective plant offices. The height of the building varies from 11 metres over the aisle to 8 metres at the northern and southern edges of the building.

Three main divisions in the built-up area consist of a main plant building, warehouse, and the office and administration block. The building is designed on a 15 x 15 metre structural grid with 1 x 1 x 0.6 metre deep precast RCC coffers. Adequate natural light is filtered into the facility, through skylights based on the module of the coffers. The fully air-conditioned building incorporates sophisticated planning of the utilities. Distribution of services is through an underground tunnel which is bifurcated into two components – one to carry electrical cables, and the other for services such as fuel oil and chilled water pipes. The external finish comprises a curtain wall on the north façade

Facing page above: *View of the magnificent glass atrium and drop-off area.*

Facing page below: *An element of verticality is repeated throughout the design, visually barricading the facility whilst regulating natural ventilation and daylight.*

Below: *Using coffered ceiling increased the clear span in the interiors.*

Left: *Expansive curtain wall allows natural daylight to flush the interiors.*

Below: *An elevational drawing of the facility.*

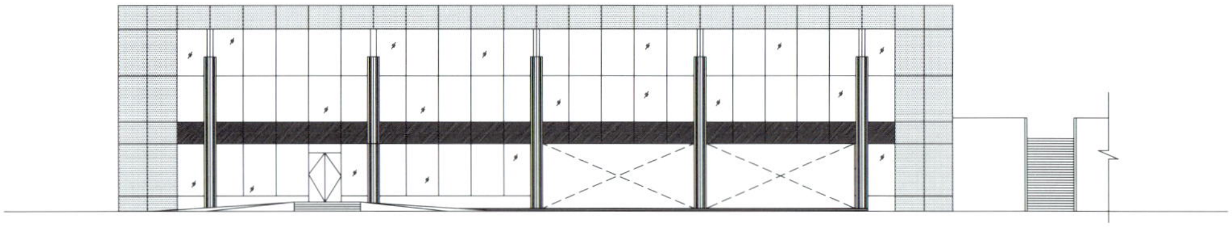

and 300 x 300 mm ceramic tile cladding on the remaining sides.

The facility is one of the first industrial buildings in the country to have its entire northern façade in curtain glazing, along with skylights being incorporated in its roof's structure. To ensure that natural light is utilized for optimum performance and provides comfortable working interiors for the occupants, the Architects proposed a completely white internal colour scheme. This meant that starting from the roof to the walls, the floor and even the equipment and pipes were painted in white. Samples of the required shade of white were created in a large quantity and shared with different vendors, ensuring uniformity across the interiors.

Another important design aspect pledged by the Architects was to guarantee proper collection and drainage of rainwater. Jamshedpur has a tropical climate, resulting in frequent rainfall. By designing an RCC pitch roof, the water could be redirected to the longitudinal northern and southern edges of the facility. The roof slopes at both ends, having a clear height of 8 metres, while the highest point provides a clear height of 11 metres. At the northern and southern ends of the industrial facility are perimeter gutters, aligned longitudinally along the façade's length, which collect the rainwater and transport the same to the ground via steel pipes. Since the pipes front the façade and are positioned outside the building, these were encased in concrete for aesthetic purposes.

The facility continues to be placed amongst the top industrial designs in the country, appreciated for its flexibility in augmentation whilst setting standards for the upcoming units. Over two decades later, the Client once again engaged the Architects in 2019, to carry out a major expansion to this facility, which includes new test cells, a cafeteria, a warehouse, augmenting of electro-mechanical systems, etc.

Left: *The loftiness of the facility is broken by an impressive glass atrium.*

Below: *Double height and curtain glazed entrance flushes interiors with daylight.*

Hero Honda Facility

Location **Dharuhera, Haryana** Site **20 acres** Built-up area **8,00,000 sq. ft.** Year of completion **1984**

Using innovative and pioneering engineering strategies, *design for the largest two-wheeler manufacturer in the world was* ***accomplished in a record breaking time of nine months***

The design of the facility for Hero Honda, the largest two-wheeler manufacturer in the world, required a method that would simplify the cumbersome process of manufacture, assembly and transportation. Keeping the demand of the Client in mind, the Architects proposed large-span interiors by designing the complex with a RCC-coffered ceiling of 15-metre grid. The complex consisted of production areas for engine manufacture, press shops, paint shops, heat treatment and assembly areas, standard rooms and engine test areas. The project's construction was completed in a highly ambitious period of nine months.

The design incorporated a compact building footprint, interspersing open areas of lush green space that regulate and maintain the temperature within buildings as well as in the vicinity. The Architects conceptualized the plan of the plant, which is able to manufacture 5,000 units per day, and accommodate a total of about 6,500 workers, based on land regeneration and minimization of overall industrial wastage.

For the first phase, a system for quick construction was devised by using RCC pre-cast waffle slabs of 1 x 1 x 0.6 metre dimension; 40,000 units were manufactured and installed in fibre-glass moulds. While the building was being constructed, these slabs were prefabricated at the site itself, reducing travel time. Clear height of the building is 9 metres which slopes down on either side to 8 metres, thus facilitating rainwater conservation.

Further, environment-friendly and innovative design strategies, such as FDV through masonry ducts, were used. These are designed to run under the floor and rise to 3 metres along the columns. High-impact flooring was used in attractive colours to enhance the work environment. The façade combined a functional aesthetic with that of a sustainable one by using design features such as niches, extended slabs and large windows.

Overall, the design strategies used across architecture, structure, lighting and ventilation created, at the time, a path-breaking approach to the design of industrial facilities, and demonstrate a level of creativity hitherto unseen in this building typology.

Below: *Use of coffered slabs enabled large clear spans in the interiors of one of the largest manufacturing plants of Hero Honda at the time.*

TATA Motors Limited

Location **Lucknow, Uttar Pradesh** Site **650 acres** Built-up area **35,00,000 sq. ft.** Year of completion **First Phase (Western Facility): 1992; Second Phase (Eastern Facility): 2005**

One of the ***largest designed assembly plants in the world***

TATA Motors Limited (TML), Lucknow, is set up in the Chinhut Industrial Area with the Deva Road cutting the plot into almost two halves, giving rise to Eastern and Western facilities. Initially, the Eastern facility was proposed to be developed as a residential area for the facility's staff. With the rise of development in and around Lucknow, TML suggested the land be developed as an industrial unit and an extension to their Western facility. Some peculiar land revenue issues incurred extremely high taxes on the Client. To resolve this, the Architects proposed to design and develop a flyover for a private enterprise over a state highway connecting both the facilities. Such a design proposal was the first of its kind and was appreciated for its fearless engineering resolve. This flyover is about 1,000 metres in length, 12 metres in width and rises to a full height of about 8 metres over the highway. Its conceptualization and design are an engineering feat, along with easing the movement of goods, and since then have been lauded across various disciplines.

The project included the design of a product engineering and training shop, administration buildings and offices along with laid-out components for the industrial facility. These comprised construction of various plant buildings such as chassis assembly shop, gear shop, heat-treatment paint shop, body shop and a large number of utility and non-utility buildings.

The Western complex was commissioned first and included facilities such as a vehicle factory (assembly plant for trucks and bus chassis), an integral bus factory (assembly plant for module buses catering to the needs of TATA Marcopolo Motors Limited and fuel building ventilation [FBV] operations), a transmission factory and a production engineering shop. A well-established training centre, which trains around 500 apprentices in various trades, and an engineering research centre with a focus on buses, were also designed. The service training centre provides training to the drivers and technicians of the separate technical units (STUs).

The Eastern facility was built at a much later stage and employs a much-advanced technological set-up than its western counterpart. It has been designed to manufacture long-haul containers and uses top-end movement to anchor material within its assembly unit. The assembly building, on its completion, achieved the feat of being one of the largest buildings in the world!

Top: *A rendered site plan.*

Left: *Cantilevered roof and large spans of windows permit diffused daylight inside the facility.*

Glaxo SmithKline Beecham

Location **Sonepat, Haryana** Site **120 acres** Built-up area **4,00,000 sq. ft.** Year of completion **2000**

A brutalist yet sculptural design, the project follows stringent ***food and dairy standards of the Dairy Board of Denmark***

Located in Sonepat, Haryana, Glaxo SmithKline Beecham (GSB) was designed as an industrial unit for the preparation of health food and dairy products. The complex comprises a total built-up area of 4,00,000 sq. ft. and was implemented in accordance with the stringent standards of the Danish Dairy Board.

The project involved design of different constituents such as production block, annexe block, general store, workshop, warehouse, along with services for cooling, firefighting, boiler room, water treatment area, etc. The first phase comprised various plant and non-plant buildings, including complex utility services, process piping, air-conditioning and FDV system. Unlike other industries, dairy manufacturing requires a vertical set-up for production. The Architects' proposal derived inspiration from a Brutalist design ideology and assimilated a design of sturdy yet sculptural edifices. By using a tiered form, the magnificence of the buildings appeared amplified, creating a never-seen-before aesthetic in industrial design.

One of the key aspects in an industrial facility's design is the ease with which services from a main utility building can be accessed and distributed to different blocks. For this project, the Architects planned the distribution of utilities from one facility to another via pipe bridges. These included services for firefighting, electrical, compressed air and processed air. The entire system of utilities was installed at a height of 7–8 metres above ground level, hampering neither the movement of goods nor the performance of the staff. Using polyurethane (PU) screed for the flooring gave a seamless and continuous appearance across the entire span of the facility, along with an assurance of dust-free interiors.

Facing page: *A rising stepped form gives softness to the facility's façade.*

Below: *A plan of the production block.*

Bottom: *Utilitarian facilities such as electric substation and water tank are also given sculptural forms.*

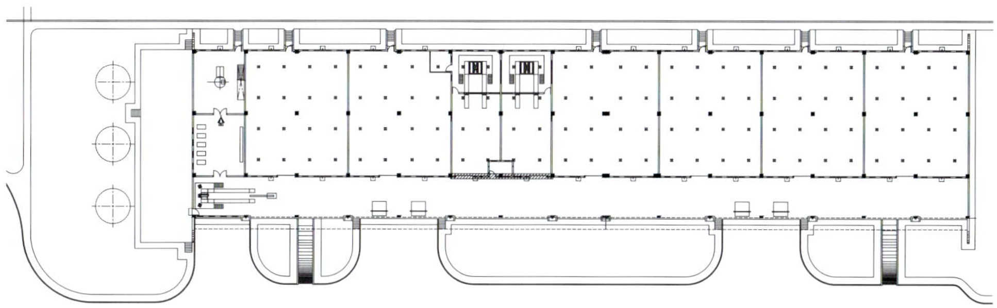

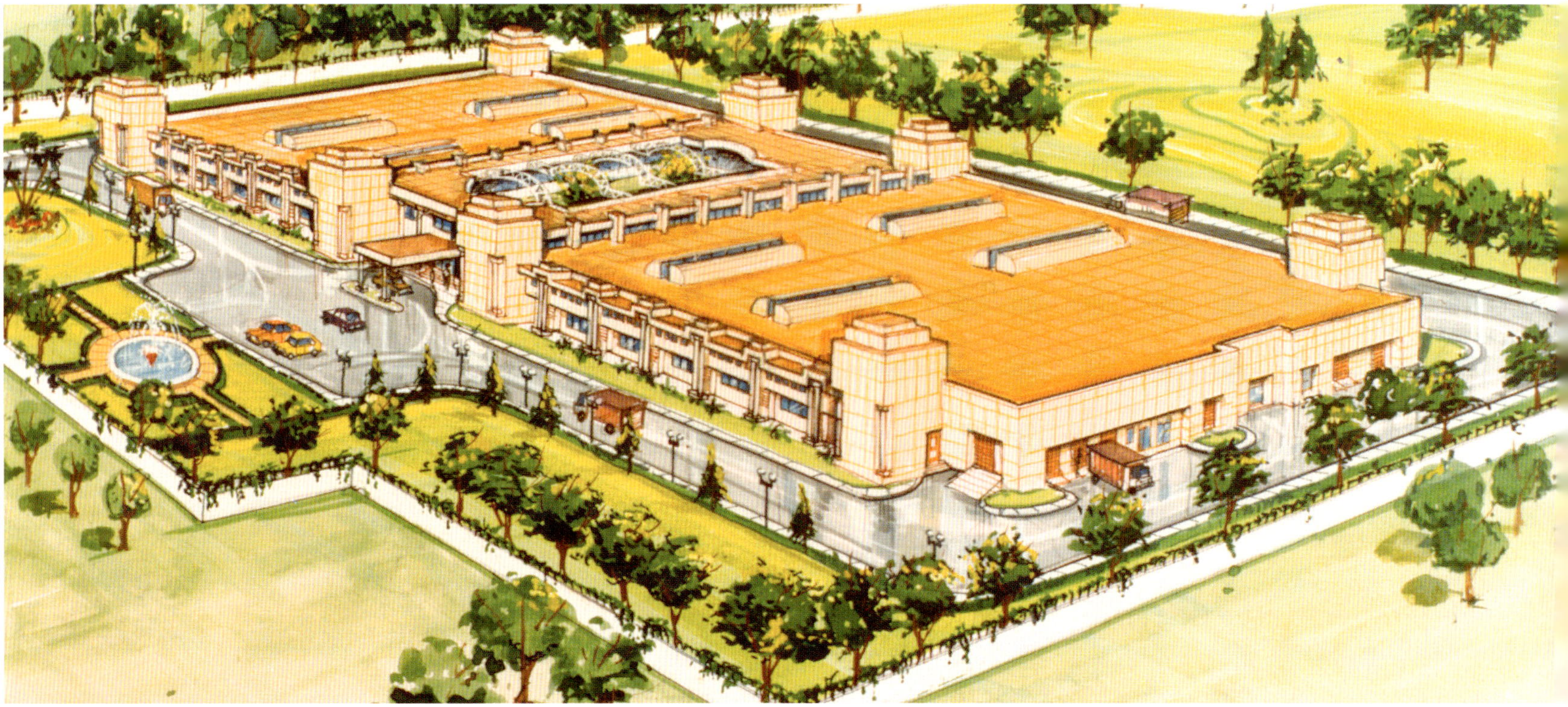

GIVO Garment Factory

Location **Gurugram, Haryana** Site **5 acres** Built-up area **2,00,000 sq. ft.** Year of completion **2000**

Unique design approach of ***integrating utilities into the architectural façade***

Set up in collaboration with Marzotto Spa of Italy, GIVO manufactures and supplies classic ready-to-wear men's suits. Using state-of-the-art equipment imported from Europe, this modern facility caters to a huge domestic and export market.

Located next to Jaipur–Delhi National Highway, the site had expansion restrictions. To counter this, along with meeting the Client's demands, the Architects proposed a longitudinal building design instead. It also helps facilitate movement of finished and unfinished goods, especially needed in a garment facility. An elaborate drop-off area was designed at the entrance, elevating its overall demeanour.

The project used pre-fabricated slabs, significantly decreasing the time of construction. This was the first-of-its-kind engineering technique used at a time when the country was still curating a modern architectural language in its landscape. The production facility was designed on a 60 x 200 metres floor plan. A single storeyed facility, it measures up to 15 metres in height.

Aligning FDV plant rooms across its longitudinal façade, the design appears sturdy with robust columnar elements. These columns were structurally designed to accommodate ducts, supporting beams on either side, to facilitate cooling in the interiors. The heftiness of these columnar elements is balanced by the horizontality of the production block. Services have been consciously placed at the roof's periphery, leaving an expansive space in the centre to accommodate skylights. Use of a white colour palette also instilled a feeling of lightweight construction. The facility consists of large production areas, raw material and finished goods stores, utilities, design centre and a canteen. The entire complex is cooled with positive pressure and has extensive utilities including compressed air, vacuum system, steam, captive power system and fuel oil handling system. Planning around central courtyards allows access to sufficient natural light from all sides of the factory. The skylights also flush daylight into the buildings, reducing overall load of mechanical energy methods.

Facing page above: *A view of the facility entrance, with lofty masses housing ventilation equipments and water tanks.*

Facing page below: *An artist's impression of the facility.*

Top: *The facility's open-sky courtyard area, which accommodates a green buffer.*

Makino India Private Limited

Location **Manesar, Haryana** Site **2 acres** Built-up area **40,000 sq. ft.** Year of completion **2006**

A first-of-its kind ***tools and skill development facility for a Japanese client***

Makino India Private Limited has been executed for Makino, Japan, a global brand leading in metal cutting and manufacturing technology. To ease communication between engineers and supervisors from India to Japan, learning the techniques and technology of Makino, and returning to the country to assemble, sell and export the machines, the owners decided to set up a training facility in Manesar.

The Technology Centre at Manesar, Gurugram, consists of manufacturing areas with a 20-metre span, a large administration block with training and seminar rooms for sale and export of machine tools, CAM (Computer Aided Manufacturing) systems, FMS (Flexible Manufacturing System) cutter and tool grinding machines, and other equipments. The complex was designed as per the stringent Japanese bye-laws for manufacturing areas.

Inside the facility, production and de-mould areas have been designed with double height, encapsulated as spacious and airy spaces. Coving on roof and floor avoids dust settling in corners and niches, easing cleaning and maintenance for a facility functioning on production and assemblage of precise and miniscule machine parts. Epoxy flooring was installed to ensure durability. The design for the facility was completed in a record of seven months.

Below: *Design of the facility juxtaposes a variety of contemporary materials.*

Choice Clothing

Location **Manesar, Haryana** Site **2 acres** Built-up area **1,75,000 sq. ft.** Year of completion **2004**

Facility for an Indo-British joint venture, *it is conceptualized keeping the* ***comfort of the users at its core***

Having completed the first factory with a built-up area of 30,000 sq. ft. in Udyog Vihar, Gurugram, for an Indo-British joint venture, the Architects were appointed to design a much larger garment manufacturing facility in Manesar by the same Client. The project includes a showroom and office areas at the front, in addition to an elaborate garment-production facility at the rear end of the building.

Even with a constricted site, the Architects were able to judiciously utilize and plan the required areas with ease. The proposed design not only catered to the Clients' functional requirements but also achieved a hospitable working environment for the staff. Façade design is a carefully crafted aspect of the project – the front façade curves inward, creating a grand and seamless skin, which presents a magnificent appearance; for those viewing the facility from the main road, it appears as a carefully crafted garment. Transparency is another feature that is significantly highlighted through the façade. Complementing the curved front façade along with elaborate curtain glazing facilities, the voids and skylights regulate natural ventilation as well.

Through this ideation, the Architects were able to present a successful example of an industrial facility with sustainable solutions, facilitating thermal comfort for the users.

Left: *A curvilinear front façade helps in maximum natural light to flush the interiors.*

Below: *A view of the facility's magnificent entrance.*

Subros Limited

Location **Manesar, Haryana** Site **9 acres** Built-up area **4,00,000 sq. ft.** Year of completion **2006**

Executed for Maruti Suzuki, the design delved into ***providing best design solutions on a highly compact site***

Subros is the approved original equipment manufacturer (OEM) for Maruti Suzuki, supplying air-conditioning for their cars. Their facility at IMT Manesar produces air-conditioners in all sizes and capacities, and comprises plant buildings, an administration block, a canteen, a utility block and site development works.

The site spreads on an area of 9 acres and is well located just off the Jaipur–Delhi National Highway. While this allowed for better visibility and accessibility, the Architects had to be weary of security concerns and circulation movement. For this, the buildings have been significantly offset from the main highway line. Buffer space in the form of an expansive green belt helps in screening dust and noise into the facility's premises. A well-planned parking space has also been accommodated in the front end of the site.

The height of the structures has been kept to two floors, keeping raw materials on ground floor while the finished goods are accommodated on the first floor. The admin block spearheads the production block, carefully demarcating accessibility for visitors vis-à-vis staff, and streamlining overall planning. A clear span of 16 metres has been designed to support the same. With a coffered ceiling, the facility opens up into a large shared hall, harbouring different functions of a production facility.

Right: *A rendered site plan.*

Below: *An expansive curtain glazing introduces a modern representation to an industrial edifice.*

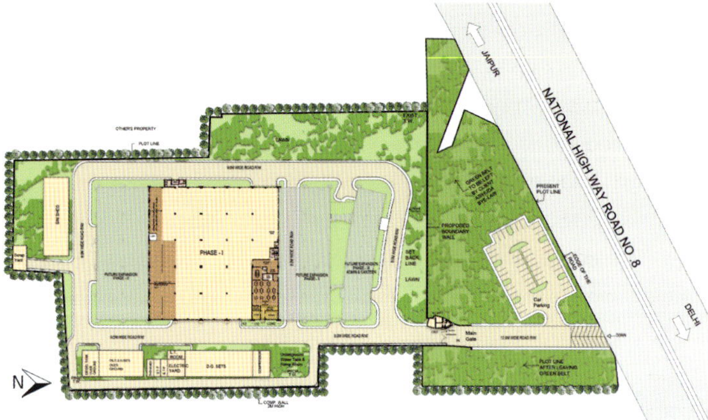

Havells Standard Electricals

Location **Haridwar, Uttarakhand** Site **11 acres** Built-up area **3,00,000 sq. ft.** Year of completion **2012**

Integrating innovative engineering strategies on a compact site, the facility emerged as ***the largest fan factory in India***

Havells Standard Electricals in Haridwar is designed as the largest fan factory of the brand in India.

The requirements in Phase-I consisted of design and development of production block, assembly line and manufacturing shop. The complex consists of independent manufacturing facilities for electrical low-voltage components, such as fans and compact fluorescent light (CFL) bulbs. It also accommodates a centralized utility block.

A warehouse with a large volume to store raw materials and finished products is provided within the complex. The structure uses a flat roof construction and has no drop-downs on the columns, which also helps in improving the utility provision across different industrial processes. Regular intervals of discreet shaft designs, with aquamarine shades of ventilators, help in bringing depth to the design.

Below: *A view of the facility, displaying a harmonious combination of a variety of natural materials.*

Sona Koyo Steerings Systems Limited

Location **Gurugram, Haryana** Site **14 acres** Built-up area **1,60,000 sq. ft.** Year of completion **1992**

Design creates a ***unique industrial character exuding modernity*** *that evolves with an artistic sensibility*

The project is an industrial building for manufacture of steering wheels and other automatic components for cars and is centrally air-conditioned.

The façade of the building has been designed using inclined brick walls and concrete members, which induce irregular cut-outs on the façade and create a unique industrial character. The facility exudes a modern character yet one that evolves from an artistic sensibility. Use of concrete members in an abstract pattern over window glazing attracts attention of the visitors whilst serving as an intriguing *jaali* design, allowing controlled daylight into the interiors. The technical administration areas in the interiors have been provided at the mezzanine level overlooking the plant area, easing supervision and instilling transparent communication between the workers and their supervisors. FDV system has been used to cool the entire plant area. Phase-II of construction involved the design and construction of an axle plant.

Above: *Use of bricks instills an earthy look to the facility.*

Below: *The design provides open spaces within the site.*

Havells India Limited

Location **Neemrana, Rajasthan** Site **48 acres** Built-up area **8,00,000 sq. ft.** Year of completion **2017**

Built with the finest engineering and sustainable design strategies, *the project is one of the first to be developed as a part of RIICO*

Built in the largest industrial area of Rajasthan NCR, Havells Neemrana was one of the pioneering set-ups to be designed and developed as a part of RIICO. Havells India Limited, established in 2004, is the largest automated water heater plant in India, with a workforce of approximately 2,500 . The Neemrana plant has four units, spread over an area of 48 acres, comprising an automated water heater plant, and industrial fan and smart lighting system.

Owing to this nature of production, the facility spreads horizontally across the site, carefully incorporating vehicular as well as pedestrian circulation areas. The project consists of production blocks for motor plant and CFL plant, utility building, compound wall and gate house, external development work comprising roads, water supply system, sewerage, stormwater, etc. Fully air-conditioned and well-planned interiors equip the facility to handle the dry, arid and extreme climatic conditions of Rajasthan. Use of skylights helps manifest natural air ventilation. This also helps the facility to emerge as spacious and airy. The structure has been designed in steel while the façade showcases a well-planned pattern of ACP and glass, rendering a modern feel to the design.

Below: *Conceptualized with contemporary materials in the sweltering heat of Rajasthan, the facility introduced a modern design in the area.*

Shriram Piston and Rings Limited

Location **Pathredi, Rajasthan** Site **22 acres** Built-up area **6,50,000 sq. ft.** Year of completion **2018**

Requiring a meticulous engineering design, the ***three phases of execution were completed in a record time of twelve months each***

Shriram Piston and Rings Limited manufactures and supplies automotive parts, such as diesel and gasoline pistons, pins, rings and engine valves, to noteworthy automobile brands. Impressed with the design and execution of their Ghaziabad facility, the Client also awarded the design of this facility in Pathredi to the Architects. With a distinctly rectangular site, the form was developed longitudinally. The three phases were completed in a record time of twelve months each.

While initially the Client had desired steel construction, considering the climatological conditions of the area as well as the micro-scale production of different components, the Architects suggested that they opt for an RCC structure. A pitched RCC roof, with drainage pipes accommodated on the sides, regulates rainwater disposal. The roof was also prefabricated to ensure no dust or water seepage would entail. Upon realizing that 12-metre-high RCC columns were to be used, jacketing of columns was done to provide support and prevent bending.

Below: *Combined use of different patterns on the façade lends an innovative approach to industrial design.*

RUJ – Skill Development Centre

Location **Jaipur, Rajasthan** Site **10 acres** Built-up area **2,00,000 sq. ft.** Year of completion **2018**

Built in accordance with high-end Swiss specifications and IGBC Gold norms, *the facility uses design to empower its workers through skill development*

Conceived as a joint Indo-Swiss venture, this futuristic design had been planned at Mahindra World City, Jaipur. The entire facility has been built in accordance with high-end Swiss design specifications and IGBC Gold norms.

The two large production blocks accommodate machines and fabrication shops, sheet-metal processing, grinding, electroplating and hardening, and provision of paint shops, besides medical device production areas.

To break the monotonous representation of yet another industrial facility, RUJ uses materials such as glass, metal container sheets and bricks to create a sustainable design solution. The volumetric play in the façade of the different blocks imparts a sculptural form to the edifices, which are well synchronized and yet have their own design values. The assembling and packaging areas have been accommodated on the first floor, which frees space for equipments and eases circulation across the work floor. Accommodating double height in the interiors allows transparency between different production and administration areas, also easing supervision from higher floors. The facility is centrally air-conditioned to ensure habitable and comfortable working conditions for the staff in the extremely hot and arid region of Rajasthan.

Below: *Meticulous use of patterns and materials gives a new definition to industrial design.*

Complete Listing of Industrial Projects

Central Warehousing Facilities for Havells, Greater Noida, Uttar Pradesh
This facility has been built for Havells as a central warehouse facility for storing over 600 in-house produced electrical and electronic products being manufactured by Havells in their various plants. The warehouse has a built up area of 2,48,000 sq. ft. with a height of 16 metres.

Hero Honda Facility, Dharuhera, Haryana
The complex is provided with both air-conditioning and FDV system. The factory complex is spread over an area of 20 acres and has a total built-up area of approximately 8,00,000 sq. ft. The complex consists of production areas for engine manufacture, press shop, paint shop, heat treatment and assembly areas, standard rooms and engine test areas. The construction was completed in a highly ambitious time period of nine months.

Glaxo SmithKline Beecham, Sonepat, Haryana
A 120-acre facility for a Nutrition Food Plant has been designed for preparation of health food and dairy products. The built-up area for phase-I is 4,00,000 sq. ft. with complex utility services, process piping, air-conditioning and FDV system.

TATA Motors Limited, Lucknow, Uttar Pradesh
Set up in the Chinhut Industrial Area, the Deva Road cuts the plot in almost two halves, giving rise to Eastern and Western facilities. Initially, the Eastern Facility was proposed to be developed as a residential area for the staff. With a site area of 650 acres, the complex includes the following plant buildings: chassis assembly shop, gear shop, heat treatment paint shop, body shop, in addition to various utility and non-utility buildings.

TATA Cummins Limited, Jamshedpur, Jharkhand
The project is a joint venture between Telco and Cummins Engine Co., USA, and spread on a 25-acre plot. The production facility is located in the industrial city of Jamshedpur and was one of the first set-ups in the vicinity. The facility manufactures high performance, reliable and durable mid-range (B&L) engines. The complex was completed in a record time of eighteen months.

Hero Cycles Complex, Ludhiana, Punjab
The project required an expansion building comprising an assembly and paint shop. The total built-up area of the expansion is 3,00,000 sq. ft.

Sona Koyo Steerings Systems Limited, Gurugram, Haryana
The project is a centrally cooled industrial building, manufacturing steering and other automatic components for cars. The built-up area is 1,00,000 sq. ft. Phase-II comprises an axle plant, the built-up area for which is 60,000 sq. ft. Both phases were completed in 1992.

Suzuki Motors Corporation, Gurugram, Haryana
The project required a facility designed for manufacturing two-wheeler vehicles. The structural design services were provided to Mitsui Kensetsu Limited.

Choice Clothing Company, Gurugram, Haryana
Located in Udyog Vihar II, Gurugram, the office and manufacturing facilities for Choice Clothing have a built-up area 30,000 sq. ft., and have been designed for an Indo-British joint venture.

Perto Industrial Facility, Jaipur, Rajasthan
With the use of low maintenance and sleek finishes, bold and contrasting colors and a strictly functional cubic form, the factory is entirely galvanized than painted to achieve a clean finish. The use of trellises and creation of central courtyards make the design well-suited to the harsh climate of the region.

Sarda Motor Industries Limited, New Delhi
The project has been designed for manufacturing PVC mouldings and car seat covers.

Subros Limited, Manesar, Haryana
With a built-up area of 4,00,000 sq. ft. on a 9-acre site, the factory's design incorporates spaces such as admin and utility blocks, plant buildings, a canteen, etc. The design juxtaposes different areas in an interesting combination of colours and materials, especially over its façade's design.

Factory for Machino TSK Nippon Cables, Manesar, Haryana
This is a joint venture project between Machino Plastics and TSK Nippon of Japan. The project was completed in a record time of five months along with electrical, firefighting, industrial piping and other utility services. The built-up area is 50,000 sq. ft.

Factory Complex for Majestic Auto Limited, Ghaziabad, Uttar Pradesh
A 23-acre unit of Hero Motors Limited, the complex serves as the manufacturing facility for 65 cc motorcycles and mopeds. It has two manufacturing and assembly blocks, and other infrastructure facilities with air-conditioning and FDV system. Phase-I was completed in a record time of ten months in 1987. Phase-II was completed shortly after.

Asian Paints, Kasna, Uttar Pradesh
The 20-acre complex for Asian Paints is the latest of their many production facilities in the country. With a gross built-up area of 5,00,000 sq. ft., the plant includes

complex buildings such as a paint house, a resin house, industrial paint units, raw material and finished goods warehouses, and non-plant buildings including canteen and administration blocks.

GIVO Garment Factory, Gurugram, Haryana
This modern facility was designed for the manufacture of ready-to-wear men's suits and dresses for domestic and export markets. It was set up in joint venture with KB&T Group in India and Thakral Group of Singapore (now Thakral Corporation Limited). It consists of large production areas, stores, utilities, a design centre and a canteen complex. The total built-up area is 2,00,000 sq. ft.

Global Auto Parts, Greater Noida, Uttar Pradesh
The 20-acre production facility is a subsidiary of Subros and produces components for auto refrigeration.

New Plant for Manufacturing Automotive Light Equipment, Dharuhera, Haryana
An industrial facility for the manufacture of automotive light fittings was set up in association with Stanley & Electric Company of Japan. The built-up area is 1,80,000 sq. ft. The project was designed for Lumax Industries Limited.

Factory Complex for Hindustan Aeronautics Limited (HAL), Lucknow, Uttar Pradesh
The complex, located in Lucknow, includes design for large manufacturing assembly workshops and production areas. RCC hyperbolic shells were used to create large span of spaces. The total built-up area of the HAL facility is 2,50,000 sq. ft. The entire process of design and execution was completed in less than eighteen months. The entire facility has been provided with central air-conditioning.

Jubilant Foodworks Limited (Domino's Pizza), Greater Noida, Uttar Pradesh
The factory was built to accommodate temperature controlled areas for food storage and processing for the popular food chain.

Factory Complex for Hindustan Aeronautics Limited (HAL), Korwa, Uttar Pradesh
Designed on a 70-acre site, the factory complex is the largest building of its kind for HAL. With a total built-up area of approximately 5,40,000 sq. ft., the centrally air-conditioned production plant has an ultra clean environment. The RCC buildings have intricate structural forms like shells, vierendeel girder, etc. The construction was completed in 1985.

Bharat Seats Limited, Maruti Complex, Gurugram, Haryana
One of the largest Maruti JV ancillary projects located within Maruti Complex, the plant has been designed for the manufacture of car seats. The complex has the main assembly building, a canteen, PU manufacturing and admin blocks. The factory has air-conditioning and FDV system. The total built-up area of the project is 1,00,000 sq. ft.

New Industrial Area (Phase II), New Delhi
The project's scope required Master Planning for development of new industrial areas for relocation of industries to Bawana area, to be designed across a site of 1,600 acres. Phase-I involved the Master Planning and layout for 5,000 industrial plots and ancillary facilities, worker housing, commercial centre and ancillary transportation infrastructure on an area spanning 450 acres. The project has been designed for the Delhi State Industrial Development Corporation (DSIDC).

JCB Facility, Jaipur, Rajasthan
Functional requirement of a large factory has been manifested through intensive mechanical engineering and has been designed in a relatively small footprint, within a harmonious and soft landscape for the JCB Group. The factory complex also has a water feature within the site, which helps manage the microclimate of the site.

J.K. Dairy and Foods Limited, Gajraula, Uttar Pradesh
The complex accommodates production, evaporator/dryer, boiler house, process and various non-plant buildings, utility blocks, transit hostel, housing, administration, canteen, development works, etc. The built-up area of the production is 1,25,000 sq. ft., and of the non-plant area is 90,000 sq. ft.

Insilco Limited, Gajraula, Uttar Pradesh
Insilco Limited is one of the leading producers of precipitated silica in South Asia. Design of the plant included a plant head, engineering functions, Environment Safety Health and Quality (ESHQ), HR and centralized accounting functions.

Automobile Components Manufacturing Facilities for Mindarika, Gurugram, Haryana
The project is a joint venture with Minda Industries and Japanese firms, Tokairika and Sumitomo. The facility includes the main plant building, a canteen building, utility and admin blocks. It has a site area of 8 acres and a built-up area of 1,15,000 sq. ft.

Jay Bharat Maruti Limited, Baroda, Gujarat
The factory complex is an ancillary project for premier automobile manufacturing companies like Ford of USA. The facility was designed for manufacturing high capacity presses.

JCB India Limited, Ballabhgarh, Haryana
The expansion of production facilities includes the design of logistics, utility and admin block. The built-up area for the project is 7,75,000 sq. ft.

Havells Standard Electricals, Haridwar, Uttarakhand
The design consists of construction of production block and assembly line M/C shop. The built-up area is approximately 1,30,000 sq. ft. in Phase-I. A built-up area of 1,18,000 sq. ft. consists of blocks for independent manufacturing facilities for fans, while the manufacturing facilities for CFL have a built-up area of 7,53,000 sq. ft.

Bundy India Limited, Gurugram, Haryana
Construction of new production facilities for Bundy India Limited at IMT Manesar, Gurugram, Haryana.

Havells India Limited, Neemrana, Rajasthan
The 48-acre project has production blocks for motor and CFL plants, utility building, compound wall and gate house, external development work with roads, water supply, storm water, sewerage, etc. The built-up area of the project is approximately 8,00,000 sq. ft.

TATA Cummins Megasite Complex, Pune, Maharashtra
The 150-acre site is an integrated industrial complex for Cummins India Limited and its subsidiaries. It has nine plants of Cummins and various subsidiaries built in different phases.

Ghaziabad Development Authority (GDA) Industrial Estates, Ghaziabad, Uttar Pradesh
The project comprises development plans for two industrial estates which include multi-storeyed flatted factories for GDA on Delhi-Meerut and Delhi-Bulandshahr roads. The area under development exceeds 1,000 acres. The Architects were cautious of providing distinct zones for heavy/medium/light and small scale industries.

Flatted Factory Complex for DCM Limited, New Delhi
The project envisaged the construction of a large flatted factory complex in the heart of the city, with a total built-up area of 15 lakh sq. ft. designed in four– and six-storeyed blocks.

DCM Engineering Products, Baddi, Himachal Pradesh
The 30 acres of factory complex consists of a toll room block, a machine shop, aluminum dye casting, forging, raw material stores, and finished product godown. Non-plant buildings comprise an administrative block, a time office, a canteen, and a Research and Development (R&D) wing.

Sriram Rayons, Kota, Rajasthan
An aviscose filament yarn production project, its built-up area is approximately 20,000 sq. ft. The production facility centre of a highly specialized nature has been conceived in a manner that it is expandable to an additional area of 50,000 sq. ft. The project also includes other ancillary structures.

Apeejay Global Logistics Park, Ballabhgarh, Haryana
Spanning across a mammoth area of 84 acres, the main purpose of the owners was to build facilities for leasing purposes. Its design parameters are synonymous with a transit storage hub for distributions services, fit for e-commerce businesses. With a total built-up area of 2,15,000 sq. ft., the project was completed in 2018.

Uptron Colour Picture Tube Factory, Sahibabad, Uttar Pradesh
A first of its kind in India, the factory complex consists of manufacturing and production areas, and utility buildings covering a built-up area of 3,22,000 sq. ft. The complex has large water treatment and effluent treatment plants. The entire complex is centrally air-conditioned with clean rooms of class 10,000 and 30,000 in 50 per cent of the areas.

Duracell India Alkaline Battery Project, Gurugram, Haryana
The project comprises plant buildings of approximately 1,25,000 sq. ft. built-up area for the manufacture of high strength alkaline batteries, set up in joint venture with Duracell, USA. The complex is centrally air-conditioned with complex utilities and services.

Asian Consolidated Industries Limited, Shahjahanpur, Rajasthan
Spread on an area of 68 acres, the complex consists of two factories: one for the production of Beer (Carlsberg) and canning of soft drinks such as Pepsi, and the other for the production of two-piece aluminium cans. The factory complex also has an admin block, a guest house and a canteen.

Sulphur Recovery Unit, Surat, Gujarat
The project consists of civil and structural design of the sulphur recovery unit for Oil and Natural Gas Corporation Limited (ONGC). It includes the design of various equipment foundations, utility buildings, pipe racks and off-site facilities. It was constructed in 1986.

Gelatine Capsule Project for Shalimar Industries, Alwar, Rajasthan
The project has the main factory building for the manufacture of hard-shell gelatine capsules, including large areas for inspection and storage of finished goods. The entire complex is centrally air-conditioned with heat and humidity control in manufacturing areas, and it also includes raw material stores, gelatin preparation block, a workshop, a machine assembly unit, and pharmaceutical factory and admin block.

Havells India Limited, Baddi, Himachal Pradesh
Built on an area of 5,75,000 sq. ft., the facilities have been designed for the manufacture of electrical switches, sockets, panels, MCBs, etc.

Makino India Private Limited, Gurugram, Haryana
Technology Centre at Manesar in Gurugram, Haryana, for Makino India Private Limited. The state-of-the-art centre consists of manufacturing areas with a 20-metre span within the centre and a large administration block with training and seminar rooms. The total built-up area is 40,000 sq. ft.

Television Glass Shell Manufacturing for Samcor Glass Limited, Kota, Rajasthan
This modern factory complex has been designed along with Corning, USA, and Samsung, Korea. It consists of heavy industrial structures with foundation for glass furnace, press machines, chimneys, silos, supporting system for conveyors platforms, etc. Phase-I, with a built-up area of 2,25,000 sq. ft., had been completed in a record time of fourteen months.

VVF Limited Plant, Baddi, Himachal Pradesh
The new production facility in Baddi has been designed for the manufacture of factory acids, glycerin and soaps. The plant has been designed for VVF Limited and is planned on a 17-acre site.

Indication Instrument Limited, Faridabad, Haryana
The factory complex is located in Faridabad and has an approximate built-up area of 5,40,000 sq. ft. in the first phase of construction. The facility has been designed for the manufacture of indication equipments for the automotive industry.

Daewoo Motors Limited, Surajpur, Uttar Pradesh
The 200-acre car plant facility consists of production buildings, engine T/A shop, aluminium casting and utilities like electrical, HVAC (heating, ventilation and air-conditioning), compressed air and processed water in all production buildings. The built-up area is 25 lakh sq. ft.

Hero Auto Limited, Manesar, Haryana
The new production facility has been designed on a site of 20 acres in Manesar, Haryana. The complex consists of plant buildings, with a built-up area of 3,00,000 sq. ft., an administration block, a utility block and provisions for future expansion. The complex also consists of an international scale R&D facility for Hero Global Design.

Expansion to Machino Plastics in J.V. Complex, Maruti Udyog Limited, Gurugram, Haryana
The expansion project has been designed to accommodate high moulding presses and is located in Gurugram, Haryana.

Nissin Brake, Neemrana, Rajasthan
The major expansion of production facilities includes logistics utility and administration block. The total built-up area of the project is 5,00,000 sq. ft.

Hindustan Thermo Prints Limited, Ghaziabad, Uttar Pradesh
The factory, Nayagaon Cement Plant, has been designed for Cement Corporation of India Limited and is located in Ghaziabad.

New Factory for Choice Clothing, Manesar, Haryana
A centrally air-conditioned garment facility with high specifications and a built-up area of 1,75,000 sq. ft. has been designed for an Indo-British venture.

Formica Laminates, Rudrapur, Uttarakhand
The project includes the design of production and manufacturing facilities for domestic and industrial laminates in the industrial town of Rudrapur, Uttarakhand. The first phase has a built-up area of 1,50,000 sq. ft. on a site of 15 acres. The project has been executed for the Bombay Burmah Trading Corporation Limited.

Havells India Limited, Haridwar, Uttarakhand
The new production/assembly plant facility is designed on an area of 10 acres and consists of a production block, stator shop, assembly line machine shop, blade paint and press shop. The first phase of the industrial facility has a built-up area of 80,000 sq. ft. The project is located in the BHEL SIDCUL area.

Automotive Research Association of India (ARAI), Manesar, Haryana
This facility is the Regional Centre (North) for ARAI and forms a state-of-the-art high-tech research, development and testing centre for various two-wheeler and four-wheeler automobiles. The complex has a built-up area of 1,00,000 sq. ft. All laboratories and testing areas are centrally air-conditioned. In addition to this, the complex has extensive outdoor testing facilities.

Nature Waste Management, New Delhi

Shriram Piston and Rings Limited, Pathredi, Rajasthan
Shriram Piston and Rings Limited is a reputed name catering automotive parts, such as diesel and gasoline pistons, pins, rings and engine valves, to noteworthy brands such as Maruti, Hyundai, etc.

RUJ – Skill Development Centre, Jaipur, Rajasthan
Conceived as a joint Indo-Swiss venture, the design of the facility is futuristic and has a total built-up area of 2,00,000 sq. ft. in Mahindra World City, Jaipur. The entire facility has been built in accordance with the high-end Swiss design specifications and IGBC Gold norms.

Havells Integrated White Goods Manufacturing Complex, Ghiloth, Rajasthan
Encompassed on 50 acres of land in the sparse and dry terrain of Ghiloth, the project proposed the design and execution of manufacturing plants for air-conditioners, refrigeration, television and washing machines along with a warehouse.

Minda Huf Limited (Unit-I), Noida, Uttar Pradesh
This is an Indo-German joint venture project for the manufacture of automobile switches and keys. The project comprises receiving and finishing stores, component assembly area, powder coating room, key manufacturing section, an administration building, staff facilities, utility services, etc.

Hella India Limited, Faridabad, Haryana
New production facilities for Hella India Limited in Faridabad include plant building, administration building and site development works, such as underground tank, road, pathways and boundary wall. The built-up area of the facility is 50,000 sq. ft.

Shriram Piston and Rings Limited, Ghaziabad, Uttar Pradesh

HOUSING

Architectural design of multi-family housing is about creating a distinctive lifestyle product – 'a boutique society'. A successful design has to ensure that at macro level, all the buildings form a coherent urban design, and at the micro level, each dwelling unit is carefully and optimally planned. Housing complexes require environment conscious design with adequate community facilities and modern amenities. The design of open spaces should address user needs of all ages. A safe and secure residential neighbourhood, which provides adequate privacy and opportunities for social interaction, creates a vibrant community.

ELDECO
Ananda
Ananda

Eldeco Ananda

Location **Noida, Uttar Pradesh** Site **2.5 acres** Built-up area **2,50,000 sq. ft.** Year of completion **2008**

Awarded by the ***Estrade Real Estate Awards, Singapore*** *as* ***a Sustainable Design Project***

Ananda, a luxurious housing project for Eldeco Developers at Sector 48 in Noida (New Okhla Industrial Development Authority), is designed for middle-income groups and is located on the fringe of the urban and suburban periphery of Uttar Pradesh. The project has intelligently devised architectural interpretations of form, space and functions, inspired by eco-friendly design concepts, to best suit the existing context and emerge as a befitting example of a sustainable design for future needs.

The award-winning design of the Ananda housing complex is a conscious attempt to bring architecture closer to nature, discovering interesting and intelligent intermixing of the two through building forms and spatial typologies. The form of the over-all complex is a spontaneous response to the boundless stretch of horizontal ground – the complex appears to rise in steps parallel to the ground. Such a design concept respects the flatness of the site, elevating slightly in the vertical direction without overpowering the spatial experience at ground level.

The design of the built form also provides space for terrace gardens that not only soften the skyline of the gated community but create green space on roofs as well, acting as 'breathing lungs' for the complex. The sinuously curved profile of the building leads to the formation of double walls, which act as heat insulators on the building façades. The landscaped terrace gardens reduce heat gain as they help control the humidity and temperature of air for the apartments below. Such an effect establishes a passive ventilation process. The beautifully designed pergola intertwined with lush green climbers and creepers is inspired by tropical architectural designs that help in cooling and humidification, providing the much needed shade to roofs as well as casting an artistic pattern of shadows against the building surfaces. The shadows, shifting constantly with the movement of sun, animate and breathe life into the aesthetics of the complex.

The complex – with seventy-two spacious apartments, a private swimming pool, health club, and most importantly, the eighteen cascading penthouses with terrace gardens, defines the true art of living luxuriously in the cradle of nature.

Facing page: *Entrance to the housing complex.*

Above: *A view of the entrance to the complex, highlighting the curvaceous edges of buildings.*

Monde De Provence – Adani Realty

Location **Gurugram, Haryana** Site **12 acres** Built-up area **10,00,000 sq. ft.** Year of completion **Ongoing**

Awarded ***'Luxury Project of the Year 2019, Residential'*** *by* ***ET NOW Real Estate Awards***

Monde de Provence is a defining statement in housing design that will revolutionize the concept of residential luxury in the coming times. The concept of housing thrives on irregularity, ideating free-flowing landscape and curved shapes of buildings to work in conjunction with each other.

The most challenging aspect of the design was the irregular trapezoidal shape of the site narrowing down to a small intersection and opening up to another small piece of trapezoidal land. The Architects decided to use this site constraint to their benefit and divided the society into two different designs. The bigger land accommodates four residential towers, a juxtaposition of clear fenestrations and transparency between indoors and outdoors for the residents. The smaller land accommodates a single Iconic Tower, seed-shaped and extruding vertically, binding itself together through a mesh of steel frames. The buildings are crowned with a harp-shaped design element which coils around the edges of the towers on the roof, while each tower looks out on to a huge green lawn.

The apartments have a built-up area of 5,500 sq. ft. while the penthouses measure 10,000 sq. ft. each. Each level houses only two apartments, concentrating on the provision of luxury of space whilst maintaining security. The penthouses are adept with state-of-the-art facilities and integrate the latest smart technologies to create smooth functioning spaces. The thirty-storeyed Iconic Tower has only fourteen duplex apartments, each double storeyed with an area of 15,000 sq. ft. These 'villas in the sky' are the ultimate in luxury living and offer the privacy of a bungalow with accoutrements of apartment living in terms of facilities. The two top floors of the Iconic Tower have club and lounge facilities for its residents. Single penthouse residences on every floor are accessible from a lift lobby outside the apartments. Each residence in this tower is provided with pool facilities and a two-storeyed lounge area. The bedrooms open up to exquisite views, accessible with balconies and full height glazing replacing the rooms' walls.

The vision of a modern and technologically adept residential development would be incomplete without carefully designed outdoors. The site is compactly packed with dense trees which act as noise barriers for the lower residences while the higher-level flats look out onto the extensive green of the surrounding areas. The site is also equipped with a club and pool facility.

Facing page: *A visualization of the thirty-storeyed Iconic skyscraper, 'Eiffel Tower'.*

Below: *A visualization of living room of the penthouses.*

Orange County

Orange County

Location **Indirapuram, Uttar Pradesh** Site **10 acres** Built-up area **1,00,000 sq. ft.** Year of completion **2008**

Combining luxury with affordability, the society catches attention with its ***upside down conceptualized clubhouse***

At a time when high-rise housing societies witnessed a surge in their numbers to accommodate the large influx of residents from surrounding states, Orange County presented the idea of residential living which was luxurious as well as affordable. Spread over an area of 10 acres, this residential development is a mix of 2 and 3-BHK apartments and penthouses.

The Architects planned the high-rise towers on the site's outer periphery, thereby creating a large central green space. The design of the residential complex builds on unique design initiatives, such as a playful and colourful form of the club, bold orange of the towers, a tropical landscape design – all of which allude to the introduction of social areas within the society, making it a prospering residential experience.

The towers are carefully aligned to avoid any overlap, providing a clear field of view to the residents and regulating light and ventilation in the apartments. A linear planning ensures balanced and equal distribution of light and wind across all levels of residences. Careful distancing of the towers from one another ensures privacy for residents. The society is furnished with facilities like a swimming pool, a club and tennis courts, to name a few.

A unique feature of the project is the upside down club, which breaks the stereotypical character of design and initiates a playful environment instead. The alignment of the building rotated upside down not only attracts the attention of the passers-by but also brings an element of dynamism to the overall urban character.

The landscape is replete with contemporary ideas of asymmetry and vivid patterns of line work, in addition to extensive areas for sports such as lawn tennis, badminton, etc. With the introduction of a swimming pool as an integral water feature within the site, the different elements – architectural and landscape – are united into a single unit of congruous coexistence. Carefully orchestrated use of bold and bright orange on the façade adds cheer to the built environment and lends a distinctive aesthetic to the development, setting it apart from its contemporaries.

Facing page: *The entrance of the housing society with the inverted club in its foreground.*

Below: *A landscaped court with outdoor seating.*

Omaxe Heights

Location **Lucknow, Uttar Pradesh** Site **10 acres** Built-up area **10,00,000 sq. ft.** Year of completion **2009**

Outward-facing in their alignment, *the* ***flower-shaped towers*** *offer far-reaching views to its residents*

Lucknow is an upcoming smart city, set to witness a large scale of urban development.

The idea of Omaxe Heights was refreshing since it was conceptualized to develop as a holistic residential space. With a well thought out typology, its residential towers have been planned around a central open space that acts as the focal point of the site. The residences are flower-shaped in design which opens up the visual span on all sides.

The form of the towers is such that it allows adequate daylight and also controls passive cooling in the residences. The apartments of each tower open out on three different sides, maintaining privacy for residents on the same floors. The two top floors of the towers have an extended slab, and a supporting pergola curving around the edges and crowning the buildings, enabling the overall character of the society with a unique element.

The sight is met with green landscaped spaces comprising a centrally located pool. The green landscape and the blue of the pool stand out at the site due to the buildings being painted in a symphony of matte white and grey. The open areas follow a hierarchy: from small, intimate sit-outs to gardens, plazas and parks. The pool is adequately landscaped to provide spaces for people to lounge in and relax, creating a common recreational ground for residents.

There is surface as well as basement parking, which restricts vehicular movement on the site, eases movability of pedestrians and ensures a safe space for kids to interact in.

Facing page: *An evening view of the residential society.*

Below: *A rendered plan of the typical 3-BHK cluster residences.*

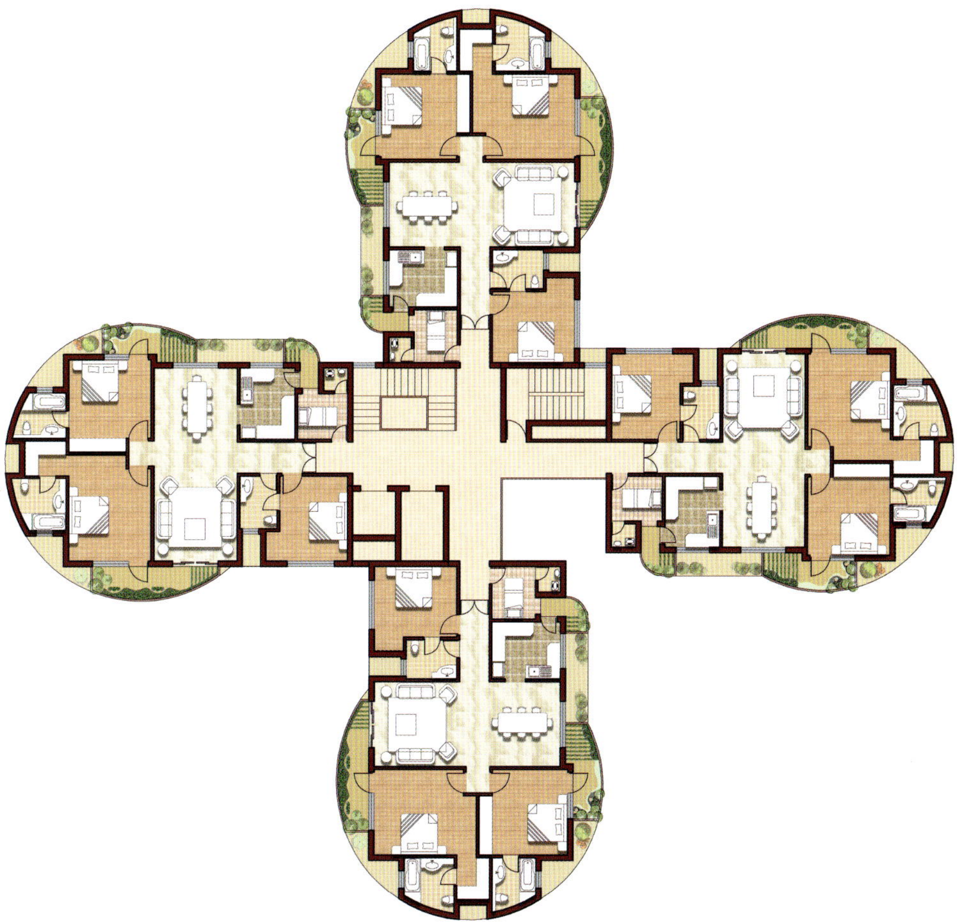

Eldeco Utopia

Location **Noida, Uttar Pradesh** Site **18 acres** Built-up area **15,00,000 sq. ft.** Year of completion **2009**

The design is curated by following sustainable ethics, *forming the façade of the edifices as flowing percurssions*

Sprawling languidly across a built-up area of 15 lakh sq. ft., on a plot of land that is conveniently located just off the Expressway in Noida, is a luxurious residential township comprising 1,000 dwelling units. Designed in a configuration of low-rise and high-rise buildings, the unusual combination of structures with varied heights – from four to twenty-two storeys – manages to look like a single balanced and cohesive unit. This landmark project was completed more than a decade ago.

Curves in the landscape design on ground level as well as over the edifices' façade that tower above it, tie the project together harmoniously. This rhythmic design element is a welcome respite from boxes of housing units, piled one on top of the other in a monotonous manner that seemed to be ruling the skyline of NCR when Utopia was built in 2009. The Architects were able to break away from the norm by incorporating a curvature in the form – a concept alien at the time – and impart uniqueness to the façades.

The mix of different types of development of varying heights succeeded in dispelling any visual barriers whilst allowing breathing space in the design. Conceiving residences in a staggered formation increased the scope for open as well as semi-covered terraces in the design. The 'twisted' plans for residences, joined at a converging point, were able to provide space for vertical circulation as well. By placing residences in this manner, the Architects were able to orient and provide privacy to each inhabitant while also ensuring an unobstructed view of the surroundings.

Like waves of musical chords, the undulating forms flow seamlessly from one end of the site to the other. The difference in planning reflects as each tower (such as Noble Towers, Sylvian View, Emerald Heights and Olympia) rises with a unique form and contributes towards a distinct design character to the society.

The façades have been further accentuated keeping green building factors in mind – for instance, pergolas to regulate daylight. Curved partitions between residences maintain privacy. The buildings have a subtle beige palette painted across the elevations,

Facing page: *The undulating façade of the residential society is a striking feature of the project.*

Right: *A rendered Master Plan of the residential society.*

Above: *The duplex apartments look out towards the housing towers.*

and create a sense of unity in diversity between the different forms of the towers.

In the case of villas, the horizontal undulation seen on the apartment towers was remodelled by using a combination of two colours and adopting a curvilinear pattern on the façades.

For the benefit of residents, maximum amount of green space was accommodated between the different housing units, while providing them with vehicular accessibility throughout the site.

The entrance to the site is a grand opening with a refreshing landscape that welcomes the visitors. The residences open to green landscapes that lie predominantly between different towers and culminate into an expansive shared green space in the midst of the site. Pruned and trimmed shrubs line the edge of a water body, which is aligned to the centre of the entrance steps to the clubhouse. Placed on the entrance axis, the clubhouse is, thus, fronted by a meticulously landscaped avenue, lined with trees and semicovered sit-outs. It is replete with facilities such as a banquet hall, a health club, a gymnasium with spa and sauna, pool facilities, etc.

The design for the clubhouse fuses curves in its columns, mimicking the curvilinear form of the towers. The form of these columns emulates a blooming flower, introducing a natural element in the building's design. The structure is clad in curtain glazing,

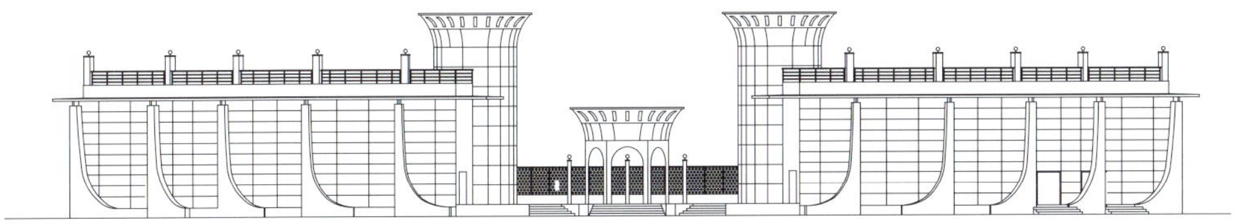

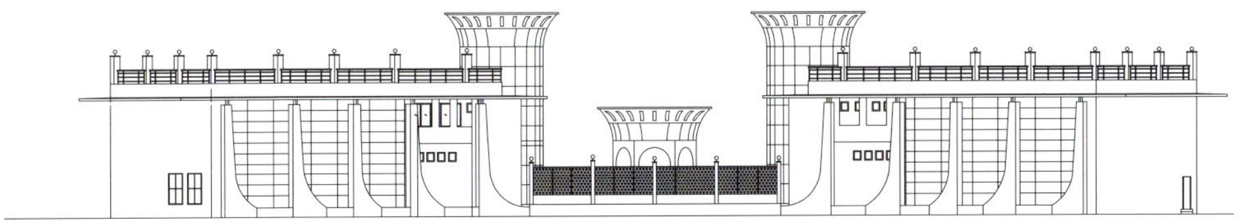

Top: *A rendered drawing of the ground-floor plan of Emerald Heights.*

Centre: *A drawing of the front façade of the clubhouse.*

Bottom: *A drawing of the rear elevation of the clubhouse.*

creating porosity between the exterior and interior spaces.

The rear side of the clubhouse has a pool for residents, landscaped with sit-outs and pergolas. Water bodies that adopt different shapes, have been dispersed across the site in order to micromanage the on-site temperature, while providing a variety of recreational areas for adults, youth and kids alike. An amphitheatre with steps (that double up as seats) going down to a stage, is the perfect place to organize activities, family functions as well as other celebrations for the residents.

There is a deliberate hierarchy of open spaces maintained with private gardens, children's areas and a central park, followed by the resort-like clubhouse with a swimming pool. The residential complex also consists of centrally air-conditioned apartments with a rooftop swimming pool.

Indeed, the entire township reflects a harmonious ensemble of built and softscape, creating an oasis of living that is utopian. Parking facilities are provided outside each of the individual blocks, making it conveniently accessible to residents.

The Palms

Location **Gurugram, Haryana** Site **10 acres** Built-up area **9,00,000 sq. ft.** Year of completion **2009**

***The colourful apex of the spires** etches its unique presence on Gurugram's skyline*

One of the first high-rise residential towers to be constructed in Gurugram, the harmony established by the combination of primary colours on the apex of The Palms has helped the soaring residential towers to be spotted from distance afar, enabling the project to etch a mark on the city's skyline.

Acknowledging the proximity of the site to the highway, dense landscape within and around the site helps cushion the towers from vehicular noise and movement. This approach also helps control energy loss from each residence and contributes towards a green design solution. The sheer height of the towers, which look far out on to the Aravalli range, enables residents to enjoy the best view while the protrusions on the façade ensure privacy between residences.

Keeping the benefit of residents in mind, the Architects planned each aspect of this compact space meticulously, down to the last detail. The circulation areas within the towers are lined with skylights on the roofs to create vibrant common spaces filled with sunlight. The Architects have broken the monotony of the rectangular site through colour-filled fauna and meandering curves of pavements.

A well-planned children's play area is an attractive feature within the site, encouraging outdoor activities for both kids and adults alike. Recreation facilities such as a pool and club are available for the residents, who have also been provided with surface and basement parking facilities, segregating vehicular movement within the site and allowing a safe pedestrian zone.

Below: *Soaring towers of the residential society surrounded by lush greenery.*

Heritage City

Location **Gurugram, Haryana** Site **24 acres** Built-up area **18,00,000 sq. ft.** Year of completion **1999**

A first-of-its-kind residential society ***infuses Persian art pattern*** *into the architectural landscape*

Situated on a sprawling 24 acres of land, the design for Heritage City, Gurugram, combines world-class luxury with a distinct architectural style.

A major advantage of Heritage City is its location. This Gurugram-based society is situated just opposite MG Road Metro Station. Additionally, it has the advantage of malls, shopping centres and healthcare facilities nearby. Some of them include the MGF Metropolitan Mall and Max Hospital. Furthermore, many attractions of Gurugram, like the Leisure Valley Park, Kingdom of Dreams and Cyber Hub, are in its vicinity.

The primary objective of the project was to design a housing complex on this vast irregular site, which allowed different towers to reflect distinct characters. The entire complex has been connected with an underlying design idea of juxtaposing art on architecture, and thus, building façades flaunt tiles with Persian art patterns. This thoughtful concept, for the first time ever, exhibited a playful demeanour on a residential society of a large scale. The harmonious variation in the heights of different towers is a visual imitation of the Aravalis in the background. Some of the apartments open to a central courtyard while some combine their core spaces (staircases, lift lobbies) to create a shared space on each floor for the residents. The eight towers comprise a total 1,200 residential units incorporating varied typology of apartments – 2, 3 and 4-BHK residences, with the built-up area ranging anywhere between 1,960 sq. ft. to 3,250 sq. ft. The project has buildings of heights varying between five to fourteen floors with extensive terraces, and is surrounded by exquisite landscaping.

The Architects ensured that the society was replete with greenscape within the site, and the earthiness of the buildings also suited the greenery around it. Wide open spaces and parks dominate the site – children along with adults find common spaces of recreation and interaction, creating a holistic environment for habitation. Facilities like a healthcare centre, a school and a shopping arcade have been accommodated within the residential complex.

Left: *The residential society infuses a harmonious concept of art in architecture.*

Krrish Provence Estate

Location **Gurugram, Haryana** Site **15 acres** Built-up area **15,00,000 sq. ft.** Year of completion **2019**

*Awarded as the **'Luxury Project of the Year 2019 – Residential' by ET NOW Real Estate Awards***

The project is a defining statement in luxury apartment housing in India. The site, measuring almost 16 acres, is located at the crossroads of Gurugram–Faridabad Highway and a major road running through South Delhi. The residential towers have been developed in a tranquil spot, nestled in the green belt of Aravallis, inspiring 'living amidst nature', and flanked by a 9-hole golf course on one side and farmhouses on the other.

The project uses environment-friendly and energy-efficient design technologies to conceptualize the residences, which comprise 3 and 5-BHK apartments ranging from 6,000 to 10,000 sq. ft. Smart planning of the residential towers enables 90 per cent of the site to dwell under greenscape, providing its residents with luscious and striking views. The configuration and alignment of each of the towers provide spectacular unobstructed views from each residence. With the landscape in focus, the towers are planned elegantly along a curvilinear axis, orienting the apartments to overlook the stunning vistas of the adjoining golf course and the Aravallis.

The Architects wanted to minimize the footprint of the built-up area. The building plans, inspired by the wings of an aeroplane deflecting strong winds, evolve into an aerodynamic shape. The homes are designed to utilize maximum amount of natural light and ventilation, which minimize the use of mechanical energy to maintain the indoor temperature. The façade adopts a modern and contemporary demeanour. The cladding combines the aesthetic of punctuated Aluminum Composite Panels (ACPs) with clear and transparent glass. The balconies are adorned with green sit-outs which act as sound buffers whilst adding a visual element of eco-conscious vertical architecture. The project introduces world-class facilities such as a personal gym, a private elevator and a plunge pool in the penthouse design. Each apartment has a pool and a private garden.

Another unique landscape feature is the introduction of a linear water body that flows along the towers' lowest floors. Vehicular access to the apartment buildings is from its rear end along a peripheral loop road, so that the interface between the buildings and the green is completely pedestrianized. The landscape also accommodates elements like playfields, swimming pool, gazebos and sit-out spaces.

Facing page: *A panoramic visualization of the estate.*

Below: *A drawing of the typical plan of the residential towers.*

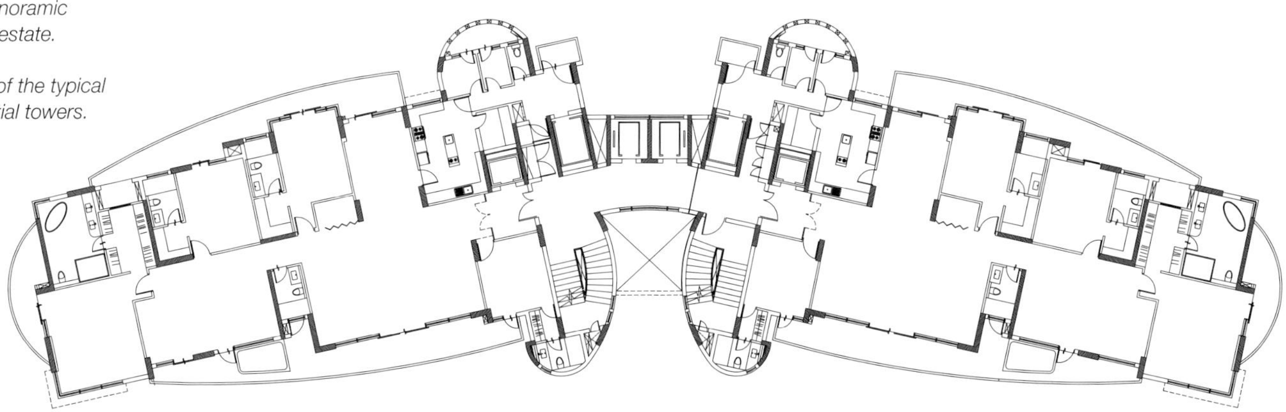

The Forest

Location **Noida, Uttar Pradesh** Site **6 acres** Built-up area **6,00,000 sq. ft.** Year of completion **2005**

***A gleaming rivulet reintroduces nature into the built footprint,** tying the towers through a seamless intervention*

An increased population density across the capital city led to an overload of development projects in the NCR. With a large volume of development taking place simultaneously, much of the housing designs failed to achieve a holistic design. Concerned with the lack of interaction between humans and their environment, the Architects conceptualized The Forest to reintegrate nature with the built environment, ensuring that a significant area of forest land remained untouched.

The project lies adjacent to over 300 acres of lush green forest area. The Master Plan is a congregation of seven towers harmoniously strung together via a rivulet, personifying pearls on a necklace. The design for the housing redefines luxury whilst allowing its residents to dwell in the lap of nature. Curvilinear forms, sweeping balconies and dramatic roofs create an eye-catching image along the Greater Noida Expressway. The Architects aimed to achieve a contemporary and futuristic architectural expression which reflects well in the undulating skyline of NCR.

Introducing innovation in residential design was kept at the core of design, following which the project became the first in the country to use ACP and glass on its façade. Unusually large balconies, glass elevators, central air-conditioning, private spas with each apartment and a 250 sq. ft. master toilet were all hitherto untouched concepts in India, witnessed for the first time in such a project.

The soaring conical turrets on the residential buildings create a distinctive form, alluding to the historical castles built at the edge of forests. The wavy outline of the buildings helps effectively control the light and wind coming into each apartment.

Each residence opens to expansive greenery on either side of the site. The penthouses are glass-clad and have a personal rooftop pool. A rivulet connects the different towers and integrates the exquisitely landscaped site with sunken courts and a state-of-the-art clubhouse with pool facilities. The rivulet is a reflection of the undulated design of the building floor plan and also helps in regulating temperature at micro level.

The Forest project design has received much praise and has been lauded for its trendsetting approach to luxurious living.

Facing page: *A view looking out to the front façade of the residential towers.*

Below: *An aerial view highlights the rivulet which flows throughout the site and binds the towers into a single ensemble.*

Silver Arch Apartments

Location **New Delhi** Site **2 acres** Built-up area **1,00,000 sq. ft.** Year of completion **1996**

The opulent ***apartments take inspiration from Persian art*** *and design sensibilities, exhibiting a striking presence*

Located along the well-known Feroze Shah Road in posh Lutyens' Zone of New Delhi, the design for Silver Arch Apartments was conceptualized to reflect an iconic residential complex. It introduced a stepped form, scooping out terraces at different levels, exposing its residents to wondrous views of luscious tree-lined avenues of Lutyens' Delhi. The extravagantly laid out, Persian art inspired mosaic work was a first-of-its-kind façade treatment to be conceptualized for a residential project in the capital city.

The building has forty-eight luxury apartments that can be accessed by glass elevators. The residences face outwards, providing each apartment with natural light and striking surrounding views. The buildings share a common courtyard, which can be entered from each cardinal direction, leading to a water body surrounding a skylight for the basement, at the intersecting junction. The towers rise up to seven floors including a stilt level. A curving wall separator maintains privacy for the residents' balconies, located on the same floor. The stepped form of the façade is complemented by and accommodates square pergola-like elements on the edges of residences, exhibiting Persian blue tile work.

Influence of the Persian style of art and architecture is translated from the buildings and onto the landscape. The apartment complex is surrounded by intimate gardens with balconies and sit-out spaces, consonant with the quiet and serene environment of the society's location. Upon entering the common courtyard, one is left stunned by magnificence of the mosaic artwork adorning the interior façade of the courtyards, well supported by walls and columns inside.

A curvilinear water body flows in the courtyard, effortlessly meandering through the landscape and creating shared spaces for the residents, thereby facilitating social encounters. Smaller shrubs are lined in the interior courtyard while dense trees line the periphery of the complex. An underground basement and stilt level have been provided within the site to accommodate parking.

Facing page left: *Watercolour illustration of the mosaic tile pattern.*

Facing page right: *Interior courtyard highlights the Persian art inspired mosaic work.*

Below: *Entrance of the apartment complex displays an imposing character of the residences.*

Aradhana Apartments (Burmah-Shell)

Location **New Delhi** Site **15 acres** Built-up area **7,00,000 sq. ft.** Year of completion **1990**

The exquisitely designed robust residential apartments ***exude an earthy character,*** *nestled in the posh area of R.K. Puram*

Aradhana Apartments is strategically located at the edge of the erstwhile diplomatic area of Chanakyapuri. Nestled in a dense cover of green, it comprises an exquisitely designed residential complex with plotted development and a premium tower with thirty-six apartments.

The buildings use brick and mortar, leaving the walls exposed on the exterior and in synchronization with the city's climate. The Architects achieved a unique distinction of employing brick as the primary and only material for construction as well as for design detail. Brick *jaalis*, balcony railings, terrace parapets, perforation designs on the club's façade etc., were all achieved using brick as the primary material.

The concise tower arrangement yet adequately spaced apartments make for an iconic design in contrast to the contemporary residential designs at the time. The brick clad buildings are hard to miss in the vast landscape, and have elevations designed in a typical façade with semicircular openings.

Eloquent bulges and curves on the apartments gracefully lead an onlooker's sight. The flats are outwardly planned, wherein each residence has an extensive balcony area, and are separated by arched partitions to maintain privacy whilst providing outdoor spaces for every flat.

The two top floors have been designed as terrace landscaped duplex penthouses. Common areas for vertical circulation (lift lobby and stairwell areas) have been provided with large windows for effective ventilation and to allow natural light to penetrate inside. The interiors have been crafted carefully with adequate number of window openings, flushing the spaces with daylight.

The extensively landscaped complex has a luxurious clubhouse, located at the rear side. The project exudes architectural finesse and structural prowess. Typical semicircular window elements became synonymous with the apartments' design. The building towers, due to their curved edges, look much more rooted to the ground. This gives a feeling of horizontal expansion on the site which is able to camouflage the apartments well in the lush and dense green cover around the site.

Below: *Magnificent brick façade of the apartments with striking semicircular openings.*

IFFCO Township

Location **Aonla (near Bareilly), Uttar Pradesh** Site **500 acres** Built-up area **12,00,000 sq. ft.** Year of completion **1985**

Spread over a large area of 500 acres, the project was ***planned and designed to accommodate different residential typologies*** *– a stadium, a clubhouse, etc., with unprecdented skill*

Master Plan for the township of Aonla, near Bareilly, is spread over 500 acres. The design includes housing for all categories of staff, ranging from 600 sq. ft. for lower staff, to 2,500 sq. ft. for the highest authorities.

The layout has been designed and planned in a way that has resulted in creation of different community neighbourhoods with clusters of twelve to sixteen units around an open space. Facilities for shopping, school, club, community centres, health centre and stadium are provided within the township.

The planning layout condenses public amenities, such as community centre, health centre, stadium, amphitheatre, shopping complex, etc., in the centre of the site while residences are placed looking outward. This allows residents to have a thriving social life and at the same time enjoy repose. Designing residences around a central courtyard also keeps interiors cool in summers with filtered daylight. By imbibing a colourful character on the façade, the Architects were able to execute a design for a housing complex which was both innovative and playful. The irregular patterns on the faces of the buildings are able to provide a distinct character to the township.

The tone of the building materials used helps to camouflage the buildings with the dense surrounding greens. The township allowed an opportunity for the Architects to gauge its different verticals (Architectural Design, Master Planning, Structural Engineering, Project Management, MEP [Mechanical, Electrical and Plumbing] Engineering and Interiors, etc.) to come together and create a landmark project.

Below: *Community centre of the township.*

Model Town Residential Redevelopment

Location **New Delhi** Site **25 acres** Built-up area **35,00,000 sq. ft.** Year of completion **Ongoing**

A design and planning proposal to redevelop one of the oldest colonies in the capital city by ***infusing principles of a smart city into its fabric***

Model Town is a well-known residential locality in North Delhi, adjacent to the famed Civil Lines and developed in the 1950s. The proposal envisages creation of a self-sufficient smart township with a Floor Area Ratio/Floor Space Index (FAR/FSI) of 4, resulting in a high density, high-rise development. Using a holistic form of urban development, it caters to different demographics of population – a leisure park for senior citizens, children's play area, affordable living spaces for entrepreneurs, etc.

Planned and designed as a township, it is replete with facilities such as a hospital, primary and secondary schools, an independent shopping centre, club and banquet. The roof-scape of the soaring residential towers opens up to the skywalks joining buildings. Fusion of art and architecture has led to a creative perspective in expression and it has been graciously used to create healing spaces.

Below: *A visualization from the top, highlighting the landscaped courtyard.*

Parsvnath Prideasia

Location **Chandigarh** Site **125 acres** Built-up area **30,00,000 sq. ft.**

The magnificent township ***reinvents living through low-rise housing design and a one-of-its-kind glass pyramid club***

The Master Plan of Chandigarh – brainchild of the legendary architect, Le Corbusier – marks wide, tree-lined avenues and quiet and meticulously segregated neighbourhood sectors. Over the years, however, Chandigarh has reinvented itself as it grows into a large metropolitan city. In such rapidly changing times, Prideasia seeks to reinterpret the way of living by allowing residents to dwell in the lap of luxury.

With all the elements that shape an integrated and holistic living environment, such as retail outlets, offices, club, health centre, school, etc., Prideasia is a microcosm of a city. The unique township is designed to define a new paradigm in sustainable living. The different typologies of residences brew a culture of residents from different social and economic backgrounds.

The township thrives on social engagement; this allowed the Architects to curate the landscape in a structured yet playful manner. The landscape has been designed in a way that encourages inclusivity amongst different age group residents, creating a holistic ecosystem. This low-rise development, where the entire township is planned within a height limit of 15 metres, has a unique landscape spine running a length of almost a kilometre uninterrupted by any vehicular traffic. The design of the linear axial lane at the entrance is laid out exquisitely, capturing one's attention as they traverse the site. The apartments are planned to allow maximum light and air with expansive balconies enveloping large glass-clad façades, offering stunning views of the Shivalik mountains and the picturesque Sukhna Lake.

The use of a subdued palette of building material for residences highlights the variety of flora used across the project. Surface parking has been provided adjacent to each residential block, easing access for the residents while restricting the vehicular movement at the centre, encouraging a healthy lifestyle.

Above: *A visualization from the grand entrance of the complex.*

HRRL Township

Location **Barmer, Rajasthan** Site **247 acres** Built up area: **21,00,000 sq. ft.** Year of completion **Ongoing**

Awarded the prestigious national ***HUDCO Design Award 2020 for 'New and Innovative Town Design Solutions/Eco Cities'***

The project, won through a national design competition, is a self-sufficient township for the employees of Hindustan Petroleum Corporation Limited (HPCL), a major Indian oil company. A joint venture company, between HPCL and Government of Rajasthan, the HRRL township is located in the interiors of Thar Desert, adjacent to an upcoming oil refinery of HPCL.

The Architects sought to change the image of a dry and parched Rajasthan and to equip the people of the region with a smart and sustainable township with a focus on water conservation and management.

The form and layout of the township sought inspiration from a *johad* (an oasis). The true meaning of that in desert environment is 'an isolated area of desert vegetation, typically surrounding a water source which provides a protected habitat for flora and fauna including humans'. A water body, meandering through the landscape, culminates in a central lake at one end and in a central oasis park on the other.

The planning for the project inspired an inward looking layout, accommodating a dense buffer throughout the periphery. The township comprises various sizes of residences, a township office, dwelling units for the Central Industrial Security Force (CISF), a shopping complex, an *Anganwadi*, a clubhouse, an auditorium, etc.

For an arid region such as Barmer, the Architects took inspiration from the surrounding urban fabric and proposed juxtaposing contemporary design aesthetics over local construction methodologies. A deep understanding of the climatological influence has been an important aspect for the Architects, who have ensured the design is able to passively regulate temperature in the interiors whilst flushing the area with maximum light. Architectural elements such as *chhatris* (canopy), *jaalis* (lattices), *jharokhas* (overhanging enclosed balconies), *aangans* (courtyards), *nukkads* (developing street corners as recreation spaces), etc., streamlined the conceptualization, integrating the vernacular into a modern, twenty-first century township.

Earthy tones of materials, such as mud and natural stone, were easy picks for their properties to quickly adapt to the dry region. The planning around *aangans,* provision of a thriving water body in the midst of the site, dense green buffers created by orienting the buildings in cardinal directions, controlling heat absorption by the texture of material surfaces and the low height of buildings have made the township a sustainable reality.

The project thrives as a regeneration model – one which revives the parched region whilst using vernacular design techniques.

Facing page: *A bird's eye visualization showing the entire expanse of the project.*

Above: *A perspective visualization of a type of residential quarters.*

Indian Foreign Services Apartments

Location **New Delhi** Site **3.5 acres** Built-up area **3,00,000 sq. ft.** Year of completion **1985**

Helming the settlements developed in East Delhi, ***the semicircular window arches provide a distinct identity*** *to the society*

A fine example of exposed brickwork in high-rise buildings, incorporating green design features that, thirty-five years later, have now become a popular concept in India.

Being adjacent to the Yamuna, the cost-conscious design has done away with basement to obviate the risk of high groundwater. Adequate parking has been provided in stilts and site periphery, creating a large, vehicle-free recreational area.

The complex houses a total of 210 units across five towers of eight floors each. Each tower conjoins three U-shaped buildings looking outwards and sharing a common vertical circulation area or stairwell. The buildings exude a sense of earthiness with extended beams supporting sweeping arched corridors and visual screens. The balconies are flanked by angular walls to provide residents with a better view. The cavity wall construction of the inner walls (two-layer sandwich panels with air gaps as heat insulation) reduce energy loads.

Below: *A view from the green courtyard, overlooking the apartments.*

Redevelopment of Air India Colony

Location **New Delhi** Site **30 acres** Built-up area **38,80,000 sq. ft.** Year of completion **Ongoing**

A unique concept to redevelop a land parcel for the country's flagship airline, *the design upgrades and uplifts the residential experience*

Air India, the country's flagship airline company owned by the government, has embarked on a process of financial restructuring which includes the redevelopment of its flagship real estate land parcel. The location is in, what is arguably the poshest residential neighbourhood of Vasant Vihar in Delhi. The project involves redeveloping this complex into a self-sustained, state-of-the-art residential township of around 2,000 apartments. As per local planning norms, the redevelopment includes a school, a health centre, the creation of a Grade A high-end commercial complex with a few luxury boutiques, an integrated food and beverage (F&B) destination as well as an office complex. These offices are designed to be leased as embassies or consular offices for various diplomatic missions.

The design responds to the specifications of the site that includes preservation of large trees on the site and limited basements due to its rocky nature which restricts excessive excavation. The greatest challenge was to create high density development which utilizes the high FAR of 3.5 while creating abundant open spaces for the landscape. All this had to be achieved within a short height limit of 26 metres due to the proximity of the airport and the land falling in the flight's path.

Below: *A bird's eye visualization of the entire site of the project.*

Parsvnath Planet

Location **Lucknow, Uttar Pradesh** Site **10 acres** Built-up area **10,00,000 sq. ft.** Year of completion **2010**

The project follows mixed-use housing, creating a ***state-of-the-art residential design development***

Lucknow's stature as a Smart City generated a significant influx from neighbouring states. It is to cater to the residential needs of this population that Parsvnath Planet has been conceptualized. The luxurious mixed-use project comprises 3 and 4-BHK, centrally air-conditioned apartments. Some of the amenities available here include a shopping mall, a clubhouse and indoor and outdoor sports facilities (gymnasium along with pool facilities).

The location of the project is well-planned: Gomti Nagar Railway Station is 2 km away, while the immediate neighbourhood is replete with healthcare, leisure and institutional facilities. The project also includes the design of a four-star hotel with eighty rooms and has been designed to be an 'inward looking' residential development.

The Architects aligned the buildings in a crescent form. This planning also helped in ensuring that each residence receives adequate amount of daylight and is ventilated properly. The residents are able to enjoy privacy and security since the towers do not overlap. Due to a concise site space, the Architects proposed high-rise towers. A dense tree line marks the boundary of the site, cutting it off visually from the surrounding areas. All vehicular movement is restricted to the peripheral road so that the interiors of the site are pedestrian-friendly. The residents are able to enjoy luscious and refreshing views of the central landscape, a hub of all social and cultural activities. The apartment towers are also interlinked with connecting bridges, easing accessibility. The landscape design introduces levels, gazebos, pergolas, etc., in its landscape to create a lively surrounding for kids and adults alike to interact and socialize in.

With a meticulously planned site, the residents enjoy lavish views of the surrounding landscape and are also provided with spacious interiors. The presence of green spaces is an efficient tool to encourage social interactions, one which the Architects have thoughtfully accommodated in the design. The provision of retail and commercial facilities within the residential site allows people to enjoy the perks of a mixed-use development.

Left: *A view from the central courtyard of the housing society.*

Kasturba Nagar Housing Redevelopment

Location **New Delhi** Site **53 acres** Built-up area **75,00,000 sq. ft.** Year of completion **Ongoing**

The mega-scale redevelopment was ***awarded to the Architects through a national competition,*** *organized by Central Public Works Department (CPWD)*

With land being a scarce resource, the mega-scale redevelopment of the General Pool Residential Accommodation (GPRA) Colony at Kasturba Nagar, New Delhi, seeks to redefine the residential experience. The project was awarded to the Architects through a national competition, organized by CPWD.

The site is situated in the heart of South Delhi. Spread over a massive area of 53 acres, the Architects sought to achieve a futuristic housing development model: a harmonious amalgamation of 'Smart' and 'Sustainable' ideologies. An example of integrated holistic living, the sustainable community, with a built-up area of 75 lakh sq. ft., is designed for 20,000 residents, with over seventy residential towers gracing the skyline of Delhi in a colour-filled ensemble. This self-contained society boasts of community facilities such as offices, retail, healthcare, primary and secondary schools. An extensive pedestrian experience and a green spine give a distinct identity to this development, which would also accommodate parking for over 6,300 vehicles, spread across the site, and over two levels of basement. The project helms as a one-of-its-kind, mega-urban housing development in the midst of the city.

Above: *A visualization looking out to the apartments.*

Below: *A rendered Master Plan of the project.*

An aerial visualization showcasing the complete project site.

Facing page above: *A visualization of one of the types of residential cottages in the project.*

Facing page below: *A rendered Master Plan of the site also showcasing different typologies of residences planned in the project.*

Tata Housing Myst

Location **Kasauli, Himachal Pradesh** Site **22 acres** Built-up area **12,00,000 sq. ft.** Year of completion **Ongoing**

The design of the housing ***sculpts the mountainous site at Kasauli*** *whilst creating an elegant residential ensemble*

The ideal location of the TATA Myst Housing allowed the Architects an opportunity of ideating a tranquil retreat space. Well placed in Kasauli, the site rests on a cliffside, surrounded by a dense forest of soaring pine trees and looking out on to the snow covered majestic Himalayan range. The Architects sought to preserve these exquisite and pristine views and took an eco-conscious design approach.

The housing uses contour as a significant aspect in the overall design, seamlessly adapting to the undulating form of the surrounding mountains. With minimal amount of cutting and filling at the site, the design prevents land pollution and adopts the contours within the residences' design to create levels. A road traversing through one end of the site to the other becomes the primary path of circulation. This restricts vehicular movement around the site and allows more freedom for pedestrian movement. The highlight of the residential complex is a lavish club located at the centre. Its design is such that it is able to function as a connecting element, becoming a shared space between residences, from the highest point of the site to the lowest.

For the Architects, the project posed the challenge of reviving a vernacular sense of design whilst providing high-end, luxury living.

Logix Blossoms Green

Location **Noida, Uttar Pradesh** Site **25 acres** Built-up area **25,00,000 sq. ft.** Year of completion **2019**

***Planned to accommodate 2,300 residents**, the design attempts to create a self-contained, sustainable high-rise residential development*

The design for Logix Group's ambitious project is a harmonious understanding of providing holistic spaces for residences in the concrete urban jungle in and around Delhi. The complex, located in Sector 143, Noida, has been designed to have 2, 3 and 4-BHK apartments. More than 70 per cent of the total site is open, creating an enormous area of thriving greenscape.

The site planning ties the built and unbuilt landscape as a harmonious unit. This orients each tower away from the other whilst allowing a clear unobstructive view of its surroundings. A vertical undulation on the façade of the towers allows privacy for its residents.

The verticality of twenty-two towers is balanced by horizontal connecting bridges, creating shared recreation spaces for residents on higher floors along with easing access from one tower to another. Use of a subtle combination of colours on the façades adds lightness to the overall outlook of the development, and the use of earthy tones subtly enlivens the environment. A state-of-the-art clubhouse provides facilities such as an outdoor swimming pool, a gym, and courts for tennis, basketball and other sports.

For the Architects, it was important to be able to provide airy and naturally lit interior spaces, achieved through careful apartment planning.

Above: *A view from the central courtyard looking out to the soaring residential towers.*

Concentrating the design on a concise footprint meant a vibrant and flourishing green landscape. This gesture elevates the project from being just another residential development to an interactive, vibrant and meaningful habitat.

Ibiza Town

Location **Surajkund, Haryana** Site **10 acres** Built-up area **12,00,000 sq. ft.** Year of completion **2019**

***Imbibing Spanish architectural elements**, the design for the residential society results in a modern yet sustainable ensemble*

On the state highway connecting Delhi with Haryana lies the prime locality of Surajkund, which in the past few decades has witnessed significant real estate growth. Ibiza Town is situated on a land parcel in this prominent area.

Inspired by the rugged landscape of the site, and with a rocky outcrop emerging from the reddish soil and wild foliage of the surrounding *Keekar* trees, the design reflects the Client's desire of recreating the experience of the Spanish town of Ibiza. The landscape also played a significant role as the building design is based on the real estate need of maximizing the built-up area and creating luxury housing towers.

Complementing the landscape of arrival courts, plazas, Mediterranean orchards, gardens and play courts is the distinct architecture of the towers. The seven residential towers, each twenty-one storeys high, have been carefully planned as linear blocks to accentuate their verticality as they become distinct icons in the skyline of the city. Further, with minimal ornamentation and clean façade design, the configuration allows maximum light to flow through each apartment and also ensures their adequate ventilation.

Even from afar, the gleaming white towers with a stucco façade appearance and an architectural vocabulary replete with Mediterranean elements of red clay tiled roofs, with cast iron balustrades, lend a fresh approach to multi-family housing, which is otherwise not visible. The society is replete with exquisite landscape elements such as semi-covered sit-out areas around a linear water body leading to the creation of boulevards and avenues. The interiors are flushed with natural light due to the expansive window façades, furnished with high-end luxury products. The boisterous height of the towers provides the residences with views of distant green landscape.

Left: *A visualization from the entrance of the housing society.*

Vasant Vihar Residence

Location **New Delhi** Site **0.1 acres** Built-up area **10,000 sq. ft.** Year of completion **2015**

A private residence that reflects ***seamless integration of art and vernacular design*** *sensibilities*

Clad in white rough granite imported from Japan, the home of architect Dikshu C. Kukreja and his wife Arunima is an interesting example of contemporary architecture juxtaposed with art installations – where each one speaks eloquently to the other. The straight and clean lines of the façade have been broken by the undulating texture rendered through a stainless steel sculpture, conceived by the architect along with the sculptor, Vishal Dhar. The sculpture exhibits linearity of the leaves of the bamboo planted in the garden, which seem to have escaped through the bushes and sealed themselves on the building, providing it with sensuality and lightness of being, apart from acting as a screen to filter out the south-east sun.

The piece de resistance of the built structure is the grand flight of granite steps that lead one to the entrance of the house, which is flanked by walls clad in quarry cut stone that rise up to a height of 40 feet, creating an impression of mystery, awe and space. Here again, at the landing, is seen another magnificent sculpture – this one by Radha Krishnan – interwoven into the stone. It has the sculptor's alter egos, *Musui* and *Maiya*, welcoming guests with fruits.

During the day, the interior spaces of the house are suffused with sunlight pouring in from all directions, especially through the 30-feet high glass ceiling of the atrium, from where the sunlight streams down on the stainless steel sculptures,

Facing page: *Clad in white rough granite, the residence encapsulates a sustainable design in a modern structure.*

Below: *At the entrance wall is a sculpture by Radha Krishnan, interwoven into the stone – it has the sculptor's alter egos, Musui and Maiya, welcoming guests with fruits.*

Right: *A grand staircase leading up to the entrance is flanked by walls clad in quarry cut stone rising up to a height of 40 feet.*

Facing page above: *Straight and clean lines of the façade are broken by the undulating texture achieved through a stainless steel sculpture.*

Facing page below: *Through high ceilings and an open to sky atrium, natural light flushes the interiors of the residence, elevating the living experience for the hosts.*

called Star Constellation, by contemporary Indian artist, Subodh Gupta. The five-storeyed house has ceilings that scale a height of 14 feet. The idea was to bring nature and greenery into the interiors and blur the boundaries defining the spaces.

Though the house is built on stilts, one does not get the impression of it being a stilt house owing to the 10-metre wide grand staircase reaching up to the first floor. The garden is perched on the first floor, giving the house a peculiar evergreen look. Due to its strategic location, it frames the canopies of trees like *Bargad, Neem, Ashoka* and *Peepal*. Yet again, one sees an interplay of nature with the interiors, rendering an 'inside-outside' feel. The wooden cladding on the elevator façade has been created as a sculptural feature, lending it a whimsical experience.

While the first floor is solely for the guests, the second and third floors have the family's private quarters, housing bedrooms (master bedroom as well as bedrooms for children) and a gymnasium. The basement is designed for recreation.

The glass balconies with their glass floors add a quiet dimension without obstructing the flow of the rough granite and steel sculpture on the façade of the building. The courtyard created in the basement has white stone going upto a height of 22 feet, giving a feel of cascading water due to the interplay of sunlight on the rough texlure of the stone. The windows of the courtyard with a height of 10 feet allow plenty of natural light to infuse the interiors of the basement, allowing an interplay of volume, light and space. But what stands out is their sensibility in ensuring that the spaces they have created are comfortable and homely.

FOREST Spa
OMAXE

Forest Spa

Location **Noida, Uttar Pradesh** Site **30 acres** Built-up area **15,00,000 sq. ft.** Year of completion **2011**

Curvaceous and bean-shaped, *the unique form of the towers creates a climate responsive design*

The Forest Spa is a unique project which had fascinating contradictions for architectural design to respond to. Firstly, it was a site which abutted a busy expressway on one side and a tranquil forest on the other. Secondly, the developers' desire was to create exclusive and privacy driven apartments in an area surrounded by many residential towers.

The Architects took all these varying conditions into the consideration of their creative process and the result is a built form which is unique in its design – three unique and exclusive twirling towers, soft and curvaceous in form. Due to a successful combination of well thought-out orientation of the towers and the arcuate outlined residential façades, the residents enjoy unobstructed views of the surrounding luscious landscape without compromising their privacy. The apartments, ranging from 4,000–8,000 sq. ft., are completely encircled by balconies that offer openness and a slice of nature to each resident. The façade is wrapped in glazing, which is shaded by the balconies, and yet blends the indoors with the outside, offering panoramic views. The twenty-storeyed towers are curiously shaped as beans, where the centre forms the circulation core.

The landscape completes the 'spa' atmosphere with a large meandering pool, a 30,000 sq. ft. club and a series of outdoor spaces, which carry one's experience away from the noise of the city into a peaceful, tranquil zone – exactly what one looks for in the peace of one's home. The extravagant pool area is furnished with seating and lounging facilities, buffered well with dense trees around.

Through this design, the Architects have been able to achieve a balanced society – one which meets the aspirations of the modern-day residents within the hustle-bustle and fast pace of the city. Adding to this endeavour is the preservation of a dense green belt surrounding the site, providing the residents with an actual forest-like experience.

Facing page: *The curvy forms of the apartments ensure exquisite views to every apartment in the society.*

Above: *The presence of a water body within the society maintains the microclimate and keeps the residences naturally cool.*

India's first transit-oriented development with the country's tallest 100-storeyed tower as a mixed-use residential development.

Complete Listing of Housing Projects

Krrish Provence Estate, Gurugram, Haryana
A condominium project comprising 3 and 5-BHK flats ranging between 6,000 to 10,000 sq. ft. Each apartment is embellished with a private pool and a garden. Premium penthouses have private elevators.

Township for Indian Farmers Fertilizer Cooperative Limited, Kandla, Gujarat
The project has 750 residential units of various typologies. Public buildings such as a club, a school, a community centre, a guest house, a post office, a hospital, etc., and external development such as roads, storm water drains, sewage treatment plant, lighting and landscape are well-planned and meticulously executed.

Krrish Montaigne, Gurugram, Haryana
With 3 and 4-BHK and duplex apartments, the residential complex is planned around a central pool and features vertical landscaping. The residents are exposed to the best luxury housing experience whilst being surrounded with natural scenic views.

Air Force and Naval Officers' Housing, Navi Mumbai, Maharashtra
Housing for officers of the Indian Air Force and Navy, it consists of 550 apartments laid out in eighteen-storey towers that are enveloped in lush green landscape. Each tower is designed to maximize the use of light and ventilation, regulating comfort for residents.

Township for Indian Farmers Fertilizer Cooperative Limited, Aonla, Uttar Pradesh
The township consists of about 1,200 dwelling units of various types. It includes public buildings such as a school, a bank, a club, a shopping centre, a post office, a police station, a guest house with thirty rooms, trainee hostel for seventy-five trainees, a community hall, a maintenance and estate office, a substation, a demonstration farm and an external development.

Ghaziabad Development Authority (GDA) Luxury Apartments, Ghaziabad, Uttar Pradesh
The complex has an ITC Group hotel located on the 150-acre land on the outskirts of Delhi. The project provides facilities such as centrally air-conditioned luxurious apartments, exclusive villas, schools, a shopping mall, a club and an entertainment centre.

Senior Diplomat Housing, US Embassy, New Delhi
The housing for senior diplomats of the US Embassy is located within the embassy premises in Delhi. The project involved renovation and refurbishing of townhouses as per modern international specifications.

Ambassador's Residence, European Union, New Delhi
The new residence of the ambassador of the European Union was designed to be located on Sardar Patel Marg near the Diplomatic Enclave.

Ibiza Town, Surajkund, Haryana
This luxury housing project has 3 and 4-BHK units and is designed on the lines of contemporary Spanish architecture. Located on the Delhi–Faridabad Highway, it has a range of exclusive facilities for its residents.

Bakshi Apartments, Lucknow, Uttar Pradesh
The apartments have been designed for Unitech Limited. They have an eight-storey tower with forty-eight units and a three-storey block with walk-up units.

Housing Complex for Regional Provident Fund Commission, Jabalpur, Madhya Pradesh
Buildings of the housing complex, which has fifty-six dwelling units, have been designed in a way that ensures the spaces are flushed with light and air.

Krrish Florence Tower, Gurugram, Haryana
The 15-acre development comprises 3-BHK units and is located in Sector 70. The project has towers ranging from twenty-five to thirty storeys. Other facilities of the development include a clubhouse, a shopping mall, multilevel car parking and school.

Monde De Provence – Adani Realty, Gurugram, Haryana
The high-end residential apartment complex has flats ranging from 5,200 sq. ft. to 15,000 sq. ft. The development has resort-like facilities and a revolutionary clubhouse.

Unitech Sun Breeze Apartments, Ghaziabad, Uttar Pradesh
With 160 dwelling units, the project has two fourteen-storey blocks planned around a centrally landscaped area with a swimming pool and a health club.

Housing for Economically Weaker Sections (EWS), Ghaziabad, Uttar Pradesh
Promoted by the GDA, a 2,000 units complex was designed to house the economically weaker sections of society and provide its residents with a well-designed house at a reasonable cost.

Township for Heavy Water Project, Department of Atomic Energy, Manuguru, Telangana
Stage I of the 250-acre township development had

2,000 dwelling units and facilities such as schools, a public infrastructure hospital, a club, a shopping centre and a community centre. Stage II had an additional 4,000 dwelling units.

Township for Nagarjuna Fertilizers and Chemicals Limited, Andhra Pradesh
Designed to have 700 residential units and public infrastructure like a hospital, schools, bank, a shopping centre, post office, a club, a swimming pool, a police station, a guest house, a community hall, maintenance/estate office, an electric substation, and a demonstration farm and development work.

Township for Indian Farmers Fertilizer Cooperative Limited, Phulpur, Uttar Pradesh
The 100-acre project has nearly 750 residential units spanning different typologies. Public buildings such as a guest house, a school, a post office, a bank and a club have also been incorporated in the planning of the township.

1000 Trees, Gurugram, Haryana
Situated in Sector 105, Sohna, Gurugram, the housing project is designed on an area of 10 acres and consists of 800 apartments of 1 and 2-BHK units. The protrusions on the façade are a unique feature for the towers.

Callidora, Gurugram, Haryana
Located in Sector 73, Gurugram, and designed for Today Homes, the project on a 10-acre plot has various types of apartments in multistoreyed towers. The uniformity in façade design is maintained to keep the towers more functional.

Dankuni Coal Complex Township for Coal India Limited, West Bengal
The township is planned for the staff and executives of Coal India Limited. It has expansive housing and all associated facilities incorporated in the design.

Krishak Bharati Cooperative Limited (KRIBHCO) Township, Hazira, Gujarat
This 100-acre township was conceptualized for the largest fertilizer project in Asia. There are 1,200 dwelling units, a training centre, hostels for 200 engineering trainees, a club, a guest house, a shopping complex, a community centre, etc. Complete land development with an independent water supply and well-planned sewerage disposal networks are the highlights of the project.

Associated Cement Companies (ACC) Township, Gagal, Himachal Pradesh
The scope for the project included preparation of the Master Plan and design of different dwelling units. These included the junior and senior staff quarters, two-room tenements housing type, a club, a bank, a police outpost as well as design of a 12-bed hospital with all modern amenities.

Friends Colony Luxury Apartments, New Delhi
An exclusive apartment complex, with independent low-rise buildings and walk-up apartments, it is nestled in the southern side of the city.

Eldeco Ananda, Noida, Uttar Pradesh
Premium-end housing complex with seventy-two flats, a private swimming pool and a health club, the project is designed in a cascade form with eighteen penthouses lined with terrace gardens. It is located in Sector 48, Noida.

Township for Western Coal Fields, Durgapur, West Bengal
The 150-acre township consists of 2,000 dwelling units and infrastructural facilities, replete with basic facilities, such as water treatment and sewerage.

Maruti Udyog Township, Sohna, Haryana
The design for the township consists of 1,500 dwelling units on a plot of 100 acres. It is essentially a low-rise development providing full infrastructural facilities for the residents.

Orange County, Indirapuram, Uttar Pradesh
Spread over an area of 10 acres, Orange County presents the idea of residential living which is luxurious as well as affordable in nature. This residential development is a mix of 2 and 3-BHK apartments and penthouses.

SARE Spring View Heights, Ghaziabad, Uttar Pradesh
The multistoreyed towers are arranged linearly on a plot area of 5.5 acres and have 2 and 3-BHK units. The elegant residential complex is uniquely planned around a landscaped podium in order to avoid extensive costs of basements on a soft soil condition.

Apartments for National Insurance Company, New Delhi
The complex comprises 278 dwelling units built in five clusters of four-storeyed blocks and one tower. The three categories of flats have areas of 750 sq. ft., 1,100 sq. ft. and 1,300 sq. ft. of built-up areas, respectively.

Gauri Sadan, New Delhi
This is a luxurious, high-end apartment complex designed near Connaught Place for Ansal Properties Limited. The complex with sixty apartments has a rooftop swimming pool. The apartment is located on plot number 5, Hailey Road.

Apartments for Vasant Group Housing, New Delhi
The complex is planned in four-storeyed buildings and eight dwelling units. Low-rise demeanour buildings are set amidst a lush landscaped area.

Apartments at Prithviraj Road, New Delhi
Exclusive high-end residential apartments designed along the prime area of Prithviraj Road, with Spanish Embassy and residence of the former President of India as its neighbours.

Indian Foreign Services (IFS) Group Housing, New Delhi
Located in Mayur Vihar, the 210 dwelling units for senior officers of the Indian Foreign Service have been built in five eight-storeyed blocks. All the external walls of the apartments are constructed as two layer sandwich panels, with air gap as heat insulation.

Township for GAIL, Vijaipur, Madhya Pradesh
A new 400-acre township for GAIL has about 600 dwelling units of various typologies designed. Other buildings included in the development are a guest house, a shopping complex, a club, a community centre and a higher secondary school.

Township for Gas Authority of India Limited (GAIL), Auraiya, Uttar Pradesh
Placed adjacent to the massive Gas Processing facilities of GAIL, the township is planned on a 3,000-acre site. It has been designed in four sectors with distinctive phasing of facilities. Complete infrastructural amenities are provided to create a self-contained township. It has been designed in association with Raj Rewal and Associates.

Eldeco Casa Italia, Sonepat, Haryana
An integrated residential township designed on a site of 100 acres comprising plotted development, group housing, schools, a hospital and a clubhouse.

Housing Complex for GAIL, Noida, Uttar Pradesh
The complex is planned on a 6.5-acre plot. It comprises four categories of units with built-up areas ranging from 600 to 1,500 sq. ft.

Uppal's Plumeria, Lucknow, Uttar Pradesh
A 20-acre of mixed-use project with a built-up area of 25 lakh sq. ft., the project comprises of 2 and 3-BHK flats planned in fourteen to eighteen storey towers. There is also a large 6-acre landscaped central park. Other facilities include a mall-office complex, an entertainment centre and a four-star hotel.

Unitech South City Heights, Gurugram, Haryana
A twelve-storeyed residential building with a cascade form creating private terrace gardens. The building, with 130 apartments, is set amidst lush landscaping.

Unitech South City, Gurugram, Haryana
With its first phase spread over an area of approximately 350 acres, South City near Gurguram, is one of the prime examples of housing development as a garden city. Besides plotted housing, the township has group housing, extensive trade and commercial areas, a club, a hospital, schools, etc.

Central University of Kashmir, Ganderbal, Jammu and Kashmir
The Central University of Kashmir is spread across 200 hectares of green field. Its institutional complex, befitting international standards, has amenities for a projected population of 14,000 (7,000 residential and 7,000 day students). With 14,000 students, 350 teaching faculty and 400 non-teaching staff on full establishment.

Eldeco Utopia, Noida, Uttar Pradesh
This is a luxurious residential township with 1,000 units in a harmonious configuration of low– and high-rise buildings. There is a hierarchy of open spaces with private greens, children's areas, a park, and a resort-like clubhouse with a pool. The complex was also one of the first in the city to introduce the concept of centrally air-conditioned apartments with a rooftop pool facility.

Mantri Meadows, Gurugram, Haryana
An exclusive golf, residential and commercial complex spread over an area of 70 acres, the project has approximately 120 dwelling units including villas, row houses, walk-ups and high-rise apartments. The development also has a 9-hole golf course, schools, service apartments, office towers and a hotel.

Sagar Apartments, New Delhi
The building consists of a sixteen-storeyed main apartment tower and a two-storeyed block built on stilts. There are a total of sixty-four 3, 4 and 5-BHK apartments in the building. Facilities like a swimming pool, shops and other recreational activities are provided in the complex. The built-up area accounts to 1,50,000 sq. ft.

Indian Oil Corporation Apartments, Noida, Uttar Pradesh
The complex consists of 320 residential apartments for the Indian Oil executives in eight multistoreyed towers. The buildings, clad in exposed brickwork, are configured around lush green landscaped gardens.

GAIL Cooperative Society Apartments, Gurugram, Haryana
The complex consists of 130 dwelling units in three categories of 800 to 1,400 sq. ft. built-up area. The project has been conceived as a low-rise development with lawns, terraces and duplex walk-ups.

Housing for Delhi WAKF Board, New Delhi
The project includes three complexes, consisting of residential apartments, in low– and high-rise structures, on behalf of the Delhi WAKF Board. They are spread across various locations in the city.

Apartments for University Teachers, New Delhi
The 110 dwelling units are designed over four floors. There are two categories of flats with built-up areas of 1,100 and 1,300 sq. ft. each. The low-rise building, landscaped gardens and shaded courtyards create a vibrant residential complex.

Heritage City, Gurugram, Haryana
This project is a 24-acre residential development designed with housing towers with five to fourteen floors, extensive terraces, exquisite landscaping, and a variegated choice of 2, 3 and 4-BHK apartments. The complex, with 1,200 dwelling units, has a club, a shopping centre, schools and community facilities.

Apartments for Parivar (Goodyear India) Group Housing Society Limited, New Delhi
The complex consists of 115 flats in four-storeyed buildings and an eight-storeyed tower. The external façade is dominated by balconies and jack arches.

Housing for Asian Consolidated Industries Limited (ACIL), Shahjahanpur, Rajasthan
Housing development for ACIL staff consists of about 200 dwelling units in various categories with public facilities like a school, a club, a shopping complex, bank, a post office and a golf course.

Silver Arch Apartments, New Delhi
An exclusive complex with forty-eight luxury apartments, the residences are served by glass front elevators. The entire building is clad in blue and white glass mosaic tiles and has a striking appearance. The project is located on 22, Feroze Shah Road, and was designed for Unitech Limited.

Logix Zest, Noida, Uttar Pradesh
Located on the Noida-Greater Noida Expressway, the location of the society makes it easily accessible. The project comprises fourteen residential towers with a total of 2,200 accommodation units. The site is spread across 19 acres.

Parsvnath Planet, Lucknow, Uttar Pradesh
The project is a luxurious 10-acre mixed-use project with a built-up area of 10,00,000 sq. ft. It includes 3 and 4-BHK, centrally air-conditioned apartments.

Residences at Shiv Nadar University, Greater Noida, Uttar Pradesh
The University is spread over an area of 286 acres. The campus accommodates residential sectors for the students and faculty members with a contemporarily designed and spacious cafeteria.

Gitanjali Apartments, New Delhi
The society has 120 dwelling units in three eight-storeyed blocks. Units of 1,100 and 1,500 sq. ft. have been designed to allow maximum light with proper ventilation. Building exteriors are in graphic patterns. The project has been executed for Hindustan Levers Limited.

Residential Facilities at Biswa Bangla Biswavidyalaya, Bolpur, West Bengal
A winning entry in a national competition held in 2017, the design treads on sustainable design philosophy. The hostels have been placed at one end of the site to ensure privacy to the students. Inward planning of the hostels helps in creation of a courtyard, which is used for recreation.

Unitech Ivory Towers, Gurugram, Haryana
This project has white marble clad sixteen-storey towers with 150 apartments. In an attempt to create something more than a compact building, Ivory Towers was envisioned to emanate a 'monumental quality'. The top of each building tapers to form a stepped pinnacle above the treetops in the vicinity, making it a dominating feature.

The Forest, Noida, Uttar Pradesh
Designed for Omaxe Group, 105 centrally air-conditioned apartments have been planned in seven towers. Each unit is designed to have a built-up area of 4,000 sq. ft. The apartment complex is equipped with a private health club and each penthouse, with a built-up area of 6,500 sq. ft., has a private swimming pool.

Apartments for Retreat (Income Tax Officers), New Delhi
Retreat complex is located in East Delhi and has 177 dwelling units. The project has been designed with eight-storeyed buildings planned around a beautifully landscaped court and a swimming pool. The treatment of the external façade with pylon-like balconies and a permanent stone finish gives it a majestic appearance.

Tarang Apartments (Built for Department of Electronics), New Delhi
In this project for the Department of Electronics, 165 apartments have been designed in two eight-storeyed and one four-storeyed blocks. The units' sizes vary between 1,000 and 1,400 sq. ft.

Apartments for Lions' Group (Punjab National Bank) Housing, New Delhi
Largely four-storeyed buildings with one eight-storeyed tower, the apartments have built-up areas ranging between 750 sq. ft., 1,150 sq. ft. and 1,500 sq. ft.

Aradhana Apartments (Burmah-Shell), New Delhi
An exquisitely designed residential complex with plotted development and a premium apartment tower with thirty-six apartments, located near the prestigious diplomatic area of Delhi. The extensively landscaped complex has a luxurious clubhouse.

Parsvnath City, Dharuhera, Haryana
A township of 15 acres, with a built-up area of 12 lakh sq. ft., it has centrally air-conditioned 3 and 4-BHK apartments, a convenient shopping arcade, a clubhouse and EWS housing.

The Palms (Unitech La Gardenia), Gurugram, Haryana
A luxurious condominium project with 530 apartments designed in eighteen-storey towers. The towers are clad in white and form a distinctive skyline, and are accentuated in different colours, making the development unique.

Residential Sectors at Jawaharlal Nehru University (JNU), New Delhi
There are sixteen residential sectors in JNU. The design of a typical one has three hostel blocks, which accommodate 600 students, and three and four residential clusters for approximately 150 faculty members. Faculty residences are placed around the hostels.

Industrial Township for Government of Himachal Pradesh, Parwanoo, Himachal Pradesh
A township planned for various light and medium industries and associated facilities on the hilly terrain of Himachal Pradesh.

Kasturba Nagar Housing Redevelopment, New Delhi
The work involves redevelopment of GPRA colony in Kasturba Nagar. The new set of flats and community facilities are being built as per norms of the Ministry of Urban Development (MoUD), which shall be at least 3-star GRIHA (Green Rating for Integrated Habitat Assessment) rating.

Model Town Residential Redevelopment, New Delhi
The redevelopment involves the design of a mini-township comprising different typologies of housing, club facilities for residents, a commercial complex, a school, religious buildings and dispensary, etc., spread over 25 acres of land.

Omaxe Heights, Lucknow, Uttar Pradesh
The housing project is spread over 10 acres of land with total built-up area of 10,00,000 sq. ft. The project comprises 2, 3 and 4-BHK apartments, a shopping mall, a hotel and luxurious spa facilities with each tower.

Forest Spa, Noida, Uttar Pradesh
A luxurious housing complex with built-up area of 15 lakh sq. ft. and a unique private spa of 30,000 sq. ft., it has apartments ranging from 4,000 to 8,000 sq. ft. and comprises four towers.

Parsvnath Bhiwadi, Rajasthan
The 10-acre project is intended to serve as a hotspot for affordable property, resulting in lucrative investment opportunities. The aim is to create a large, open area to slowly replace concrete with greens. Towers with affordable and compact 2 and 3-BHK flats overlook a large green area at the centre.

Army College of Medical Sciences, New Delhi
A new medical college designed to support the modern facilities such as a 1,200 seater auditorium and hostels for 600 students.

BPTP Princess Park, Faridabad, Haryana
The towers comprising 2 and 3-BHK apartments are painted in bright colours, making the dream abode idyllic. The project covers a total area of 18 acres with twelve towers designed with fourteen to nineteen floors.

Air India Colony Redevelopment, New Delhi
With increased urban development in the city, housing has been proposed for the Air India employees and other Central Government bodies. For this purpose, a 30-acre site in Vasant Vihar area of Delhi has been selected for the redevelopment of the Air India colony.

Omaxe Grand Woods, Noida, Uttar Pradesh
This housing project has been planned on a 30-acre land with approximately 1,300 apartments. The complex is completely furnished with amenities like a swimming pool overlooked by a state-of-the-art club.

Austrian Embassy Complex, New Delhi
The complex consists of the chancery, ambassador's residence and staff quarters. Executed in association with the Austrian architect, Mr. Heinz Scheide.

Parsvnath Prideasia, Chandigarh
The project is a Chandigarh township for Parsvnath Developers Limited. Located in the Rajiv Gandhi Chandigarh Technological Park, the township is spread over 125 acres of land. The township comprises apartments, a seven-star hotel, a shopping mall and other amenities, designed with a built-up area of 30 lakh sq. ft.

Gautam Buddha University (Residential), Greater Noida, Uttar Pradesh
This prestigious university is developed on an area of over 511 acres. The facilities also include hostels for 5,000 students and 500 faculty members. It has been awarded as a 'sustainable campus' by various national and international awarding committees.

Township for HRRL, Barmer, Rajasthan
Won as a part of a national competition, the township is conceptualized by taking inspiration from the local design strategies and sensibilities.

Vasant Vihar Residence, New Delhi
Clad in white rough granite imported from Japan, the home of architect Dikshu C. Kukreja and his wife Arunima is an interesting example of contemporary architecture juxtaposed with art installations, where each piece speaks eloquently to the other.

TATA Myst Luxury Housing, Kasauli, Himachal Pradesh
Perched atop a private hill, Myst is India's first residential development overlooking the Himalayan foothills. The housing has been designed using the concept of biophilic architecture: an approach which creates luxurious spaces that bring residents closer to nature.

Logix Blossoms Green, Noida, Uttar Pradesh
The high-rise residential development uses landscape as a means to develop the site, planning the towers around it. The project kept close to 72 per cent of the total land under open area and is spread across 25 acres of prime land.

Pearls Gateway Towers, Noida, Uttar Pradesh
Designed across a site area of 9 acres, and located in Sector 44, Noida, this housing society uses a unique combination of coral blue and green to conceptualize eleven residential towers.

Indian Law Institute Apartments, New Delhi
Apartments for the Indian Law Institute staff with forty-two dwelling units in a multistoreyed block, with areas of 1,200-1,800 sq. ft. of coverage area were designed and executed in Karkardooma area of Delhi.

SPR Imperial Estate, Faridabad, Haryana
Completed in 2013, the Architects designed 372 housing units spread across 10 acres of prime land in Faridabad. The design uses a harmonious combination of brown and beige on the façade of the eighteen-storeyed high-rise towers.

Indian High Commission, Abuja, Nigeria
Design for the chancery complex and high commission residence in the new capital city of Abuja, Nigeria; the project was awarded to the firm through an international competition.

Indian High Commission Complex, Lagos, Nigeria
The project consisted the design of chancery and staff housing. The chancery has been designed around two atriums, which, in good weather, form interesting assembly areas within the building.

Finland Embassy, New Delhi
The project consists of chancery, ambassador's residence, and housing for the Finnish and Indian staff. Designed in association with Rili and Riema Pietila of Finland.

South Campus, University of Delhi, New Delhi
The campus is designed on 75 acres of prime land near Dhaula Kuan, South Delhi. The residential facilities comprise students' hostel (boys and girls), faculty housing, with shared facilities such as a library, a shopping centre, a recreational complex, etc.

Diplomatic Residences, Canadian High Commission, New Delhi
The project involved design for the housing for senior diplomats in the premises of the Canadian High Commission at Chanakyapuri, New Delhi. The white mosaic finish on the exterior façade gives the complex a stately appearance.

Housing Facilities at Indian Institute of Management (IIM), Lucknow, Uttar Pradesh
Among the premier management training institutes in India, this IIM is a 200-acre campus near Lucknow city. Hostels for 2,000 students and 500 faculty residences are part of the complex. The project was selected as the Best Designed IIM by the *Outlook* magazine.

Indian Institute of Mass Communication, New Delhi
The first premier housing institution is on a 15-acre site adjoining the JNU Campus in Delhi. The expansion programme of the institute comprises an air-conditioned guest house for eighty persons and faculty housing, an auditorium to seat 1,500 people, a lecture and seminar complex.

Human Resources Development Centre, Greater Noida, Uttar Pradesh
The Human Resources Development Centre is an educational nerve centre of DPS Society for the 'In-service Teachers' Capacity Building' programmes.

Residential School, Jaipur, Rajasthan
A residential school with advanced facilities and fully equipped with on-campus housing for 1,500 students and faculty.

East Delhi Hub, New Delhi
East Delhi Hub in Karkardooma is a 15 million sq. ft. project located on a site area of 60 acres which was originally conceived as the pilot project for Transit-Oriented Development (TOD) in India. Integrating concepts of advance technology in architecture, the complex includes the tallest tower in India with 100 storeys.

Denmark Embassy, New Delhi
Inspired by the international style of architectural design, the project uses clean lines in the plan and façade of the buildings. The chancery and apartment blocks were incorporated harmoniously in the design.

Indian Institute of Technology (IIT), Guwahati, Assam
The IIT in Assam near Guwahati is the sixth premier institution of this kind in the country. The Master Plan for this 200-acre campus has been developed with the academic complex, faculty and student housing and a uniquely innovative technology park.

Sri Aurobindo College of Commerce and Management, Ludhiana, Punjab
An institution of higher learning being developed on 12 acres of land on the outskirts of Ludhiana city. The campus comprises a learning centre, an auditorium for 1,000 students, a hostel for 500 students, faculty residences, a meditation centre and clubhouse facilities.

SCI Maritime Training Institute, Mumbai, Maharashtra
This project was designed for the Shipping Corporation of India Limited. It consists of an academic block, staff housing, hostel blocks, a gymnasium, a guest house and specialized survival training facilities.

Residential Blocks at Indian Institute of Technology (IIT), Jodhpur, Rajasthan
The Development of a permanent campus of IIT Jodhpur includes buildings for residential zone, hostel zone, and related utilities and services. Boasting of a zero carbon footprint through a 'Net Zero' design concept, IIT Jodhpur is designed to be a self-sustainable, 'Smart Eco-Campus'.

Central University of Rajasthan, Ajmer, Rajasthan
Spread over 500 acres along the Jaipur-Ajmer road in Rajasthan, the campus has a hostel for 10,000 students and housing for 1,000 faculty members.

Punjabi Saudagar Housing Society Limited, New Delhi
A group housing project of 110 dwelling units designed for a trading community. The apartments are located in Mayur Vihar, Delhi.

Tata New Haven, Bahadurgarh, Haryana

Township for Oil and Natural Gas Commission (ONGC), Ahmedabad, Gujarat
The 100 acres township has 2,000 dwelling units. The complex has well laid out roads, landscaped greens, and residential buildings ranging from three- to eleven-storeyed towers.

Township for ONGC, Ankleshwar, Gujarat
Within the existing township, additional 200 dwelling units and the township's extension with 1,600 dwelling units have been executed.

Township for ONGC, Baroda, Gujarat
In the existing township, additional multistoreyed buildings with 1,500 dwelling units have been designed.

Township for ONGC, Mehsana, Gujarat
A residential township with 1,200 dwelling units planned for employees of ONGC.

Supertech Czar Suites, Greater Noida, Uttar Pradesh
The residential complex for Supertech in Greater Noida consists of 2, 3 and 4-BHK typologies of apartments and penthouses. The built-up area of the apartments varies between 870 sq. ft. and 3,447 sq. ft. The complex also has a clubhouse, a gymnasium, a swimming pool and tennis and badminton courts.

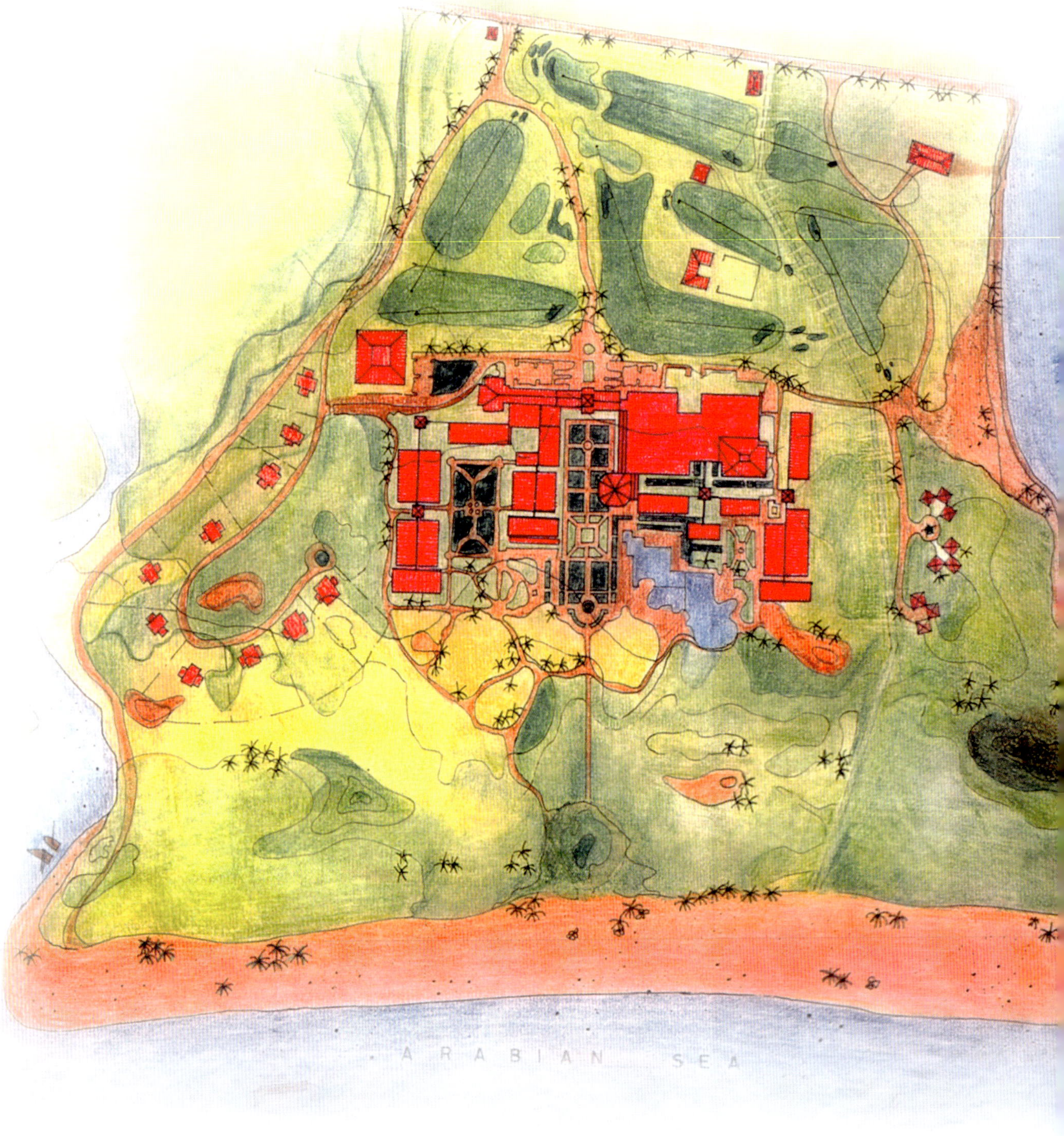
ARABIAN SEA

LEISURE

Leisure and entertainment design combines the architectonics of a place, a journey and a dream. In an age which makes far-off locations virtually accessible, the Architects strive to teleport those experiences and formalize them in the actual realm. This category includes designs for projects such as hotels, forest resorts, country-side clubs, shopping malls and multiplexes.

Aerocity

Location **New Delhi** Site **65 acres** Built-up area **90,00,000 sq. ft.** Year of completion **2014**

Detailed ***Master Planning of an integrated, one-of-its-kind hospitality district***

Aerocity in Delhi is a unique project redefining the urban experience of the city. Establishing itself as a gateway to visitors who arrive by air, both international and domestic, the development is the first and last impression of the city and the country. In terms of scale, it is the largest planned development that Delhi has witnessed since the establishment of the capital city by the British in 1911. With such significance, the Client, a consortium of the government and the private concessionaire, the GMR Group, floated a global competition for selecting the Master Planner and the infrastructure designers. The Architects won both the contracts.

The Architects took this unique opportunity of not just creating a Master Plan for the hospitality district but for the entire conceivable mixed-use development of 250 acres. Thereafter, the design developed for the 65-acre hospitality district, defined the urban form of each land parcel, detailing the creative realm of the complex. The design strategies included creating a vibrant pedestrian promenade, which starts from the metro station at the southern end and runs through the entire area like a spine. By opening up the complexes of different hotel properties, instead of planning them as separate and gated blocks, the Architects developed Aerocity as a complete and one-stop public recreation centre, an exemplary concept for the city. The Architects created a novel idea in their urban design wherein the Food and Beverage (F&B) and retail of each hotel opened onto the pedestrian promenade.

The seamless traffic circulation, creation of the plazas, the novel designs of street furniture, landscape plantation, water features and public art, all come together to what has truly become one of the most sought after public places in Delhi and NCR.

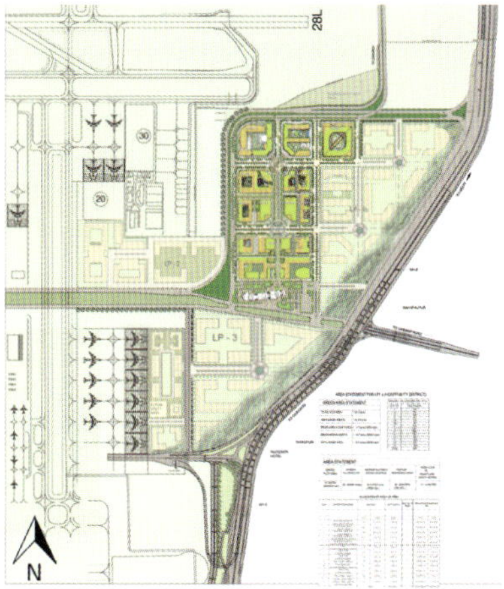

Facing page: *The visitors are greeted through an entrance boulevard.*

Above: *Master Plan of the Aerocity urban complex.*

Below: *The Architects followed an iron-grid planning for the project.*

JW Marriott

Location **New Delhi** Site **4.5 acres** Built-up area **10,00,000 sq. ft.** Year of completion **2012**

Situated in Aerocity, the hotel is the ***largest of its five hotels in India*** *with more than 500 rooms*

JW Marriott, located at Delhi Aerocity, adjacent to the Indira Gandhi International (IGI) Airport, is a major gateway infrastructure that aspires to become a new destination with an international ambience. This hotel not only attracts arrivers at the airport, but is also an iconic building that welcomes visitors to Delhi, upholding the proud image of a rapidly growing modern India.

The site for JW Marriott is located at a corner plot directly adjacent to the central spine which runs as a major artery through the Aerocity. Being one of the newest luxury hotels in Delhi offering five-star amenities, the architecture called for an aesthetically pleasing design that expressed a relaxing escape into an oasis of intriguing décor and a tranquil atmosphere, and away from the hustle of city life. The hotel at the Aerocity is the largest of its five hotels in India with 523 rooms spread over 4.5 acres.

The site was envisioned to contain 10,00,000 sq. ft. area spread over seven storeys. The building has been organized in an H-shaped configuration. The north-eastern boundary incorporates the leasable office and retail building, framing a semi-enclosed courtyard, which is also shared by the office and hotel blocks and has been designed as a prime feature and focal point for F&B facilities. The visual and physical link to the central pedestrian plaza forms a major axis through the heart of the hospitality district and enhances the public space network within the complex.

Common public spaces, such as the main lobby, ball room, meeting rooms, business centre, F&B outlets, retail, gym and swimming pool, allow a great public life within the complex which promises activities, engagements, and hence, a warm and hospitable ambience. The courtyards are not only open spaces that balance the heaviness of the built mass on the site, but also act as a central green area that allows a feeling of a getaway into the openness.

The design, with its vocabulary of sandstone, aluminium and glass captivates both contextuality of the site and the global identity that the project attempts to deliver. The design strategy of creating a lush landscaped courtyard, which infuses a reprieve much like an oasis, sets the design apart from the surrounding buildings in this hospitality district.

With a modular construction technology focusing both on sustainability and ease of construction, this hotel was the first to be built and operational in the entire hospitality district.

Facing page: *A view of the façade of the building.*

Below: *Use of high window openings allows natural daylight into the interiors, complementing the rich brown decor of the hotel.*

The LaLiT Golf & Spa Resort

Location **Goa** Site **85 acres** Built-up area **4,00,000 sq. ft.**

Year of completion **2005**

A Baroque-Portuguese styled resort, *spread over 85 acres of site, synchronized with the existing design language of the region*

The five-star resort hotel, designed for Bharat Hotel Limited, is located on the Raj Baga beach in Canacona, along the pristine South Goa coast. Burrowed amidst the confluence of the Talpona river and bordered by the glorious Sahyadari range, the resort is surrounded by picturesque views. Sharing a kilometre long and exclusive beachfront along the Arabian Sea, the Architects wanted the design to least interfere with its surroundings.

Keeping Goa's well preserved cultural sense as one of the strongholds in their proposal, the Architects proposed following a Baroque-Portuguese style of design. The design demonstrated preservation of the urban character of the area whilst retaining an ecological balance, which has allowed for the landscape to seamlessly grow and complement the design language of the hotel. The project harnesses local architectural techniques

Facing page: *An evening view of the resort exhibiting the rhythmic arches on the façade.*

Below: *An initial conceptual sketch of the resort shows the structural membranes used to support the roof.*

Top left: *The cottages are designed with pool facilities and are surrounded by a serene landscape.*

Bottom left: *An interior view of one of the suites.*

Above: *The façade balances vernacular elements borrowed from the Portuguese style of design and aptly suited to the Goan landscape.*

Following page: *An aerial view of the resort.*

and includes design elements like spacious verandahs, huge arched openings and pitched roof structures whilst allowing water as the ultimate entity, percolating into the fabric of the resort and unifying it into a single harmonious ensemble. From afar, the canary yellow and red laterite juxtaposition of the buildings stands out against the plush greenscape of its vicinity. This colourful intervention is well in sync with the scale and expanse of the resort over 85 acres of land.

Respecting the loose soil conditions, the Architects resolved to expand the resort horizontally, maintaining the height to two storeys. The rooms have been planned to face the sea, offering a striking and unobstructive view of the lush greenery expanding onto the serene sea beyond. The sparsely placed built structures within the site are balanced by the heavy detail work on the face of the buildings. Locally inspired stucco patterns adorn the outer walls and columns across the verandah.

Climatological influence is well visible in the hotel. The verandah space regulates passive cooling, supported by large spans of openings for the rooms. These openings are also an effective way of keeping humidification levels in the interiors in check while naturally ventilating the spaces. The interiors are opulent and generous in their use of rich textiles, handicrafts and wood, sourced from the local region and projecting a Goan-Portuguese design sensibility. The location allows the rooms to stay cool while the orientation permits glare-free daylight inside. Through the use of a subtle combination of materials, the absorption of heat is effectively minimized.

The different outdoor spaces have been designed to accommodate various recreational facilities, and decks and grass paved with meticulously pruned foliage act as transition and connecting spaces. The other facilities provided at the resort vary from restaurants, banquet hall, business centre, meeting rooms, shopping amenities, a spa and a casino.

The design style of the resort offers permeability between different zones within the site, resulting in a singular design language and making it one of the biggest design strengths offered by the Architects. The project is a successful example of a world-class luxury resort, designed using vernacular techniques, sensibilities and aesthetics.

The LaLiT Grand Palace

Location **Srinagar, Jammu and Kashmir** Site **15 acres** Built-up area **1,30,000 sq. ft.** Year of completion **1998**

The resort was awarded ***'The Best Luxury Hill Resort'*** *in 2017 at the* ***Outlook Traveller Awards***

Pine covered dense mountains surround the valley where The Lalit Grand Palace sits nestled in serenity, away from the chaos and hasty city life. Overlooking the breathtaking Dal Lake, the palace was originally built in 1910 for the royal family. It was readapted and renovated to accommodate 122 rooms, including sixteen suites and a host of guest facilities, a 9-hole golf course and a jogging track, over 4,000 sq. ft. of banqueting space, conference facilities, a shopping arcade and a luxurious spa with an indoor swimming pool. The site is landscaped comprehensibly with an array of trees and plants, displaying a colourful palette of visuals in summers while a blanket of white snow envelops the space in winters. The Architects were conscious of its surroundings and wanted to preserve the natural sanctity. As one enters the site, they are left spell bound with the spectacular panoramic view. The vast expanse of the front lawn creates a dramatic visual experience. The resort is painted white with red-brick tiles that stand out brightly from the overall building's character. A large lotus pond acts as a drop-off area, leading the visitors into the elaborate atrium and reception space. The building is divided into sections – coffee shop, restaurant, kitchen, dining spaces, etc., are on one side of the reception, while the other side discreetly leads the visitors to guest rooms and private cottages. The interiors are furnished as an exuberant spectacle with wood being the primary design material. Moving through the space, one realizes that the design retains the grandeur of a palatial residence while the redesign brings in a vernacular and local aesthetic to the overall character. With minimalistic intervention, the Architects have successfully been able to execute a sustainable transformation of the space.

Facing page: *The entrance of the resort greets visitors with a colourful embrace while the backdrop is a striking view of the Himalayan range.*

Below: *A drawing of the ground-floor plan of the Club House.*

Bottom: *The front façade of the resort enveloped in snow.*

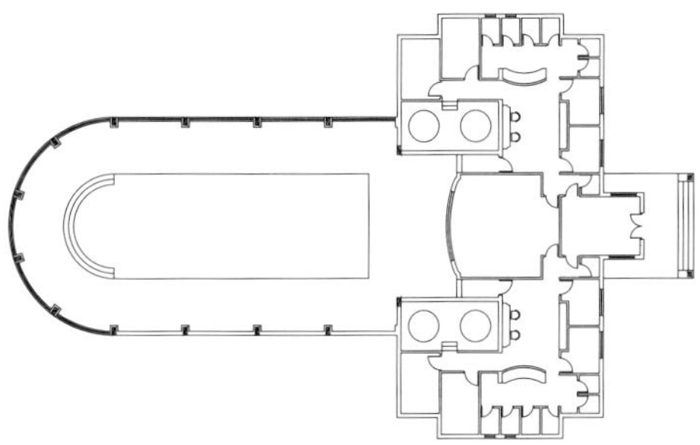

Logix Riviera

Location **Noida, Uttar Pradesh** Site **7 acres** Built-up area **15,00,000 sq. ft.** Year of completion **Ongoing**

The design proposes to ***juxtapose the searing business tower with the whirling mall*** *below*

This mixed-use commercial and hospitality complex, located on a prime land in Sector 105, Noida, boasts of luxury four– and five-star hotels, a premium shopping and entertainment centre and a high rise corporate office tower. The Architects hoped to challenge the norms of mixed-use design and its perception by proposing an organic design with an impeccable futuristic sense.

Technological finesse was incorporated to conceptualize a design which thrives on meeting futuristic requirements, juxtaposing the soaring business tower with the whirling mall below. The design seamlessly ties the two functional aspects of the complex into a single capsule. With an iconic tower, it is a landmark statement in the character of the skyline.

The Architects used fluidity in form to create vibrant, interactive courts within the hollow of the concave curves of the building. While the mall is enveloped in a patterned mesh over a glass façade, the business tower uses a combination of tinted and transparent glass cladding, creating a well-proportioned edifice. Façade design combines undulating surface of the mall with hologram-like effect of offices.

The buildings are designed to enhance the recreational experience for people living in the surrounding area, which is one of the largest expanding localities adjoining metropolitan Delhi. The design echoes a holistic sense of living, working and co-existence.

Below: *An aerial visualization of the design, integrating technology into its façade.*

Gold Souk Mall

Location **Gurugram, Haryana** Site **3 acres** Built-up area **1,80,000 sq. ft.** Year of completion **2005**

The shimmering design demeanour complements the ***first-of-its-kind mall designed in India to host jewellery stores*** *from across the country*

A unique concept, Gold Souk is India's first speciality jewellery mall with over 100 leading jewellers and luxury brands from across the country in a single place. The design accommodates 1,00,000 sq. ft. of outdoor area and an expansive plaza, which makes it a one-of-its-kind recreation space.

For the first time, 22 feet high retail shops with pre-designed structural elements, which allowed a part mezzanine to be created, were attempted in India. This addressed the specific need for owners to be physically present in their stores while monitoring from the mezzanine. A striking design idea translates the name of the mall onto its façade with gold coloured Aluminium Composite Panels (ACP) and establishes it as a landmark in Gurugram. The design of the building is inspired by an oyster, which holds within itself a precious pearl. Likewise, the two curved forms of the twin buildings 'hold' an atrium which becomes the centre of all activities.

Gold Souk's prime location, in the vicinity of MG Road, makes the mall well placed and easily accessible for visitors. It is equipped with the most advanced technological and security systems while also comprising a grand atrium, exhibition hall, conference facilities, food court and terrace garden. Destination cafes and luxurious dining spaces make the experience much more fulfilling for visitors. The evening light turns the building into a shining gold, jewel-like sculpture.

Below: *The entrance atrium of the mall is guarded by two imposing building segments.*

Bottom: *The interiors of the mall use gold tint, representing the metal mostly used in jewellery.*

Spirit Global Mall

Location **Ludhiana, Punjab** Site **4 acres** Built-up area **4,00,000 sq. ft.** Year of completion **Ongoing**

The Architects staggered different recreation spaces in the shopping mall to create ***an innovative amalgamation of façade,*** *giving a distinct identity to the mall*

Spread over an area of 4,00,000 sq. ft., this shopping mall has a hypermarket, anchor stores, retail, food court and an entertainment centre. The building is planned as a multilevel facility with an interestingly designed atrium which connects the various levels and is staggered in different parts of the complex.

The pleated outlook of the façade reflects an abstract, deconstructive demeanour for the building, instilling a playfulness in the design.

The concept for the project sought to break the monotonous and flat image associated with mall designs by chiseling the edges of the façade. The deconstruction in the design was translated onto planning as well, creating an interesting path for indoor circulation.

The wired and irregular façade reflects as a precious stone supported by an intricate pattern of *jaali,* which cocoons the mall and creates a playful ambience of filtered natural light in the building. The building's skin stands as one of the highlights of the design and helped the Architects to achieve a unique and iconic distinction for the mall.

The Architects wanted to make a departure from the conventional mall designs, which were often stereotypical approaches of lining shops along a central atrium and using the façade only as a medium of advertising. In Spirit Global Mall, the design explores the possibility of converting a building typology of a shopping centre into a thriving public space, both with the variety of functions encapsulated in the space as well as the dynamic volumes created internally and externally.

Below: *A visualization of the mall's façade which takes inspiration from deconstructivism.*

The LaLiT & World Trade Centre

Location **New Delhi** Site **8 acres** Built-up area **9,00,000 sq. ft.** Year of completion **1982**

A pioneering architectural and ***structural marvel of its time,*** *the twenty-eight-storeyed edifice is still* ***one of the highest buildings in the capital***

A super deluxe five-star hotel designed for Bharat Hotels Limited, the Lalit Hotel and its adjacent World Trade Centre are located in the posh area of Connaught Place. The drop off area is shaded by a coffered 15 metre projection, a structural marvel of its time. Well supported by robust columns, the imposing and elevated entrance porch doubles up as an outdoor swimming pool on the fifth level.

Rather than adopt an easy design approach of aping what had already been done abroad, the Architects experimented with a design which would reflect the local culture and Indian architecture. The volumetric play – as the building rises and creates terraces at various levels – with the central volume soaring skywards, is reminiscent of the *shikharas* in Indian temples. The skyline is punctuated with *chhatris*, recalling the charming architectural element used historically in public buildings in India. Combining beige and red sandstones made the building a part of the architecture of Lutyens' public buildings in Delhi, which used the same material.

Conceived in the late 1970s, it was designed as the tallest building of Delhi and one of the largest hotels with 540 rooms and suites. A six-storeyed, air-conditioned shopping mall with over 600 shops was unprecedented. The hotel has five multilevel restaurants, exclusive glass capsule elevators, a 60-feet high atrium with a waterfall, executive club and roof gardens.

The twenty-eight-storey tower used inventive construction technology. Dewatering the area, which has a high water table, for building two basements within the deadline for the 1982 Asian Games – being hosted by India at the time – was a difficult challenge, and for this purpose, the Architects opted for modular construction and chose slipform technology for constructing the floors at a rapid pace.

One of the first flagship projects for the Lalit Group of Hotels, over the years they have now expanded to over twenty properties across India and abroad, with the Architects' involvement at many significant locations.

Below: *A night view of the front façade of the hotel reflecting a Brutalistic architecture, a rising concept in post-independent India.*

Delhi Gymkhana Club

Location **New Delhi** Site **27 acres** Built-up area **5,00,000 sq. ft.** Year of completion **1999**

One of the most prestigious and highly coveted clubs of the capital, ***the Architects sought to revive the Indian design sensibility within the imperial premises***

The club, originally called the Imperial Delhi Gymkhana Club, is located in the highly guarded locality of Lutyens' Delhi on Safdarjung Road.

The project required the renovation, refurbishing and planning of new facilities for the historic complex built under the British regency. The Architects' concept for the project was aimed at preserving the existing character of the club whilst upgrading its existing facilities to the latest designs. The project thus included Master Planning of the entire complex, Structural Improvements, Renovation and Interior Design of the main club building, cottages and staff housing.

The single-storey structure of the club building expands horizontally across the site. The low-rise appearance of the club is well complemented by the functionality of the shining pristine white edifices with red-tiled roofs.

The club is fronted by a magnificent lawn, appropriate for hosting get-togethers and high-tea events, creating a dramatic scale of entrance for visitors. The entrance porch of the main building is an extravagant space designed by extruding a slab from the building and supported by four robust columns.

The Architects were cautious of seamlessly translating the colonial demeanour into the interiors as well. As a recreation project, it was ensured that the planning allowed ample scope of sit-out spaces wherever possible, balancing the built-up area to landscape ratio.

Left: *Façade of one of the cottages of the club reflecting the colonial flavour.*

Monarch Hotel

Location **Ootacamund, Tamil Nadu** Site **4 acres** Built-up area **1,00,000 sq. ft.** Year of completion **1990**

The 100-bed hotel, *tucked away in the misty hills of Ootacamund (Ooty), was* ***designed for film actor Mithun Chakraborty***

Perched atop the magnificent Nilgiris, the Monarch Hotel offers striking views of the surrounding expansive tea gardens, establishing itself as a perfect choice for a romantic escapade. The 100-room hotel was designed for film actor Mithun Chakraborty and has extensive terraces and glass capsule elevators. The mist hovering over the prolific tea plantation allowed the Architects to conceptualize a design which did not interrupt the balance of the natural surroundings while providing its visitors with prime leisure services.

The rooms are lined along the length of the building, soaking in natural daylight and unobstructive views of the surrounding exuberant landscape. The hotel is equipped with super deluxe facilities, including banquet hall, two restaurants, party rooms, health club and discotheque. The hotel embraces a white demeanour and an elaborate façade, paying close attention to Colonial Era inspired design details. The royal look spreads from the outside to the inside, providing visitors with a lavish and elaborate experience. The grandeur of the hotel leaves a long-lasting impression, establishing the hotel as a landmark in the lush valleys of Ooty.

Above: *An initial sketch for the hotel from an aerial perspective.*

Omaxe Terminal

Location **Ludhiana, Punjab** Site **5 acres** Built-up area **4,00,000 sq. ft.** Year of completion **2010**

The location of the mall along the highway towards the airport helped ideate a ***design which paid careful attention to ease in circulation***

For the conceptualization of a mall to be designed in Ludhiana, the Architects wanted to break away from the predefined and preconceived glass-boxed typology of mall complexes. Located on Ludhiana GT Bypass Road, the favourable placement makes the mall easily accessible for shoppers from in and around the cty.

The Architects restricted the use of glass, ideating a play in form and materials and bringing together a congregation of an innovative design. The concept of the mall allows the front façade, visible from the Bypass, to appear as an accordion, folding the displays of advertisement panels over it. The entrance façade supports a glass curtain wall, allowing natural light into the interiors, and also facilitates as an element of permeability for visitors from the outside. This induces a playful ambience in the overall fabric of the building. For the Architects, it was essential to translate the leisurely function of the project into a playful and appealing form on an otherwise awkwardly linear site. The staggered advertisement panels over the façade are backlit which helps set the evening mood in the landscape.

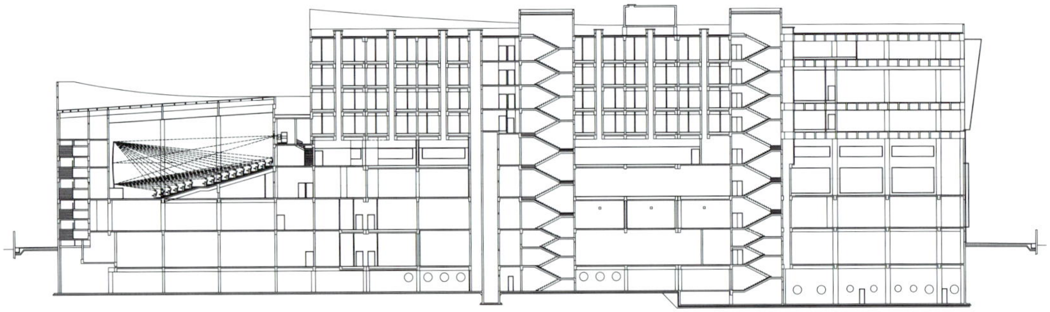

Above*: A drawing of the cross-section through the mall.*

Top*: A visualization of the front façade of the mall.*

Westin Hotel

Location **Kolkata, West Bengal** Site **8 acres** Built-up area **4,00,000 sq. ft.** Year of completion **2015**

Designed as a world-class complex and soaring as ***one of the tallest buildings in Kolkata,*** *the mixed-use development is a striking addition to the city's skyline*

A world-class mixed-use complex, the project consists of a five-star Westin Hotel, service apartments, premium residential apartments of 5,000 to 7,000 sq. ft. each, a shopping mall and a four-star vedic resort.

Located on the Biswa Bangla Sarani in Rajarhat, New Town, the multi-tower hotel complex on the eastern fringe of the city is spread across an area of 8 acres. The lavish property overlooks an ecological park with a water body, with the skyline of the cityscape in its backdrop.

The project is one of the tallest buildings in Kolkata. The planning of the hotel is such that each room is able to enjoy a striking view of the outdoors whilst enjoying amenities such as a spa, world-class gym, a high-end restaurant and an outdoor pool. The pool's placement on an elevated level is another one-of-its-kind experience for the visitors to enjoy. The 30,000 sq. ft. banquet is one of the largest in the city.

Through a minimalistic design conceptualization, the soaring towers exude magnificence in scale. The two towers are connected by an elevated pool. The project is conceived as an urban recreational experience with hotels, retail, entertainment, hanging gardens, performance spaces and a crafts bazaar.

Left: *The monumental scale of the edifice is highlighted as one views the thirty-two-storeyed and Kolkata's tallest tower from bottom to top.*

Omaxe Value Mall

Location **Amritsar, Punjab** Site **4 acres** Built-up area **3,55,000 sq. ft.** Year of completion **Ongoing**

Using an accordion as a design inspiration, *the mall breaks the typical glass-box typology for shopping complex designs*

The project is a mixed-use commercial complex located on a prominent site along the highway leading from the airport to the city. A 1,000 seater multiplex and 150-room hotel have been incorporated into the design fabric of the shopping mall.

An array of staggered profiles of panels on the façade instill a playful design aesthetic. The Architects minimized the use of glass, instilling a unique character to the mall. This also helped curb any visual or audio disturbance from the highway traffic outside.

The side facing away from the highway has been given a resplendent form and used as an entrance for the hotel. The mall distributes the masses of different blocks to achieve a proportionate and breathable ensemble of development.

For a progressive city such as Amritsar, these recreation spaces support a futuristic model for growth and revenue generation. The project, therefore, is a prestigious and first-of-its-kind endeavour to uplift the social spaces in the city.

Below: *An initial drawing of the front façade of the mall.*

Bottom: *A perspective visualization of the façade of the mall highlights playfulness on the building's exterior.*

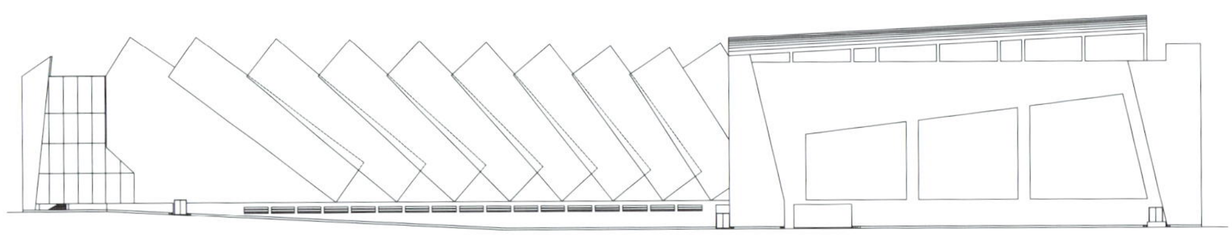

Ansal Royal Plaza

Location **Jodhpur, Rajasthan** Site **1 acre** Built-up area **1,36,000 sq. ft.** Year of completion **2007**

***Designed for the Maharaja of Jodhpur, the complex derives inspiration from the traditional Rajasthani patterns** for its façade*

The first such complex in Jodhpur, it has been designed for the Maharaja of Jodhpur. Indulging in creation of an abstract element over its façade, the geometric design takes inspiration from the popular colourful patterns of Rajasthani designs. The site's location at the junction of two main roads inspired the Architects to approach the possibility of breaking the façade into different sections. The different sides of the building are conjoined at different angles, which increased the overall surface area of the front façade and provided the mall with an expansive feature wall to showcase the abstract element in the design.

Designed for the Maharaja, the mall was required to exude finesse and luxury in its amenities. From the abstract exterior to the well-planned layout, the mall is a one-of-its-kind recreational development in the city. The popular Rajasthani design pattern has been used with a contemporary connotation, giving the building a personalized indigenous appeal. A frame of stainless steel originates from a single central point and expands horizontally. The use of glass adds a modern outlook to the mall's design.

The widely used floral and vibrant illustrations have been assimilated and flattened into a one-of-its-kind and striking representation of the state's cultural aesthetics.

Staggered volumes of spaces, juxtaposition of different materials accommodating a slew of design elements allow the complex to be a successful example of a landmark edifice.

The project includes a shopping mall, multiplex, food court, entertainment centre and an office complex. The effect of the evening light displays a subtle picture of the interiors and allows the mall, through its geometric pattern, to shine as a sparkling chiseled spectacle in the urbanscape of the city.

Below: *The view of the mall as seen from the main road.*

Unitech Club

Location **Gurugram, Haryana** Site **5 acres** Built-up area **30,000 sq. ft.** Year of completion **2000**

A high-profile resort club for Unitech Limited, ***the design exudes architectural finesse, seamlessly tying the indoors with the outdoors***

A prominent resort club located in the South City Township, the Unitech Patio Club has a well-equipped health club, restaurant, bar, banquet hall and guest suites, party lawns, a large swimming pool and indoor and outdoor sports facilities. It is an oasis of quietude in the fast-paced urban setting of Gurugram. Nestled between a cover of thick green foliage and surrounded by high-rise residential complexes, the club offers an ideal getaway and a place of solitude within the city.

The design approach involved the Architects creating an ensemble of spaces, using an intricate understanding of volumes and planning a seamless transition in-between. With a low-rise demeanour, the Architects restricted the built expanse on the land, resulting in a vast swathe of open space and, in the process, creating a sculptural edifice.

While moving in and around the club, one is able to gauge 'space' as an essential design element, around which the Architects ideated their design. Starting from the drop-off area, which curves into a grand space under an impressive protruding vault, the visitors are left in awe of the design. The double height of the drop-off is balanced by the low-height entrance lobby which leads the visitors, once again, to a double-height central courtyard. The carefully curated and planned volume of spaces strikes as an impressive understanding of spatial design. The architectural finesse lies in allowing the built and unbuilt to come together in a synergy and provide a unique visual experience to visitors. The pristine white façade is accentuated with a mosaic work of Persian blue tiles on the side walls, complementing the green landscape.

The vault roof of the club acts as skylight and regulates natural ventilation and daylight inside the building. The inner courtyard beneath has been extravagantly landscaped – a curvaceous water body unifies the different elements such as the bridges, open sit-out spaces and the dense greens. The architectural design approach of fusing the structural expressionism with delicate mosaic works integrates the landscape and provides a memorable experience for any visitor.

Facing page: *Skylight roof covers the exquisitely landscaped central courtyard of the club.*

Below: *The entrance of the club is dramatized by an imposing drop-off area.*

Parsvnath City Centre Mall

Location **Ranchi, Jharkhand** Site **5 acres** Built-up area **10,00,000 sq. ft.** Year of completion **Ongoing**

One of the first mixed-use development spaces to be designed in the city with ***five-star luxury standards***

Ranchi witnessed a boom in its infrastructure development, propelling it as a thriving centre for business and design opportunities. Emerging from the same phenomenon, the design for the Parsvnath City Centre comes across as a refreshing break in the urban fabric of the city. The Architects ideated a space that will be a convergence of leisurely engagements.

One of the most prestigious projects to be developed in Ranchi, the project comprises a shopping mall and entertainment centre which includes retail, anchor stores, hypermarket, multiplex, bowling alley, food court and other entertainment facilities. Though the shopping centre restricts the use of glass on its façade, the commercial and office block rising as an eleven-storeyed edifice, in contrast, uses glass as its primary building material. This accentuates the character of the project as a progressive centre of public space. The City Centre also has a five-star hotel and luxury housing with 100 apartments. The total project has a built-up area of 10,00,000 sq. ft.

A unique design element of the project is the creation of one of the largest aquariums in India to be built on the façade of the building. This aims to create a sense of dynamism and drama in the City Centre besides becoming an attraction for the visitors.

Below: *Visualization of the entrance of the mall.*

DB City

Location **New Delhi** Site **7.7 acres** Built-up area **30,00,000 sq. ft.** Year of completion **Ongoing**

A striking example of a ***high-density mixed-use development*** *situated in the multi-district site of Aerocity*

DB City project is a striking example of a high-density development. As land crunch in cities leads to increasing Floor Area Ratio/Floor Space Index (FAR/FSI), the design challenges have shifted to exploring new sustainable development models. DB City project posed many design challenges. With a site area of less than 8 acres, the development guidelines of this plot of land permitted a built-up area of 30 lakh sq. ft., resulting in an aspect ratio of ten, hitherto never before developed in the city.

Further, the development guidelines mandated a pedestrian promenade bisecting this plot, leading to greater challenges of ground level site circulation of both vehicles and pedestrians. The project brief required a 1,200-room hotel, the largest in the country, a 2,000 seater convention centre, a banquet hall and a parking for 1,400 cars. All this had to be accommodated within only seven floors above ground due to proximity to airport runway. Such restrictions led to a design wherein, for the first time in India, the complex has seven basements.

With all these architectural and engineering design challenges, the project still endeavours to be iconic as it is strategically located adjacent to the IGI Airport and the Delhi–Gurugram Highway, becoming the first commercial building that greets visitors landing in Delhi.

Top: *A linear façade of the hotel.*

Above: *A view of the internal courtyard with a swimming pool, around which the hotel's design is centred.*

Club Mahindra Pristine Peak Resort

Location **Baldeyan, Himachal Pradesh** Site **6 acres** Built-up area **70,000 sq. ft.** Year of completion **2017**

Nestled near Shimla, the Neo-Classical edifice, ***built on one of the steepest slopes of Himachal Pradesh,*** *is the perfect getaway from one's urban space*

Celebrating the design ideas of Neo-Classical architecture, the resort is an ideal destination in the mountains. The project is situated in Naldehra, a town 18 km north-east of Shimla, placing the location away from the noise of the city.

The Architects wanted least intervention in the present site's form and altitude, and hence, sought to adapt to and adopt the variation of contours into the resort's design. Going forward, this emerged as one of the strengths for the entire project, which also gave a magnanimous demeanour to the resort.

The design also continues the legacy of the colonial style of architecture, of which the impression is visible in the entire urban development of Shimla. The resort is segregated into an activity centre and hotel room block, and the buffer of green space ties the spatial layout of the built area seamlessly. Through this, the Architects were also able to provide a shared recreation space in the outdoors. Careful planning of the hotel also allowed each room to have an unobtrusive view of the splendid landscape and the breathtaking snow-covered Himalayan peaks.

The well-preserved natural surroundings were a source of inspiration for the overall design. The typical pitch of the resort's roof design takes inspiration from the spectacular form of the surrounding Himalayan range. The façade uses a combination of rhythmic pattern of French style windows, which is pleasing to the eye whilst also displaying a subtle and serene sensibility in design to the visitors. The colour palette of the edifices imitates and preserves the charm and quaint aura of the surroundings. A combination of pastel shades of white and brown on the façade are accentuated by the decorative Greek columns, the delicate beading around the windows and horizontal trimmings lining the building through and through.

Facing page: *The resort, with its turrets and intricate lattice, overlooks the majestic Himalayan range.*

Below: *A watercolour of the awning detail which supports the colonnaded corridors.*

Complete Listing of Leisure Projects

Atrium Palace Hotel, Ekaterinburg, Russia
A 200-room super deluxe business hotel located in the vibrant city of Ekaterinburg (earlier known as Svervdlovsk). This hotel is planned around a six-level landscaped lobby. The façades have been built with local bricks while the building form has been articulated to blend with the site contours and environment. The hotel has a heated swimming pool, two restaurants, a business centre, sauna and health club, banquet hall, two bars as well as a thriving commercial office space.

Guest House (Gas Authority of India Limited [GAIL]), Lakwa, Assam
For a new gas-processing complex established by GAIL in the tea gardens of Lakwa, Assam, a guest house containing rooms and suites and associated facilities has been designed. It uses the traditional Assamese building design philosophy to conceive a vernacular yet contemporary design on stilts.

The LaLiT & World Trade Centre, New Delhi
The project is a super deluxe five-star hotel for Bharat Hotels Limited, with 540 rooms and suites, five multilevel restaurants, exclusive glass capsule elevators, atrium, lobby, banquet halls, party rooms, executive club, meeting rooms, health club, swimming pool and roof gardens. A unique feature of the hotel complex is a six-storeyed shopping mall, which has over 600 shops and extensive office areas. The hotel and shopping complexes are provided with a two-level basement parking for 700 cars. The total covered area is 9,00,000 sq. ft.

East Delhi Mall, Ghaziabad, Uttar Pradesh
The multilevel mixed-use complex includes retail shops, department stores, hypermarket, food court, a 1,200-seater cineplex, banquet halls and a sixty-room hotel. The project also has conference facilities and speciality restaurants. The total built-up area is 4,50,000 sq. ft.

Entertainment Centre, Ludhiana, Punjab
An integrated entertainment centre for Aerens RJ Groups with a built-up area of 15 lakh sq. ft., the project comprises a shopping mall, hotel, exhibition halls, multiplex, restaurants and an IMAX facility.

Omaxe Value Mall, Amritsar, Punjab
The design for the project includes a shopping mall, a 1,000-seater multiplex and a 150-room hotel designed on a prominent site along the highway leading from the airport to the city. The total built-up area is 3,55,000 sq. ft.

Monarch Hotel, Mysore, Karnataka
The five-storey hotel has been designed for tourists and business travellers, and has single, deluxe and presidential suites along with banquet facilities, restaurants, party rooms, discotheque, business centre, health club and a swimming pool to facilitate a comfortable space.

Monarch Hotel, Ootacamund, Tamil Nadu
In the sylvan landscape of Ootacamund (Ooty), this exclusive 100-bed hotel has been designed with extensive terraces and glass capsule elevators. The hotel is equipped with super deluxe facilities including banquet hall, two restaurants, party rooms, a health club and a discotheque, among others.

Defence Colony Club, New Delhi
The club is a part of the Defence Colony residential area in Delhi. It has been designed as a single and, partially, two-storeyed building in exposed brick. It has lounges, a bar, space for indoor games and a swimming pool.

Shopping Mall and Office Complex, Ambala, Haryana
A five-storey centrally air-conditioned shopping mall cum office complex, the project is a landmark building in Ambala. With two floors consisting of a shopping mall at lower levels and modern offices on upper levels, the total built-up area is 75,000 sq. ft. It also has a multiplex and a lavish rooftop restaurant.

Interstate Bus Terminus (ISBT), Dwarka, New Delhi
The multi-modal transit facility located in Sector 22, Dwarka, integrates an interstate and intercity bus terminal and a cluster bus depot under one roof to create this para-transit hub. The interplay of masses to create its grand form and the use of dynamic LED façades makes this building a landmark. This project has been designed for the Delhi Transport Infrastructure Development Corporation Limited.

Savoy Suites, Manesar, Haryana
A first-of-its-kind project, it accommodates an outlet mall and service apartment complex along the Delhi–Jaipur National Highway. The mall has outlet stores for branded retail, a food court, a banquet hall for 1,000 persons' capacity and a service apartment complex.

Spirit Global Mall, Ludhiana, Punjab
This is a shopping mall of 4,00,000 sq. ft. with a hypermarket, anchor stores, retail, food court and complete entertainment centre. The building is designed as a multilevel facility with an interestingly designed atrium that connects various levels while being staggered in different parts of the complex.

Aerocity, New Delhi
Spread over an expansive area of 65 acres, Aerocity has been planned and designed as a one-of-its-kind integrated hospitality district. The project comprises the planning and integration of retail spaces, convention centres, offices, areas of recreation, restaurants, etc., in addition to 5,000 rooms which are spread in different hotels, ranging from seven-star super deluxe category to budget hotels.

Sikkim House, New Delhi
Prominently located in Chanakyapuri, Delhi, the four-storey guest house complex is centrally air-conditioned and has forty guest rooms and suites. The architecture is distinctly reflective of the culture of Sikkim.

Westin Hotel, Kolkata, West Bengal
A world-class complex consisting of a five-star Westin Hotel, service apartments ranging between 5,000 to 7,000 sq. ft. each, a shopping mall and a four-star vedic resort. It is one of the tallest buildings of Kolkata.

Ambience Mixed-Use Complex, Gurugram, Haryana
A high-end commercial and recreational centre, it has been envisaged to be a landmark destination consisting of a five-star hotel with 225 rooms, shopping mall, restaurants, cineplex and a convention centre.

Grand Mansion Hotel, New Delhi
The project is an exclusive five-star hotel and entertainment complex and, besides accommodating the facilities of a super deluxe hotel, the project consists of a shopping mall, a multiplex and a food court. The hotel has been designed in association with Wimberly Allison Tong & Goo (WATG), London.

Mixed-Use Complex, Dehradun, Uttarakhand
The first-of-its-kind integrated township in Dehradun, with a built-up area of 30 lakh sq. ft., it comprises a shopping mall, a multiplex, a budget hotel and housing, varying from 2 to 4 bedrooms.

IFFCO Club, Aonla, Uttar Pradesh
The IFFCO Club in Aonla has been designed to cater to the township population of 10,000 and has extensive facilities for indoor game activities besides a swimming pool. Apart from space for sports like badminton, squash and billiards, the club also has a library and reading rooms for members.

The LaLiT Golf & Spa Resort, Goa
A five-star resort hotel designed for Bharat Hotels Limited with 270 rooms and suites, bungalows and exclusive villas each with an individual swimming pool. The beach resort has a casino and an 18-hole golf course and is developed on 85 acres of land in South Goa. The project is extensively landscaped with native vegetation.

Gold Souk Mall, Gurugram, Haryana
A unique shopping mall, it houses jewellery stores from all across India. The project, with the most advanced technological and security systems, also comprises a grand atrium, an exhibition hall, conference facilities, food court and a terrace garden.

Integrated Entertainment Complex, Reis Magos, Goa
A unique residential and entertainment centre, it is designed on a 30-acre hilly site. It has exclusive landscaped facilities, connected by a cable car within the complex. With an artificial lagoon and beach, the complex has a 100-room hotel, exclusive villas, a retail village, a spa and an ayurvedic centre.

KRIBHCO Club, Hazira, Gujarat
Located in the township of Krishak Bharati Co-operative Limited (KRIBHCO), it is one of the most actively utilized public buildings in the township. It has an Olympic-size swimming pool and facilities for all the conceivable indoor and outdoor games such as table tennis, squash, children's play rooms, library and an indoor badminton court.

Surat Multi-Modal Transportation Hub, Surat, Gujarat

The project is a first-of-its-kind multi-modal transportation hub, with 100 lakh sq. ft. of development. The project emphasizes on world-class infrastructure with an integrated and efficient transportation hub. The roof over the platforms symbolizes fluidity, designed with an inspiration from the image of woven fabric. The twin towers, which are also the 'Gateway to the City', have an envelop of perforated membrane over their façade.

MMR, Noida, Uttar Pradesh

The project is a mixed-use development and comprises nine cinema halls, an underground shopping mall, which is a one-of-its-kind design proposal, and office spaces. The project seeks to add luxury and variety to the thriving culture of Noida.

Le Meridien, Goa

The project is a five-star super deluxe beach resort. It was designed to have 250 rooms and 125 villas along with facilities such as restaurants, pool, offices, etc.

Delhi Gymkhana Club, New Delhi

The project included the Master Planning of the entire complex, Structural improvements, Renovation and Interior Design of the main club building, cottages and staff housing.

The LaLiT Grand Palace, Srinagar, Jammu and Kashmir

A former palatial residence of the Maharajas, this five-star hotel, owned by Bharat Hotels Limited, overlooks the famous Dal Lake and is within close proximity of the Governor's House. It has 122 rooms, including sixteen suites, and a host of guest facilities. The project also includes a nine-hole golf course and a jogging track. Additional facilities include private cottages, a health centre, an indoor swimming pool, tennis and squash courts.

Oswal Towers, Ludhiana, Punjab

This is a six-storeyed shopping and commercial complex located on the busy Mall Road. The terraced building has a high-class shopping centre spread over four floors around an atrium. The building will house the corporate headquarters of Punjab Woolcombers Limited.

Ansal Royal Plaza, Jodhpur, Rajasthan

A first of such complexes in Jodhpur, it has been designed for the Maharaja of Jodhpur and the Ansal Group. The project includes a shopping mall, a multiplex, a food court, an entertainment centre and an office complex.

India International Convention Centre (IICC), New Delhi

In order to capitalize on the vast meetings, incentives, conferences, and exhibitions (MICE) market potential and to drive India's economic industry, associating itself with programmes such as Make in India, promoting tourism, trade and commerce activities, the need for a large scale Exhibition cum Convention Centre (ECC) was felt. IICC is located in Dwarka, Delhi. The project built-up area is more than 1 crore sq. ft. of development.

Parsvnath City Centre Mall, Ranchi, Jharkhand

The project comprises a shopping mall and an entertainment centre which includes retail, anchor stores, a hypermarket, a multiplex, a bowling alley, food court and other entertainment facilities, a five-star hotel, luxury housing and a sophisticated spa and club. The total project has a built-up area of 10,00,000 sq. ft.

Unitech Club, Gurugram, Haryana

A high-profile resort club in South City Township, it was designed by the Architects for Unitech Limited. The club has a well-equipped health club, restaurant, bar, banquet hall, billiards and guest suites. Outdoor sports facilities have also been provided, including a large swimming pool.

JW Marriott, New Delhi

JW Marriott is located at Delhi Aerocity, adjacent to the IGI Airport. The site is spread over 10,00,000 sq. ft. area. It is the largest of its five hotels in India with 523 rooms over seven storeys.

DB City, New Delhi

DB Hospitality project is a high-density mixed-use development situated in the multi-district site of Aerocity. The project brief required a 1,200-room hotel, the largest in the country, a 2,000-seater convention centre, a banquet hall and a parking for 1,400 cars. All this had to be accommodated within only seven floors above ground due to proximity to the airport runway. Such restrictions led to a design wherein, for the first time in India, the complex has seven basements.

Redevelopment of Pragati Maidan, New Delhi
The project entails the development of exhibition-centred areas, an iconic convention centre, along with spaces for well-designed public circulation and recreation facilities.

Shalimar Bagh District Centre Complex, New Delhi
The district centre complex at Shalimar Bagh for Delhi Development Authority includes offices, a vast multilevel shopping centre, a hotel, offices of the city authorities, a bus terminus and other facilities on a site of 25 acres with 2 million sq. ft. built-up area.

Gomti Nagar Railway Station Redevelopment, Lucknow, Uttar Pradesh
The 1,000 crore project has state-of-the-art architecture and technology amalgamated into an integrated, efficient and smart transportation hub. The project is the first-of-its-kind in the country, with income generated through retail facilities contributing to the station's redevelopment.

Gandhinagar Railway Station Redevelopment, Gandhi Nagar, Gujarat
This project involves the redevelopment of the existing Gandhinagar Capital Station (GNC) building through various passenger amenities and facilities, including a 300-room hotel above the station tracks.

Logix Riviera, Noida, Uttar Pradesh
A mixed-use commercial and hospitality complex, located on a prime land in Sector 105, Noida, it boasts of luxury four- and five-star hotels, premium shopping and entertainment centres and a high-rise corporate office tower.

City Bus Terminal (CBT), Noida, Uttar Pradesh
This prestigious urban infrastructure project in Noida lies along the highway. A richly landscaped foreground leads to the terminal, which features a shopping mall, a 1,000-seater multiplex and a 150-room hotel with a built-up area of 10,00,000 sq. ft. The architectural expression is inspired from Indian design sensibilities and uses lattices and colonnades.

Logix City Centre, Noida, Uttar Pradesh
A prestigious mixed-use project in the prime location of Sector 32, Noida. It comprises a five-star 300-room Starwood Westin Hotel, an Olympic-size ice-skating rink, retail with multiplex, 150-room Fairfield Marriott Hotel, high-end offices, extensive recreational and food court facilities. The project is spread over 6 acres with a total built-up area of 15 lakh sq. ft.

India Pavilion, World Expo 2020, Dubai, UAE
India Pavilion at the World Expo 2020 is a national competition winning entry. The Expo seeks to represent the potpourri of cultures housed by a country. The project would encompass offices, meeting rooms, display booths, shopping and eating areas, etc.

Interstate Bus Terminus (ISBT), Anand Vihar, New Delhi
Designed for Delhi Integrated Multi-Modal Transit System Limited, the redevelopment project for this bus terminal aims to cater to the staggering volumes of passengers it would serve for the next four decades. With a built-up area of over 10,00,000 sq. ft., it includes state-of-the-art retail and office facilities and a hotel. With a capacity of 300 buses, both on and under the ground, it is integrated to the Delhi Metro and Anand Vihar Railway Station, truly making this project a para-transit marvel.

Club Mahindra Pristine Peak Resort, Baldeyan, Himachal Pradesh
Nestled in the valley of Shimla, and spread over 6 acres, the design of the resort plays with the contours at the site whilst offering exquisite and serene views. The green spires of the roofs mimic the steep Himalayan range in its backdrop.

GBP Centrum, Zirakpur, Punjab
The project is spread over 4 acres of land and is a mixed-use development. It has been designed to provide commercial, office and retail spaces in Zirakpur, Chandigarh. Showrooms, SOHO (Small Office Home Office) spaces, restaurants, spas and a four-star luxury hotel are being included in the property that is also set to be the tallest in Zirakpur with nineteen storeys.

Interstate Bus Terminus (ISBT), Noida, Uttar Pradesh
The inception of ISBT Noida, the design for which is an integrated facility of different services – commercial, retail, transport, etc., has been inspired by the boom in real estate development in NCR over the past decade. The project is spread over 50 acres of prime land parcel.

Incredible!nd

MISCELLANEOUS

Certain projects defy inclusion in a broad typological categorization. It is more interesting to collate them as miscellaneous, leaving an open end for the future. The scale and function of these projects are also such that they are better suited in a special curation. The projects in this category range from diplomatic missions, religious places, legislative assemblies, international pavilions and high commissions to exhibition and convention centres, and transit-oriented developments, in addition to many others.

Karmapa International Buddhist Institute

Location **New Delhi** Site **1.2 acres** Built-up area **60,000 sq. ft.** Year of completion **1990**

Built for His Holiness, the 16th Gyalwa Karmapa, *the monastery is* ***a striking representation of traditional Sikkimese architecture*** *in the city's urban landscape*

There is an undeniable dichotomy within the urban fabric of Delhi, as its rich heritage coexists with the chaotic and unplanned development of the city. The Karmapa International Buddhist Institute is an oasis of calm and serenity in such a context, and was built for His Holiness, the 16th Gyalwa Karmapa, in 1990.

The site was carefully selected and aptly suggested for a project of this demeanour. The Institute is located in Qutab Institutional Area, overlooking the Sanjay Van. The location, nestled in a thick cover of greenery, is an inspiration for the students, who are offered magnificent views of the expansive green cover. The design was conceptualized as a seamless integration of this natural cover with the built form.

The four-storeyed edifice leaves a striking impression on the visitors from the very first glance. The stupendous scale of the front façade imposes itself on the visitors, leaving them spellbound with the beauty of an edifice influenced by traditional Sikkimese architecture. The flow of volume in spaces is seamless, traversing with fluidity between the exterior and interior. A harmonious rhythm in the alignment of different rooms creates a sense of serenity within the Institute.

As one enters the campus, one is engaged in a balanced symphony of a combination of colours and textures. The Architects derived their inspiration for design sensibilities from the Buddhist philosophy. The space had to be a confluence of meditative contemplation juxtaposed with high-spirited energy. The inwardly designed campus is, thus, an inspiration for the students to indulge in meditation practices, encouraging them to look within themselves, while the symphony of colours incorporates an exuberance in the atmosphere.

The central courtyard is a hearty extension of the colourful façade from the vertical face of the building to the horizontal landscape. Its terrain is designed with neatly lined and pruned flower shrubs whilst providing common space for faculty and students to bask during the sunny winter mornings in the capital.

The imposing blocks at the entrance act as guards to sieve energy flowing from the exterior of the Institute to its interiors, creating a safe haven for those practising Buddhism. The main block of the Institute consists of a large prayer hall, classrooms, meditation rooms and

Facing page: *A view highlighting details of the columns inspired by traditional Sikkimese architecture.*

Below: *A detail of the artwork on the ceiling of the monastery, made using natural pigments.*

Top: *A watercolour showcasing the intricate carving detail on the capital of the columns.*

Facing page top left: *A view of the interior courtyard.*

Facing page top right: *Carved details on lintels of the doors.*

Facing page bottom left: *Frontal façade of the monastery.*

Facing page bottom right: *The detailed carving and use of typical Buddhist colours on the ceiling, columns and doors impart vibrancy throughout the project.*

a library. Located on the first floor, the library has been designed as a 'knowledge centre', offering a wide selection of religious and dharma books. The prayer hall is a magnanimous space which opens up to magnificently and opulently designed interiors. The ornate mouldings and traditional art motifs translate effortlessly from the exterior façade of the Institute to the interior of the hall. Surrounded by *thangkas*, the hall hosts a magnificent statue of Buddha at the centre. A clear demarcation between the worshipping students and monks from the holy deities has been established through a difference in levels, where the deities are placed at a higher platform. The dining hall is in the basement of the building, with an uninterrupted span, to allow students and the faculty to feast together. The rooms for students surround the main building and have been designed to accommodate 300 persons at a given time. They are divided into two types: small rooms with an attached private bathroom and common rooms with shared bathrooms. It was ensured that all rooms were equipped with a minimum of two beds, a desk and chair, book shelf and wardrobe.

As one moves through the corridors, one is greeted by the interior courtyard in individual blocks, which allows for transparency, ease of visibility and unobstructed flow of air between different floors. For the months of extreme heat and humidity, students are engulfed in a state of thermal comfort with naturally regulated ventilation channelled through the Institute. Since the design brief for the classrooms and meditation halls was to accommodate a significant number of students, they are expansive in their spans. Through large window openings, natural light flooding the interiors makes them spacious and airy. Additionally, provision of wide window openings passively regulates the temperature in the rooms.

In order to replicate the intrinsic architectural features of the original Rumtek Monastery in Sikkim, around fifty highly skilled local craftsmen from Sikkim were engaged, giving them an opportunity to showcase their workmanship, thereby empowering them. This project placed special focus on sustainability as only natural dyes and pigments were used to create artwork in the building. Inspired by the Monastery, which was built almost entirely in timber and stone, the Architects recreated the Tibetan architectural vocabulary in brick and concrete, more suitable to the climate of the capital city.

ARMAPA INTERNATIONAL BUDDHIST INSTITUTE

East Delhi 'Smart Transit-Oriented Development' Hub

Location **New Delhi** Site **60 acres** Built-up area **1,50,00,000 sq. ft.** Year of completion **2023 (Estimated)**

A first-of-its-kind transit-oriented development to grace the urbanscape of the capital city, this ***100-storeyed tower is the tallest in the country***

Born out of contemporary urban dynamics are ambitious demands that urban planners seek to fulfil through innovative and path-breaking design concepts. For instance, the search for auto-adjustable, spontaneous and responsive people's architecture for our contemporary cities still continues to exercise the imagination of our architects, planners and urban designers. There is an urgent need for smart built environments, economic sustainability, energy and resource conservation in tandem with state-of-the-art infrastructure that is suitable for all.

East Delhi Hub in Karkardooma, envisioned for the Delhi Development Authority (DDA)/NBCC, attempts to live up to such ambitious demands. A comprehensive design approach contributed to the Architects winning this prestigious project in an international competition.

This project aims to create an architectural typology that responds to transit network and movement patterns of the city. To enable this, the project has incorporated findings from studies on density control, urban massing and public space network that define the architecture supporting circulation networks within a city.

The use of 'organic density' as a tool for spontaneous adaptation to environmental and economic diversity, and as an auto-adjustable controlling measure for the population influx and activities within the urban complex, lies at the crux of this revolutionary vision. This also involves a deep understanding of the circulation pattern of visitors and residents in and around the site.

By studying and mapping the surrounding transportation centres, the Architects were able to improve planning for urban movement as well as circulation within the site. The circulation network follows axial planning, which is an unobstructive and efficient form of planning. Another important factor was the concept of an inclusive high-rise housing complex. By designing areas of social recreation on higher levels, the Architects were able to resolve the issue of creation of silos in high-density urban areas.

The development of this project is a successful example of harnessing and integrating technology. This not only encourages a more nuanced and high-functioning security system and user-comfort spaces, but also helps in the overall management of the site. In addition, a smart system of technology equips the residential and commercial towers with a high-speed connection and communication mechanism for its residents. This includes

Facing page: *An aerial visualization of the transit-oriented development (TOD).*

Below*: A rendered Master Plan of the development.*

Above: *A visualization of the design showcasing the high– and low-density urban massing wherein the volume is softened by interspersing greenery within different levels of the façade.*

efficiency in information regarding pollution levels, weather conditions, occupancy within different blocks and traffic news updation in and around the site.

The project seeks to thrive as a green and futuristic hub of development, aspiring to bring back the lush green cover, vital to regulate water percolation into the soil, benefitting the depleting levels of ground water. With the burgeoning of green spaces horizontally as well as vertically, the expansive green cover within the site impersonates a forest ensemble, absorbing carbon dioxide and significantly reducing the heat island effect.

This design is being achieved through an interesting combination of high– and low-density urban massing distributed at different vertical levels, which allows myriad public activities to take place at different levels. The idea of a high-rise development is aimed at creating vertical neighbourhoods that would free up considerable area of open, green spaces horizontally – a resource that is depleting in the city more and more with every passing day. These green spaces will become vibrant public spaces that contain different leisure and multi-purpose activities. The squares and plazas are lined with commercial development in order to ensure 'eyes on the streets', rendering the public areas safe for everyone.

In an attempt to bring landscape to the upper floors, vertical gardens and green terraces have also been proposed to provide 'green for all'. The vertical greens also create an interesting elevation treatment – a skin made with a combination of man-made materials and natural plantations. The façades use a combination of two or three layers of *jaali* in different patterns to trap dust and create standing waves that damp out any noise from the nearby Anand Vihar terminus and the high-speed corridors around it.

The building masses of tower are designed to create an interesting pattern of urban solids and voids that allow natural light and ventilation

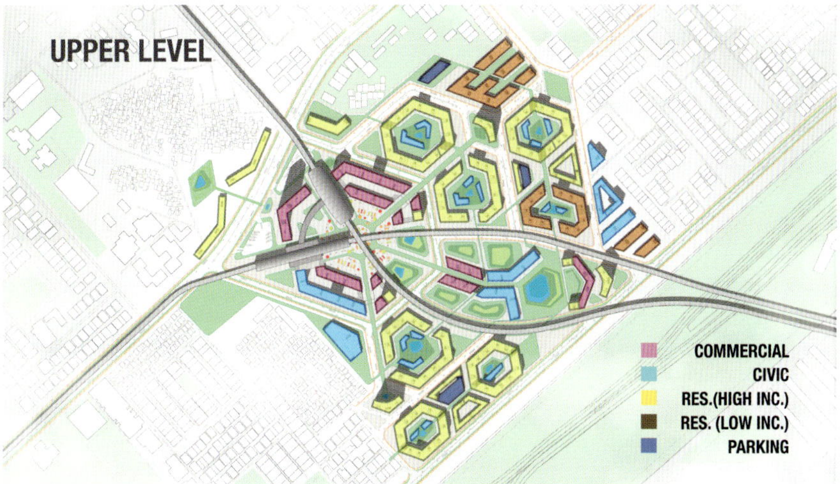

Top: *Zoning to highlight different areas of functions on the tower level.*

Centre: *Zoning to highlight different areas of functions on the upper level.*

Bottom: *Zoning to highlight different areas of functions on the street level.*

within the complex all year round. The towers soar high above the landscape, connecting the city with the sky. These towers are envisioned to also function as 'watch-towers', contributing to smart urban surveillance.

The project uses clean and green technology as one of its virtues, accommodating water and waste management systems. With most of the waste being segregated on site, the biodegradable waste is recycled, grey water is used on-site, and rainwater is stored and harvested for the residents to benefit from. Today, the East Delhi Hub is emerging as a fine example of smart, green urban architecture and a forerunner of the Smart City Movement in India.

East Delhi Hub is not only a miniature Smart City, but a definition of 'living organic architecture' on real ground. In fact, East Delhi Hub will show the way for smart, auto-adaptive and responsive architecture in the days to come. This project has been dedicated to define the art of smart living for smart communities of our future generations.

India International Convention Centre

Location **New Delhi** Area **225 acres** Built-up area **1,22,00,000 sq. ft.**

Year of completion **Phase 1: 2021; Phase 2: 2025**

A first-of-its-kind urban scale mixed-use development, the ***state-of-the-art Convention Centre is Asia's second largest and third largest in the world,*** *with a capacity to host 10,000 people*

Despite India's sustained levels of growth and immense economic potential, the exhibition industry has not grown in tandem with the economic expansion and urban development in the capital city. A need was felt to provide a space which could be a common ground for interaction between Indian businesses, investors and buyers to catalyse existing economic activities in the country. To exhibit India's growth and achievements at an international level, the India International Convention Centre has been conceived as a smart and efficient mixed-use urban development which would help support the country's GDP growth in the long haul. The concept has been curated as a successful juxtaposition of varied nature of developments such as exhibition, convention, retail, hospitality, offices, museum and many more, and is designed to cater to the indigenous as well as the international exhibitors.

Envisaged at the scale of a Central Business District (CBD), the design of this massive project pays close attention to creating connections with Indian culture and tradition while aiming to embody the ambitions of a forward looking nation through a contemporary interpretation of Indian planning principles and architecture. Multiple accesses to this complex create porosity and permeability to the urban context, thereby integrating it to its vicinity.

The state-of-the-art Convention Centre is Asia's second largest, and third largest in the world, with a capacity to host 10,000 people at any given time. The centre is designed to host the G20 Summit and other such mega international events in India, along with international conferences, exhibitions and trade shows. With a site area of 225 acres, the project also boasts of mixed land use such as retail, commercial spaces and 3,700 hotel rooms as well as a 20,000 seater, one-of-its-kind, world-class indoor arena with a retractable roof, which would be built in India for the first time.

Not only is the scale of the project vast, but also the parameters with which the design is being tailored are innovative and futuristic: Green Building principles and IGBC (Indian Green Building Council) Platinum rating standards are being used as a benchmark for formulating the design.

The project is strategically located adjacent to the international airport and at

Facing page: *A visualization of the aerial view of the project.*

Below: *A visualization of the exhibition halls in a stepped form giving a sense of buoyancy to the building.*

Above: *A visualization of the Convention Centre with the 'LED Crown' roof design.*

Facing page: *A visualization of the metro station with solar panels on the roof, making it energy efficient.*

the crossroads of Gurugram and Delhi. A major transportation hub has been created in the heart of the site which offers great public connectivity. The government hopes that the mega-scale urban project in the capital city will act as a catalyst for industrial growth in the country and catapult India as a global meetings, incentives, conferences, and exhibitions (MICE) destination.

The building envelops are designed to communicate an image of contemporaneity inspired by tradition. A thoughtful skin system is proposed to achieve sustainability, along with synthesizing each facet of the project, such as materiality, constructability and budget. It is mainly focused on performance and constructive optimization. All façades are proposed to be layered in two orders: the first one will be a regular system attending to all static conditions, and other will be a structural system, optimized to be integrated as the building structure.

The mobility at the micro level has been kept hassle-free with a car free zone, pedestrian walkways and availability of electric transport. Pedestrians are provided with shades and views through the green boulevards and semi-open spaces, which encourage user interaction whilst providing naturally inspired recreational spaces. Water features run parallel to the green

Above: *A visualization of the* jaali *detail used throughout the project.*

Facing page: *The indoor arena's exterior membrane is reminiscent of a saree.*

landscape, complementing the design and breaking the monotony of the static hardscape and also influencing the microclimate of the area.

The Convention Centre fronts the site at the northern end. The exhibition centre is a collection of a sequence of five exhibition halls, fronted by a large arched lobby. The roof is shaped into a series of leaning arches, fusing a mix of contemporary design with ethnic sensibilities, which changes with movement of the observer. The arches also provide spaces for skylights, penetrating natural daylight inside the halls. One of the most talked about design feature includes crowning of the Convention Centre with, what is poised to be the world's largest, LED video wall. Specially engineered for the project, the video wall LEDs will be accessible from behind, and grating catwalks would be provided for ease of maintenance.

Adding to the long list of features designed as per international standards, the exhibition hall has a 4,200 seater auditorium, which is furnished with retractable seats and stage area and can serve as a multipurpose hall when the requirement arises. The façades of the halls would be a combination of three dimensional and flat Glass-fibre Reinforced Concrete (GRC) panels, which would serve as a responsive system towards thermal control, structural energy and acoustic regulations.

The sustainable approach in design thinking also reflects through an effort to recycle and reuse waste being generated at the site, and effectively manage solid waste produced through a comprehensive management plan. The design utilizes abundant solar energy through power and water heating systems.

The design is a representation of an integration between traditional architectural elements – like *jaalis*, stepwells, green open spaces, a lotus motif embossed on the retractable roof of the indoor arena, to name a few – projected with a contemporary outlook through forms and spaces at the site. Walkability has been kept at the core of landscape design with paths lined with local plant species, creating green boulevards and courtyards wherever possible, shading areas with colonnades and canopies, keeping in mind a universal accessibility for users. Façades have been designed intelligently in order to regulate diffused sunlight in public areas. Water bodies throughout the site help passively cool the environment while complementing the green spaces. The design and materials for the pavement are conceptualized to make percolation of water possible. The idea is to push for methods which can help in stabilizing the otherwise parched water table of the region.

The project is a futuristic development model to catapult India as a forerunner in sustainable design practices while also providing an arena to display its spectacular innovation and engineering skills. The project, with its revolutionary ideas, is being touted as a fine example of development of a mini-cityscape, thriving as an urban biodiversity in the midst of a concrete jungle.

Redevelopment of Pragati Maidan

Location **New Delhi** Site **125 acres** Built-up area **65,00,000 sq. ft.**

Year of completion **2020**

An homage to one of the city's iconic developments, the redevelopment ***infuses a vernacular aesthetic with the latest technology,*** *curating a design which is a futuristic leap for the country*

The Pragati Maidan Exhibition Complex has been an icon for the capital city for decades and has played host to innumerable exhibitions and conventions, besides the world famous India International Trade Fair that is held every November. Over the years, the need for the expansion of the complex and a resolve to ease its adaptation to modernistic sensibilities of the present times has been felt. In accordance with the same, the Ministry of Commerce, Government of India, decided to redevelop the facility into an international-level integrated Exhibition cum Convention Centre (ECC).

The Pragati Maidan Convention Centre is located in the heart of Delhi. The complex is spread across approximately 125 acres, overlooking the historic Purana Qila and flanked by the famous Mathura Road and Bhairon Road on either sides. It is also in close proximity to the Supreme Court of India. The Architects were entrusted with the responsibility of detailed design of architecture, landscape and engineering for the project, based on the concept by Aedas.

For a noteworthy site such as this, a balance between contemporary design ideas with the historical identity of the location became one of the influential aspects of design ideation. Design proposal for the prestigious project, thus, was carried forth keeping the particular requirements in mind to create an iconic centre of recreation and business.

Facing page: *The seamless span of the front façade of the Convention Centre provides a striking panoramic view of the city.*

The magnificence of the built edifices is softened by the impressive landscape which balances and ties the design into a congruous conglomeration. The favourable location of the project contributes towards an ease of urban mobility. Boulevards and semi-covered recreation spots are created using long spans of pergolas and gazebos. The design thrives by accommodating expansive open spaces, using water as one of its primary landscape features which, channeling through the site, effectively regulates and maintains its thermal comfort.

Within the existing geometric constraints, a structurally efficient framing system has been identified. Formulating a structural system to achieve the unique profile of the building with minimum disruptions to the functional layout is adopted. Structural member sizes are optimized to maximize stiffness and minimize weight to control overall building stresses and movements under wind, seismic and gravity loads to within acceptable levels. This also ensures satisfactory performance under seismic and wind loads for human comfort.

The Mechanical, Electrical and Plumbing (MEP) system selection and design focuses on reliability, maintainability, energy efficiency and optimum cost. For instance, fresh air is pre-cooled by energy recovery unit through exhaust air, thereby reducing the air-conditioning load. The heat transfer is through the heat recovery wheel.

The Convention Centre is proposed to be a world-class state-of-the-art iconic building, which derives its architectural form from the rich heritage of Lutyens' Delhi. It is proposed to become a landmark building for Delhi, accommodating best global facilities and design features in line with modern convention centre requisites. The Convention Centre is being completed in a record sixteen months time period. The striking curve of the front façade provides a panoramic view for the visitors through its seamless span of glass. The use of natural red sandstone as the primary building material helps retain the surrounding urban character while the imposing and robust steel columns hold the large cantilevered edifice intact.

The Convention Centre's infrastructure has been designed to host prestigious and international summits, conclaves, conferences, etc. Strips of sandstone on the façade help mould and strengthen the profile further, enhancing the overall demeanour. The Architects were extremely cautious of incorporating/integrating MEP facilities in the edifices so as to not interfere with these intricate design details.

The design includes spaces such as lobbies, ticketing pre-function and public circulation spaces, VIP rooms and backstage waiting areas, various sizes of meeting rooms, a 1,000-seater lecture theatre, amphitheatre, and a 4,000-seater multipurpose hall. Other amenities include Food and Beverage (F&B) outlets, business centres and meeting rooms, and presidential and VVIP lounges at podium, plenary and terrace levels. For a project that seeks to achieve a distinguished stature in the capital, the Architects imbibed a meticulous MEP design. This ensures thermal comfort for distinguished dignitaries and VIPs using the space, as well as the general public visiting the exhibitions, conventions, etc. The building exterior at night time is envisaged as an iconic object appearing to 'float' over the landscape.

The landscape design of the Convention Centre has been used as an integral element to frame the overall concept. A stream of water flows through the contoured landscape fronting the Centre, producing an effervescence in the atmosphere. This entrance path is lined with dense foliage on either sides, creating an intimate boulevard with the Convention Centre in the front and the vast sky above. The interaction which so ensues allows visitors to feel one with their built environment.

The exhibition halls are designed as large two-storeyed halls which can easily

Left top: *A visualization displaying the expansive landscape leading to the Convention Centre.*

Left centre: *An interior visualization of the auditorium.*

Left bottom: *A visualization of the exhibition halls.*

Facing page: *A visualization of the entire site through an aerial view.*

accommodate industry exhibitions, trade shows, product demonstrations, corporate events and related activities at both national and international levels. The transparency used in the design easily regulates the circulation and allowance of natural light, and ventilation inside the buildings. The unobtrusive height and the simplistic yet striking design of the exhibition halls project a poised ensemble, balancing the project's flamboyant design.

The project proposes an elaborate basement spanning over an area of approximately 18 lakh sq. ft. The basement is to have an approximately 100 feet wide city tunnel connecting the Purana Qila Road to Ring Road to enable decongestion of traffic. The basement has a parking facility for 46 buses and 3,200 cars.

The project reinforces India's global image as a fast developing nation which is poised to occupy centre stage in trade, commerce, conventions and exhibitions. The sensitive approach undertaken to redevelop the urban land catapults it to a one-of-its-kind archival project, while the customized technology incorporated into the fabric of the project leaves visitors with a first-of-its-kind experience.

Indian High Commission

Location **Abuja, Nigeria** Site **5 acres** Built-up area **1,00,000 sq. ft.** Year of completion **2015**

Design adapts and ***reinterprets Indian architectural sensibility*** *juxtaposed in the foreign lands of Abuja*

The design for the chancery complex and High Commission residence in the new capital city of Abuja, Nigeria, was awarded to the firm through an international design competition.

The Indian High Commission in Abuja is situated in a pristine area, surrounded by embassies of other countries. The design has been selectively curated using ideologies hand-picked by Architects from Indian architecture which work well within the context of the site.

On visiting the site, the Architects discovered that the plot allotted to the project happened to fall on the axis along which two prominent hillocks of the city formed a backdrop. This unique opportunity became the genesis for the design which was then developed as a symmetrical composition along this central axis.

One is able to immediately establish a visual connect with India as typical elements, such as *jaalis* and *chhatris*, adorn the façade of the chancery. The chancery building is crowned with a dome, a significant architectural element in important government buildings in India. Another aspect of the dome is that it echoes in its built form the bulbous shape of the twin hillocks.

In an extreme climate such as that of Lagos, the Architects felt it was necessary to keep sustainability at the core of design conceptualization. Utilizing a combination of design elements successfully enabled the rooms with passive thermal comfort. The design lies low to the ground, expanding horizontally to make areas within the building easy to access. The use of subtle hues of local yellow sandstone is pleasing to the eyes in the sore and dry heat of the region. A darker shade of yellow on trims and borders helps highlight façade features, whilst complementing the stronger hues of subdued yellow. The constant endeavour to modulate elevation through levels on the façades reduces the overall area directly exposed to sunlight by creating shadows, thereby reducing the overall heat gain in the building. The use of *chajjas, chhatris* and *jaalis* was also significant in effectively regulating the passive technology in the overall design.

The chancery, thus, stands against the wide and empty skies of Abuja, dominating the skyline with its subtle yet fierce presence, etching its own mark.

Above: *Showcasing the different Indian architectural elements in the front façade of the High Commission.*

Sikkim Guest House

Location **New Delhi** Site **3 acres** Built-up area **70,000 sq. ft.** Year of completion **1988**

*By using **vernacular design aesthetics of Sikkim,** one feels transported away from the hustle and bustle of the city*

Sikkim is located amidst the pristine beauty of Himalayas, where the landscape is an essential part of buildings. The same concept has been followed here, whereby a colourful harmony of engagement through design ensues, making visitors exhilarated to stay within the campus for a quick and peaceful getaway.

Sikkim is a combination of two Limbu words: *su* or 'new', and *khyim*, which means 'palace' or 'house'. Located in the prime location of Chanakyapuri in New Delhi, the four-storeyed complex is a fine representation of the culture and architecture of Sikkim. Surrounded by embassies of other prominent countries, one gets glimpses of the building with its typical bordered moulding on the roof through the dense foliage.

The Architects of the complex wanted its design to reflect the simplicity of Sikkim's culture that makes the state one of the most sought-after destinations in the country. It is centrally air-conditioned and has 40 guest rooms and suites. The façade reflects the traditional charm of Sikkimese architecture, which derives its inspiration from Tibet. The rhythmic and symmetrical placement of windows define a distinctive Tibetan architectural pattern. With intricately carved frames, the windows act as important regulators, facilitating daylight and ventilation to the interiors. They are carved on the inside in tiers and a play in illusion comes into view for visitors. Decorated and carved richly, these framings are given special status in Tibetan architecture and are iconic elements in the design of local architecture in Sikkim.

Below : *A view of the front façade of the guest house showcasing a modern adaptation of the typical Sikkimese window design.*

Sikkim Legislative Assembly

Location **Gangtok, Sikkim** Site **5 acres** Built-up area **1,00,000 sq. ft.** Year of completion **1993**

The design is ***reflective of serenity yet the highest authority of power*** *it holds in the region*

The design for the Sikkim Legislative Assembly was proposed to reflect the combination of the rich architectural and cultural heritage of the region. The foundation stone of the building was laid by the late Giani Zail Singh, President of India, on 30 November 1985 and inaugurated by Admiral R.H. Tahiliani, Governor of Sikkim, on 3 March 1993.

The Legislative complex comprises an assembly hall, committee rooms for the political parties, offices for the chief minister and members of the cabinet and a large conference complex.

The site is located amidst a vast expanse of dense greens on one side, providing lush and far-reaching views away from the city. It is perched atop the edge of the mountain range which makes the Legislative complex one of the first built forms one is able to locate in the city's skyline from a distance. The other side faces the city, sitting at the head of all the buildings, establishing the legislative as the ultimate people's representative.

Upon entering, one is guided from the entrance gates to a drop-off area which is shaded by a majestic porch, held firm by four columns. The capital of the columns are an exquisite combination of mouldings and carvings, fused with colours. These columns are in stark contrast to the otherwise subdued colour palette of the building. Walls are washed in white, a pristine colour imparting an environment of serenity. The roofs are tapered in typical Sikkimese architectural style and painted green, partly camouflaging the building with the greenery of the surrounding hills.

The architectural design of the buildings borrows from the typical Tibetan style, where the windows have stepped wooden frames with swinging roofs with huge overhangs, symbolic of the vernacular architectural style of the region.

The landscape adds to the beauty of the whole campus. Seeded through the front and back lawns, one receives a colourful welcome in the shades of flowers filling up the ground and the finely trimmed grass carpet, influencing movement between buildings. The landscape has been curated in a fashion which engulfs the building complex from the movement outside the site and fosters a politically charged atmosphere within its premises.

The landscape design complements the architectural approach to the built form. Majestic lawns with abundant native plantation and large trees create a foreground for the edifice, magnifying its status as a supreme building of the state.

Below: *A view of the Assembly sitting atop a hill.*

Finland Embassy

Location **New Delhi** Site **5 acres** Built-up area **80,000 sq. ft.** Year of completion **1986**

An ***abstract design of combination of the Lake Kitkajärvi in Northern Finland and the Himalayas in India,*** *binding the two countries through architectural uniqueness*

Located in the diplomatic area of Chanakyapuri, the design for the Embassy of Finland breaks away from box-typology pattern of the surrounding sites and comes into view as a range of snow-clad mountains nestled amidst the green cover of the city.

The prestigious project has been designed in association with architects Raimi and Reila Pietila from Finland. The project consists of a chancery, the ambassador's residence, and housing for the Finnish and Indian staff.

The concept for the design – 'snow speaks on the mountains', won a lot of acclaim as it tied the two nations through their most symbolic natural national reserves. The roof is an abstract design of a combination of the Lake Kitkajärvi in Northern Finland and the Himalayas in India. Irregular and contorted yet sculpturally pleasing, this innovative roof design established a common architectural ground. Through the heights achieved in the roof, skylights neatly tucked in the folding clefts emerge through.

The walls are streamlined with diamond-cut shaped stone cladding, subtly supporting the design of the roof structure. The roof has also been extruded beyond the walls forming large spans of overhangs or *chhajjas* which deflect the sun rays, controlling the entry of light from the exteriors. The Architects had the unique opportunity to associate again with this project three decades later when the Government of Finland decided to undertake a major renovation of the entire complex. The design challenge this time was to deal with this project extremely sensitively, since it had been accorded a heritage status, considering the importance of the original design approach of this project.

Top: *An evening view of the ambassador's residence.*

Above left: *Lush landscape surrounds the design.*

Above right: *A side view of the residence showcasing the deconstructed abstract form of the roof.*

Cultural Centre at Bodhgaya

Location **Bodhgaya, Bihar** Site **13 acres** Built-up area **2,50,000 sq. ft.** Year of completion **2021**

Deriving inspiration from the prevalant Buddhist philosophy in the city, ***the design brings together culture, faith and nature into a single vector***

Bodhgaya is an important pilgrim and tourist destination, and attracts millions of domestic and international tourists. It caters especially to the Buddhist community under the overarching theme of: *'Trailing the footseps of the Buddha: Celebrating the lives contributing to the birth of Buddhism in Bihar'.* Sensing this trend, the Swadesh Darshan Scheme by the Union Ministry of Tourism aims to promote, develop and harness potential tourism here.

A cultural centre facility for Buddhist pilgrimages has been proposed to be developed at this destination to spread art and cultural awareness of the practice as well as to hold performances with historical and spiritual themes. At present no facility of this demeanour exists, and the presence of such a centre will mean significant upgradation of facilities for tourists in the region. It will also add to the attraction and success of Bodhgaya as an important destination of the Buddhist community in Bihar.

The design concept uses elements such as stupa, toranas, *chhatra*, etc., and integrates them in a contemporary view. The project comprises a world-class convention hall of a capacity for 2,000 persons, and smaller halls for seating 500 persons, seminar halls, meeting and conference rooms, dining hall, cafeteria and banquet facilities with outdoor event lawns.

The design approach is to explore synergy between a rich Buddhist architectural vocabulary and a modern, twenty-first century public facility. The design celebrates the rich, historically significant local context of the 'birthplace' of Buddhism where Lord Buddha attained enlightenment.

Below : *A visualization of the front elevation of the Centre.*

Canadian High Commission – Diplomatic Residences

Location **New Delhi** Site **17 acres** Built-up area **1,50,000 sq. ft.** Year of completion **2000**

***Pristine white edifices nestled in dense greenscape of the capital city** are able to provide the residents with thermally comfortable spaces*

The Canadian High Commission, located in the posh area of Chanakyapuri in New Delhi, stands facing the beautiful Shantipath Lane. The project involved the design of the housing for the senior diplomats within the premises. The entry for the building is far offset from the main road, first buffered through dense trees guarding the service lane and next by the high-rise boundary wall which guards the buildings. The prestigious project was executed for the Government of Canada.

The concept for the building takes on volumetric play. The planning of the residences is such that it is concentrated on a compact land parcel, allowing for more green and open spaces, culturing a vibrant environment for the residents. The ground floor residents are provided with private courtyards while for the residents on the upper floors, terrace gardens become an open space for recreation. Extensive lawns are variegated across the overall landscape, reducing the ratio of hardscape within the site and in doing so, also creating a sustainable habitat.

The form of the edifices is such that it is able to provide the viewers with a new view as they change their position. The buildings are placed far into the site to maintain the security of the Commission and the high-profile delegates accessing it. The immaculate white shade for the housing was adopted to reflect serenity and tranquility in the crowded sphere of the city. The centrally air-conditioned apartments, built to international specifications, are planned as a low-rise complex. The white mosaic finish on the exterior façade gives the complex a stately appearance. Once inside, the visitors are greeted to a perfectly trimmed and well-maintained front lawn which is ideal for events and as a community recreational space.

The different blocks are connected through pergolas acting as semi-shading devices to ease and encourage pedestrian movement within the site. A swimming pool area has also been provided within the complex. Replete with a carefully designed and well-furnished expansive deck, the pool becomes another point of attraction for community gathering and for social recreation.

Above: *A view of the diplomat residences.*

India Pavilion, Expo 2020 Dubai

Location **Dubai, UAE** Site **1.2 acres** Built-up area **1,00,000 sq. ft.** Year of completion **2021**

Representing India on an international platform at the ***Expo 2020 Dubai, the Pavilion is one of the largest at the Expo, at par with countries such as the USA and China***

The Expo 2020 Dubai is a global stage for renowned architects from all over the world to represent countries whilst showcasing their design finesse. With an overarching theme of *'Connecting Minds, Creating the Future'*, it is a platform promoting partnerships for innovation, inclusion and understanding. For the prestigious design, CPKA, principal architects of the project, have amalgamated ethos of the country's mobility with technology, infusing a sensory stimulus into the Pavilion. It is one of the largest pavilions at the Expo, at par with pavilions of countries such as the USA and China. It is among one of the three pavilions at the Expo that will be retained for posterity in Dubai's legacy phase as an Indian centre.

To represent one of the fastest growing nations in the world, the design of the Pavilion imbibes the theme of *'India on the move'*. With a moving façade that celebrates India's seventy-five years of Independence, the Architects used the design as a platform to showcase the diversity in India's cultural heritage. The building's façade is made up of 600 individual blocks that move using kinetic architecture. Seventy-five stories have been identified which would engage visitors through the charm of storytelling through the day, familiarizing them with the history, geography and literature of the country. In the evening, the façade will turn into a vibrant show with sound, light and projections, as if hosting a festival. The trapezoidal form of the site enables the creation of a visual memorabilia. The vastness brought forth by India's culture and cityscape

Left: *The kinetic façade of the Pavilion uses 600 moving blocks, adapting as a platform to showcase the diversity in India's cultural heritage.*

is condensed within the site. Different design elements, such as the radiant sun-dial and the elaborate amphitheatre, are seamlessly tied into a single harmonious unit. The Pavilion is designed to facilitate economic, social and investment opportunities for the country. Through the Pavilion, the Architects foster the idea of India as a pool of opportunities for investment and collaboration and, at the same time, pay homage to the cultural multifariousness.

The interior design makes the journey inclusive and interactive for the visitors by employing the use of the latest, cutting-edge and innovative technologies. The visitors will get to witness both physical exhibits as well as immersive digital content, which would showcase various sectors in the thriving Indian economy. Programmes such as Make in India, Digital India, Skill India and Start-Up India campaigns would be featured as the key highlights, displaying the country's capabilities on an international level. Muse International designed the interiors. The *India experience* inside the pavilion is designed under eleven themes. As one enters the building, one is fascinated by the starry space guiding them through India's journey in space exploration. As a land of tranquillity and healing, live yoga performers will have projections of mandalas behind them. A walk inside a giant radium will help the visitors to understand the many benefits of Ayurveda. On the first floor, the colours of India in an immersive environment will be showcased with LED walls enveloping the visitors in a heritage experience. Such mesmerizing installations will also help exhibit India's diverse culture. The second floor will display India as a land of endless opportunities. A state-of-the-art theatre hall will be open for meetings, conferences, cultural shows, reception and film screenings.

India Pavilion at Expo 2020 Dubai amplifies India's position on the global map as a thriving hub of limitless possibilities, integrating futuristic approach and mobility while projecting the Indian story in a global narrative.

Right: *Different design elements, such as the radiant sun-dial and the elaborate amphitheatre, have been used as cafeteria and lounge spaces.*

Cultural Centre, Chinese Embassy

Location **New Delhi** Site **10 acres** Built-up area **1,00,000 sq. ft.** Year of completion **1985**

A descriptive exhibit of Chinese architecture, the Cultural Centre follows an ***irregular eye-catching design form***

The Cultural Centre complex within the Chinese Embassy compound is designed in ceramic tile façades and has exhibition spaces, an auditorium, art gallery and offices of the cultural wing of the Chinese Embassy. The entire area is exquisitely landscaped and is a distinctive structure within the Diplomatic Enclave of New Delhi.

The Cultural Centre's façade is a playful rendition of staggered levels, both vertically and horizontally. With an irregular plan, the design is easily able to regulate natural light and ventilation in the interiors because of which a dynamic and playful façade emerges. The volumes of these stepped forms are uniformly arranged on the façade, bringing a balanced element to the design.

Traditional Chinese architectural forms and elements have been very interestingly yet simplistically juxtaposed in a modern architectural language. The main entrance and windows are flanked by an extension, an abstract rendition taking inspiration from the traditional Chinese gateway, the Paifang. This striking feature imposes its scale on the visitors, lending an element of grandeur to an otherwise simplistic form. A horizontal expansion creates a magnificent scale for the onlookers, and it also eases out circulation within the blocks. The Architects' proposal to incorporate a water body, which outlines the centre, came from an understanding of uplifting the design aesthetically. Presence of water would help keep interiors and the surrounding space thermally regulated. Interspersed with green lawns, the Cultural Centre creates pleasant outdoor spaces for events, gatherings, exhibits, etc.

Below: *The front façade of the Cultural Centre showcasing a modern adaptation of Chinese architecture.*

Denmark Embassy

Location **New Delhi** Site **2 acres** Built-up area **70,000 sq. ft.** Year of completion **2019**

***Vertical and horizontal elements synchronized harmoniously** present a contemporary design aesthetic*

Located in the distinguished area of Chanakyapuri, the prestigious project involved design of the embassy as well as the diplomatic residences.

The Architects carefully segregated the site into two parts – chancery and residential blocks. Taking advantage of a relatively wide frontage of the plot, the design allowed both blocks their independent accesses as well as provided security and privacy. The design of the chancery blocks follows inward planning around an open-to-sky courtyard. The façade has been designed using vertical louvres, dismissing any kind of elaborate ornamentation, with minimalistic and functional elements – a very Scandinavian concept. A careful orientation regulates natural ventilation and daylighting within the interiors with ease. A controlled duality in the materials and colour palette used for the edifices highlights the potential and usefulness of minimalism even for a project of this stature. In doing so, the aspects of Danish architecture are highlighted – a modernistic design sensibility, which incidentally, came in for praise from the Former Hon'able Prime Minister of Denmark, Mr. Lars Løkke Rasmussen, when he inaugurated this embassy.

Above: *The front elevation of the Denmark Embassy.*

Below : *A capture of the diplomatic residences.*

Austrian Embassy

Location **New Delhi** Site **5 acres** Built-up area **54,000 sq. ft.** Year of completion **1982**

A modern derivation of traditional design elements *such as* chhajjas, jaalis, *louvres, has helped curate a contemporary scultptural edifice*

Surrounded by a dense landscape of greens, the pristine white demeanour of the Austrian Embassy reflects a sense of serenity in the urban chaos of the city. It is located in the diplomatic area of Chanakyapuri. For the design of the embassy, the Architects sought to juxtapose Indian design elements over a contemporary planning, creating a unique modern edifice.

The design is climate responsive, incorporating design elements such as vertical louvres on the façade, extended slab of roof (*chhajjas*), central courtyard planning, terrace gardens, to name a few. The interiors are spacious and airy and the careful orientation of the buildings allows natural daylight to liven up the mood. Sunlight entering the interiors is broken into fragments by the vertical louvres on the façade, creating diffused light. By keeping the height of the edifices low, the design works positively in this endeavour and ensures optimum light and wind circulation. Along with this, the surrounding cover of trees also maintains privacy for the embassy and its residents.

An undulating façade and distinct perforations on *chhajjas* and balconies create unique and playful patterns, showcasing an intricate understanding of architectural influences on the project by the Architects. A project done in collaboration with Austrian architect, Heinz Scheide, the simple yet striking design of the embassy enables it to seamlessly blend with its surroundings.

Below: *Front façade of the embassy.*

Paryatan Bhawan

Location **New Delhi** Site **9 acres** Built-up area **2,00,000 sq. ft.** Year of completion **Ongoing**

Magnificent sweeping roof structure, cantilevered delicately, *exudes engineering par excellence whilst establishing an architectural marvel*

Located opposite the iconic Birla Mandir in Delhi, is the site for Paryatan Bhawan (Ministry of Tourism, Government of India). The Architects were given a unique design brief wherein along with the development of the office building, they had to plan for a multilevel parking facility of 500 cars for the general public, who mostly visit the adjacent temple.

The Architects responded to the universal client brief by creating a sculptural edifice which sits majestically along the garden and away from the historic temple, allowing the open space in-between to form a buffer. The building's design is an amalgamation of contemporary and local architecture, creating dynamic forms that stem from the deeply rooted design elements of Indian culture.

The sweeping pergola is an eye-catching feature, the robustness of which creates a powerful impression representing an idea of progress and development. It also exhibits the engineering finesse of the firm, at par with international design ideation. Yet, Indian elements such as traditional ornate moulding, terracing and lattices bring back a familiarity to the cultural roots, not just as a cosmetic decoration but also as integral components to the overall planning and design of the building.

The landscape has been exquisitely designed with spaces for exhibitions, cultural events as well as a ridge ecology, establishing it as a memorable design.

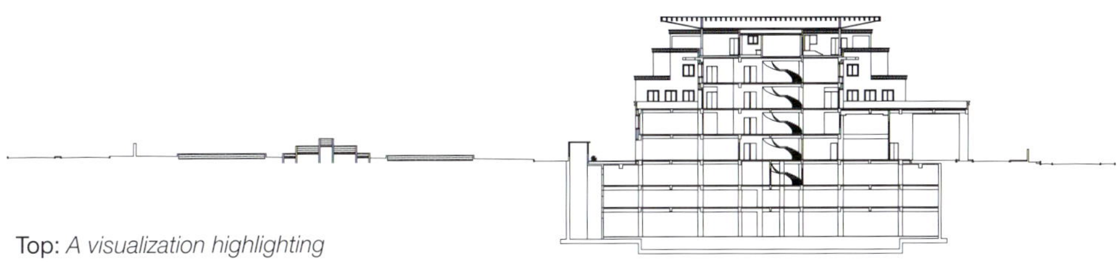

Top: *A visualization highlighting the sweeping roof structure.*

Above: *A sectional drawing through the entire site of the project.*

Indian High Commission

Location **Lagos, Nigeria** Site **3.5 acres** Built-up area **40,000 sq. ft.** Year of completion **1989**

Adapting to the harsh climate through** an understanding of **Lagosian concepts and tropical architecture

The design for the Indian High Commission in Lagos had to be a reflection of the culture, art and architectural sensibilities of the country represented on an international scale. In seeking to derive a design that suited the Nigerian landscape, the Architects used a combination of forms weaving Indian design elements into the overall planning. The project consists of design of the chancery and diplomat housing.

The façades have a distinctive Indian architectural character. Full-height arched columns form semi-covered recreation and shared spaces. Each of these columns are arranged rhythmically, at equal distances from one another, forming a visual pattern. The windows are ornamented with a pattern inspired from the local art and aligned in the centre of each of these arches. The chancery has been designed around two courtyards which, in good weather, form interesting assembly areas within the building.

The Architects wanted the High Commission to be a sustainable endeavour. The same was achieved through the use of vernacular design principles and techniques of construction. A pattern of uniformly laid windows, which have an outer layer lattice work, allow controlled but adequate natural light and ventilation. Further, the courtyards play a similar role in controlling the amount of light and ventilation through louvres on the windows of the building. Such features have ensured successful operations of the embassy without complete dependence on electrical power supply, something which was a local challenge in the times when this embassy was built in Nigeria. A continuous semi-shaded corridor around the main Commission building cools the air before it enters the building and helps regulate the temperature naturally. The building also sits nestled in a landscape of dense foliage, also acting as a visual and a noise barrier.

Left: *A view of the High Commission showcasing the beautiful confluence of Indian and Nigerian architectures.*

US Embassy – ACSA Facilities Centre and Diplomatic Residences

Location **New Delhi** Site **6 acres** Built-up area **50,000 sq. ft.** Year of completion **2002**

***Modern materiality complements an Indian design aesthetic** and elements to inspire the residences*

The American Community Support Association (ACSA) is a co-operative which manages the facilities centre for the US residents within the US Embassy complex in New Delhi. The ACSA facility has been redesigned in entirety and the new design includes a 150-seater restaurant, a bar, party rooms, a totally refurbished kitchen, video library, health club and changing rooms.

The housing for senior diplomats of the US Embassy is located within the embassy premises. The project involved the renovation and refurbishing of the townhouses as per modern international specifications. The Architects seeked to collate a design using tropical design elements which would suit the climatology of the city as well.

Elements such as trellises, courtyard spaces, etc., have been used extensively. These design elements are essential in contributing towards sustainable living as the city's temperatures vary on extreme fronts while a well-thought out incorporation of the same translates into an idyllic space for the residents.

The residences are fronted by well-landscaped green spaces which double up as private and shared outdoor lawns. The design of the residences comprises two floors. While the lower floor comprises public areas such as the kitchen, den, dining room and living space, the upper floor is reserved for private areas such as bedrooms. The residences are constructed using brick and mortar which complement the city's climate and check the absorption of heat into the interiors.

A distinctive design element for the project is a continuous trellis which envelops the residences, acting as a second skin for the buildings. It not only shades the residences but, as it extends from the vertical façade into a horizontal plane, also helps to create semi-covered outdoor recreational spaces, perfect for spilling over from the private confines of the indoor spaces. The creepers and foliage interspersed between the trellises help provide a visual buffer for the residents, safeguarding the view from visitors, whilst the dense nature of the same absorbs noise and screens the overall sound within the residences. The idea to allow a membrane of louvres to become an integral part of the entire project was a unique concept, blanketing the residents with a warm embrace, especially in the winter months of the city.

Left: *The embassy harmoniously integrates vernacular elements such as trellises, louvres, central courtyards, etc., to derive a design which is a comfortable residential space for international diplomats.*

Complete Listing of Miscellaneous Projects

India International Convention Centre, New Delhi
In order to capitalize on the vast MICE market potential and to drive India's industry, associated with programmes such as Make in India, promoting tourism, trade and commerce activities, etc. the Delhi Mumbai Industrial Corridor Development Corporation (DMICDC) has proposed the need for a large-scale ECC in Dwarka, Delhi.

Atrium Palace Hotel, Ekaterinburg, Russia
The project is a 200-room super deluxe business hotel in the vibrant city of Ekaterinburg (earlier known as Svervdiovsk). It has an atrium hotel planned around a six-level landscaped lobby. The building form is articulated to blend with the site contours and environment with locally machined bricks used for the façades. The hotel has a heated swimming pool, two restaurants, a business centre, sauna and health club, banquet hall, two bars as well as some commercial office space.

Gomtinagar Railway Station Redevelopment, Lucknow, Uttar Pradesh
The 1,000 crore project has state-of-the-art architecture and technology amalgamated into an integrated, efficient and smart transportation hub. The iconic arch form is introduced as its skin as well as a structural element over the outer face of the terminal. The curvilinear roof of the railway station building is influenced by traditional domes used in Awadh architecture and has been adapted in a contemporary form.

India Pavilion, World Expo 2020, Dubai
India Pavilion at the World Expo 2020 is a national competition winning entry. The Expo seeks to represent the potpourri of cultures housed by the country. The project's mission is to showcase India's future, innovation and research by turning a didactic exhibit into a sensory experience for the visitors.

East Delhi Hub, New Delhi
East Delhi Hub is the first transit-oriented development (TOD) in Delhi and experiments with the new TOD policy drafted by the DDA. It has been envisaged as a 'Smart City' that incorporates an 'organic density' by introducing extensive mixed-use vertical development and the tallest tower in the country of 100 storeys to tackle the issue of high density of population and ensuring safer public spaces.

Finland Embassy, New Delhi
The project consists of the chancery, the ambassador's residence, and housing for the Finnish and Indian Staff. It has been designed in association with Rili and Riema Pietila of Finland and was won through a national competition.

US Embassy – ACSA Facilities Centre and Diplomatic Residences, New Delhi
ACSA is a co-operative which manages the Facilities Centre for US residents within the US Embassy complex in New Delhi. The ACSA facility was redesigned in its entirety and the new design includes a 150-seater restaurant, a bar, party rooms, a totally refurbished kitchen, video library, health club and changing rooms.

Karmapa International Buddhist Institute, New Delhi
Also known as the Rumtek Monastery, the building is an outstanding example of Sikkimese architecture and is a religious institution as well as a house of the Buddhist culture.

Interstate Bus Terminus (ISBT), Dwarka, New Delhi
The multimodal transit facility in Sector 22, Dwarka, integrates an interstate and intercity bus terminal and a cluster bus depot under one roof to create this para-transit hub. The interplay of masses to create its grand form and the use of dynamic LED façades make this building a landmark. This project was done for the Delhi Transport Infrastructure Development Corporation Limited.

Gandhinagar Railway Station Redevelopment, Gandhinagar, Gujarat
This project involves the redevelopment of the existing Gandhinagar Capital Station (GNC) building through various passenger amenities and facilities, including a 300-room hotel above the station tracks. This project is set to be a landmark in the country and uses its axial relationship with other notable places in the vicinity, such as Dandi Kutir and Mahatma Mandir, to create an integrated Master Plan.

Surat Multi-Modal Transportation Hub, Surat, Gujarat
The project is a first-of-its-kind multimodal transport, with 100 lakh sq. ft. of development. The project emphasizes on a world-class infrastructure including an integrated and efficient transportation hub. The roof over the platforms symbolizes fluidity, designed with an inspiration from the image of woven fabric. The twin towers, which are also 'Gateway to the City', have an envelope of perforated membrane on their façade, enclosing the functions within.

The LaLiT & World Trade Centre, New Delhi
A super deluxe five-star hotel for Bharat Hotels Limited, with 540 rooms and suites, five multilevel restaurants, exclusive glass capsule elevators, atrium lobby, banquet hall, party rooms, an executive club, meeting rooms, health club, swimming pool and roof gardens. A unique feature of the hotel complex is a six-storeyed shopping mall, which is centrally air-conditioned and has over 600 shops and extensive office areas. The hotel and shopping complex is provided with a two-level basement parking for 700 cars. Total covered area is 9,00,000 sq. ft.

City Bus Terminal (CBT), Noida, Uttar Pradesh
This prestigious urban infrastructure project in Noida lies along the highway, linking the airport to the city. A richly landscaped foreground leads to the terminal, which features a shopping mall, a 1000-seater multiplex and a 150-room hotel in a built-up area of 10,00,000 sq. ft. The architectural expression borrows from Indian design sensibilities by using elements such as lattices and colonnades.

Cultural Centre, Chinese Embassy, New Delhi
The Cultural Centre complex within the Chinese Embassy compound is designed with ceramic tile overs its façade, and has exhibition spaces, an auditorium, art gallery and offices for the cultural wing of the Chinese Embassy.

Indian High Commission, Abuja, Nigeria
The project involved the design for the chancery complex and High Commission residence in the new capital city of Abuja, Nigeria. The project was awarded to the firm through an international competition.

Redevelopment of Pragati Maidan, New Delhi
The project entails the development of an exhibition centre area, convention centre, spaces for public circulation and support facilities. CPKA were entrusted the responsibility of detailed design of architecture, landscape and engineering for the project based on the concept by a Singaporean firm.

Sikkim Guest House, New Delhi
Prominently located in Chankyapuri, New Delhi, the four-storeyed guest house complex is centrally air-conditioned and has forty guest rooms and suites. The architecture is distinctly reflective of the culture of Sikkim.

East Delhi Mall, Ghaziabad, Uttar Pradesh
The multilevel, mixed-use complex includes retail shops, department stores, hypermarket, food court, a 1,200-seater cineplex, banquet halls and a sixty-room hotel. The project also has conference facilities and speciality restaurants. The total built-up area for the project is 4,50,000 sq. ft.

Delhi Metro Rail Corporation, New Delhi
The design for Line 2 consisted of four underground stations – Delhi University, Old Secretariat, Civil Lines and Kashmere Gate, and associated tunnels for 4.4 km corridor. For Line 3, the metro corridor was extended for 23 km, from Barakhamba Road to Dwarka. The scope of work also included the planning and design of the underground station at Barakhamba Road.

German Embassy, New Delhi
For the project, the design of a new visa section and renovation of existing facilities was included in the scope of the Architects. The external façade of the embassy was designed keeping in mind the climatological factors in the city whilst experimenting with louvre design.

Indian High Commission, Lagos, Nigeria
The design consists of chancery and staff housing. The chancery has been designed around two atriums which, in good weather, form interesting assembly areas within the building. The façades have a distinctive Indian architectural character.

Austrian Embassy, New Delhi
Consisting of the chancery, ambassador's residence and the staff quarters, the project was executed in association with the Austrian architect, Heinz Scheide.

Logix City Centre, Noida, Uttar Pradesh
A prestigious mixed-use project in the prime location of Sector 32, Noida, the Centre comprises a five-star 300-room Starwood Westin Hotel, an Olympic-size ice-skating rink, retail with multiplex, 150-room Fairfield Marriott Hotel, high-end office spaces, extensive recreational and food court facilities spread over 6 acres, with a built-up area of 15 lakh sq. ft.

Shri Kanchi Kamakoti Temple, New Delhi
The temple design is conceptualized on the lines of equal opportunities to all, regardless of caste, age or economic conditions. The acharyas, through charitable trusts, help aid the economically weaker background individuals and families to arrange for marriages, provide homes for the aged and a space for those seeking medical treatment.

Cultural Centre at Bodhgaya, Bihar
A cultural centre facility is being developed in the holy city of Bodhgaya, on a 13-acre site, to spread art and cultural awareness of Buddhism, as well as to hold performances with historical and spiritual themes. With a built-up area of 2,50,000 sq. ft., it will add to the attraction and success of Bodhgaya as an important destination for Buddhist community from all over the world.

Denmark Embassy, New Delhi
Inspired by an international style of architectural design, the project uses clean lines in the plan and façade of the buildings. The chancery and residential blocks were prime requirements in the design.

Logix Riviera, Noida, Uttar Pradesh
A mixed-use commercial and hospitality complex located on a prime land in Sector 105, Noida, it boasts of luxurious four– and five-star hotels, a premium shopping and entertainment centre and a high-rise corporate office tower. The design for Logix Riviera proposed to juxtapose the soaring business tower with the whirling mall below.

Paryatan Bhawan, New Delhi
Located opposite the Birla Mandir, the office building for Paryatan Bhawan has been proposed for the New Delhi Municipal Council (NDMC). Translated as the 'Environmental Secretariat', the complex is unique in its ideation as the office building is enveloped within a magnificent park.

Interstate Bus Terminus (ISBT), Anand Vihar, New Delhi
ISBT, Anand Vihar is designed for the Delhi Integrated Multi-Modal Transit System Limited. With a built-up area of over 10,00,000 sq. ft., it will include state-of-the-art retail and office facilities and a hotel. With a capacity of 300 buses, both on and under the ground, it is integrated to Delhi Metro and Anand Vihar Railway Station, truly making this project a para-transit marvel.

TRANSPORTATION

With India's focus on an international level of development, infrastructural projects have gained significant momentum. The transportation modes have expanded from traditional railway stations to metro stations, multimodal transport hubs and transport-oriented mixed-use developments. The Architects have been at the forefront of such development with involvement in various projects. The participation of the firm ranges from planning to designing. By using advanced building management systems, the Architects are able to anticipate precise calculations well in advance to expedite and improve the quality of the construction process.

Gandhinagar Railway Station Redevelopment

Location **Gandhinagar, Gujarat** Site **20 acres** Built-up area **4,00,000 sq. ft.** Year of completion **2021**

The design sets the benchmark for an ***innovative land use*** *with a* ***world-class hotel facility above the railway tracks,*** *a first-of-its-kind in the country*

The redevelopment plan for Gandhinagar Railway Station or Gandhinagar Capital Station (GNC) is one of Prime Minister Narendra Modi's dream projects. A vanguard in mixed-use redevelopment of public infrastructure facilities, it involves conversion of the existing building into a world-class railway station. A first-of-its-kind redevelopment, it is to be followed by similar restructuring of 6,000 railway stations nationwide.

Design of the station with a hotel facility, which is in tandem with the Platinum-rated LEED (Leadership in Energy and Environmental Design) standards, sets the benchmark for an innovative way of land usage. The site enjoys excellent connectivity with the city as well as with prominent state and national highways. The airport is located 20 km from the site, and the famous Dandi Kutir Museum and the Mahatma Mandir Convention and Exhibition Centre are located at 300 metres. It is also the terminal point of the 3-km axis drawn from the Gujarat Legislative Assembly complex. The entire stretch is developed as Central Vista or Swarnim Park – the greenest part of Gandhinagar with parks, gardens and cultural spaces. The balanced axial geometry of the central axis, threading Mahatma Mandir and Legislative Assembly complex, symbolize the global spirit and one world philosophy of *'Vasudhaiva Kutumbakam'* – the world is one family.

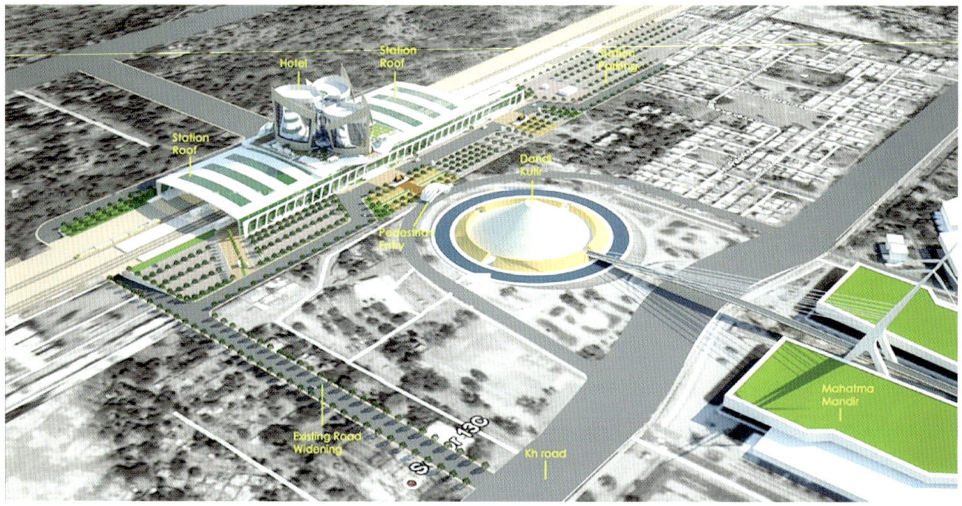

Above: *A visualization of the alignment of the railway station on the axis which connects it with Mahatma Mandir Convention Centre.*

The three wings of the triquetra shape, also referred to as the trinity knot, symbolize the potent and powerful virtues of love, honour and protection – the philosophy, tradition and essence of India. The wings swirling up to the pinnacle are expressive of India's rapid positive growth in its prime sectors.

At a height of 65 metres, the multifunctional aspect of the 300-room Leela Palace Hotel makes it sustainable in concept whilst providing a range of facilities. The GNC includes a new departure and queuing hall, offices for staff, shops and cafeteria, new toilet blocks, a prayer room, a first-aid room, escalators, elevators, modern building management systems (BMS) facilities, Wi-Fi provision and CCTV monitoring, all nestled amidst the lush green landscape. The transit hall for passengers has a seating capacity of over 600. An elevated ramp outside the building segregates the traffic, demarcating areas for pick-up and drop-off facilities. Carefully planned parking ensures safety of pedestrian movement within the site. The design for the building also encourages local artisans and craftsmen to display their art and crafts.

The project has addressed various design challenges – from constructing the tallest building of Gandhinagar over operational railway tracks with uninterrupted train movement, to creating one of the largest single-span roof structures in the country. The sheer power of this harmonious structure, thus, leaves visitors spellbound.

Delhi Metro Rail Corporation

Location **New Delhi** Site **192 km** Year of completion **Yellow line: 2004 (Phase I), 2010 (Phase II); Blue line: 2006**

A revolutionary proposal for the traffic congested capital city, the ***Architects became the pioneers to design major metro stations on the Blue and Yellow Metro lines***

Above: *A visualization of the section showing different levels of an underground metro station.*

The Delhi Metro Rail Corporation (DMRC) proposed a metro system to cover 192 km across the capital's cityscape. Designed by incorporating world-class standards, state-of-the-art facilities and the highest level of safety requirements, Delhi Metro comprises three parts – underground sector, the ground sector and the elevated sector. The first phase saw the construction of Line 2 – a metro corridor consisting of ten underground stations from Vishwavidyalaya in the north to Central Secretariat in the south. The Architects designed four of these stations – Vishwavidyalaya, Vidhan Sabha, Civil Lines and Kashmere Gate, including the 4.4 km intermediate tunnels.

The Architects were later involved in the construction of Line 3 – the East-West corridor with underground stations at Barakhamba Road and Mandi House. Both these stations, located in the heart of the capital, cater to a large number of commuters.

In the next phase, the Architects designed nine underground stations – from Central Secretariat to Qutub Minar, and six stations of the Airport Express Line from New Delhi Railway Station to Terminal 3 of the Indira Gandhi International (IGI) Airport.

Each of these stations required an unconventional design approach that involved the integration of highly sophisticated engineering services including large column-free spaces, tunnel ventilation, ambient air control, fire-fighting facilities and an efficient evacuation system. Successful incorporation of these along with salient aesthetic considerations give each station its unique character.

The Architects sought to create a symbiosis of a functional, technologically savvy, modern public space with a sensitive response to the urban character of the vicinity.

Interstate Bus Terminal

Location **Noida, Uttar Pradesh** Site **50 acres** Built-up area **75,00,000 sq. ft.**
Year of completion **Ongoing**

An ***integrated multilevel bus terminal*** *with provision of* ***facilities of offices, retail, entertainment blocks, hotels and apartments,*** *helps establish it as the gateway to Noida*

With Noida having grown into a large self-sustained region, a need has been felt to create a modern Interstate Bus Terminal (ISBT), which acts as a grand terminal for the city. The Architects have planned this facility not simply as a transport hub, but as an integrated multifunctional destination which truly becomes the gateway to Noida. This development, planned over an area of 50 acres, comprises a state-of-the-art, modern, multilevel bus terminal along with high density development of offices, retail facilities, entertainment blocks, hotels, service apartments – all creating a vibrant, multiverse destination for the city.

A strong need for an efficient transportation system led to the conception of the ISBT in Noida. Careful planning helps in segregating vehicular traffic, including bus movement, from well-designed and abundantly landscaped public plazas. The creation of this much needed public space in the city allows for a variety of public activities. Musical fountains, performance plazas, amphitheatres, outdoor exhibition spaces – all offer opportunities of expansion of this project from a mere transportation and logistics facility to becoming an iconic destination in the city. A free-flowing, resplendent form of curved roofing spans the entrance of the site, unifying the different structures into a harmonious design. The design projects an extravagance which is so different from any other transportation hub in the city. The light show in the evening would be unlike any event in the city, displaying a dazzling addition to its skyline.

Facing page: *A visualization of the front façade of the development.*

Below: *A drawing of the plan of the concourse.*

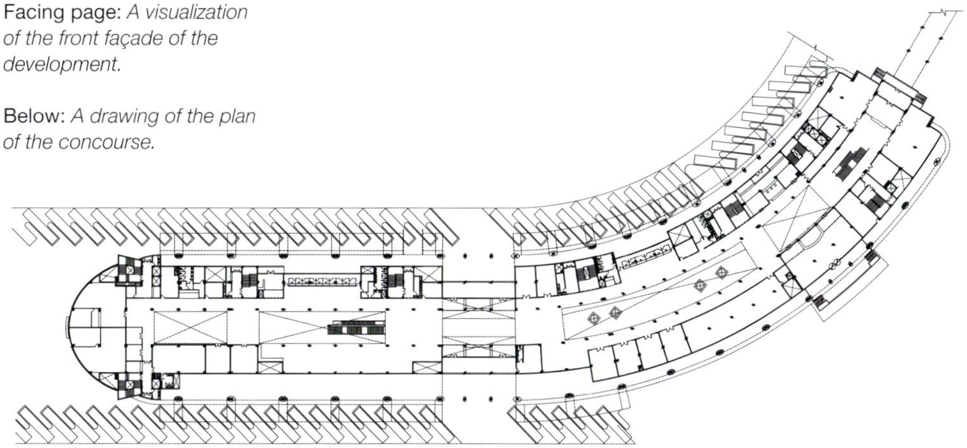

Interstate Bus Terminal

Location **Dwarka, New Delhi** Site **25 acres** Built-up area **75,00,000 sq. ft.** Year of completion **Ongoing**

An imposing yet balanced conceptualization of ***striking forms inspires a futuristic design development***

The multimodal transit facility at Sector 22, Dwarka, integrates an interstate and intercity bus terminal, and a cluster bus depot under one roof to create this para-transit hub. The project has been designed for Delhi Transport Infrastructure Development Corporation Limited. The site is located near the Delhi–Gurugram highway, making it accessible to daily commuters. Boarding, alighting and parking facilities for more than 650 buses have been provided at the site.

The building is segregated into different segments which distribute the overall mass of the built-up area over the landscape, with the interplay of masses creating its grand form. The building's design restricts its footprint to less than 40 per cent on the site, allowing maximum space for circulation and parking.

Bold curves dominate the overall façade, which adds to the magnificence of the project in the vicinity. It widens the view for visitors, exhibiting a panorama of the surrounding expansive cityscape. The use of dynamic LED façades, thus, makes the edifice a landmark and an icon for futuristic urban development.

Below: *A visual interpretation showcasing the dynamism over the façade.*

City Bus Terminal

Location **Noida, Uttar Pradesh** Site **10 acres** Built-up area **10,00,000 sq. ft.** Year of completion **2021**

The architectural expression of the city's bus terminal is ***inspired from the influences of traditional Indian architectural sensibilities***

The City Bus Terminal in Noida is a prestigious urban infrastructure project located in Sector 82. Designed for buses, the design focuses on ease of movement in and around the limited site area. The design integrates a bus terminal facility with a mixed-use commercial complex comprising a shopping mall, a 1,000-seater multiplex and a 150-room hotel.

A richly landscaped foreground leads to the structural edifice, the architectural expression of which reflects the influences of traditional Indian architectural elements such as lattices and colonnades. The curvaceous design of the building broadens its span without projecting an imposing demeanour. An intricate *jaali* on the façade encases a glistening glass edifice. A bright chrome entrance becomes the focal point while the remaining building is flushed with subdued colours. The concourse has been restricted to the ground floor while the upper floors accommodate commercial activities.

With separate access points for the offices at the complex and for the bus terminal, the circulation in and around the site becomes hassle-free.

Below: *A visualization of the front façade displaying the confluence of Indian design elements with modernity.*

Gomti Nagar Railway Station Redevelopment

Location **Lucknow, Uttar Pradesh** Site **40 acres** Built-up area **36,70,000 sq. ft.** Year of completion **2021 (Estimated)**

The design pays an iconic homage to the city; the redevelopment plan is a ***railways upgradation project integrating a 40-acre commercial land parcel with the railway station infrastructure***

Capital of Uttar Pradesh and the potpourri of Nawabi culture, Lucknow is home to impeccable educational, commercial, financial and legal infrastructures. Listed as one of the cities in the Government of India's Smart City Mission, Lucknow attracts a great influx of people in information technology (IT), banking, retail, construction and other service sectors.

The Gomti Nagar Railway Station, located 12 km away from Lucknow, currently serves 40,000 passengers every month. Owing to its proximity to the city, a plan to redevelop and upgrade its facilities was proposed. Lucknow has an Awadhi architectural sensibility reflected in its heritage and prospering cultural fabric. The conceptualization revolved around the redevelopment as an extension of the existing design language, albeit one which needs to be revived keeping the present city's requirements in mind.

The redevelopment plan is a railways upgradation project integrating a 40-acre commercial land parcel with the railway station infrastructure. The revenue generated by the sale of services developed on the retail side of the land parcel is envisaged to facilitate the economics of the project.

The Architects began working on the project in September 2017. The façade derives its inspiration from the grandness of Awadhi architecture. The *jaali* adorning the face of the complex spans the station's entire length, perforated by a pattern which appears timeless in appearance. It is complemented by the introduction of arches, while at the same time, accommodating them into the structural element of the terminal's exterior. Taking inspiration from traditional domes, the roofs lined with photovoltaic cells follow a curvilinear shape.

The façade has space for advertisements that would help generate and contribute to the revenue of the project, while kiosks and exhibition halls would provide a platform for local artists and agencies.

This project is an iconic model of transportation infrastructure, with its unique feature being hassle-free circulation. The concourse areas are divided into levels to avoid confusion between incoming and outgoing passengers. An elevated road leads passengers to the drop-off area, from where they make their way through the ticket counters and information desks to arrive inside the departure hall. Waiting facilities like seating and kiosks are provided here. The passengers may then walk through the concourse and take the escalators going downwards to

Facing page: *An aerial view visualization of the project.*

Below: *A render of the Master Plan of the redevelopment.*

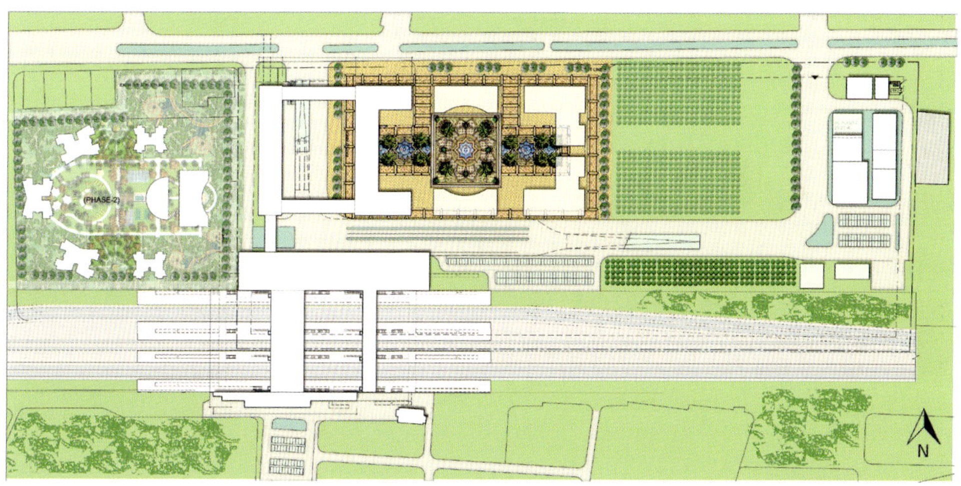

Above: *A front view of the railway station highlighting the intricate Awadh-inspired* jaali *pattern.*

Facing page below: *A visualization of the retail areas.*

reach their respective platforms. On the other hand, passengers arriving at the platforms would be required to walk down the subways, which open up into the arrival halls. These have meet and greet areas, pick-up facilities and, subsequently, lead towards the exits of the station.

Distinguishing arriving passengers on the ground floor from departing passengers on the first floor, helps free the station from hindrances caused due to passenger movement. This also facilitates a pedestrian friendly design, creating a safe and secure zone for the elderly and disabled. There are resting and medical room facilities available in addition to buggy and pre-paid taxi services.

The design also strives to model itself as an efficient transportation hub which is both technology driven and energy conscious. To work towards this, the walls are conceptualized on the basis of a 'living wall' design, which promote fluidity in landscape from a horizontal surface to a vertical one. The buildings have large spans of rooms that welcome natural daylight and ventilation inside.

Another highlight of the structure is the connectivity of the station building with the retail complex. Passengers can seamlessly

walk from shopping and office areas into the railway station and vice versa. This allows them to enjoy entertainment spaces, kiosks and retail shops while making their way in or out.

Gomti Nagar is now developing as the commercial and IT hub of mainland Lucknow, providing ample scope for implementation of a green design proposal on an urban scale. It is also a first-of-its-kind railway project where the railway station is integrated with retail outlets. The presence of such a complex would be a model to follow while boosting the economy of the region.

Airport Express Metro Line

Location **New Delhi** Site **22.7 km** Year of completion **2010**

*The metro line for the **airport express spans six metro stations,** saving significant travel time for commuters*

From conceptualization to design to engineering, the Architects have established a revolutionary design for city commute with the Delhi Airport Express Metro Line or the Orange Line (DMRC). The line resolves the long-standing issue of delay in travel for commuters traversing to and from the airport within the city. All six metro stations on the line, spanning the New Delhi Station-Dwarka Sector 21 corridor, are known as City Airport Terminals (CATs).

The Architects were called upon for a detailed design consultancy for five underground stations – New Delhi Railway Station, Shivaji Stadium, Dhaula Kuan, Aerocity and Indira Gandhi International Airport. Of the 22.7 km line, 15.7 km is underground while 7 km is overhead. The Architects designed the stations keeping in mind the convenience of the specially-abled and the elderly. Full height platform screen doors not only prevent untoward incidents but also provide for better air-conditioning. A network of CCTV cameras help the station control room, security control room and operations control centre maintain close vigilance for the safety of the commuters.

The Airport Express Line, with its cloakroom facilities expediting the process of check-in for passengers, is first of its kind in South Asia.

Below: *An aerial view of the Express Line.*

Mumbai Metro Rail Corporation Limited (MMRC)

Location **Mumbai, Maharashtra** Site **34 km** Year of completion **Ongoing**

For a metropolitan city struggling to solve its traffic woes, ***the introduction of Metro as a commuting option is a futuristic resolve***

For a city infamous for its traffic congestion and unregulated intra-city travel, a strong need was felt to boost the public transportation system and create a network which could provide a long-term solution. This inspired the inception of the mass transit project of Metro Rail in Mumbai.

The Mumbai Metro Rail aims to provide fast, reliable and easy public transit to the commuters of the city. The underground stations of the Chhatrapati Shivaji Maharaj International Airport (CSIA) Domestic and International Terminals, Dadar, Shitladevi Temple, Siddhi Vinayak and Sahar Road will redefine the dynamics of their surroundings, creating opportunities for high density, transit-oriented development in the years to come.

With the firm's trusted record of expertise in designing and executing Metro projects, the Architects were assigned to helm the prestigious urban project. The scope of work involved designing Mechanical, Electrical and Plumbing (MEP) for six underground metro stations, and integration of services such as Fire Fighting, Air-Conditioning, Ventilation System and BMS. The corridor covers a great length of distance and considerably reduces the commute time, which has been one of the most welcoming changes brought forth by the project.

Below: *A view of the Mumbai Metro Rail.*

Interstate Bus Terminal

Location **Anand Vihar, New Delhi** Site **25 acres** Built-up area **10,00,000 sq. ft.** Year of completion **Ongoing**

Aiming to cater to a staggering volume of passengers for the next four decades, it has a ***capacity to house 300 buses***

Anand Vihar is one of the busiest and most frequented bus terminals in the capital region. Keeping in mind the growing demands of commuters, the dilapidated terminus required not only redesign but also an upgraded model of facilities. Designed for Delhi Integrated Multi-Modal Transit System Limited, the redevelopment project will cater to staggering volume of passengers, to be served over the next four decades. With a built-up area of 10,00,000 sq. ft., it includes state-of-the-art retail and office facilities, a hotel and has the capacity of housing 300 buses, both on the surface and under the ground. It has been integrated with Delhi Metro and Anand Vihar Railway Station, making this project a para-transit model for commuting.

One of the biggest concerns of the Architects while designing this terminus was achieving a smooth transition and movement of transport facilities and passengers between different spaces. Conscious of the adjoining metro station, the Architects were careful to keep its traffic separate from that of the terminal. Foot overbridges for pedestrians have been used to join railway and metro stations, and ensure safety and ease of movement to and from different concourses. The alighting bay has been placed near one end of the site, facilitating the movement of commuters and buses. The taxi and auto stands have been segregated and are adjacent to this alighting bay. Provision of parking for the same, along with inquiry booths, frees congestion within the site at different nodes.

Access and movement of interstate buses has been segregated from that of Delhi Transport Corporation. Along with this, there is a car ramp planned around the station for ease of underground vehicular exit. Office commuters would enter the site directly into an underground parking spot from where they will have access to ramps and lifts to reach their offices. The VIPs accessing the terminus have been allowed a drop-off area from where they can enter. A filling station has been provided within the site, and its exit route is a ramp from under one of the boarding bays. Inquiry booths have been provided at different points within the site; these also act as information points for passengers.

The design, thus, takes a leap from conventional protypes and planning methods while creating a world-class transportation facility.

Below: *Cantilevered projection displays remarkable engineering.*

Bottom: *The sweeping and seamless façade of the ISBT.*

Surat Multi-Modal Transportation Hub

Location **Surat, Gujarat** Site **60 acres** Built-up area **1,00,00,000 sq. ft.** Year of completion **Ongoing**

A unique ***integration of urban transport development such as Transit Oriented Development (TOD), multi-modal development and last mile para-transport connectivity***

The Surat Multi-modal Transportation Hub (MMTH) is a first-of-its-kind transit development, both in terms of function (integrating nine different modes of transport) and scale (a facility with a mammoth built-up area of 100 lakh sq. ft.). This project is a unique demonstration of urban transport development, such as TOD, multimodal development and last mile para-transport connectivity, combined in a unique model of public-private partnership.

Its world-class infrastructure, including an integrated and efficient transportation hub, draws upon Smart City model and an iconic architecture. It promotes efficient mixed land use based development through planning for the unplanned areas, containing a range of compatible activities. The state government has enabled some flexibility in land use and built by-laws to adapt to change. The hub is conceptualized to integrate technology and energy management along with state-of-the-art architecture. The free-form of the MMTH easily blends with the rigid and imposing scale of the office and residential towers, etching a bold line in the skyline of Surat.

The hub comprises *zari* pattern screens and sharp, chiselled parametric façades. The vertical twin towers at the centre, which are also a 'Gateway to the City', have an envelop of perforated membrane. The idea, which derives inspiration from the typical embroidery style and famous diamond-cutting expertise of the city, showcases a unique perspective of the city to the visitors. The flowing volumes give the railway station a dynamic form. The roof over the platforms symbolizes fluidity, inspired from the image of woven fabric. The sculptural expanse introduces large column-free spaces, creating a mirrored design identity of the edifices and facilitating lighting and ventilation in the interiors. The Bus Rapid Transit (BRT), railway station and the Gujarat State Road Transport Corporation (GSRTC) have been neatly segregated for the convenience of commuters.

The design takes a leap into futuristic architectural and engineering innovation by seamlessly introducing green spaces into the fabric of the built. Vertical garden walls, landscape podium plazas and rooftop gardens will add beauty and softness to the transport hub.

Below: *A night visualization of the different forms of the buildings coming together to give dynamism to the transportation hub.*

Following pages: *An aerial visualization of the hub.*

Sustainability and India

Sustainability, Green Buildings, Net Zero Buildings, Environment Conscious: these words have become the most read, heard and spoken terms in recent times. Climate change being the most important topic for earth's future, the world has now started taking tangible steps towards addressing these important issues. In recent times, various countries have taken different approaches to tackle these concerns. On one hand, developed countries are focusing on doing research to find effective ways to reduce, reuse and recycle natural resources; on the other hand, developing countries are trying to learn from the mistakes of developed countries to ensure they have a lower impact on environment in future development.

India has also started making significant contributions in the matter. Very recently, the country hosted COP14 attended by the heads of UN, international organizations, leaders of states and ministers from many countries. Alongside with other countries, India has promised timebound contributions to the movement. Clean Energy Program, Environment Clearance to check the impact of buildings on environment, green ratings to promote environment friendly designs are some of the positive steps taken by the country.

It is not now that India has become energy conscious. Historically, we have been living in harmony with nature for centuries. Our food, clothing, rituals and way of life were always environment sensitive. *Vastu Shastra*, the ancient knowledge on building design and construction, meritoriously combines the knowledge of astrology, universal energies, human energies and many subtle aspects of life in easy-to-use principles. It also has a unique way of ensuring its implementation: the rules subtly integrate with spiritual practices and daily rituals.

These days, everyone is claiming to have found techniques to reduce demand and innovate products to generate clean energy. Many declare themselves as the most environment-friendly country, product or company. There are hardly any advertisements which do not claim to be non-environment-friendly or non-innovative. However, most of these claims are far from reality and offer very expensive solutions which are not sustainable for developing countries.

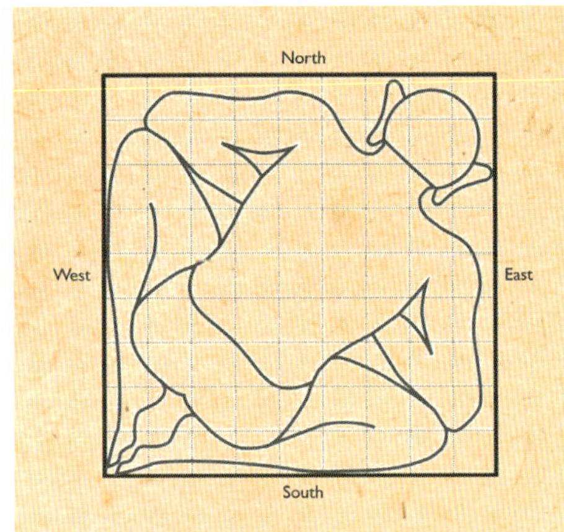

Facing page: *Lessons in environment-friendly concepts from ancient India inspired designs of heritage, such as Hawa Mahal, Rajasthan, and Adalaj ni vav, Gujarat.*

Below: *Historical learnings combined with latest design tools and technologies.*

It is an irony that the solutions which need to be contextual are bought from completely non-contextual countries or companies. Rather than looking for answers from our history, our available resources and our way of life, which have a proven record of sustainability in our climate, we are looking for answers from countries or companies that are completely different in all of these aspects. This trend demonstrates non-belief in our own historic knowledge and lack of confidence in our capability to develop that knowledge to recent needs. It is not wise to ignore available knowledge and blindly follow what is being sold to us.

There is no denying that learning from our historic knowledge has some limitations. The scale, function, right use, comfort parameters, construction materials, etc., are very different from those used historically, but these still offer relevant fundamental principles. Orientation specific to location, wall thickness and openings related to direction, allocation of functions related to wind direction, shading systems related to sun movement, building proportion linked to construction material, food habits and clothing related to outdoor temperature developed historically – all these still provide a relevant starting point for the design. The need of the hour is to wisely use applicable historic principles, overlap them with latest technologies and develop a well-balanced solution.

CPKA has a rich history of designing climate responsive designs. Our founder, Ar. C.P. Kukreja, laid a strong foundation, demonstrating how to utilize historic principles in building design. His book *Tropical Architecture* has been acknowledged by not only Indian architects but is also used as a reference book in prestigious institutes like MIT and Harvard. Moving ahead, we at CPKA are determined to effectively build upon this foundation and develop it further to make it effective in today's new age architecture. For the first time in Indian architectural history, our firm has established an 'Innovation Studio' to carry out research and development in the field of sustainability. We have a dedicated team, equipped with latest tools and technologies, which ensures that each building designed by CPKA goes through a rigorous process of brainstorming, development, implementation and validation of sustainable principles. We are confident that in years to come, we will be able to significantly contribute to shaping a sustainable and nature-friendly environment for India and for the planet.

Sameer Divekar

Executive Vice President at CP Kukreja Architects (CPKA)

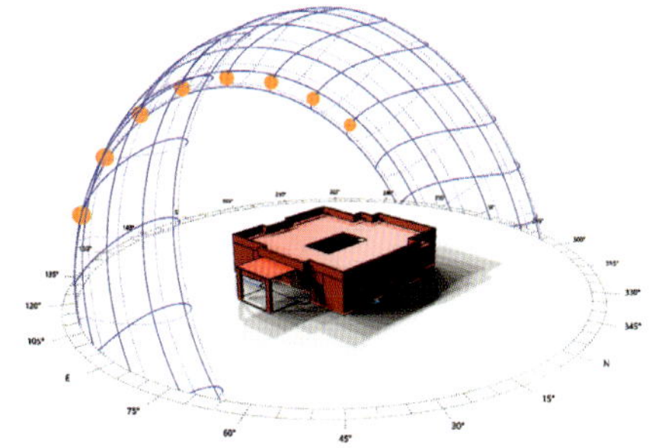

Orientation

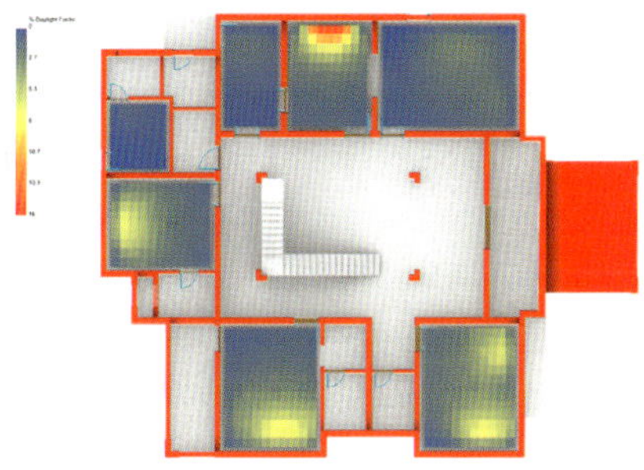

Daylight

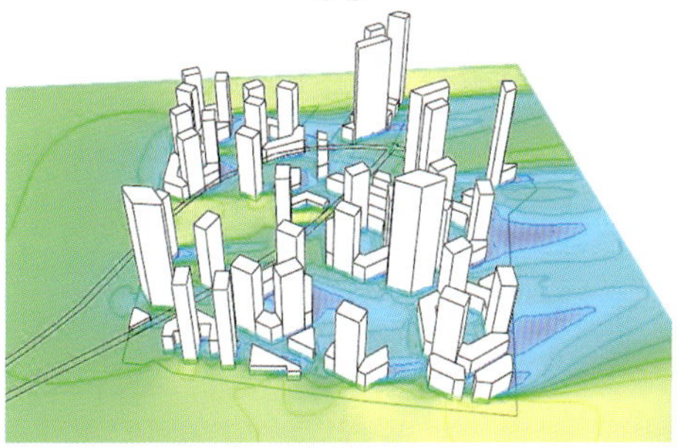

Wind

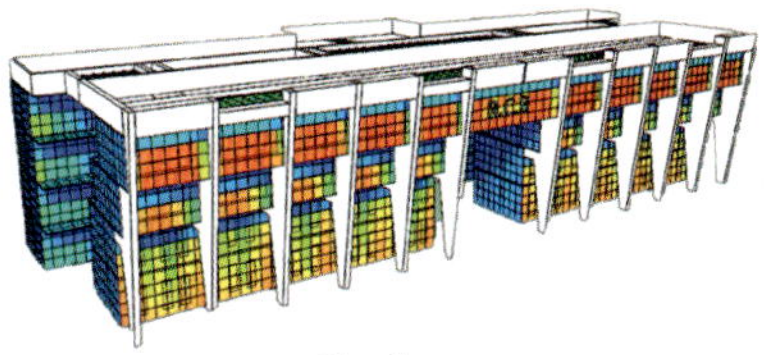

Shading

Team CPKA

Leadership
C.P. Kukreja, Founder

Ar. C.P. Kukreja, a legendary architect, made significant contributions to the field of architecture in the last five decades, not just in India but also at the global level. What he started as a modest two-man firm has today become not only one of India's largest architectural practices with over 200 professionals, but has also been continuously recognized amongst the top 100 architecture firms in the world.

Mr. Kukreja's high academic achievements strengthened his resolve to work hard and achieve scholarships. With these, he travelled to far shores to achieve the best in education. He received his scholarship to attend the prestigious Melbourne University for his Town & Regional Planning degree. He also received scholarship to obtain his Master's Degree in Architecture from University of Manitoba, Canada.

Winning the national design competition for the prestigious Jawaharlal Nehru University, New Delhi, in the year 1970 propelled him into the spotlight. A success of diverse projects followed: Ambadeep Towers, New Delhi; Rumtek Monastery, New Delhi; IFFCO Township, Aonla, Uttar Pradesh; Indian Institute of Management, Lucknow; international embassies in New Delhi as well as industrial projects for TATA and JCB across the country, and many projects across the globe. In a deep urge to propagate the virtues of environmentally sensitive principles of design, he penned down many of his philosophies in his book *Tropical Architecture* (published in 1978 by Tata McGraw-Hill), a celebrated book on 'Environmental Architecture' and a popular reference book in the libraries of prestigious institutions like Harvard University and MIT. Altogether, a completely new revolution was started by him in the field of post-independence Indian architecture, prioritizing concepts like sustainability, energy efficient design, renewal of natural resources, responding to natural context and blending tradition with modernity that made his projects contextually relevant.

He made a pioneering effort of establishing the first Indian architectural magazine called *Architecture + Design (A+D)* in 1984, followed by an interior design magazine titled *Indian Design & Interiors*. To strongly spread his message beyond his homeland, he even delivered speeches and lectures abroad in various institutions, such as Harvard, which he believed could make a serious impact on architectural thinking and theorization. He was the founding governing body member of the Sushant School of Art & Architecture, Gurugram, India.

Mr. Kukreja also contributed immensely to the post-earthquake reconstruction work of Gujarat. He was the highest contributor, recognized by the Indian Institute of Architects, for his financial contribution to the 2004 tsunami victims. His immense philanthropic efforts include active contribution in various disaster relief campaigns and organ donation drives.

He was the founding member of the Manav Chetna Kendra, which has been instrumental in spreading the words of Swami Paramananda. For his immense contribution to Indian society, he was felicitated by the former President of India, Shri. K.R. Narayanan, for his lifetime contribution to architecture and environmental awareness.

Awards Conferred to Ar. C.P. Kukreja

- 'Lifetime Dedication Honor' awarded by Society Interiors Honors in 2015
- Felicitated by the Foundation for Architectural & Environmental Awareness for his 'Lifetime Contribution in Promoting Architectural Academics & Journalism'

- Felicitated with the 'Baburao Mhatre Gold Medal', awarded by the Indian Institute of Architects in December 2012
- Featured in *Who's Who of Asia*

- 'Life Time Achievement Award' for contribution to Architecture of India, awarded by Union Urban Development Minister, Mr. Kamal Nath, in 2011 (received by Mr. Dikshu C. Kukreja on Mr. C.P. Kukreja's behalf, as seen in the photo above)

- 'Building Industry Leadership Award 2008', felicitated by Builder Information Bureau (BIB) and presented by Ms. Aarti Mehra, Former Mayor of Delhi

- Conferred with the title 'Titanic Genius Award 2007' by BIB

- Awarded 'Lifetime Contribution in Architecture and Environmental Awareness' by Foundation for Architectural & Environmental Awareness, felicitated by Former President of India, Shri K.R. Narayanan, in 2005

- Felicitated amongst 'Best Personalities of India Award – Icons & Reflections of Architecture' by Hettich

'You see, at the macro level, nature basically is made up of elements such as space, air, light, water and earth. The activities of existence are being centred around these elements, in varying proportions. At the micro level also, if you study the physical and mental requirements of man, he essentially follows the same stream of line. Therefore, this relationship is nearer to true architecture. This is the truth to me.'

Ar. C.P. KUKREJA
Founder of CP Kukreja Architects

Leadership
Dikshu C. Kukreja, Managing Principal

Ar. Dikshu C. Kukreja received his B. Arch Honours as Gold Medalist from School of Planning & Architecture, New Delhi. He was selected amongst the top few to attend the prestigious Taliesin Fellowship at Frank Lloyd Wright School of Architecture, Arizona, USA. Shortly after, he received his Masters of Architecture & Urban Design from Harvard University. He was elected the founding vice-president of Asia GSD, which grew to become one of the largest student organizations at Harvard University. Also pursuing his interest in international relations and business management, he simultaneously took courses at the School of Business and Kennedy School of Government, Harvard University. He was elected as the youngest president of Harvard Club of India – the first architect to achieve this distinction.

Travelling across Europe as a part of his Master's curriculum, he worked in France as well as USA before returning to India and joining CPKA. He started out his journey with revered projects such as the Gymkhana Club, New Delhi and The LaLiT Grand Palace, Srinagar, Jammu and Kashmir, and steadily moved up. Presently, he is leading some of the country's prestigious projects such as: India's tallest residential tower and the country's first transit-oriented development; India International Convention Exhibition Centre, Delhi, with the world's third largest Convention Centre of 10,000 capacity for hosting G-20 summit; India Pavilion at the Dubai World Expo 2020, Dubai, to name a few.

He has been selected as the 'Young Icon of the Decade', 'Best Citizen of India', and most recently, as the 'Face of 21st Century Architecture in India', and has featured in *Who's Who of Asia*. He was selected as the Cultural Ambassador by the Government of Finland. He is also Member, Governing Body, of one of India's best architectural institutions – Sushant School of Art & Architecture, Gurugram, India.

Mr. Kukreja actively engages and partakes in discourses surrounding urban spaces and environmental issues. He was featured by CNBC TV on the programme 'Young Turks'. In continuation to this endeavour, he is often invited as a keynote speaker or panelist at prestigious national and international conferences, conclaves, summits, and is also a regular guest on various media portals (television, print and digital). He has been a guest writer for national newspapers like *The Times of India and Hindustan Times* on urban issues.

Mr. Kukreja deeply cares about youth development in the country through academia. He has started a foundation, 'CP Kukreja Awards for Design Excellence', for students of design, to encourage ideas from youth for improving our cities. It gives design students highest cash prizes and opportunities to intern abroad.

One of his latest initiatives include promoting an awareness and sensitivity towards design. For this, he curated a breakthrough design series, 'Deciphering Design with Dikshu', in collaboration with one of the country's leading media channels, *NewsX*. The series focused on discourse with globally renowned and leading personalities hailing from varied backgrounds of heritage, such as culinary art, fashion, transport, business, and who have contributed immensely to their respective fields.

Awards and Recognition Conferred to Ar. Dikshu C. Kukreja

- Bharat Shiromani Award 2019 for 'Excellence in Architecture', presented by Lord Swraj Paul in the presence of Ambassadors of Iceland and Slovenia

- Felicitated amongst 'Top 11 Architects in the Country' at the 12th CW Architect & Builder (CWAB) Awards 2017

- Selected amongst '101 Notable Personalities Amongst Professionals' by World of Business Magazine in 2016

GLOBAL ECONOMIC PROGRESS & RESEARCH ASSOCIATION (GEPRA)

- 'Bharat Seva Ratan Gold Medal Award 2016 for Outstanding Individual Achievement in Architecture', awarded by Global Economic Progress & Research Association (GEPRA)

- 'Society Interiors Honors Award 2015 for Outstanding Contribution to Architecture' awarded by Society Interiors

- 'Excellence in the field of Architecture (Young Architect)' awarded by GPS Achievers Award 2014 and felicitated by Dr. Manmohan Singh, Former Prime Minister of India

- Presented with the honour of 'Best Designed Residential Skyscraper' at Infra & Realty Sutra Award 2014 by Mr. Nitin Gadkari (current Minister for Road Transport and Highways and the Minister of Micro, Small and Medium Enterprises)

- Awarded Business & Community Award for 'Quality Excellence and for Outstanding Achievement in Sustainable Development' by All India Business & Community Foundation in 2014

- Felicitated as the 'Young and Most Sought After Architect in India' by then Union Urban Development Minister, Mr. Kamal Nath, in 2011

- Presented with the 'Indian Achievers Award 2010 for Outstanding Achievement in Business Excellence & Quality Achievements' at the 24th Indian Achievers Summit

- Awarded 'Best Citizen of India' by International Publishing House in 2010

- Awarded 'Young Icon of the Decade'

- Awarded 'Face of 21st Century Architecture'

- Featured in *Who's Who of Asia*

- Appointed as the Cultural Ambassador by the Government of Finland

- Featured by CNBC TV on the programme 'Young Turks'

Awards Conferred to CP Kukreja Architects

- Placed amongst 'Top 100 Architects in the World' by World Architecture for the year 2021
- The proposal of Central Vista Redevelopment and the new Parliament design, New Delhi, awarded the distinguished international World Architecture Award (35th Cycle)
- HRRL Township, Rajasthan awarded the prestigious national HUDCO Design Award 2020 for 'New and Innovative Town Design Solutions/ Eco Cities'
- Placed amongst 'Top 5 Architects in Asia' by World Architecture, a UK-based institution, for the year 2019
- Placed amongst 'Top 100 Architects in the World' by World Architecture for the year 2019
- Project of Human Resources Development Centre, Uttar Pradesh, felicitated as 'Outstanding Concrete Structure 2019, Uttar Pradesh' by Indian Concrete Institute, Uttar Pradesh
- Felicitated as 'Most Outstanding Urban Design Firm 2019 – India' by Global Business Insight Awards 2019
- Provence Estate, Haryana, awarded 'Luxury Project of the Year – Residential (2019)' by ET NOW Real Estate Awards – Best Luxury Projects
- Gautam Buddha University, Uttar Pradesh, placed as winner in the 'Institutional Category (Built)' by international platform, Rethinking the Future 2018
- Vallabh Bhawan Secretariat, Madhya Pradesh, selected as 'Best Indian Institutional Project' by BUILD 2018 Architecture Awards
- CP Kukreja Architects felicitated as 'Most Innovative Indian Architectural Design Firm, 2018' by BUILD Architecture Awards

- Vallabh Bhawan Secretariat selected as 'Architectural Design of the Year' by Construction Week India Awards 2018
- Placed amongst 'Top 100 Global Architects' by World Architecture for the year 2017
- Awarded as 'Best Architecture & Urban Design Firm in India' by BUILD for the year 2017

- Felicitated with 'BUILD Excellence Award for Healthcare Projects' 2017 by BUILD

- Received the 'APAC Excellence Awards 2017' by *APAC Insider* Magazine

- Placed amongst 'Top 100 Global Architects' by World Architecture for the year 2016

- Felicitated with award for 'Innovation in Institutional Archicture, India' by BUILD 2016 Architecture Awards
- Gautam Buddha University felicitated as 'Best Eco-Friendly Indian Institutional Project' by BUILD 2016 Architecture Awards
- Felicitated as 'Best Multi-Disciplinary Architecture & Engineering Firm Project' by Build News, London, UK in 2016

- Awarded for having designed the 'Best Sustainable Campus' of Gautam Buddha University, Greater Noida, by Build News, London, UK in 2016

- Felicitated as 'Architect of the Year – North' at the Indian Property Award 2015

- Recognized as 'Architect of Sustainable Design Project: Eldeco Ananda' at the Estrada Real Estate Awards 2015, Singapore
- Awarded by Real Estate Awards 2013 as 'Architectural Firm of the Year (North India)'

- Awarded as 'Best Architecture Firm, India' by IDE Award 2012

- Felicitated as 'Best Architecture Firm of the Year' at the 5th GIREM Leadership Award 2012

- Awarded 'Best Architects for Residential Building' at CNBC Awaaz Crisil Real Estate Awards 2007

- Presented with 'Innovative Design' For Pathways World School, Aravali Hills, Haryana, by International Design Share, USA, in 2003

Acknowledgments

- Arunima Kukreja for research, creative design and content
- Megha Balooni for research and text
- Maria Louis, Founder Editor, *Architect and Interiors India*
- Aedas for association in the Redevelopment of Pragati Maidan, New Delhi
- Idom for association in East Delhi Hub, New Delhi, and India International Convention Centre, New Delhi
- Raili and Riema Pietila for association in the Finnish Embassy, New Delhi
- MO-OF for association in TATA Housing Myst, Kasauli
- Mr. Heinz Scheide of Austria for association in the Austrian Embassy, New Delhi

CP Kukreja Architects
D-1, Green Park, Ashirwad Complex
New Delhi – 110016, India
Ph: +91-11-41759907/41004554
E-mail: cpka@cpkukreja.com
Website: www.cpkukreja.com

ISBN: 978-81-949691-3-6

SHOWCASE
Roli Books

Published by Roli Books 2021
M-75, Greater Kailash-II Market
New Delhi-110 048, India
Ph: +91-11-4068 2000
E-mail: info@rolibooks.com
Website: www.rolibooks.com

Editor: Ekta Chadha
Layout Design: Supriya Saran
Pre-Press: Jyoti Dey
Production: Lavinia Rao

Printed and bound at Samrat Offset Pvt. Ltd., New Delhi

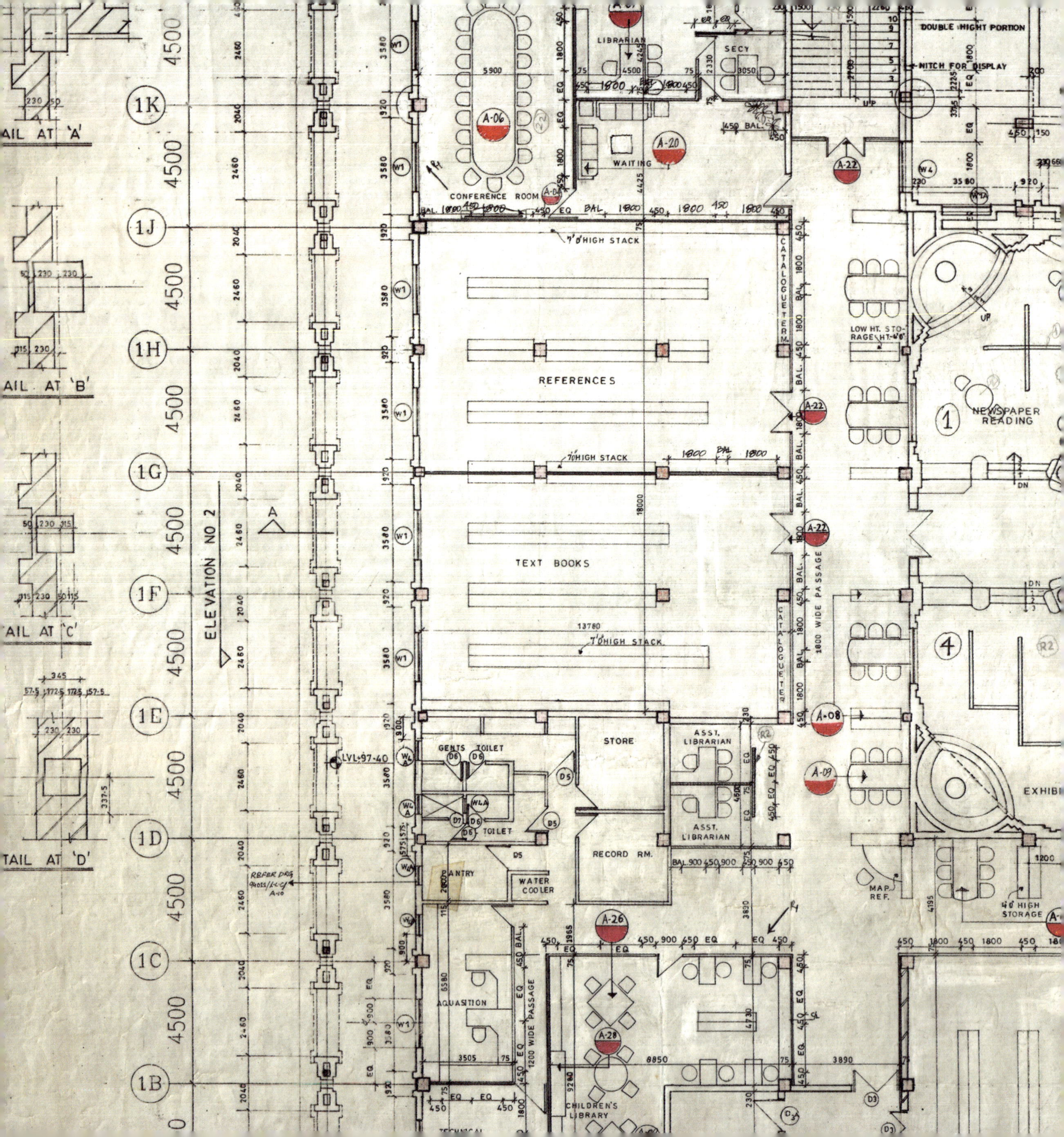

CONFERENCE ROOM
LIBRARIAN
SECY
WAITING
DOUBLE HIGHT PORTION
NITCH FOR DISPLAY
UP
7'0"HIGH STACK
REFERENCES
CATALOGUE TERM.
LOW HT. STORAGE HT. 4'0"
NEWSPAPER READING
TEXT BOOKS
1800 WIDE PASSAGE
13780
18000
ELEVATION NO 2
LVL-97-40
GENTS TOILET
TOILET
STORE
ASST. LIBRARIAN
ASST. LIBRARIAN
RECORD RM.
PANTRY
WATER COOLER
MAP REF.
4'0" HIGH STORAGE
EXHIBI
AQUASITION
1200 WIDE PASSAGE
CHILDREN'S LIBRARY
AIL AT 'A'
AIL AT 'B'
TAIL AT 'C'
TAIL AT 'D'
1K
1J
1H
1G
1F
1E
1D
1C
1B
4500